THE SWAFFS
FROM
THE SHIRES

THE SWAFFS

FROM

THE SHIRES

*A fully illustrated
history of the Swaffield family
from 1728*

Written and published
by Natalie Wheatley

First published by Natalie Wheatley, 2003

ISBN 0 9544680 0 7

Page make-up by Don Friston

Printed in Great Britain by
Richardson Printing Ltd
44 Pinbush Road
South Lowestoft Industrial Estate
Lowestoft, Suffolk NR33 7NL

Author's summary

The intention of this book is to record a 'family history' through the ages.
There may be variation in dates and spelling concerning places, people and
events. Readers may object to today's 'politically incorrect' entries sustained
for historical accuracy. I have made efforts to acknowledge all copyright
holders; anyone inadvertently left out should contact me after publication,
and I will arrange an acknowledgement should the book be reprinted.

DEDICATED TO THE MEMORY OF MY FATHER
FRANK EXTON (TONY) SWAFFIELD
who loved me so much

For our children, Susina, Simon, Andrea and David,
my long-suffering husband, Michael
and, particularly, for my grandchildren
Laurence, Nicholas, William, Jackson, Fay, Thomas
and future grandchildren
who, I hope, will continue to chronicle their own family history

Bardie Swaffield
b 1916

George Swaffield
1841–1936

Audrey Swaffield
b 1917

Clifford Swaffield
b 1922

Fred Swaffield
1888–1963

Ann Swaffield
b 1848

Jo Swaffield
1882–1965

Tony Swaffield
1899–1975

Natalie Swaffield
b 1938

Ben John Swaffield
1845–1896

Some key people in the formation and recording of the Swaffield family tree

Foreword and Acknowledgements

Material for the compilation of this book has come from a multitude of sources. I have written to many family members requesting short autobiographies, notes about parents and relatives, comments on events that have affected their lives. I have also requested photographs. I have had lengthy telephone discussions with people who find talking easier than writing, and electronic mail has produced details from younger members of the family. The response has been wonderful and I am grateful to them all. My most sincere thanks go to Malcolm Boyer, husband of Margaret Swaffield 1949, who generously offered to scan in all the visuals. I am sure he had no idea there would be over 450 faded and creased photographs, photocopies, crumbling letters and yellowed cuttings. His task has been enormous and without his freely-given time, cheerful attitude and technical ability this book would never have become a reality. Malcolm has worked with Don Friston, book designer and fan of social history, who has taken such an interest in the writing and produced a quality layout. Last, but not least, Andrew Underwood, family historian, who provided support and encouragement when I needed it most.

Much written material, to substantiate the stories, has been destroyed and it has only been the occasional defining diary, scrapbook or cache of letters which has set things straight. The advantage is that of understanding the family culture from the inside, of knowing instinctively how different circumstances might play out in a family to whom the author is intrinsically tied by blood. There are a few obvious gaps mainly due to lack of time, or interest, to contribute to this project.

I have relied almost entirely on the genealogical information painstakingly researched over several decades by Audrey Bartron, née Swaffield. She is a devoted genealogist and has worked with Clifford Swaffield who shares her interest in names and dates. It was Clifford who started me off by drawing out a huge family tree which had my name on it. In 'The Swaffs from the Shires' there are bound to be inaccuracies, misquotes and anomalies. For these I apologise and state that I have taken the greatest of care to get things right, but can ultimately take no responsibility for misinformation. Interviewing [often elderly] relatives and sifting memories, at times, proves the unreliability of the spoken word. Perhaps the old fashioned E&OE printed on bills will suffice – Errors & Omissions Excepted. I hope so.

In order to keep the book to a manageable size I have adopted the usual conventions of following the male line, giving preference to those with the Swaffield name. But there are several interesting women who have played an important role and, where I have found them, they have their share of space and are identified by their maiden names. To realise the complexity of writing such a family history, here is an interesting point. If an average Swaffield 'family had two sons and two daughters, after five generations there would be 32 Swaffield sons and 992 other descendants'.

It has been a long road to completion, it has been written with affection and loyalty, and spurred on by family acceptance of the idea. Sue Swaffield 1956 puts the essence of the family into a nutshell: 'The best thing that ever happened to me was to have been born into my family, with its unique and extraordinary special blend of nature and nurture.'

I like the Swaffs, their ways and their wanderings, their humour and diversity. Thorough research has enabled me to write the Swaffield story, but much is written by themselves and, of course, it has no end.

Natalie Wheatley, October 1999 to July 2003

Contents

Introduction

"And then there is also a need that each should
understand where he came from and what he is
– and what will become of him."

Wulfstan, Archbishop of York from 1002–1023

When I started researching my family's history in 2000 in Yeovil, I spotted a book 'Crewkerne in Old Photographs'. I picked it idly from the shelf, and nearly fell over, for inside the front cover was a crackled photograph of a blonde, curly-haired little boy called Bill Swaffield from the garage business, J H Swaffield & Sons, founded in East Street around 1905. This initiation into what I had believed to be a relatively small clan made me realise that there are Swaffield's galore. There is certainly a great crowd from Shipton Gorge, most of whom seemed to be Masons and Builders. Indeed the link of inn-keeping holds fast as a Swaffield ran the Mason's Arms in the village. This story, however, focuses on some of the offspring of one Beaminster couple, John and Betty [Gillingham] Swaffield.

Mainly farming folk, after several agricultural depressions, the men eventually scattered to different parts of the country namely Derbyshire, Bedfordshire, Northamptonshire, Hampshire and various British Shires and Cities establishing themselves in new careers and starting new families. Local history has been documented where necessary and family houses, farms, schools, graves and churches have been located. I have walked family land, trodden the streets, visited the homes and become very acquainted with those I chronicle – those both long gone and those very much alive.

Academic writer, W G Sebald, pinpoints historical research: 'The truth emerges very slowly … it makes us realise that an investigation of the past, of what is lost, is crucial to our present sense of identity.' Simon Swaffield 1952 lives in New Zealand and wrote, 'I think that a long generational cycle is critical to the understanding of the family, and its characteristics.'

On the north Norfolk coast is a small village, Swafield, known as Swafelda 1086 and in the Domesday Book as Suathefeld – *c*1150 – described as 'open land characterised by swathes or tracks.' In Olde English *c*450–*c*1100 it is described as Swaeth+feld.

The Swaffields possibly came from a Rhine Valley tribe who settled in Dorset, however Julian de Swafeld 1201 was recorded in 'Pleas Before the King and His Justices, Norfolk' between 1198–1202, and William de Swafeld from the County of Bedfordshire is recorded in the 'Placita De Quo Warrant' [Warrant awarded to hold markets and fairs] during the reign of Edward I 1272–1307 and, in 1406, Robert de Swafeld in the 'Inquisitions Post Mortem' [After-Death Inquests]. Dorothy Swaffield, baptised 22 March 1567, daughter of Ralphe came from Maiden Newton. On 21 July 1580 it is recorded that Agnes Swaffeylde married Miles Morgan in Power-stock and, in 1662, Thamasin Swaffield was included in the Hearth Tax Returns also in Dorset.

There are Dorchester Swaffields dating back to Joseph Swaffield 1679, but it has been difficult to make a connection with our own roots. Joseph was Mayor of Weymouth. His son, George, married Kezia Overly from Westminster at St George's Church in Mayfair in 1750. One by one, year after year their seven children were wrapped in the family christening robes, and carried to the fonts of St Botolph's Church, Bishopsgate and then to St Peter Le Poer in London. George's brother, John, Deputy Paymaster, was also born in Dorchester, and married Theodocia Gould at St Peter Le Poer in 1774. He was a determined Swaffield for, when his grandchildren were born, no matter their sex or given surname, he insisted in his Will that all should be called Swaffield. His daughter, Eliza, married Charles Orton at St Marylebone in 1805 and they produced a son, John Orton Swaffield. Before he died prematurely, Charles Orton reached the position of Gentleman of the Pantry to King George III. John Orton Swaffield's daughter, Eliza Mary Josephina, married Robert Hassall-Owen, Royal Marines – Lt Major of the 31st Foot – from Shawbury in Shropshire. They produced fourteen Owen-Swaffields, seven of whose published Wills plot their travels and wealth. John, the fourth child, was a Lieutenant in HM 51st Regiment of Foot and resided at 'Jackattelah', Neilgherry Hills [Nilgiri], East Indies, and Sidney was 'late of Kurachee' [Karachi]. Both these boys died at the age of 21. Adelaide and Octavia were born in France and left substantial legacies. George was a Barrister at Law, Harriet bequeathed over £6000 and, Eliza, the unbelievable sum of £35,488 13s 7d.

Another Swaffield connection is The Halle at Braunston in Rutland. This large property was built about 1100 and was the residence of William atte Halle in 1300. From him it came into the Swaffield family, who were resident in Braunston until the end of the 16th century. A Military Survey in 1522 states 'Simon Swaffield, Gent, hath lands £11, in Goods £20'. He had 13 tenants, including in 1524 'Symon Swafield, Gent, hath lands £17'. This Symon left a Will (written in Olde English) dated 1538. Records show that Augustus Swaffield, descendant of the Swaffields of The Halle, was both Curate and Lord of the Manor, Braunston. He sold the Manor in 1607.

And there are other Swaffields, accounts of which have appeared in undated and unsourced press cuttings. A generous Swaffield called James of Salt Hill Drive, Slough left most of his money to his housekeeper, Florence Curteis, and very little to his children, and a naughty Swaffield *c*1920s:

'Benjamin Holmes Swaffield describes himself as a poet, but there seems very little poetry in smashing plate-glass windows. He was charged at the Mansion House with committing damage of that description. When previously before the court he addressed the alderman in a poetic effusion in which he begged him to temper mercy with justice, and the gaoler said that in the cells Benjamin freely indulged in rhyming. He was very subdued now.

"Were you drunk?" asked the Alderman.

"Well," said Benjamin, "In the ordinary acceptation of the word I was. It unfortunately runs in my family."

He goes to prison for three weeks, or in the ordinary acceptation of the 'term' – twenty-one days hard.'

The web has spread wider with the discovery of Swaffield Harbour between Coats Island and Mansel Island in the Hudson Bay, Canada. The Manitoba Geographical Names Program has material submitted by the Dominion Geodesist in 1946, that the harbour was named after Mr Albert T Swaffield who was in charge of the Hudson's Bay Company post in that area around 1936. The Geodesist, one who studies portions of the earth, wrote, 'He is, I believe, the only white man to have wintered on Mansel Island with the Inuit people.' There is a Swaffield School in Wandsworth built in 1895, a Swaffield Close [after Sam 1802] and a Swaffield Bridge [after HRJ] in Ampthill , Ronald Swaffield, Composer and Sir James Swaffield, who was Director General of London County Council. All these, and a multitude of others.

AUTHOR'S NOTE

In 1949, when I was eleven years old, my father took me to Ampthill in Bedfordshire 'to meet the Aunts'. I also met the tall and hooky-nosed Great Uncles and other members of a very large, cheerful, accepting family. Wartime petrol shortage had kept us apart – but the visit stuck in my mind like no other visit before or after. My father died in 1975, my mother in 1995. It was then I found old Swaffield family photographs tucked away in shoe boxes. Groups in the garden, stiff and still, women in bombazine dresses and big hats, the men with heavy moustaches and smoky pipes, the children dressed in calico and lace. I wanted to know more about these people, much more. They were my ancestors and immediately special to me.

In the intervening years between my first visit to Ampthill and my second to renew family friendship, I have married, lived an austere, lonely bush life in rural Africa and India for twenty-five years and given birth to four children. Dr Spock became my closest friend, Twi and Telugu were my languages, and I bargained for goat meat and pineapple in the village bazaars. At five-years old each of our children was heart-breakingly packed off to Mission School in the Nilgiri Hills, a three-day journey by steam train. Later they travelled to East Anglia to complete their education. We all know about crying 'Goodbye' and shouting 'Hello'.

Our life in alien lands has been fulfilling but difficult. We have experienced mutiny, cyclone, riot, tropical diseases, cockroaches, rabid dogs, cantankerous servants and nerve wracking travelling. Worse has been the separation from our children, the lack of squabble and laughter in our lonely homes. But it has taught us the true value of family life, and of how precious we are to each other. In writing this book about mine and other Swaffields, I have regained my ancestors and I have learnt a little of what makes them, and me, tick. It has been a long journey, and has answered some of my questions. But, like all families, the questions can go on for ever.

NW

Natalie Wheatley is the daughter of Frank Exton Swaffield. She was educated in Wales and trained as a secretary. Widely travelled, she lives in Suffolk with her husband, Michael, and works as a multi-subject freelance writer. This is her first book.

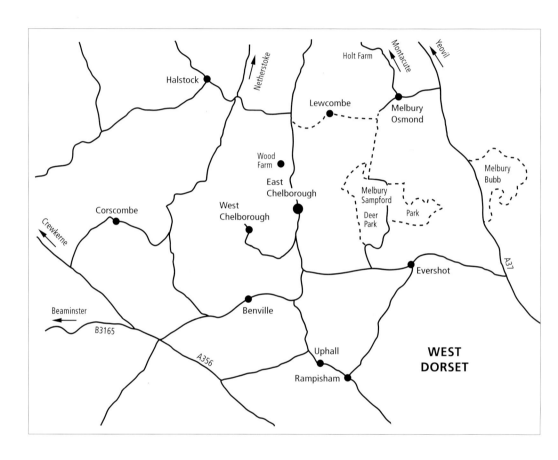

Chapter 1

DORSETSHIRE ~ EAST CHELBOROUGH
John (Swaffel) Swaffield 1731 and the family of his youngest son, Benjamin 1767

St Mary's Church, Beaminster, Dorset

*John Swaffield and Betty Gillingham
both of this parish were married by Banns in this Church
this 18th day of May 1755*

s/o *John Adams, Curate*

*This Marriage was solemnised between us
John Swaffield and Betty Gillingham
in the presence of us Henry Slade and John Ford*

Both signed the Register John (1731–1818) and Betty (1728–1812)

Beaminster is a pivotal town in our Dorsetshire story: Before John and Betty's marriage it was described as:

'A praty market towne in Dorsetshire and usith much Housbondry and lyith in one streat from North to South; and in another from West to Est. Netherby is the Paroch Chirch to it, and Bemistre is a Prebend to the Church as Saresbyri [Salisbury]. Bemistre is but 4 miles from Crookeshorn [Crewkerne] a market in Somersetshire, by north from Bemistre.' Fires ravaged the town particularly in 1700 when the Parliamentary Army saw 'the pittyfullest spectacle that Man can behold, hardly an house left not consumed'.

When our John Swaffield was born, George II had been on the British throne for four years, Robert Walpole dominated politics, Bonnie Prince Charlie's uprising was savagely cut down at the Battle of Culloden in 1746, and Robert Clive helped to lay down the foundations of British India. We have no previous affirmation of young John's parentage or birthplace. Many church

A contemporary view of The Square, Beaminster

records were lost in flood or fire. Nor do we have knowledge of Betty (Elizabeth) Gillingham. Their wedding, when the apple trees were full of blossom in May 1755, was a simple affair with family and friends attending. St Mary's Church is close to the main square, up an incline, with a fine tower. Inside there is a magnificent window behind the altar, its coloured patterns through filtered sunlight, brightened the faces of the young couple, John at 24 and Betty at 27. After some time they left Beaminster and moved to Chelborough Farm in East Chelborough in the parish of Lewcombe [low-coombe = deep valley]. It was a quiet place after the bustle of Beaminster.

St Mary's Church, Beaminster

Dorsetshire is traversed by the north and south Downs. The soil is mainly chalk, gravel and sand, but is very fertile in the valleys. When the young Swaffields settled in East Chelborough, wheat and barley were the standard crops and immense flocks of sheep were pastured. Dairy farms were large and animal husbandry carried to a high point of perfection. It was good breeding ground for a future generation of competent Swaffield farmers. Small industry included sailcloth, sacking, flax, nets, paper, linen and silk, also malting, brewing and iron-founding.

In 1744 John Hutchens wrote that 'Lucomb' was: 'A little vill, distant about two miles north from West Chelborough' and that East Chelborough was: 'A little hamlet, a mile south from Lucomb, with a parish containing 948 acres, two-thirds being pasture, meadowland and copses. The remainder arable. It is 2½ miles in length from north to south, a mile in breadth … It seems to be Celberge in the Domesday Book and belonged to Roger Arundel.'

There is no mention of the Swaffields so they did not pay the Poor Tax, nor were they rich and notable. The Swaffs were Yeomen, a term sometimes misunderstood because:

' … a curious belief prevailed, and still exists, that a yeoman was permanently anchored to a medium-sized holding of 100–150 acres embalmed, as it were, in his virtues of diligence, prudence and shrewdness. Clearly a man so noteworthy amassed enough capital to pay the entry fines and there was nothing to stop him accumulating lifeholds, especially before 1750, when there was less competition from townsmen.'

East Chelborough once had two medieval castles on the barrow-like mound. Iron relics were found, but the castles have disappeared, and the stone was used to build Chelborough Farm and nearby houses. The farm has a construction stone dated 1607. Originally built as a small T-shaped manor house, with a cottage addition, it had five-paned mullioned windows. The curved roof-

supporting beams are second-hand from a cruck house and marked with Roman numerals. There was a porch and adjoining is a large wooden grain storage and wagon shed. It is a pretty, low-lying house, fitting well into the countryside. It is easy to imagine the thump of heavy boots, the whinnying of horses, the cries of babies and the smell of cooking emanating from the kitchen, mingling with that of the privy in the yard. It has the appearance of a happy home, one that can comfortably squeeze in yet another child. And many children were squeezed in.

In the roof of the grain storage is a vertical wheel which hauled up sacks of grain. Here some visitors feel a presence:

> One experience is 'of a 'little man with his hands on his hips' and another 'a little male person, dark haired, with his hands in his pockets and a benevolent spirit'. Someone else has felt 'a child, protecting two little grandchildren'. The occupiers wonder if gangs of seasonal reapers camped in the barn, and perhaps a child fell from the beams?

A typical Dorset farmhouse

Chelborough Farm as it is today

Opposite the house, facing east, a brick crypt was built between 1720 and 1745. Inside were leather bound lead-lined studded coffins and a skull. Previous owners of Chelborough House in the 19th century were Lilian Digby of the Digby Estate, and it was rented to the Ridout family. The present owners describe their home as 'old and crumbling, but we love the family feel of it'. Their tiny parish church of Lewcombe is buried in this medieval pocket of Dorsetshire, and reached by travelling up and down narrow banked lanes through tiny hamlets dotted with 17th century cottages, the rolling land wooded and laced with small rivers and streams.

John and Betty had three boys, one unmarried, who pre-deceased their parents leaving two younger sons, Joseph and Benjamin, widows and eleven grandchildren. Their only daughter, Elizabeth, lived until she was over seventy, having had the heartache of losing many of her nineteen babies. Like her elder brother John, she married into the Neal family of Wood Farm, and the two families co-existed closely, all worshipping at St James. Of John and Betty's two surviving youngest boys, Joseph became a Master Carpenter in Rampisham, later Halstock. He married and had five children by an untraceable cousin, Mary Swaffield. Most of his family remained firmly in Dorsetshire and its villages until the end of the 19th century, when they had died, or the land could no longer sustain them. Dorsetshire still holds the heart strings of many of Joseph's descendants. He was registered in the 1841 Benville census, aged 77, as 'agricultural labourer' and, in the 1851 census he was still labouring at Halstock aged 87, finally to die in his boots, at the ripe old age of ninety. Life could be hard and cruel. One lad in Melbury Osmond was convicted of breaking into a bakery, sentenced to death at Dorchester Assizes and publicly hanged. Another resident, Benjy Miller, kept a diary. He was born in 1776. His family scratched a living and 'allmost [sic] starved to death'. He went from village to village looking for work and finally returned home and 'larnt to wave' Eventually he 'went gloving' in Yeovil before he joined the Royal Artillery in 1795, and fought in the Peninsular War against Napoleon.

John Swaffel 1731–1818 and Elizabeth Gillingham 1728–1812

Thomas	John	George	Elizabeth	Joseph	Benjamin
born	born	born	born	born	born
1756	1758	1761	1762	1764	1767
bap 19.4.1756	bap 27.3.1758			bap 24.8.1765	bap 24.7.1768
Beaminster	Corscombe			Lewcombe	East Chel
d 5.9.1788	d 1805	d 6.3.1792	d Aug 1835	d 1854	d 5.4.1840
					Wootton Fitzpaine

The first son, Thomas, was born in Beaminster a year after John and Betty's wedding. They then moved to Corscombe, where John II was born and, finally, into Chelborough Farm where they settled and the other children came along. In the mid-18th century most people in Britain lived in small villages. The only city of any size in England was London, with a population of 500,000. The rural majority earned their money by farming in ways which had hardly changed since the Middle Ages. They were ploughmen, shepherds and waggoners. Labourers did seasonal work, and even the youngest children would scare away crows, drag turnips or glean after harvest. Birds and rabbits were trapped, fish were caught in the ponds, honey collected from nests, and herbs from the waysides.

Lewcombe and East Chelborough are described as abandoned villages, although once there was a string of cottages housing a baker, wheelwright, blacksmith and carpenter. One building was a schoolroom with a teacher and a few pupils. In the nearby hamlet of Melbury Osmond another school was started by Lord Ilchester, so most of the village children received some education. Printed matter was expensive and lighting in homes was primitive. Lights were made from precious beeswax or peeled rushes dipped into warm mutton fat, producing smoky, smelly flames lasting a bare half-hour, making it difficult for children to study. Both John and Betty could read and write, and were determined that their own children should receive an education to a reasonable standard.

The villagers worshipped at their parish church, St James at Lewcombe. This building is said to have been built in the 16th century on the site of a 12th century chapel. Both John, and his

Melbury Osmond Village

youngest son, Benjamin, are recorded as churchwardens. It is the sixth smallest church in England and situated on private land. It has no steeple, but a small bell turret and, up high, pretty circular windows. In the churchyard so many of our Swaffields are buried or have memorial stones. Altogether thirteen family names can be identified, as well as those associated, such as Neal, Matthews and Cridge. To reach St James the family walked across the fields in summer, and travelled a mile by cart along the tracks, and down the hill to the tiny church in the valley on cold winter mornings. They stamped the mud off their boots, the girls straightened their bonnets and smoothed their skirts, and the babies were hushed. The church is so small, that the consolidated Swaffields must have been bursting out of the doors.

> There are eight small oak pews on one side and four on the other. Nikolaus Pevsner, art historian, wrote that the 'Parish church of East Chelborough is situated in a very secluded leafy spot. The site is only one mile west of Melbury Osmond, but there is no road from there.' Inside the church it is recorded that '… there is a superstition that it was attempted to build the church at East Chelborough but the fairies, every night, removed what had been built during the day down to the present site.' The fairies ensured that the family had a good tramp to church each Sunday, uphill all the way back.

As well as education it was important to keep the children healthy. The only energy at the time was that of human and animal muscle, water and wind. Medical care was minimal, there were no antiseptics or anaesthetics. Hospitals in Crewkerne or Yeovil were archaic, and patients had little chance of leaving alive. They housed the poor, insane, drunk and contagious. Patients were minded, not nursed, in unsanitary and overcrowded conditions by untrained staff. Childbirth was always at home, with a local midwife relying on her common sense to deliver a baby safely, "You just keep on pushin', gow arn now, push again moy luv, do yew not give up, 'tis painful Oi know." Once the baby was wrapped in clean cloths, with the other little ones poking its eyes and wiggling its toes, it was then up to the mother to suckle and nurture – and cook, launder clothes and sweep. Many babies died, some buried before baptism.

The youngest son, Benjamin, married Hannah Burdett, from Membury in Devonshire, in 1791 at Halstock, and they were fortunate to rear eleven healthy children, who whooped around

Halstock Church, where Benjamin Swaffield and Hannah Burdett were married in 1791

Date of Births of the Children of Benj[n] & Hannah Swaffield
Thomas Son was born July 18th 1791 at a quarter to ten in morning
Hannah Daughter born 30 Nov[r] 1792 at Ten oClock at night
Mary Daughter born 7th June 1794 at 7 oClock in morning
Robert Son born 10th of August 1795 at 12 oClock at night
Benj[t] Son born 30 of October 1797 at 11 oClock at night
Elizabeth Daughter born 5 of August 1799 at 10 oClock at Night
Judith Daughter born 6th February 1801 at One oClock in morning
Samuel Son born 15 of August 1802 at One in the Morning
Martha Daughter born 7 of February 1804 at 9 oClock in evening
Sarah Daughter born 11 June 1805 at 4 oClock in the Afternoon
John Son born 10th December 1806 at 10 oClock in morning

Written list of the 11 Benjamin Swaffield children 1791–1806 – Courtesy Andrew Underwood Collection

Chelborough Farmhouse, tripping over the dogs, fluttering the chickens, and fighting with their many cousins.

A good diet and a sensible mind was the key to a healthy household, and there were books to help. Farmers set broken bones by picking and grating slimy comfrey roots. The fractured limb was agonisingly set by the pull-push method, and the comfrey mash covered the injured area until it set. Constipation and piles were another problem, eased by roasting quick snails in their shells, picking out the meat with a pin, and beating them in a mortar with some powder of pepper to a salve. The dried and powdered roots of Pilewort were added, 'strewn thin' on the plaster and applied as 'hot as you can suffer it.'

Household heating and cooking was provided by wood or peat fires. Betty urged young Elizabeth, the only girl, to chop vegetables and wash the wooden platters, and the boys were instructed to fill the water pans. Countrymen had rights to remove dead wood by 'hook or by crook'. Water came from streams and pumps in the yards. Domestic wells were shallow and often became contaminated. At

Betty's kitchen at Chelborough Farm

Chelborough Farm there was a three-seater privy in an outside hut in the muddy yard, full of puddles after rain. The family washed occasionally before the fire, one by one in the same water. Food was cooked in wall fireplaces, next to which was a warm cupboard with an iron door. The grate was cleaned out early in the morning, riddled and relit if necessary. Betty chivvied her children to help, whilst John stamped around, grumbling, waiting for his dinner.

Bread and cheese was a staple diet, and rennet was made to curdle new milk for cheese. This was complicated, but a recipe well worth keeping when the corner shop is shut. For Elizabeth it was agonising, as one of the soft, sweet young calves had to be sacrificed. The baby animal was allowed to suck as much milk as it wanted from its mother before it was killed. The calf's full stomach bag was removed and left, covered in stinging nettles, until it turned red. When the milk had curdled it was poured out and left standing. The stomach bag was washed, salted inside and laid in salt for a further twenty-four hours. The curdled milk was washed in fresh milk, put back into the bag with '… four streakings, the last milk from the cow, a beaten egg, twelve cloves and a blade of mace'. The bag was skewered and hung up in a pot. Meanwhile another pot was boiled with half a pint of salted water, six tops of blackthorn and burnet [plant] and two of sweet marjoram. When cooled this liquid was poured into the hanging bag with egg and milk, and then soaked in the rest of the liquid in the pot. This residual liquid finally became rennet and '… the bag can be filled and left to exude another six or seven times before the action of the stomach juice lessens.' The fresh cheese was eaten with coarse home-made bread and onions from the fields.

The first son, Thomas, did not marry but the rest of the family extended with weddings which produced thirty-two grandchildren born between 1781 and 1806. Five were named Elizabeth, four named John, three named Mary or Benjamin and two named Joseph, Edward, Thomas or Hannah. New babies often appeared annually, certainly every two years. The Swaffield family to this day can be considered a prolific one of longevity, nurtured by good humour. Family conversations were complicated:

"Mornin' George, 'ow's yor new babe, John?" asked John.

"Doin' well, John and, may Oi arsk, 'ow's yor little 'un, John?" replied George.

"He be foine, George. Little John looks just like his grandad, John Swaffel," said John.

George was puzzled, "Hmmm. That's what moy Betty said 'bout our little boy John, just like John Swaffel, she say." He wandered off, scratching his head trying to work it out.

They were a hard-working lot and pursued trades such as farmer, master carpenter, miller, quarryman, sailcloth maker, postman, inn-keeper, weaver and baker. The Lord of the Manor, Lord Ilchester, who oversaw Melbury Bubb, Melbury Osmond and Melbury Sampford – all bordering East Chelborough and Lewcombe on private land – helped the Swaffield boys get good jobs. A verbal testimony from such a respected local dignitary was worth its weight in gold.

The family of Benjamin Swaffield 1767–1840 and Hannah Burdett 1765–1857

Thomas	Hannah	Mary	Robert	Benjamin	Elizabeth	Judith	Samuel	Martha	Sarah	John
1791	1792	1794	1795	1797	1799	1801	1802	1804	1805	1806
1859	married	married	1857	1879	1831	married	1863	1877	1856	1891
m Harriet	John Rugg	John	Charlotte	m 1) Frances	m	Robert	Harriet	George	Ephraim	Elizabeth
Guppy on	from	Gard	Farmer	Chubb 1829	James	Meech	Nash	Squibb	Matthews	Otton
18.3.1818	Montacute		1799–1869	m2) Frances	Storer		Exton		1796–65	1821–89
				Watkinson						

We have no silhouettes of our Dorset forbears, although at local fairs amazingly accurate profiles were created using black paper and scissors. The cost could range from a shilling to a guinea. The family loved the fairs where stallholders sold furniture and ironmongery. The little girls picked up the shiny jewellery and silver, and felt the soft silks and muslins, toys and millinery. Horse fairs drew in gentry, farmers and dealers alike, a good horse was worth a king's ransom. Yeoman farmers travelled by cart, richer people by carriage. The Swaffields travelled to Evershot in the south and, occasionally, northwards to Crewkerne, their nearest town. Betty Gillingham Swaffield lived until she was eighty-four, although her gravestone states 83, and the burial register states 85. Her husband, daughter Elizabeth and her two surviving sons, Joseph and Benjamin, attended her funeral, on a chilly March day at the little church, accompanied by a great crowd of Swaffs, Neals, Guppys, and a lot of bemused children squawking for their food. News travelled fast by word of mouth, a galloping pony, and passing carts. The youngest of the grandchildren, John, son of Benjamin, was just six.

Five years later grandfather John Swaffield drew up a Will. He left £50 (£3500 in today's terms) to be shared between his surviving children and grandchildren.

The double grave of Betty and John lies quietly to the left inside the gate of Lewcombe Church.

The grave of Elizabeth & John Swaffield, Lewcombe

St James Church, Lewcombe

~o~————————————————————————~o~

In Memory of ELIZABETH the wife
of JOHN SWAFFIELD Sr who died
March 26th 1812, aged 83 years.
Also of THOMAS the son of
John & Elizabeth Swaffield who died
Sept 5th 1788 aged 32 years.
Also of GEORGE the son of
John & Elizabeth Swaffield
who died March 6th 1792
Aged 31 years

In Memory of JOHN SWAFFIELD Sr
who died May 14th 1818 aged 86 yrs.
Also of SARAH MATTHEWS
daghter [sic] of Benjamin and Hannah
Swaffield and grand-daughter of the
above named John Swaffield who
died February 12th 1856
aged 53 years
"The Lord is Righteous in All His
Ways and Holy in All His Works"

~o~————————————————————————~o~

Benjamin had worked alongside his father, and took over the farm when John became too old and ill to work. The family vacated the property on John's death, and moved to live with the youngest son, John, who was tenant of Manor Farm in Wootton Fitzpaine, near Lyme Regis, on the south coast. The families of Joseph and Benjamin, remain the focus of our story.

Wootton Fitzpaine was the starting point for Benjamin's sons, Ben aged 27 and Sam aged 22, to journey by stagecoach to London in 1824. Thanks to Lord Ilchester, they had connections with the Duke of Devonshire [Ben became his Head Bailiff] and Lord Holland of Ampthill [Sam became his Steward].

Thomas, their elder brother, applied for a marriage licence and was wed to Harriet Guppy [Huguenot – Goupe] from Halstock. She was the daughter of Christopher Guppy and Ann Nanny. Tom was a miller and farmer at Lower Holt Farm, and resident in Melbury Osmond for upwards of 40 years. In the 1851 census he employed 10 labourers. He and Harriet had three children. Their eldest, John Guppy, was also a miller, and was persuaded by his Uncle Ben to try for work in Derbyshire. There John met and married Eliza from Marylebone. She was employed in the Duke of Devonshire's household at Chatsworth. The marriage is registered in the Leek District in 1846. But John did not settle, and the couple moved back to Dorsetshire to farm at Melbury Osmond, and then Charminster, where John worked his mill and made bread. They had four children, the last born in 1860. The marriage was a failure and John deserted Eliza in 1865. He is recorded as dying at Melbury Osmond, Yeoman. His Will was proved by Thomas Randall of Winfrith, Gentleman, and Arthur Dibble of Woolcombe, Yeoman. Eliza returned to her more familiar Derby, along with the children. Her son, Herbert James, lived there too in Rosehill Street with his wife Lucy Jane. Herbert was Assistant Secretary to Samuel Allsop & Sons, Brewers. Eliza died on 1 July 1881 in Derby and her Will was proved at St Helens, County Lancaster by her daughter, Mary Eliza Swaffield, spinster, of Wood End House, Cromford.

The rest of the family remained close to their roots and had plenty of opportunity to meet for births and marriages, for high days and holidays and at times of sadness when loved ones died.

Benjamin Swaffield was a wonderful father – visiting, writing letters and remembering his eleven children, trying to do his best for them. In 1835, he wrote to Ben Bailiff, living at Edensor on the Chatsworth Estate. Ben's wife, Frances Chubb, had tragically died three years previously. The 'Miss Chubb' referred to twice must be one of Frances' sisters, sent from Evershot to care for Ben's surviving daughter, Sarah Seaward Swaffield who, in 1835 was 4½. Preserved by the Derbyshire Swaffields, the letter and others, have been passed down.

The letter, detailed below and overleaf, consists of two sheets folded carefully to the size of the address and fastened on the back with black sealing wax. This was before envelopes and stamps. Ben would have paid the postman 10d, or more, as a delivery charge.

Wotton Fitzpaine 11 Sept 1835

Dear Son

I now take an opportunity of writing to you and I hope this will find you your dear child with Miss Chubb all quite well, we are all well at Wotton except myself. I hath been laid up in the Gout for the last week but not severly I have it in one foot only at present but I expect it with go further before it will have me for good. I am sorry to inform you that your Aunt (Anne) Neal is no more she died about three weeks since she was seased suddenly and fell down in to fit and laid eight days before she died, she will be a great loss to John and Edward [b 1794] as they have no one else to do for them, Captn Jennings buried his youngest daughter about a week since and it is thought that he himself will not be down stairs any more till he is brought down also Mr John Warr of Beaminster is dead and buried. Mr Pattens old servant Peggy is also no more, she have been dead about two months, Sam [from Ampthill] was down with us in the begining of the sumer for the good of his health and he found great benefit by the change of air, we sent him home quite … and Mr Rowland told him he hoped he would not have ocasion to go to Uncles House any more, John [b 1806] Rec^d a letter from him about a fortnight ago he was continuing much beter then, how are you off for grass we have had the dryest summer that I ever knew in my life allmost all the Cow Cattle in this part of the country have been served with Hay for a considerable time past we have no raine till the last two or three days past Crops of Corn are very good in this part how is the Wheat selling in your markets, we cannot get more than from 4/6^d to 5/- per Bushell here, but we get a good price for the Oats I have been selling at 28^d Quart. I have between 3 and 4 Thousand Bus^{el} of Wheat by me now, Tollerdown Fair was last Monday the largest N^o of Sheep that ever was seen there in one Fair, they went off dull at reduced prices and it is supposed the Old Ewe trade will be a bad one this fall, I have put my Derby Ram that you was kind enough to send me with 50 off the best of my Ewes, he is like to make a very good sheep, I saw … G. Squibb, Robt Meech [2 of his sons-in-law] at Tollerdown they was all well there, we shall be glad to hear from you the first half our you have to spare, your mother, Sarah [b 1805] & John join me in kindest regards to you dear little Child and Miss Chubb.

Benj Swaffield

NB When you go on the Moores shooting remember me to the heath …

Grandfather's letter.
Novbr 1837.

Mr Benj Swaffield
Edensor
Bakewell
Derbyshire

Wotton Fitzpaine 11 Septr 1835

Dear Son,

I now take an oppertunity of writing to you and I hope this will find you your dear Child with Miss Chubb all quite well, we are all well at Wotton except myself. I hath been laid up in the Gout for the last week but not sceerly I have it in one foot only at present but I expect it will go further before it will leave me for good I am sorry to inform you that your Aunt Neal is no more she died about three weeks since she was seased suddenly and fell down in a fit and laid eight days before she died, she will be a great loss to John and Edward as they have no one else to do for them, Captn Jennings buried his youngest daughter about a week since and it is thought that he himself will not be down stairs any more till he is brought down

how is the Wheat selling in your markets, we cannot
get more then from 4/6 to 5/ pr Bushell here, but we
get a good price for Oats I have him selling at 28 pr Quar
I have between 3 and 4 Thousand Bus.s of Wheat by
me now, Tollerdown Fair was last Monday the
largest N.o of Sheep that ever was seen there in one
Fair, they went off dull at reduced prices and it
is supposed the Old Ewe trade will
be a bad one this fall, I have
put my Derby Ram that you was kind enough
send me with 50 off the best of my Ewes, he is like
to make a very good Sheep, I saw Tho.s G Squibb. Rot.
Meech Jr. at Tollerdown they was all well tho—, we shall
be glad to hear from you the first haff our you have
to spare, your Mother, Sarah, & John joine me in
kindest regards to you dear little Child & Miss Chubb
NB when you go on the Moores shooting
remember me to the heath poults
Benj Swaffield

Shown left is the Derbyshire address and the first page from the letter showing the date

Above is the final page showing the second reference to 'Miss Chubb' and the signature of Benj Swaffield

Benjamin died at Wootton Fitzpaine in 1840, and Hannah later in Allington, Bridport where she
was described as an Annuitant – 'a person who receives or holds an annuity'. Her son, Robert,
was described similarly, when he died at Corscombe in 1857. Their bodies were brought to the

family church at Lewcombe, and they occupy the centre gravestones of the row of the Swaffield three. The inscriptions read:

~o~————————~o~

To the Memory of BENJAMIN SWAFFIELD
Yeoman
Who was born at Chelborough Farm in this
Parish where he resided for upward of
60 years. Died April 5th 1840 at
Wootton Fitzpaine in the County
Aged 73 years.
Deservedly respected by large circle of
friends and acquaintances and much lamented
by his family.
"My friends were many and few were my foes
My path was chequered amidst a world of woes
And now my Life's short thread is spun
My virtues imitate my vices shun"

~o~————————~o~

~o~————————~o~

To the Memory of HANNAH wife of
Benjamin Swaffield who died
October 5th 1857 aged 92 years.
"Thou Shall guide Me With Thy
Counsel & After That Receive Me
With Glory"

~o~————————~o~

Described as 'Yeoman' Benjamin Swaffield left a fair Will which he signed on 30 January 1840. He died the following April and was carried by cart to be buried at Lewcombe. It took time for the sad news to reach Ben and Sam so many miles away. Grief filled their hearts – their father was a worthy man, and had made great efforts to regularly visit his two sons, who had moved so far away from home. He also wrote monthly letters sending them all the family news. His Will was proved at London on 27 June 1840 by Thomas, his eldest son, and John, his youngest son.

Seven years after his father died at Manor Farm, John was a bachelor of 41. He met and married Elizabeth Otton who was then twenty-six years old. We have an image of this couple, a

Painting of John Swaffield and Elizabeth Otton's wedding in Chideok Church
Courtesy Andrew Underwood Collection

pretty oil painting which hangs in Chideok Church, showing them leaving the churchyard under a cloudy blue sky. Their wedding day was on 28 June 1847.

Elizabeth's father, John Otton of Devonshire, could not give her away as he had died in 1831 at Catherston Lewston, but was buried at Wootton. In the spring of 1866 John, Elizabeth's husband, wrote a congratulatory letter to Ampthill from Wootton Fitzpaine, on the occasion of the wedding of his nephew, Henry Richard James Swaffield, eldest son of his own brother, Sam. HRJ married Emmeline Jepson of Rowsley, Derbyshire. The Jepson family had met John's elder brother, Ben, and his family in Bakewell.

The Parish Church, Wootton Fitzpaine – 1846

John Swaffield's grave, and that of his wife, Elizabeth Otton, is easy to find in the small churchyard of Wootton Fitzpaine, north of Lyme Regis. The day before our April visit it had been snowing heavily, but we found a pretty sun-filled place, the grass sprinkled with daisies, primroses and shiny celandines. In the tall trees a cacophony of demanding crows almost drowned out the chorus of songbirds. The inscription reads:

~o~————————~o~

'In Loving Memory of Elizabeth
wife of John Swaffield, Wootton Fitzpaine,
who entered into rest January 7th 1889 aged 68

–

'Until Day Break and the Shadows Flee Away'

'Also of the above named who died March 10th 1891
aged 84. For 60 years occupier of the Manor Farm'

~o~————————~o~

indicating that he moved from Chelborough Farm when he was 25. John died at West Allington, Bridport but was buried at Wootton Fitzpaine. John willed to his niece, Sarah Seaward Milward, daughter of his brother Ben of Chatsworth, his three oil paintings – portraits of herself, her father and her mother, Frances Chubb.

THE WILL OF JOHN SWAFFIELD 1732–1818

I JOHN SWAFFIELD SENIOR of East Chelborough [alias LUCOMB] in the County of Dorset, Yeoman, being of sound and disposing [sic] mind memory and understanding do this ninth day of July in the year of our Lord One Thousand Eight Hundred and Seventeen make publish and declare this my Last Will and Testament.

I give and bequeath unto my grandchildren, children of my son George Swaffield [3rd son died aged 31] the sum of fifty pounds to be divided equally between them share and share alike, that is to say, John Swaffield, Elizabeth Slade, George Swaffield and Benjamin Swaffield or so many as shall be then living or surviving at my decease.

Also I give and devise unto my son Joseph Swaffield, Cottage Garden and Orchard with the appurtenances situated and lying at Glandvilles Wootton in the County of Dorset.

Also I give and devise my household goods (of which an Inventory was taken and signed by me the eighth day of April in the year of our Lord One Thousand Eight Hundred and Eleven) to my son John Swaffield, my daughter Elizabeth Neal, my son Joseph Swaffield and my son Benjamin Swaffield to be equally divided between them.

And I give and bequeath all my monies, securities for money and personal estate and effects whatsoever and wheresoever after payments thereout of my just debts legacies testimonial and funeral expenses unto my son John Swaffield and my daughter Elizabeth Neal and my son Joseph Swaffield to be divided between them share and share alike and I make constitute and appoint my son Benjamin Swaffield and my good friend William Daw of West Chelborough Gentleman of the County of Dorset Executors in Trust of this my last Will and Testament revoking all former Wills and Bequests by me heretofore made declaring this and no other to be my last Will and Testament.

IN WITNESS WHEREOF I have hereunto put my hand and seal the day and year first above written

SIGNED SEALED AND PUBLISHED

Declared by the said named Testator
John Swaffield as and for his last
WILL AND TESTAMENT in the presence of us

John Swaffield

Chris G Daw
Elizabeth Genge

Then a CODICIL was added:

WHEREAS I have in my said WILL given to my grandchildren John Swaffield, Elizabeth Slade, George Swaffield and Benjamin Swaffield the sum of Twelve Pounds Ten shillings each. In addition to the said Twelve Pounds Ten Shillings I give and devise to my Grandchildren before mentioned the further sum of Fifty pounds to be divided between them share and share alike being a part of a Note of Hand now in my possession against my Grandson Thomas Swaffield of Halstock if the same is recoverable from the said Thomas Swaffield by my Executors

WITNESS my hand and Seal

This third day of May 1818

IN THE PRESENCE OF

X the cross of John Swaffield

Hannah Swaffield
Susanna Neal

Although he could write, John Swaffield was too ill to sign his name and died just eleven days later.

THE WILL OF BENJAMIN SWAFFIELD 1767–1840

This is the Last Will & Testament of Benjamin Swaffield of the parish of Wootton Fitzpaine in the County of Dorset, Yeoman on this day January 30th 1840. To my wife Hannah all my interest in Sutton Mills situate in the parish of Sutton Bingham [nr Yetminster] in the County of Somerset. Daughter Sarah £20. In Trust for my grand-children, sons and daughters of my late daughter, Mary Gard, the sum of £100 to be equally divided among them when 21. Wife, son John and Sarah my daughter, all the household furniture, plate, linen, china, glass, pictures, books, wine and liquors in the said dwelling house. Goodwill or lease of Wootton Farm to my son John. John, all my outgrown crop of wheat at the expiration of the said lease by paying to the rest of my sons and daughters that are now living the sum of £25 cash, if deceased their children. Leave the sum of £100 in the hands of my son John until the expiration of the lease of the said farm which expires on the 25th day of March 1844.

John to pay my dear wife £20 yearly until the lease expires. After this all my children and Mary's, my late daughter, children to pay my dear wife £20 a year.

IN WITNESS WHEREOF I have hereunto put my hand and seal the day and year first above written

SIGNED SEALED AND PUBLISHED   *Benjamin Swaffield*

Proved at London June 27th 1840 by Thos. & John Swaffield, sons.

PART OF THE WILL OF ELIZA SWAFFIELD, w/o JOHN GUPPY SWAFFIELD 1820

'Administration was granted, limited to all such personal estate and effects as the deceased acquired after 15 September 1865, being the time of commencement of desertion by her husband, John Guppy Swaffield. The testatrix left £508 4s 10d. She also left her own portrait in oils to her eldest daughter, Evelyn Anne who had married John Aday Wheatcroft and '... the residue of my estate to daughter Mary Eliza, both real and personal, for her own independent use independent of any husband she may marry.'

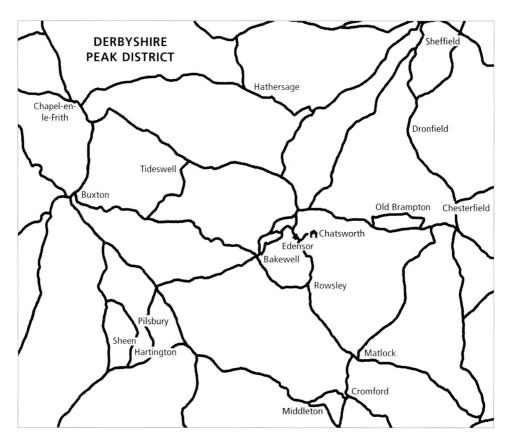

Chatsworth House and grounds c1700s – Courtesy Chatsworth Settlement

Chapter 2

DERBYSHIRE ~ CHATSWORTH
Ben Swaffield, Bailiff, 1829–1853

Benjamin Swaffield 1767–1840 and Hannah Burdett 1765–1857

Thomas	Hannah	Mary	Robert	Benjamin	Elizabeth	Judith	Samuel	Martha	Sarah	John
1791	1792	1794	1795	1797	1799	1801	1802	1804	1805	1806
1859			1857	1879	1831		1863	1877	1856	1891
m Harriet Guppy	John Rugg	John Gard	Charlotte Farmer	1) Frances Chubb 2) Frances Watkinson	James Storer	Robert Meech	Harriet Nash Exton	George Squibb	Ephraim Matthews	Elizabeth Otton

Ben was twenty-one when his grandfather, John, died and he and his family moved to Wootton Fitzpaine to tenant another farm. He continued to help his father, Benjamin, and learn new agricultural skills, such as animal husbandry and crop management. The family fitted well into the community, made contacts, and prospered. Ben's education progressed, he could comprehend well, write legibly, and understand and keep accounts. He was single and 27 years old when he finally left the family homestead, to seek a successful livelihood elsewhere. He had made up his mind to take up work in Derbyshire as recommended by the highly connected Lord Ilchester. He and his younger brother, Sam, travelled together as far as London, where they parted, Sam to travel to Ampthill in Bedfordshire.

For Ben, the journey from Dorsetshire to Derbyshire in 1824 was long. The Dorsetshire coach left Cartgate for Lad's Lane in London. He stopped overnight, near Charing Cross, and travelled on next day, on the inside, paying 5d a mile. Hostelries and stable boys had one minute to remove exhausted horses at each stage, and harness up a fresh team. The coachman drove the horses, and the guard was responsible for passengers and mail bags. A guard could travel up to 150 miles a day and receive 10 shillings a week, relying on tips from the inside passengers to supplement his wage.

Ben made contacts and took up work near Bakewell. In 1826 he returned to East Chelborough to witness his sister, Martha's, wedding to George Squibb of Melbury Osmond. The other witness was his future wife, Frances Chubb. Ben was a personable, hard-working young man, and soon became established. In 1829 he was employed as Bailiff on the Chatsworth Estate. The 83,000 acreage was inherited, at 21, by the 6th Duke of Devonshire, William Cavendish, Marquess of Hartington. Known as the Bachelor Duke [Hart to his friends], he was the only son of Duchess Georgiana, the politically involved, dynamic, attention seeking, loose living daughter of the 1st Earl Spencer.

A chance meeting with landscaper, Joseph Paxton, at the Horticultural Gardens at Chiswick, initiated his real interest in gardening. Hart employed Paxton, a Bedfordshire boy born at Milton-Bryant near Woburn, two years after Ben. Whilst Ben managed the land and the tenants,

A painting of the 6th Duke as a teenager – Courtesy Chatsworth Settlement

A painting of Sir Joseph Paxton – Courtesy Chatsworth Settlement

the Duke and the Gardener transformed the grounds. Botanists were sent to the Americas and the Far East to bring back rare plants. Great rockeries and flower beds were introduced. The Conservative Wall glasshouse was built, as well as the Great Conservatory which was constructed of wood, iron and glass, covering three-quarters of an acre. This conservatory was the forerunner of the Crystal Palace, which Paxton built for the Great Exhibition of 1851, in Hyde Park.

Hart went to Russia as Ambassador for the Coronation of Tsar Nicholas I in 1826. There he saw the Peterhof Fountain, the highest in the world. He told Paxton about it, and the two planned a more powerful sky-scraping jet. It proved Paxton's engineering skills, and their Emperor Fountain reaches over 280 feet on a calm day.

These three young men, Hart, Ben and Joe, with their diverse backgrounds, developed much of the Chatsworth Estate as it is today:

> 'From whichever way the Estate is approached, it is obvious that it sits in a man-made landscape on a huge scale. Hedges are in a uniform pattern, the villages, be they built of locally available dark gritstone, soft buff limestone or grey limestone, have houses with their original doors and windows, and all painted with blue woodwork. There are heather grouse moors, fertile valleys and narrow limestone dales. The fields are full of humps and bumps of old lead-mine workings, and the jagged grey and white dry-stone walls, which line narrow lanes, end as mysteriously as they begin. The flora, and the occasional ash tree and thorn on the heights, inhabited by larks and hares, are a land apart. So are the farms on the gated road from Hartington to Pilsbury.'
>
> *The Estate – 'A View from Chatsworth' – Devonshire, Deborah Duchess.*

Church banner at Evershot

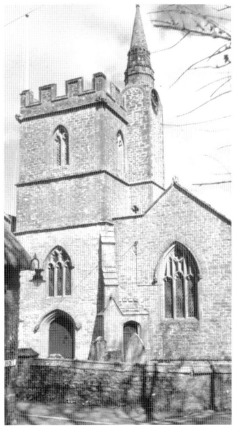

St Osmund's Church, Evershot

Ben returned briefly to Dorsetshire and, on 19 March 1829, at St Osmund's Church, Evershot he married 31 year old Frances Chubb. In the previous century, George Crabbe, poet, had been Rector at St Osmund's. He had a sympathetic understanding of country people, similar to the grandparents of the Chubbs and the Swaffs, '… life had not been all milk and honey' – and he wrote:

> 'Go then, and see them rising with the sun,
> through a long course of daily toil to run,
> Like him to make the plenteous harvest grow,
> And yet not share the plenty they bestow …'

Within a few days, they travelled to Derbyshire. For Frances, daughter of James and Ann Chubb, this was like a journey to the other side of the world.

Insignia of the Trustees of the Chatsworth Settlement

The archivist of the Trustees of the Chatsworth Settlement wrote:

'The first mention of Benjamin Swaffield is in 1829 when on October 15 he was paid £27 1s 6d 'for travelling expenses from Dorsetshire to Chatsworth and back.' Despite this October date, it seems that he actually began work earlier in the year, because his predecessor as Bailiff here, Henry Worrall, was reimbursed – for tolls and petty expenses for one quarter ending at Lady Day – whilst Swaffield was – paid for the like to Midsummer. Presumably the latter began his employment here on Lady Day – March 25 1829. It is interesting to calculate, from the same account book, that Benjamin Swaffield's wages were £120 per year, much the same as those of Joseph Paxton and very much more than his predecessor, Henry Worrall who only earned £72 per year. I am puzzled at this very large increase, just as I am by the very generous allowance listed as – Furniture for the Bailiff: Ranging from £2 for cutlery, £4 for barrels, £27 for ironmongery to £104 for upholstery. The total payment for Mr Swaffield's furniture and fittings was £165 16s 6d., or approximately £7,000 by today's equivalent rates, magnanimous indeed!

'As Benjamin Swaffield was Bailiff [Farm Manager] he would have worked on the whole estate which was much larger than the Estate is today [35,000 acres] We are not sure where he lived, but his children were born at Edensor, a village within the Park, so we would surmise that is where the family resided.'

Benjamin Swaffield 1797–1879 and 1) Frances Chubb 1798–1832

Anna Maria	Sarah Seaward
b March 13 1830	b April 16 1831
d February 15 1832	bap May 15 1831

That village of Edensor was then, in the 6th Duke's eyes, 'a ragged conglomeration of nondescript buildings unworthy of a well-run estate'. He had plans for a model village, but that was to be later.

Ben and Fanny soon had two little daughters, but their mother died young, as did little Anna Maria, leaving Ben a widower at thirty-five with a one-year-old toddler, Sarah, and a tiring, responsible job. He was heartbroken. The double grave is close to Edensor church. In spring, the sandstone memorial is softened by a swathe of golden daffodils.

Anna Maria and Fanny's gravestone at Edensor

~o~————————————————————————————~o~

Sacred To the Memory of Frances
The WIFE of Benjamin Swaffield who died Feby 4th 1832 Aged 34 Years.
Also of Anna Maria Daughter of the above who died Feby 15th 1832.
AGED 1 YEAR and 11 MONTHS.

As if a silv'ry Planet left the sphere.
It cheer'd with calmest brightness leaving there
An empty unblest darkness; ever so
Didst thou, from thine afflicted husband go;
And thy fair Satellite, thy darling child.
So quickly follow'd from this gloomy wild
To Regions fairer: brighter: Fare thee well
Fanny: no epitaph thy worth can tell.

~o~————————————————————————————~o~

Four years later, Ben married Frances Watkinson at the church of St Thomas, Old Brampton, a small village on the Chesterfield road, east of Baslow. They waited nine years for Frances to produce the first of their four boys. Sarah, Ben's fourteen-year-old daughter, was then able to help look after the babies. They all lived at Edensor until Benjamin John was eight.

Benjamin Swaffield 1797–1879 and 2) Frances Watkinson 1812–1893

Benjamin John	Clement Edward	Thomas Watkinson	Sylvester
Dec 5 1845	Nov 23 1847	March 14 1850	Dec 31 1851
Jan 26 1896	Aug 6 1921	Sept 5 1905	1931
Farmer, Hartington	Corn Merchant	Railway Clerk, Derby	Solicitor, Chesterfield
m Sarah Ellen Moore	1)Annie Rutter	Alice Swaffield	Catherine Marie

Hart '… liked to share his demesne with his cottagers.' He knew what he wanted. Buildings that conformed, a village that was kept tidy. Tidy it may have been, but the houses were designed for their outward appearance rather than their inner comforts. Squashed into high damp banks, they had oddly shaped rooms with doors everywhere. The present Duchess, Deborah, describes them as '… extremely inconvenient. To protect the picture-book ideal there were no vegetable gardens or pigsties, but allotments were provided up the hill …'.

George Gilbert Scott, who designed the Albert Memorial in London, created the new Edensor church for the 7th Duke. The churchyard was extended. Paxton's tomb is centrally situated and fit for a King. Less prominent are the Cavendish memorials and the grave of Kathleen Kennedy, sister of John F Kennedy – 35th President of the United States. Kathleen married Billy, elder brother of the present Duke. Billy was a Major with the Coldstream Guards and killed in action in Belgium, just four months after his marriage to 'Kick', her family nickname. She was tragically killed in an air accident in 1948, aged twenty-eight. In October 1963, John Kennedy visited Kathleen's grave one month before he was assassinated by Lee Harvey Oswald in Dallas, Texas.

During Ben's early years at Chatsworth, the monarch was the dotty, unconventional William IV. His gouty brother George IV, known as 'Swellfoot the Tyrant', died in 1830 presenting William with a kingdom for seven years. Known as the fun-loving nautical Duke of Clarence, William had spent twenty-one carefree years with the actress, Dorothy Jordan. She cheerfully gave birth to five sons and five daughters, all surnamed FitzClarence. The liaison faded, and William sensibly wed Adelaide of Saxe-Meiningen. Both daughters of this

St Peter's Church, Edensor

marriage died in infancy. Dalliances were ignored and William's subjects grew fond of their bluff, gross, loud-mouthed Jack Tar. One described him as, 'A little old, red-nosed, weather-beaten, jolly-looking person, with an ungraceful air and carriage.' Washington Irving, an American man of letters, guest at a ball given by the Duke of Wellington observed that, 'His Majesty has an easy and natural way of wiping his nose with the back of his forefinger which, I fancy, is a relic of his middy habits.' Nicknamed 'Coconut', he had a pointed and red-thatched skull. He loved wandering round the London streets peering into shop windows. An Irish whore tried to kiss, him while a passer-by shouted, "Go it King!". The King, and his Queen Adelaide, were crowned in 1830. Hart, then living in Chiswick, tilted the inkstand so that Coconut could prod in his quill and sign his wobbly name.

Cartoon of Coconut 1795

Dorothy Jordan

William and Adelaide did not visit Chatsworth, as Hart spent most of his time in London mixing widely with the aristocracy and in Royal circles. Meanwhile work at the Estate continued at full pace, and the archives of the Chatsworth Settlement continue as from the first entry in 1829:

> 'Benjamin Swaffield occurs in the Chatsworth account book for every year thereafter, supervising the sale and purchase of livestock (and all other things agricultural), travelling to shows and sales from Yorkshire in the north to Hampshire in the south, and checking and approving the entire 'Chatsworth Farming and Grazing Account' on December 31 each year. In 1843 his wages increased to £150 pa, plus £10 allowances in lieu of perquisites."

Agistment, or joisting' (grazing), was the established practice as the following extract explains:

> 'The park itself is partly devoted to (the villagers) comfort, the best of it being reserved for the cows of the cottagers and labourers on the estate. The rates paid by the labourers for joisting a cow are from 50s to 55s, which are very moderate, and must add much to the comfort of the labourer's fireside. Another part of the park, about 300 acres in extent, is joisted to the tenants, who are thereby enabled to ease their farms of young stock in summer, and to reserve part of their grass for hay. The late and present Dukes of Devonshire have, for many years, kept stallions for the use of tenants and the neighbourhood.'

The Estate – 'A View from Chatsworth' – Devonshire, Deborah Duchess.

The horses were sturdy giants which provided power on the land. There were also dairy herds, cattle for fattening, pigs, game, deer, goats and chickens. There were blacksmiths and farriers, stockmen, stable lads, coachmen and granaries, barns, dairies, kennels and sheepfolds. The Estate and its outlying farms were a complete agricultural world, and Bailiff Ben was a very important person within it.

'Tenant records were kept in 'terriers' or letting books, the names pencilled in and crossed out as generations succeeded one another. This pattern of tenure gave rise to fields being named after occupants of long standing. Measurements of holdings were in acres, roods and perches documented in fine English copperplate writing. The smallest details such as ditches, stream banks and roadsides were noted.'

The Estate – 'A View from Chatsworth' – Devonshire, Deborah Duchess.

The other Monarch during this time was Queen Victoria. She, with Prince Albert, visited Chatsworth in December 1843. Notice given was so short that all the staff, inside and out, had to work at full tilt to prepare the house and grounds. The diarist, Mary Frampton, at the first dinner sourly observed '… how unbecoming was the Garter ribbon round the Queen's plump little figure when she danced'.

On the final evening, wrote Hart's biographer:

'The Queen was led to a window of the state drawing room at the east corner of the south front to view the spectacle prepared for her in the garden. She stood on a stage which elevated her to the height of her husband standing behind. Three thousand Russian lights had been attached to trees. The Cascade, a staircase of tumbling water, was lit like a ribbon of descending fire. The fountain in the canal pond was brilliantly illuminated. And while cannonfire echoed from the hillside, fireworks were visible to thousands in the park and pleasure grounds. The Duke of Devonshire, deeply moved by his own handiwork and the resource of his head gardener, exclaimed, "Paxton has outdone himself". The Duke of Wellington [the Iron Duke] kept repeating with emphasis, "I have seen Versailles and La Granja the Queen of Spain's, but I never in my life saw anything so beautiful as this fête."'

Nor perhaps had Ben from Lewcombe or Frances from Brampton. They stood, starry-eyed and marvelled at the effects of lights on water backed by fizzing fireworks. From then on the garden and grounds were opened to the public.

'The Duke has expressly ordered the waterworks to be played for everyone without exception. This is acting in the true spirit of great wealth and enlightened liberality; let us add also, in the spirit of wisdom.' Tourists came in the summer of 1849 when the railway arrived at Rowsley station and 80,000 people travelled in horse-drawn buses or on foot to see the house and the garden.

Little Emmeline Jepson was seven years old when the railway line opened. Her father, John, had managed the Peacock Hotel at Rowsley, three miles south of Chatsworth. The Peacock was where Emmeline grew up, and it is a grand building for a little Victorian girl to run around. Originally built as a Manor House in the mid-17th century, it was a dower house for the Duke of Rutland, the peacock being taken from the family crest. It then became an hotel in 1820. One fine day Emmeline, and her elder sister Sarah (Sally), and, the youngest, Charlotte Page Jepson, were dressed in their best and taken to see the wonders at Chatsworth. Ben Swaffield had also

Rowsley, the Peacock Hotel

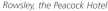

Right: Emmeline Jepson aged 17 – photo by Will Houseley, Bakewell 1859

befriended Emmeline's grandfather, William Jepson, who had, previously, been at The Nags Head in Mansfield. William is recorded in the 1861 Census, as Innkeeper [Edensor Inn], Malster and Farmer of 250 acres. He employed a barmaid, ostler, postboy, boots, groom, waiter, two chambermaids and a gardener. This connection led to the marriage of Emmeline Jepson to Ben's nephew, Henry Richard James Swaffield of Ampthill, son of his younger brother Sam. St Peter's, Edensor, where Ben's first wife is buried, was where baby Emmeline had been baptised in 1842, and she was married there to HRJ in the spring 1866. Emmeline's sisters also married. Sally to a haulage contractor, Martin Smith, and Charlotte to George Horn of Bedford. This gave Sally ample opportunity to frequently visit her Bedfordshire sisters. The alliance between HRJ and Emmeline started the linkage of Swaffields, Jepsons, Pages and Milligans which has extended the family throughout Britain.

After twenty-five years, having reached the rank of Head Bailiff at Chatsworth, Ben decided to retire.

TESTIMONIAL TO MR. BENJAMIN SWAFFIELD

——— ~o~ ———

The Subscribers to this object are respectfully informed that the above Presentation will be made at Edensor Inn, on Friday, the 29th inst., when a Dinner will be provided for the occasion.

SIR JOSEPH PAXTON WILL TAKE THE CHAIR

Dinner on the Table at four o'Clock — Tickets Three Shillings and Sixpence each.

Gentlemen intending to dine are requested to apply for Tickets on or before Thursday.
Edensor Inn, April 21, 1853.

Included in the List of Subscribers is Sir Joseph Paxton £2 10s 0d, Mr William Jepson £2 0s 0d and Mr James Milward 5s. In total £64 2s 0d was given by over seventy subscribers. The occasion was reported in the Derby Mercury on 4 May 1853:

PRESENTATION OF PLATE TO MR BENJAMIN SWAFFIELD

On Friday evening a party of about 25 gentlemen sat down to a sumptuous dinner at Mr Jepson's, The Edensor Inn, for the purpose of presenting Mr Swaffield, farming agent to His Grace The Duke of Devonshire with a testimonial of respect for his uniform excellent conduct during a quarter of a century. A superb dinner at 5 o'clock followed by a choice dessert including purple grapes and other choice fruit of uniform excellence, and wines of the first quality. Sir Joseph Paxton presided and proposed the toast to the Queen. 'God Save the Queen' was sung by the Sutton-in-Ashfield Glee Singers and then a toast to the rest of the Royal family.

Several Glees were sung including 'The Fine Old English Gentleman', 'The Red Cross Knight' and 'Banish Oh Maiden' followed by various toasts to the Duke, the Queen and Joseph Paxton, '… whose fame was world-wide to Kamchatka and the Antipodes.'

'The presentation service of plate consisting of a tea pot, coffee pot, cream ewer and sugar vase was handed round for inspection by the company to unanimous praise of the chaste design and elegance of workmanship reflecting great credit on the silversmith, Mr Moss of Sheffield. Inscription: "To Benjamin Swaffield by his friends and neighbours on his leaving Edensor for the uniform and faithful discharge of his duties during a residence of twenty-five years – April 29th 1853."

The Chairman (Paxton) presenting the service remarked that twenty-five years earlier, the farming of the Duke was on a limited and irregular scale. The village had driven the farm away and scarcely anything worth calling a farm at all remained. A gradual change, year by year, of arduous duties brought order, regularity and system, and Chatsworth could now boast one of the most complete homesteads in the kingdom, especially cattle and sheep gaining the admiration of our county and country at large. Benjamin Swaffield was now leaving the Duke's service to become tenant of one of the best farms [Pilsbury] on the Duke's estate. It had given Mr Swaffield pain to ask permission to leave, but having a numerous young family to provide for he thought it prudent to endeavour to do the best he could for them etc.

Mr Swaffield replied: At a loss for words because of the happy, warm and cordial manner of the Chairman, he feared his feelings would overcome him. He would treasure the gift while he lived and hoped and trusted that his children after him would long continue to cherish and preserve the kind pledge of esteem with which he had just been presented. He had endeavoured to do his duty in all transactions in connection with Chatsworth. Briars and thorns had occasionally sprung up and had been eradicated by perseverance. He had received every possible kindness and assistance from Paxton. He trusted that he had never lost a friend in 25 years at Chatsworth and would only leave to be His Grace's tenant. The chances were that his friends would never all assemble again together, but he hoped to meet them hereafter in the land where 'the wicked cease from troubling and the weary are at rest' .... continued applause.

LIST OF SUBSCRIBERS TO THE PRESENT TIME.

	£	s.	d.		£	s.	d		£	s.	d.
Sir Joseph Paxton, ..	2	10	0	Mr. Anthony Taylor,..	1	0	0	Mr. B. J. Blockley, ..	0	10	0
The Rev. H. J. Ellison,	2	2	0	Mr. John Royal, ..	1	0	0	Mr. Thomas Wyld, ..	0	10	0
Joseph Nicholson, Esq.	2	2	0	Mr. Charles Coote, ..	1	0	0	Mr. George White, ..	0	10	0
W. P. Thornhill, Esq.	2	0	0	Mr. Lingard, ..	1	0	0	Mr. George Kirkham,	0	10	0
John Brown, Esq. ..	2	0	0	Mr. J. Hodgkinson, ..	1	0	0	Mr. Ralph Dain, ..	0	10	0
Mr. William Jepson,..	2	0	0	Mr. T. P. Wood, ..	1	0	0	Mr. J. Goodwin, ..	0	10	0
Mr. John Kirkham, ..	2	0	0	Mr. Charles Cawton,..	1	0	0	Mr. G. Robinson, ..	0	10	0
Sydney Smithers, Esq.	1	1	0	Mr. W. Hattersley, sen.	1	0	0	Mr. Thomas Gould, ..	0	10	0
W. Condell, Esq. ..	1	1	0	Mr. W. Hattersley, jun.	1	0	0	Mr. Gilbert Gould, ..	0	10	0
William Unwin, Esq.	1	1	0	Mr. Samuel Potter, ..	1	0	0	Mr. William Barker,..	0	10	0
Henry Unwin, Esq. ..	1	1	0	Mr. William Barber,..	1	0	0	Mr. John Wright, ..	0	10	0
E. C. Bright, Esq. ..	1	1	0	Mr. J. Mower, ..	1	0	0	Mr. Gregory, Longstone	0	5	0
Frederick Ward, Esq.	1	1	0	Mr. Gregory, ..	1	0	0	Messrs. Darwent, ..	0	5	0
Thomas Turner, Esq.	1	1	0	Mr. W. Greaves, ..	1	0	0	Mr. Richard White, ..	0	5	0
J. J. Rowley, Esq. ..	1	0	0	Mr. Robert Sybray, ..	1	0	0	Mr. James Bampton,..	0	5	0
John Roebuck, Esq...	1	0	0	Mr. Robert Thornhill,	1	0	0	Mr. Thomas Housley,	0	5	0
John Rodgers, Esq...	1	0	0	Mr. Joseph Winson, ..	1	0	0	Mr. Henry Milner, ..	0	5	0
John Cutts, Esq. ..	1	0	0	Mr. Peter Furniss, ..	0	10	0	Mr. E. Clark, ..	0	5	0
William Wyatt, Esq...	1	0	0	Mr. T. M. Leech, ..	0	10	0	Mr. James Milward,..	0	5	0
Messrs L. & G. Furniss,	1	0	0	Mr. Michell, ..	0	10	0	Mr. R. Sedding, ..	0	5	0
Mr. W. Tomlinson, ..	1	0	0	Mr. T. Gardom, ..	0	10	0	Sums under 5s. each,..	1	10	0
Mr. John Cocker, ..	1	0	0	Mr. Beardmore, ..	0	10	0				
Mr. Thomas Burgoine,	1	0	0	Rev. C. Smith, ..	0	10	0				
Mr. A. Wheatcroft, ..	1	0	0	Mr. Frederick Parker,	0	10	0				
Mr. William Burkitt,..	1	0	0	Mr. William Bark, ..	0	10	0				

List of Subscribers, Edensor Inn, April 1853

Archives from the Chatsworth Settlement continue:

'The last entry for him (Benjamin Swaffield) is in 1853, when on June 11 he was paid £100 salary to this date. Obviously this was when he left Chatsworth because on the next line is the entry 'June 11 … Paid Benjamin Swaffield a gift from His Grace £500 0s 0d' – (£37,000 in today's terms). A golden handshake of this magnitude is testimony again to just what a valued employee Mr Swaffield obviously was. It is difficult to track down Mr Swaffield's exact movements after this date although he moved eventually to Pilsbury Grange near Hartington. He is listed as being there in Francis White's Directory of Derbyshire 1857. Pilsbury Grange is a large farm on the gated road between Hartington and Pilsbury in the Dove Valley, owned by the Duke of Devonshire.'

All was hustle and bustle at the village of Edensor. The Swaffields were leaving, not going far, only to Pilsbury – but Pilsbury was a good journey by wagon, over the hills and farm tracks, and more than a long walk. Neighbours came in and cared for the little boys, whilst Ben and Frances packed up their belongings in trunks and wooden boxes. Sarah's mind was elsewhere, grown now to a pretty girl of 22, she was mooning over books with James Milward, the Librarian at Chatsworth. Moving home is a big event, getting married is another, and both had to be achieved that year. Ben loved his only daughter, they had managed well together since Sarah's mother, Fanny, had died so long ago.

So the Swaffield-Milward wedding took place, with many friends, and family from Dorsetshire and Bedfordshire who had travelled up for the occasion. The workers on the Chatsworth Estate sent baskets of dried rose petals, and Sarah's bouquet was gathered in the gardens. Ben was a proud man to give his daughter away, and his little sons excited at the gathering of so many happy people.

Then Ben did his rounds of the vast estate, and said his farewells to the many farmers and labourers, with whom he had been linked for nearly a quarter of a century. He assured them, "We're not going far, just you come and visit us when we're well set at Pilsbury." Frances was sad to leave, it was a comfortable, friendly life in the village. Her friends brought baskets of food, wooden toys for the children, and warm embraces.

"We'll miss you all. Goodbye, good luck," they shouted, "Yon look after those dear little boys, Frances, love, you take care, and Ben my man don't you forget us!"

Ben wiped his eye and raised his hat, pulled at the reins and clicked his tongue, "We'll be back," he shouted, as the horses clopped through the narrow gates of Edensor village. 'Edensor' lives on in the Swaffield family, for many have named their homes, all over the land, after the 'workers village' on the Chatsworth Estate. Does it speak of peace and plenty, of comfort and warmth – or does it tell of a little bit of England that has become home? One hundred and twenty years since the birth of his great-grandfather, John Swaffel 1731, from the small Dorsetshire town of Beaminster, another strong branch of the extensive family tree was established in the Peak District of Derbyshire.

The magnificent view from Pilsbury Grange in the Dove Valley

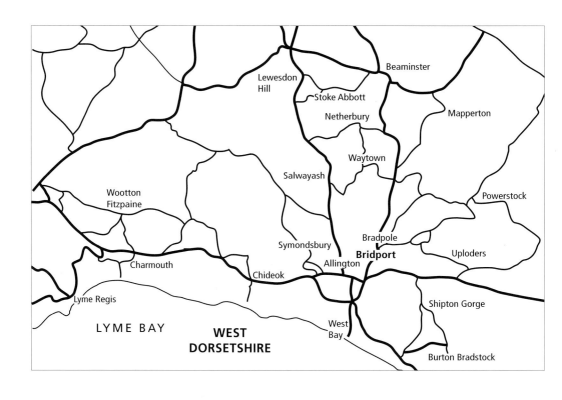

Beaminster

Lewesdon
Hill

Stoke Abbott

Netherbury

Mapperton

Waytown

Salwayash

Powerstock

Wootton
Fitzpaine

Bradpole

Symondsbury

Uploders

Bridport

Charmouth

Allington

Chideok

Shipton Gorge

Lyme Regis

West
Bay

LYME BAY

**WEST
DORSETSHIRE**

Burton Bradstock

Chapter 3

DORSETSHIRE ~ 1761–1936
Rampisham, Stoke Abbott and Beaminster

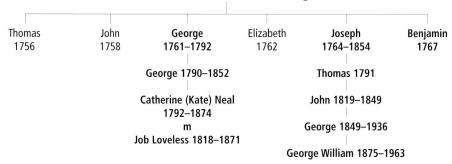

The third son, George who married 'a Betty' at the age of twenty, died when he was thirty-one, having fathered seven children. His son George 1790–1852 married his first cousin, Catherine Neal, a close neighbour from Wood Farm in East Chelborough. They had five surviving children from a brood of eight. They moved to Witcombe, near Martock in Somerset and he worked as a dairyman. The children were brought up in Witcombe, Halstock and Swillits in Broadwindsor. Catherine (Kate) 1819 married Job Loveless, baptised at Ash, Netherbury, in January 1844. Job was the son of Sam [whose original name was Lovelace] and Susannah Guppy. Job moved his way up from labourer to farmer and dairyman. He prospered and could afford house servants to help Kate with chores and children, of which there were seven. But his health was poor, and he died of stomach complications in South Street, Crewkerne aged only 53. Seven years later, Kate also died, after being paralysed for a period of twelve days. The children were well educated, and moved away from the land. When she was 24, Mary Loveless 1856, was working for Thomas and Emma Caftyn, owners of a Grocer and Drapers shop in Handcross, Sussex. They had eleven other staff, and Mary was employed as an assistant and milliner. Samuel George married Elizabeth Norman and they had nine children. Sam became a coal merchant and remained in Axminster for the rest of his life. Job was a flax dresser, a labourer and then became Licensee of the Railway Tavern in Crewkerne. John Swaffield Loveless was a butcher and, latterly, publican of the Crown Hotel, South Street, Crewkerne. He married twice and had a total of seventeen offspring. His first

wife, Mary Bessy James, died aged 42 after having eleven babies. Her second child, William John Loveless, joined the butchery business and delivered meat around the town using a horse and cart. But business was bad and could not sustain two families. By then William, and his wife Blanche, had three children running around. They decided to move to Cardiff in 1908, settled in Canton, and eventually both died there in 1961.

But our story focuses on the two youngest sons of Benjamin Swaffield and Hannah Burdett, Joseph and Benjamin. Joseph was born at Chelborough Farm and married a cousin, Mary Swaffield, in May 1787, when he was twenty-two. Three children were born at the farm, and three at Rampisham where Joseph established himself as a Master Carpenter. Thomas, followed his father's trade and, when he was twenty, married Mary Whittle, a Dorchester girl, and they moved to Closworth. After eight years a son, named John, was born in 1819.

This John was a weaver making ships sails. When he was twenty-two, he married Caroline Canterbury from Stoke Abbott.

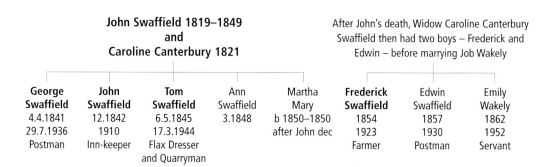

John Swaffield 1819–1849 and Caroline Canterbury 1821					After John's death, Widow Caroline Canterbury Swaffield then had two boys – Frederick and Edwin – before marrying Job Wakely		
George Swaffield 4.4.1841 29.7.1936 Postman	John Swaffield 12.1842 1910 Inn-keeper	Tom Swaffield 6.5.1845 17.3.1944 Flax Dresser and Quarryman	Ann Swaffield 3.1848	Martha Mary b 1850–1850 after John dec	Frederick Swaffield 1854 1923 Farmer	Edwin Swaffield 1857 1930 Postman	Emily Wakely 1862 1952 Servant

Caroline Canterbury and her Swaffields – circa 1880
Top L–R, John [inn-keeper], Frederick [farmer] Edwin [postman] Emily Wakely, Tom [flax dresser and quarryman]
Bottom L–R, George [postman] Caroline Canterbury [widow of John 1819] and Ann

Her family name can be traced to the 16th century, and is still connected in several ways to the Dorsetshire Swaffields. John signed his name in the vestry and Caroline marked with a cross. She was then heavily pregnant with George, who was born in Stoke Abbott the following month. During the next seven years John and Caroline had John, Tom and daughter Ann. The year after little Ann was born her father died. His Death Certificate records – 'Died December 20th, 1849 – Gun Shot Wound in Heart'. The tragedy forced an inquest which was reported in the Dorset County Chronicle & Somerset Gazette, back page, col 2 under Inquests in January 1850:

'On Thursday last a poor weaver, residing at Stoke Abbott, was on his way to Blackdown, accompanied by George Symes, a neighbour, both having guns in their hands as their ostensible purpose was to sell a spaniel to A Pinney, Esq., and when near their destination John Swaffield fell in such a manner that his gun exploded and the contents entered his chest in a most singular manner, killing him on the spot. His body was taken to a cottage at Coles Cross, where it waited the Coroner's Inquest. On the following morning, S S Cory, Esq., Coroner for the Western Division of the County of Dorset, arrived. The corpse presented the body of a fine young man, under 30 years of age, dressed as a labourer – no-one had seen the wound. The Coroner ordered the body to be undressed and then saw a wound under the left collar bone, in such a position that after passing the finger in the direction of the shot hole, it was difficult to reconcile the mind to the circumstance, but from evidence, it was clearly proved that no person was near enough to have fired the shot, and it was an impossibility for the man to have done it wilfully: He must have fallen, and the gun exploded whilst he was on the ground. Verdict – Accidental Death'.

George was twenty-five when he courted and married Harriet Wakely. They celebrated their simple wedding at the Hope Chapel in Weymouth, where Harriet was working as a cook. She returned home to Stoke Abbott to collect her boxes. She then walked the whole way from Stoke to Beaminster, two miles or more, dragging a very lazy donkey, hee-hawing frantically, trying to lie down or throw off her possessions.

1888 – Harriet Wakely and George Swaffield with 8 of their children – awaiting the arrival of baby Nancy
Top L–R, Rose, Het, Jen
Bottom L–R, Jack, Emily, Harriet with Nell on her knee, George with Tom on his knee and George William

They had fifteen children in twenty-two years. One of the excuses given for the birth of so many children in those days, is that some were expected to die, as they did in George and Harriet's case. Insurance companies started selling policies to cover funerals of deceased children. One little Swaffield was still-born, four died at birth including a set of twins, and one daughter, Julia, survived only three years. George was a good husband and father but unemotional. He was not one for hugging or having a child on his knee, but kindly and fair. As a grandfather, he would take the little ones for walks to pick foxgloves. The countryside then was still exquisite. Wild flowers made carpets of glory on the verges of winding lanes, disturbed only by the clop and rattle of a pony and trap. Some remote areas of Dorset were literally unchanged since Stuart times.

George Swaffield 1841–1936 and Harriet Wakely 1845–1929

Ann Rosetta (Rose)	Julia Jane	Still born	Mary Jane (Jen)	Caroline Esther (Het)	George William [Boer War]	John James (Jack)	Fred'k Job (Fred)	Emily Eliza	Harriet & Tom	Emily Agnes	Ellen Harriet (Nell)	Thomas Edwin (Tom)	Annie Louisa (Nancy)
1867	1868	1870	1871	1873	1875	1877	1879	1880	1881	1882	1884	1886	1889
1951	1871	1870	1966	1969	1963	1969	1879	1880	1881	1966	1917	1961	1975

Harriet struggled with continuous pregnancies, bringing up their large family. She had all her babies at home, confined with a midwife. She had a basic knowledge of first aid, and knew all about hygiene. She kept some medicines in her cupboard – sal volatile [smelling salts], ipecacuana for coughs; opium [or laudanum] as a painkiller. Even babies were given laudanum in 'soothing mixtures' if they cried. First they lived at 20, St Mary Well Street in Beaminster, then at No 27, next they resided in Shorts Lane and, finally, in East Street. George had an allotment but sold most of the vegetables, irritating Harriet who needed the carrots and cabbages for soups and stews.

George Swaffield in his allotment

Known as 'Mam', Harriet was a dear, a loving mother and grandmother. Mam called her daughters and daughters-in-law, Little Maids. Slowly the children moved away looking for work, but visited often with their families. They would wander round the town, meet the neighbours and catch up with the local news. Harriet liked to take her grandchildren to see the little piggies in the nearby orchard. Nancy, her youngest daughter, was almost sick when the butcher came and cut the pigs' throats, chasing them round the apple trees as they bled to death to 'keep the meat white'.

George's mother, Caroline Canterbury, worked hard and saved up to send him to the Penny Dame School from the age of eight to twelve years. Each pupil brought a penny a day to pay for tuition. The unqualified teacher passed on basic knowledge of reading, writing and arithmetic. With such limited education, it is surprising what George later achieved. Nearly three-quarters of the population verged on illiteracy until compulsory education was introduced in 1870 and 1880. George was satisfied when he was given the job of postman. Such a man, with literacy and numeracy, was a well-trusted member of the community. George took his job seriously and, for forty years, he walked delivering and collecting from Beaminster to Salwayash, a route of nine miles each way. Later he had a pony and trap. He was strong, upright, burly and bearded. A strict teetotaller, he was a pillar of the Congregational church and a Sunday School Superintendent. He was also a keen Liberal, and became involved in heated arguments during elections, resulting in street corner tussles, quite out of character with his Victorian values. He would horrify Harriet by stumbling home with a bloody nose, bruised cheeks and the odd black eye.

Beaminster Band – 1895 – Top right – George William aged 20

George belonged to the Debating Society and started the Beaminster Town Band in 1878. He taught himself the trumpet, driving everyone mad with the noise, and then he mastered other instruments. His sons and nephews soon learnt to play along with him, and all had musical ability. Then he taught the village boys and eventually formed the Band, which was still in existence until fairly recently. Every year, the Band successfully contested at Bournemouth, Torquay and Bristol. Encouraged by his prowess as a musical leader, George bought one of the earliest gramophones, and a record of 'Pomp and Circumstance' by Edward Elgar. He was so enthralled with the music he played it over and over again to everyone's annoyance, "Turn that ol' player off," they implored, "We're goin' stone deaf with the din!". George turned his back, muttering, wound it up and played it again. It was probably the first time he had heard a full orchestra play.

The best fête for the band to perform, was at Stoke Club held at Stoke Abbott on the first Friday in June. Another regular engagement was at the Litton Cheney Fête, but they insisted on ten players. Sometimes the Beaminster Band could only muster nine, and were nervous they would not

In 1938, two years after George died, the Beaminster Band formed a Guard of Honour at the marriage of his great-niece, Kathleen Swaffield to Frederick Collin.

get their full fee. So they gave the coach driver a drum, and prodded him to bang it now and then. George was the choirmaster and loved singing. His favourite song was 'By Killarney's Lakes and Fells':

> By Killarney's lakes and fells,
> Em'rald isles and winding bays;
> Mountain paths and woodland dells,
> Mem'ry ever fondly strays.
> Bounteous nature loves all lands,
> Beauty wonders ev'rywhere;
> Footprints leaves on many strand,
> But her home is surely there!
> Angels fold their wings and rest,
> In that Eden of the west.

He loved it so much, he decided to visit Killarney. The journey took a long time, by train and by boat. When he arrived, his heart sank, "Where are the Em'rald isles and winding bays?" he moaned, standing in the whistling rain, his beard stuck to his chin, "This is not what I expected. I should have stayed with the song, and not come," he grumped.

Harriet loved the Stoke Fete and returned to her village every year with her children. She spent time with her sister, Hannah Harris, who would proffer a jar of cider along with the food she had prepared. The children played with their cousins and the two women laughed, giggled and enjoyed good times together. George didn't go but came to meet them. Nancy remembered

1902 – George, proud of his long service six chevrons

that Mam had drunk a little cider, something she never did at home. George took one look at her wobbly steps, turned the trap and trotted home alone. "You can all walk," he shouted gruffly. It reminded Harriet of her wedding day, but instead of a lazy donkey she was dragging tired and hungry children. One day George's pony bolted as he started his round. He fell, holding the reins, and the wheel went over him. But he wouldn't let go, he held on like grim death until the pony stopped, and he was able to stagger up and get home, badly injured.

He was an enterprising man, and clever, and became a self-taught, area repair agent for Benson's, the watch and clock company. He was skilled and kept accurate accounts. During his morning postal round on the rural Beaminster–Salwayash route, he gathered up clocks and watches; then repaired them at Salwayash in a little cottage he rented to use as a workshop. If the faults were minor, he would deliver the repaired items whilst collecting the post in the evening.

Some needed more attention, so he prepared a working area in his attic and did more repairs, under very poor light, at night. The rusty tools and equipment were still enshrined there on his death in 1936. He was diligent, hard-working and community minded. The Post Office awarded him a total of six chevrons, and he wore them proudly on his dark uniform.

George kept a diary and in 1881, when he was forty, he recorded:

'Great snowstorm and severe frost early on Tuesday morning January 18th, and continued until evening of the next day. There was a fearful cold wind blowing the whole time and freezing as well. All the roads far and near were impassable for several days. (On 21 January Exeter recorded a temperature of minus 30F). No letters came to Beaminster for two days and then only by men bringing them on their backs from Bridport. The carrier's cart did not run for nearly a week nor yet the bus. Hundreds of men were set to work clearing the roads.'

That same year George and Harriet lost their twins, Harriet and Tom. George was a frequent visitor to London, to see the sights, and make his annual report at the Benson's office in Clerkenwell. He often made it a family outing travelling by train.

August 1886: 'Went to London taking three eldest daughters with me to see the Colonial and Indian Exhibition at South Kensington and a glimpse of the Great City. We started at 3am Friday from Beaminster and arrived at Misterton Station [outside Crewkerne] at 4 45am. Started soon after – fine – had a very pleasant ride to Waterloo stopping only at Salisbury and Basingstoke to take in water. Arriving at Waterloo Station we made our way over Waterloo Bridge and had a glimpse of the obelisk on the Thames Embankment. Then passed Somerset House. Knife for John (Jack) bought near St James's Park, knife for George [George William] bought at the Exhibition, scissors for Mary Jane (Jen) bought ditto, brooch for Caroline Esther (Het) bought at the Crystal Palace.'

The Exhibition was at South Kensington, and was opened by Queen Victoria on 4 May 1886. In his prayers, the Archbishop of Canterbury spoke of Dominions stretching from 'sunrise to sunrise', and a notable feature of the pageant was the singing of the National Anthem in Sanskrit, the representative language of India. The three eldest daughters – Ann Rosetta 19, Mary Jane 15 and Caroline Esther 13, were besides themselves with excitement to see to the great city, and absolutely exhausted on their return home. Harriet, nursing new baby Tom, had sent them off with a basket of food.

In January 1891 the River Exe was frozen from Exeter and Topsham, and the Teign to Newton Abbott. Several ships were frozen at the entrance to the Exeter Canal.

March 1891: 'Another great snowstorm began on Monday March 2nd about midday and continued with very little cessation till early on Wednesday morning – the wind was very high. The snow in some places was from 10 to 12 feet high. The weather began to break the following Wednesday when a mild thaw set in, but the snow did not entirely disappear for a month afterwards. I saw one or two relics of it on the roadside on April 17th.'

Between 1897 and 1916, Harriet and George married off eight of their children, five of them daughters. First was Het, who married George Slade in 1897 and they had three girls, Lilian Rosetta Penelope, who inherited the musical genes and sang beautifully. Kathleen Thyrza was the middle daughter. She married Doug Collow and emigrated to New Zealand, where the whole family settled. The third was Gwyneth who married John Boss in 1941.

Het in later life

Left: New Zealand – Kathleen Slade and Doug Collow's Golden Wedding 1985.
Top L–R, Linda and Henry Perkins, Mary, Melissa and Andrew Collow, Janet Perkins.
Bottom L–R, Hayden Collow, Doug and Kathleen, Graham Perkins

Below: Beautiful hats and pretty dresses. Jen marries William Ascott in 1897
Top L–R, George William, Emily Agnes, Jack, Rose, George Slade, Het
Centre, Tom, Harriet (Mam) William Ascott, Jen, George
Front L–R, Nell, Nancy

Then it was Jen, when the family was living at Shorts Lane. She married Cumberland William Sebastopol Ascott, a Beaminster man, fifteen years her senior. After their wedding they moved up to Wealdstone and had four children.

Various family members lived with the Ascotts whilst finding jobs, and Jack married Cecilia (Cissy) Edmonds in 1906. They managed to squeeze over thirty faces into their wonderfully posed group, with a flurry of

Jack and Cissy's family wedding at Wealdstone in 1906

trimmed hats, flowers, lace collars, and crisply clean children in cotton dresses, sailor suits and baby bonnets.

Perhaps George's longevity was due to his chilly and vigorous daily ablutions which started his day, and the hot brick from the oven, wrapped in flannel, which warmed his bed and gave him a peaceful night's sleep. Tasma Joan, remembers her grandfather as '… a very old man, blind, with spotless white hair and beard. He washed every morning under the pump which was between the East Street kitchen door and Pony Rose's stable. Grandad used Pony Rose with his Post trap, and took his family on outings with her, though they had to walk up the hills. He loved his grandfather clock, and dutifully felt his way to wind it every evening, sadly scratching the dial whilst fitting in the key. Strangely I recall how he loved pears which my mother, Nancy, always posted for his birthday.'

Pony Rose with the trap outside the East Street home. Setting off to West Bay.
L–R, George Swaffield holding reins, granddaughter Phyllis, Jack, Rosetta, Nell, Mam, Cissy and Ethel Weaver.
Photo taken by Nancy c1923

News cutting – February 3rd 1927:

Married 60 years. Congratulations to Mr and Mrs G Swaffield

'Mr & Mrs G Swaffield of East Street celebrated their Diamond Wedding on Thursday, having been married in 1867 at Hope Chapel, Weymouth. The unique event aroused a good deal of interest in the town of Beaminster and congratulatory messages were showered on the old couple from all directions, and they were specially pleased with the letter of congratulation from His Majesty the King [George V].

He was a lover of music and it may be of interest to many to learn that he was the founder of the Beaminster Brass Band in 1878. The band paid him the compliment of playing a selection of music outside his residence on the evening of his Diamond Wedding.

Mr & Mrs Swaffield, whose ages are 85 and 82 respectively, have up to a few years ago enjoyed good health, in fact 'Dad' as he is affectionately called by everyone, hardly had a days illness up to his 82nd birthday, but since then his sight has gradually failed, and he is now totally blind.'

1927 – Mam and George

1936 – George aged 95

As many children, and grandchildren as could be mustered, attended their Diamond Wedding celebrations. Harriet died six years before George. She was a sweet, patient person and someone had made her a padded brush which she used as a crutch under her right arm. She had a round face, and often looked tired. She wore her grey hair with a centre parting, pulled down tightly over her ears into a small bun at the back.

George enjoyed his radio set provided by the charity 'Wireless for the Blind'. He had 10s a week pension from the Post Office. After Harriet died, a Mrs Hunter became his housekeeper and George told his young grandson, Bill, ' I wouldn't mind dying now, all my friends have died many years before.' He went in his sleep, without any illness, and had been very fit all his long life.

News Cutting 1936: George Swaffield

'A postman who was reputed to be the oldest Post Office pensioner has just died at the ripe age of 95. He was appointed a rural postman on the Beaminster–Salwayash route in 1866 and performed the same journey until he retired in 1902 aged 61.'

George William 1875 was their first son and the sixth child. He fought in the Boer War which lasted from 1899–1902. George Swaffield joined the Dorset Regiment and, along with members of the 1st Northumberland Artillery, they sailed to South Africa on Tuesday, 3 April 1900 when his father had just reached his 59th birthday.

Young George kept a journal: 'On the ship were 200 horses destined to pull the field guns. In the Bay of Biscay many of the chaps were sick, and the poor horses suffered the most when the ship rolled. They were tossed from one side to the other. We could not sleep as the horses were over our hammocks and made an awful noise.' There were three stowaways on board, 'rather sharp boys from North London' and that 'on Sunday we had to throw a horse overboard.'

Queen Victoria, a passionate lover of animals, was concerned principally for the troops sent to the Cape but, as early as 11 November 1899, she recorded in her Journal, 'We lamented bitterly over the loss of so many horse, and I made him [Lord Wolseley] promise to see that everything was done in the ships for their safety and comfort. But it is at best a great risk transporting so many such a great distance by sea.'

Finally the Dorset Regiment arrived in South Africa:

'We got on the hill and stopped the night in trenches where we could hear firing. We had an awful night what with fire and wind. We had to fight against the grass fires, but it was no use and we had to carry our things through the flames on the burnt grass next morning. We had to make more trenches to protect ourselves and before long we were under fire. We had a lot of Boer snipers all round us, and as soon as we showed ourselves we had a shower of bullets. It was our first experience under fire. Hawker and Dunn were hit. We all had a narrow shave. Neither of them was wounded seriously. They were both sent back to Base. We had to spend another night on that hill – the wind and rain was awful, also the dust was blinding. We could not see any difference, it was all the same, just dry and burnt grass.' On 11 June he wrote, 'Fifty-four men wounded and twelve killed in the attack on Almond's Nek [sic] in the 2nd Dorset Regiment.'

Previously the English lost the Battle of Colenso. Losses amounted to 1,045, of whom 102 were officers. Many were sent home with enteric fever. Major Prince Christian Victor of Schleswig-Holstein, a favourite grandson of Queen Victoria, died of enteric fever at Pretoria, 29 October 1900.' When the volunteers returned safely to Beaminster, there was great rejoicing, and George resumed his interest in the Beaminster Football Club. The year after the war ended, George married Daisy Wheeler of Wokingham, and they had five children.

1936 – George's funeral
L–R, George William, Het, Jen, Rose, Nancy, Emily, Jack. Not pictured is Tom, who had to run off and catch a train

Ampthill Town

Chapter 4

BEDFORDSHIRE ~ SAMUEL SWAFFIELD 1802–1863
Agent to Lord Holland of Ampthill

Benjamin Swaffield 1767–1840 and Hannah Burdett 1765–1857

Thomas 1791 1859 m Harriet Guppy	Hannah 1792 John Rugg	Mary 1794 John Gard	Robert 1795 1857 Charlotte Farmer	Benjamin 1797 1879 1) Frances Chubb 2) Frances Watkinson	Elizabeth 1799 1831 James Storer	Judith 1801 Robert Meech	**Samuel 1802 1863 Harriet Nash Exton**	Martha 1804 1877 George Squibb	Sarah 1805 1856 Ephraim Matthews	John 1806 1891 Elizabeth Otton

The Swaffields from Dorsetshire, by their endeavours and early education, fared better than many. Sam was the eighth of eleven children. He was ten years old when his grandfather died, and they lost the tenancy of Chelborough Farm. They packed up and left, and his father Benjamin took a farm in another small village, Wootton Fitzpaine, near Lyme Regis. His father's elder brother, Joseph, whose family story runs parallel, stayed in Dorsetshire and followed the trade of a Master Carpenter. In those days it was not expected for a man to retire, nor did he expect to. It was work, work, work until you dropped. So Joseph laboured on, finally doing agricultural work. His son, Tom, followed his father's carpentry trade. He was three years older than his cousin Sam, married young, and had a son, John, in 1819. This John's marriage to Caroline Canterbury of Stoke Abbott, firmly cemented the Joseph branch of the family in Dorsetshire, into Beaminster, Stoke Abbott and surrounding areas.

For Sam, and his older brother Ben, this was not enough. They were, ambitiously, looking at new horizons. Sam was serious, took care of himself and had a friendly disposition. His benefactor, Lord Ilchester, identified the potential of this confident Swaffield lad. Ilchester was a member of the Fox family, a relative of Lord Holland of Ampthill [Henry Richard Fox, 3rd Baron, and Liberal statesman]. He offered Sam the position as his Land Agent, a promise taken up eagerly by the twenty-two year old. In 1824, Sam left home, with brother Ben, by coach to London. Ben went on to Derbyshire, and the brothers kept in firm touch with each other throughout their lives. It is because of their close relationship, that the Bedfordshire Swaffs and the Derbyshire Swaffs remain so affectionately intertwined.

Sam kept immaculate accounts. Within them is a veritable golden egg of social history, employment, furtherment, social habits, food and drink, fashion and day-to-day activities. There are few personal details, no additives, no fun. But reading through the pages is fascinating, and thoroughly interesting. This is a young man, far away from home probably for the first time, leaving a large and affectionate family circle, and a collection of gentrified friends and neighbours with whom he felt comfortable. He has a systematic mind and excellent handwriting, and is forging his way into a job, a new place to live, finding a wife, building up his assets and interests, and achieving.

Sam's accounts date from his journey to, and employment in, Ampthill. The first page states:

> Household account and an Account of all other my Expenses and Incomes from the 15th January to the 31st Decr. 1824. S. Swaffield

We have records up until 1836 after his marriage, and the birth of the first of seven children. There are more, tucked safely away in the Bedford Record Office, neatly scripted in copperplate writing with a fine black pen. My copy is more modern, typed painstakingly by an interested descendant, on yellowing flimsy foolscap with a cloth ribbon.

Sam started out with £21 2s 6d of his own, and was paid an annual salary of £70 plus £2 travelling expenses, the latter paid in arrears. He left in the coach Defiance, sitting outside, from Cartgate to the Golden Cross Inn, Charing Cross, London paying a fare of £1 10s 0d, and expenses to guard and coachman of a further 12s. A night at the Golden Cross was 15s 11d and waiters and porters were 5s. Preparing for his new job, he purchased a Hoppus' Measurer and a Ready Reckoner also, vital for him, Acct. books etc, papers and a new trunk. He travelled by coach to Woburn and 'paid a man 3s to carry my trunk from Woburn to Ampthill Park, this being a distance of 5 miles' [sic – actually 8]. Seven days after leaving Wootton Fitzpaine, he found lodging with a Mrs Peacock at 5s a week. He made regular payments to Mrs Peacock until his marriage in April 1834. After that his regular monthly payments were to 'Mrs Swaffield – cash paid for her bread, washing etc – 16s 9d'.

After three years he had been presented with the lease for cottages, one being, 'Westley', and he received regular rents from tenants. It was due to Sam's negotiations, that he was presented with these as a reward. Lord and Lady Holland started planting an avenue of lime trees in the 1820s. They had liked the avenues they saw in Spain, and this new project was called Alameda. A hundred years later the Ampthill War Memorial was placed amongst the pine trees at one end. Unfortunately the Boughton family owned land right across the proposed avenue, and did not want to part with it. But Sam was persuasive, and managed to exchange the 'avenue' land with another plot elsewhere.

The Alameda showing remaining cottages in the background

11th April 1827

LEASE FOR LIFE   Lord Holland to SS

Two cottages in Woburn Street occ Jos Westley and Jn Wildman, lately purchased of
Richard Boughton and w Martha

He was an enterprising young man and, by the end of the first year, he had already earned extra
cash by doing valuations [timber]. His salary then was £90 per year and went up regularly by
£10 annually. His income increased with further rents, sale of pigs, sale of clothes, surveying and
money lending. He also regularly received cash – £15 – from Reverend J Allington for estate
management at Marston Moretaine, and from various other small estate owners. He was also
quite canny. Some of his 'income' is disguised in a weird shorthand – looking a little like
Pitman's – which I cannot decipher. Indeed Pitman's first 'Phonetic Journal' was not published
until 1842. But, in nearby Woburn, Thomas Gurney had created a system in the mid-18th century
which led him being known as 'The First Official Shorthand Writer', although Thomas Shelton
is reputed to have devised the first alphabetic system in 1630. Maybe Sam got sight of this work,
as he certainly had a particular code in his own accounting. In 1831 there is income from Colonel
Webster for 'skso'of £2 10s 0d – maybe shooting or hunting. In 1832 a payment was made to
J Bull for a pair of 'oejuw' and a 'Hmwx' costing £2 6s 0d. J Bull was a Bedford jeweller, so the
first item could have been earrings for his intended – or another admirer – or cufflinks for
himself. The second perhaps a watch, as he had a penchant for timepieces. By 1835, the year

before he married Harriet Nash Exton, his annual income
had increased to £270, his year's expenditure had been £173
5s 8d, and he had savings amounting to £526 19s 10d. Harriet
came from a long-established Ampthill Quaker family. They
were bankers and eventually became a part of Barclays.
Quaker offspring were often sent to other communities as
part of their education. When Sam first became acquainted,
Harriet was in Hitchin, the two communities were close and
prosperous. Sam had set his sights on a very 'suitable' girl.

Samuel Swaffield, aged 61. Courtesy Andrew Underwood Collection

His father, Benjamin, was a regular correspondent, posting his
letters at Wootton Fitzpaine. Each letter cost young Samuel 10d to
receive, and he paid the money to the postman as a delivery charge.
It was not until 1840, that letters were paid for before despatch by
buying a stamp, and the Penny Post was introduced. At times he
was unwell, and on 4 March 1825 he paid 2s 3d for two boxes of
Dr Roberts' Pills, and another box cost 1s 1¾d. Things improved
and he paid 12s 11d for a gallon of gin and 11d for cheese. Sam
travelled home to Dorset once a year to 'see my family and friends'
and took presents with him. He also visited his elder brother, Ben,
who was Head Bailiff at Chatsworth – himself becoming a worthy
man of means. The family communicated regularly by post,
brothers and sisters visited, Sam went to London and to Liverpool, Yorkshire and Suffolk.

Penny Black stamps

Mrs Peacock provided bed but no board, as there are frequent entries for beef, bread, mutton, moist sugar, tea, cheese and flour. As the years go by, and he becomes more established, the food improves to 'fat goose – 5s' and '2 roasting pigs – 18s', 'leg of lamb – 4s 10d', 'salmon – 9s 6d' and 'stuffed teal – 5s 0d', 'bread, cake & biscuits – 8s 0d' and a 'barrel of oysters 6s 6d'. All this rich food led to boxes and boxes of Dr Roberts' Pills being swallowed. Sam too, enjoyed a drink, and evenings at the White Hart Inn. He bought gin, rum, sherry and brandy by the gallon, wine by the dozen and Port by the crate. He was something of a connoisseur as he laid wine down, certainly six bottles in 1830 with 'papers round their necks explanatory of what they are'. He also collected Port and stored several dozen of 'Ashby's old bottles', in various cellars. He received a letter from Sir Jas Parke [Lord Wensleydale], at that time a tenant at Park House, 'I have some Brandy which is old and excellent and I have ordered 12 bottles to be sent to you …'. As a pimply boy from East Chelborough, cleaning out the byres and lugging in the buckets, he had become a man of taste, style and means.

The White Hart, Ampthill

His accounts are meticulous, his demeanour was immaculate because he did not deny himself clean linen, new hats, silk gloves and top boots. The days of muddying his fingers was over. Every week he paid Mary Smith for 'washing and mending'. He walked great distances as his entries for the 'repair of boots and shoes' appear weekly. He had his silver watch regularly checked and cleaned, he bought new pens and paid for the 'stropping of razor'. If he was unwell, he paid to be shaved and had his hair cut regularly. He was particularly fond of head gear and, in eight years, he purchased 14 hats, 6 night caps and a shooting cap. He shot rooks and rabbits. His toilet was important with a regular supply of brushes, combs and toothbrushes, and he had new suits tailored regularly. He liked gloves, mostly kid, and purchased 34 pairs, as well as 23 pairs of stockings and 6 pairs of cotton cambric drawers tied up with string.

Then he started courting, and travelling to Hitchin to woo Harriet Exton, his intended. Mr Wonfor, proprietor of the White Hart, town vet and general tradesman, supplied newspapers, booze and various foods, also provided a gig or a chaise and other services. Sam, unofficially, tied the knot by paying her an amount of '£5 paid to HNE' prior to their wedding, possibly for an engagement ring. In 1834 he married Harriet, then aged twenty-seven. She was the daughter of George Exton and Harriet Nash, who themselves married three years before her birth. Harriet was baptised with both parents names on 5 October 1807. George Exton had previously been married to Mary Albright, a Quaker, and they were both Members of the Society of Friends, Ampthill. George is recorded in the 1797 Land Tax Assessments when he paid £2 10s 0d for the house, 'Foulislea', which he was occupying, while the farm and other properties he had leased to other tenants were assessed at just over £10. Foulislea was built in 1742 by Mrs Catherine Coppin, a clergyman's widow. Later it was leased to tenants, one being Reverend Charles Cavendish Bentinck who, through his second marriage, became the Queen Mother's (Elizabeth Bowes Lyon) grandfather. By 1960, Foulislea and its cottage belonged to the Wingfield Club, formerly the United Services Club, owned by Sir Anthony Wingfield of Ampthill House, which was in dire straits. [Mabel Swaffield, w/o Leslie, Sam's great-grandson, bought it as a potential retreat to get away from her father-in-law. The cottage has since been purchased by Andrew Underwood, great-grandson of Ben George.]

Foulislea
Courtesy Andrew Underwood Collection

Generous and, as aspiring gentry, Sam subscribed to charities and started paying into the 'Birmingham Infirmary'. Before he wed, he bought furniture and household effects, a rosewood bookcase £5 10s, a pair of decanters and a pair of stuffed pheasants as well as a 'pr of toilette bottles 13s.' On May 7, 8, 9 1834 he paid out £20 'for the total amount of my marriage expenses'. The wedding was at St Mary's Church, Hitchin. on 7 May 1834. It had taken Sam ten years to become established and settled, and to find a bride. They had seven children and thirty-two grandchildren:

Samuel Swaffield 1802–1863 and Harriet Nash Exton 1807–1867

Mary Emmeline 1836–48	Harriet Exton 1837–1916	Henry Richard James 1839–1909	Benjamin George 1842–1898	Samuel John 1846–1914	Alice and Edward twins 1849

Sam had stayed at Mrs Ann Peacock's lodgings for ten years. Six years later he acted as Executor to her Will. He and Harriet then moved into 'The New Cottage' in Ampthill Park, the original Steward's house which had been extended. They made themselves comfortable with linen, a paliasse, 18 yards of druggett, a dining table, looking glass, bed posts, counterpanes, a feather mattress, wine glasses and kitchen utensils. Altogether, the comfortable furnishing of the house cost over £380. A year later young Mary Emmeline arrived, and her safe delivery is eventually marked 'new bonnett [sic] for my child' and 'toy 1s 0d.'

Women were seen as inferior to men and expected to marry. When they married, everything they owned became their husband's property. [In the 1851 census, Victoria describes her relationship to the head of the family as 'Wife' and simply lists under Rank, Profession or Occupation: 'The Queen']. Soon after marriage Samuel paid '...the travelling and other expenses incurred by my Wife going to Chatsworth for a fortnight to visit my brother Ben' – which included a visit to Manchester, Sheffield and Liverpool – together with '...my expenses in going to Chatsworth with her and meeting her on return to Leicester which altogether cost £22 10s 0d.'

Queen Victoria on her wedding day

19th-century kitchen

In 1835 Samuel paid his annual haircutting bill to J Gascoigne, Barber which amounted to 5s and 'for shaving when ill 4s' After a year he gave Harriet a silk dress as a Christmas present. He celebrated the festive season with a bottle of brandy and three bottles of soda water for 8s. After baby, Mary Emmeline, arrived a maid was employed to help in their house at Ampthill Park. Her name was Martha Stapleton and, in October, she was paid four guineas [£306 in today's terms] 'for half a year's work due this day'. Martha, and the other servants, toiled from six in the morning, when they stoked the fires polished everything polishable, and boiled the big iron kettle hanging from a hook above the fire. The cook kneaded dough for breakfast bread, the hem of her rough dress and apron brushing the cold flagged floor. She made porridge and hot tea, and the maid carried heavy trays. Martha soothed the baby, washed her tiny clothes in a wooden bucket, and cuddled her when she cried. Mending took up her evening until, at nearly midnight, she staggered up to the attic and sank onto her thin hard bed in a room hardly big enough to turn around in. In 1835, Sam took out an insurance policy covering his household furniture, and also 'negligence and carelessness of servants in causing fire, for which they can be committed to the Common Gaol for the space of eighteen months, and there to be kept to Hard Labour'. Mary Emmeline was christened in August, and a horse and chaise was hired for the occasion from Mr and Mrs Lee. The church clerk was paid £1 15s 0d for arranging the service.

Sam was keen on a good education for his boys, and tutoring in singing and music for his girls. HRJ went to Belvedere House Academy in Stony Stratford, and there is an arithmetic book to prove it. He was keen on sketching, and always kept a diary. The youngest twin boy, Edward, also went to Belvedere House and his sister, Alice, was educated by Miss Charlotte Weight and received 'Board & Instruction' at 40 guineas per annum. Samuel John went to the Bishop Stortford Collegiate School – Board 30 guineas per annum. Eventually Sam John moved up to London to work and wrote to his elder brother, HRJ, in 1903 from an address in New Southgate:

'As to business, I am sorry to say it is fearful in London ... there are thousands out of Employ ... I am trying to lessen my expences [sic] all I possibly can, discharged a man last week ... I could not afford to pay him 28s per week ...'

Despite his father's adequate income, Ben George was admitted for a free education into the Bluecoat School – Christ's Hospital. The place should have gone to HRJ, but was transferred to his brother because of HRJ's 'ill health'. This condition, in his future life, did not impair the production of a clutch of children, nor the ability to manage his father's extensive affairs with enthusiasm but, perhaps, far less perceptivity.

An oil painting of Benjamin George whilst a student at the Bluecoat School c 1855.
Courtesy Andrew Underwood Collection

So it was Ben who attended for six years, nominated perhaps by John Brooks, the Flitwick Squire whose estate Sam managed. Sam put up a good case for avoiding school fees, pleading poverty, almost pauperism, having no known means to support or educate his son, although his detailed accounts prove that his annual income was well over the £5000 mark. Despite his perseverance, his son Ben George, did not make a success of scholastic life, left under a cloud with his father paying a final bill of £1 15s 0d. Ben George was showing the family wilfulness, apparent in later generations of independent Swaffield personalities. In the year of his father's death, Ben George married Eliza Annie Smith, daughter of Sam Smith, a grocer from Newport Bagnell, Buckinghamshire. Ben George, unlike his prudent father Sam, was irresponsible and hopeless with money, 'nags and the devil drink' perhaps being of more interest to him than a steady job and family life. He tried farming but failed, and ended up with almost nothing.

To protect Eliza Annie, his brothers, HRJ and Samuel John, set up a Marriage Settlement, with themselves as trustees. The financial situation was not helped by the family moving from pillar to post, all over the County of Bedfordshire, ending up in 29 Arthur Street, Ampthill where Ben George died of throat cancer. His children renounced all interest in his household effects in favour of their mother. She had a hard time making ends meet, and took in dressmaking. Rumour has it that Ben George sold off personal family silver, such as his christening mug, in order to pay debts. The silver came into the possession of

Eliza Annie Smith, at home, 33 Church Street, Ampthill c 1900.
Courtesy Andrew Underwood Collection

the County Court bailiff, Richard Upton, who, knowing the family circumstances contacted HRJ. He, in turn, apparently redeemed some of the pieces, which eventually found their way back to Ben George's family.

Their second daughter, Harriet Exton Swaffield, was born in 1837 the year King 'Coconut' William IV was buried. Sam was a close friend of one of the King's illegitimate FitzClarence daughters, Mary, married to Major General Fox. He and Sam had an amusing friendship, shooting and socialising. In 1856, after the death of Major General Fox, Sam was surprised to receive a gift from the Fox family, as listed in Bedford Record Office:

Benjamin George Swaffield, photo taken the year before he died, aged 56.
Courtesy Andrew Underwood Collection

Gift to SS in 1856

> [A] School exercise book *c* 1776, inscribed inside by General Fox – "[This book is] One of Prince William Henry's [later Duke of Clarence and King Wm IV]. This was [found] at Bushy House where the Duke lived till he came to the Throne. It was then given to his son Adolphus FitzClarence [and] on his death to his sister Mary Fox, and I [now] give it to my old Friend, the Pitcher Sam Swaffield." [Sgd Fox]

Queen Victoria succeeded William IV when she was 19. She married her first cousin, Albert of Saxe Coburg-Gotha in 1840, when Lord Holland's estate was in the process of being sold to the Duke of Bedfordshire. In 1841, Victoria and Albert visited Woburn and, it was suggested, '… ought Swaffield and the Ampthill tenantry join the welcome to the Queen at Woburn Abbey?' An invitation difficult to refuse. The young Queen became a role model for young women. She had a precocious maturity and a surprising firmness of will when required.

In 1861, when Victoria was 42, Prince Albert died from typhoid. She was heartbroken. Generally women went into deep mourning for at least a year. They wore heavy black, and left the house only to visit relatives or go to church. Funerals were expensive, glass hearses were elaborate and black horses had silver trimmed harness and black ostrich feathers on their heads. The 'mutes' who walked with the hearse were employed because of their especially glum faces. The family presented mourners with special gloves or scarves, or necklaces and bracelets fashioned from the dead person's hair. Victoria remained firmly in mourning for Albert for forty years, until her own death in 1901. Not a day went by without her feeling totally bereft and grief-stricken.

As well as being agent to Lord Holland, Sam took on other contracts as agent to landowners, and also did a great deal of surveying work for the North Western & South Midland Railway Companies. In the 1861 census at Ampthill, Samuel, aged 58, was described as 'Land Agent, Brickmaker and Farmer of 850 acres employing twenty-nine men and fifteen boys on the farms.' All his children are included, except Benjamin George who had been sent away to the Bluecoat School. Also listed is Julia Mundy, aged twenty-one, a house servant from Oxfordshire. Sam was a charitable man and paid for singing classes, heating the church with gas, donated towards a reformatory school, subscribed to the 'Indian Fund', gave the children 3s 6d, and had a Rifle Suit made for Henry (HRJ) to wear when he took part in parades with the Rifle Volunteers.

Queen Victoria's reign was a time of peace and prosperity for Britain. The Crimean and Boer wars were fought far away from Britain and, apart from the Indian Mutiny of 1857, even the conquest of the Empire proceeded relatively peacefully. The Industrial Revolution transformed people's lives, and Britain became the greatest trading nation in the world. Some farm workers moved to cities seeking their fortunes, but many were forced to eat food scraps from rich people's kitchen doors. Some even collected dogs' mess and sold it to tanneries where it was used to darken animal hides. Bedfordshire folk were less inclined to make for the cities, and scratched a living from the land.

Harriet and Sam lived a comfortable life, nevertheless, their first daughter, Mary Emmeline, died aged twelve. She lies in solitary state, poor little thing, in a great family table tomb in Ampthill churchyard, sheltered by a cedar tree. The rest of her family elected to be buried elsewhere. The second daughter Harriet Exton never married, and the third, Alice, married a cousin and had no children. Both are buried in Derby. Big brother, HRJ, made up for them all by fathering fourteen. Childbirth was considered dangerous, one newborn in six died, as did so many mothers. Henry Richard James [Henry Richard after Lord Holland and James after Charles James Fox], was born in 1839, followed three years later by Benjamin George who predeceased HRJ by eleven years. Meanwhile, Sam was possibly getting itchy feet, wondering whether to emigrate to 'the promised land' – Australia. He was an efficient correspondent, annotating letters coming in with the date of their arrival, and the date of his response.

From Hen Badcock, 3 Apple Street, Sydney, N S W. Dt 30th May 1849 – to SS

'Oh how I wish all I loved were here. It is the finest country in the world. It is winter and there is plenty of everything even greens in abundance. Our passage was a very pleasant one, marked with little or no variety. We had 7 deaths and 9 births during the time. I assure you death has a great effect on all at sea: all feel a gloom cover over them. As to the births, the ladies seemed to care but little: about above deck in the day, confined in the night and again up in two or three days well and hearty … we also had a mutiny on board but that was quelled without bloodshed. The sight of loaded guns looked anything but inviting. All the cabin passengers had two guns each. There were five of us beside the Capt and about five men, but there were 40 seamen and some of the emigrants seemed inclined to join them … we could not have come out any a better time.'

From Hen Badcock 10th January 1850 to SS

'I like the life very well and intend to take a station myself … fortunes are to be made out here and I venture to say that if you or R Furze were out here with moderate capital, you would soon make a handsome one. I advise no man to come out without capital, a thousand pound with any expectation to make money, but I advise every poor man who can obtain passage to come out to a land of plenty. Oh send out your starving poor instead of paying it all away to poor rates and county rates to keep your prisons and unions full. …The rate of wages for common sheppards [sic] is £20 a year with rations: it was £40. Everyone is saying invest your money now, but I mean to wait for more time. Remember me kindly to R Furze and all who care for the little Capt.'

Endorsed (Answd 29th Sep '50 SS)

In 1850, Sam received a letter from Major General Fox:

'Sam – Marmaduke Tees has just informed me that one of the Partridges you held up as having shot after we left you in the Rain was found dead and not shot by you but found by Tom the Marker. You know you never shot it! Oh Sam! Oh Sam! Oh Sam! George says that you told him to leave the Hares at Canfields, none are come up at all and three Partridges instead of two with Canfield. Oh Sam! Tees approves of this letter. George says you did not tell him to leave them, but desired they to be kept in the Larder and there they are but I write to Master Canfield to send them up by this post. Lady Mary has a parcel for you, how is it to be sent?

Yours (when you are a better boy) C J F'   no date.

29 Jan 1851 – from General Fox

'Dear Paragon, Lady Mary is very well at Nice, so am I here ....'

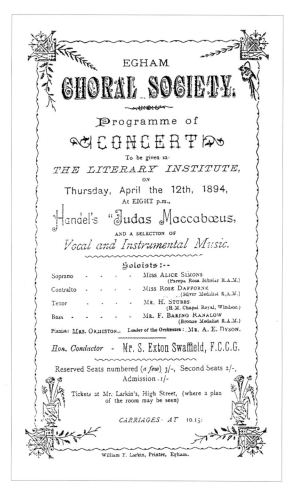

Programme from the Egham Choral Society featruring
Mr S Exton Swaffield as Hon. Conductor.

Ben George's son, Samuel Exton, obviously inherited the Dorsetshire musical ability as he played at society concerts, and was organist at Slough. In April 1894, he conducted the Egham Choral Society when they performed Handel's 'Judas Maccabaeus'. Seats were sold at 3s, 2s and 1s. Between 1898 and 1936, when they moved to 26 Church Street, Ampthill, Samuel Exton and his wife Eliza Jane, had sixteen changes of address. Samuel Exton's Will was proved by Albert Grimmer, retired motor engineer – £345 12 11d. Albert was married to Sam Exton's sister, Annie. Sam Exton's youngest unmarried sister, Eva May, was a music teacher, sang with local operatic societies and played dance music on the piano. The sister in between these two, Laura Harriet, eventually settled in Middlesex married to John Gee, a blacksmith and docker, a veteran of the Afghan Wars.

Samuel Swaffield from Dorsetshire, worked hard for sixteen years as Steward, but on Lord Holland's death and after the sale of the estate, he then became a tenant of Ampthill Park Farm and of Lye Mead Farm on the top of Millbrook Hill. He

Laura Harriet, aged 13 and her little sister Annie, aged 5.
Courtesy Andrew Underwood Collection

Below: Park House

lived at this farm, and built up Park Farm at the bottom of the hill, a property with Georgian/Regency proportions. The lake in the park provided 'running water', in that it was pumped to a tank on the roof and fed a bathroom, toilets and the kitchen. Harriet ran her household from the parlour, and there kept her account books. She often referred to her illustrated copy, inscribed 'H.N. Swaffield 1861' of Eliza Acton's 'Modern Cookery for Private Families, Reduced to a System of Easy Practice'. Sewing was an important skill, and the keeping of scrapbooks. Illustrations were stuck in with flour and water glue. Painting watercolours was another genteel hobby, as was the pressing of wild flowers and making dried flower arrangements.

c1863 Harriet in her invalid chair outside the front door of Park House. Courtesy Andrew Underwood Collection.

Reading was a popular pastime. Favourite authors were Charles Dickens and Mrs Gaskell. Charlotte, Emily and Anne Brontë were well-known writers and, because of the bias against women, used the pseudonyms of Currer, Ellis and Acton Bell, and were published from 1834. All died relatively young. Charlotte wrote 'Jane Eyre' at 39, Emily wrote 'Wuthering Heights' at 30 and died from tuberculosis. Anne Brontë wrote 'The Tenant of Wildfell Hall' when she was 29. She was a cautious girl and advised 'Keep a guard over your eyes and ears as the inlets of your heart, and over your lips as the outlet, lest they betray you in a moment of unwariness'.

Charlotte Brontë

With their good contacts, and Sam's aptitude for management, Harriet and Samuel had a fortunate life. Over the course of thirteen years Harriet gave birth to two girls, three boys and twins. She always complained she had 'too many children' and blamed her later ill-health on 'childbirth'.

"Nothing that a hysterectomy could not have cured," mocked a stout female relative in later years. But for Harriet, the pain and discomfort she suffered, was probably preferable to the fear of major surgery, although Ampthill was then well supplied with competent doctors specialising in various complaints. Well-to-do people, such as the Swaffs, could subscribe to the Nursing Association, paying the salary of a visiting District Nurse. But for Harriet it was too late, exhausted, she spent the last three years of her life in a wheelchair.

Sam did not enjoy good health, despite the much improved medical facilities. In 1860, aged fifty-eight, he felt ill and had a solicitor draw up his Will. Closely handwritten, and carefully worded, it thoughtfully provided for everyone until they were independent. Provision was made for the whole family from the working income of his farms.

Sam was a good man and an excellent businessman, well connected, respected and appreciated. Maybe he did not take quite enough of Dr Roberts' Pills, for he died relatively young in a family that has many octogenarians. He is buried on top of the hill in Millbrook churchyard, overlooking the acres of Ampthill Park, which he faithfully walked in his innumerable pairs of boots and shoes, pulling up his kid gloves and tipping one of his fourteen hats.

Millbrook Church

On his father's death, HRJ wrote in his diary on 22 March, 'My poor Father died this morning ¼ to 9 o'clock. He was seized yesterday about ¼ past 1 o'clock in the Pony Chaise and never spoke or was conscious afterwards.' On 27 March, 'My poor Father was buried this afternoon at Millbrook about 3 o'clock. Ben, Sam, Ted, Uncle Ben, Messrs Furze, W Seabrook, F Seebohm, J T Green, Collingwood, J Morris, Wynter & Collier followed. Dr Maule performed the service. Blustery wind.

Four years afterwards, Harriet joined Sam in Millbrook Churchyard on top of the hill, with sweeping wooded views and horses grazing in the fields below. The church can be approached by a track from the A507, but it is better to climb through the tree tunnel and up the footpath.

At the top there is no sound of traffic, but a small and pretty garden, and a wooden bench on which to rest. The headstone is impressive and we stripped away the ivy fast growing up it. The dedication is simple:

~o~——————~o~

In affectionate memory of Samuel Swaffield of Ampthill Park
March 22nd, 1863
Also of Harriet Nash Swaffield
Wife of the Above
Born August 1807
Died August 1867

~o~——————~o~

THE WILL OF SAMUEL SWAFFIELD 1807–1867

THIS IS THE LAST WILL AND TESTAMENT of me Samuel Swaffield of Ampthill Park, Bedfordshire, Gentleman. I appoint my eldest Son Henry Richard James Swaffield, my brother Benjamin Swaffield [of Hartington, Derbyshire] and my friend Robert Furze [of Steppingley, Bedfordshire], Farrier, Executors of this my Will.' He allowed nineteen guineas [in today's terms = £1346.13] each as a slight acknowledgement for the trouble they may have in execution of the trusts of this my Will.'

'I give to my said Son the silver tea service consisting of a Tea Pot Coffee Pot Sugar Basin and Cream Ewer presented to me by the tenancy of the late Lord Holland.'

'And give to my Wife Harriet Nash Swaffield the sum of two hundred pounds sterling [circa 2000 = £13,461.36] to be paid to her by my Executors within one calendar month next after my decease and I give to my said Wife for her own use and benefit absolutely all my household furniture household stores plate linen and other household effects which shall be in or about my dwelling house at Ampthill aforesaid at the time of my decease.'

In 1862 he added a codicil:

'I give to Giles N Collier my Farm Bailiff at Milbrook if in my employ at the time of my death fifty pounds [£3365.34 in today's terms] free of legacy duty. I give to Thomas Collier my farm bailiff at Wootton if in my employ at the time of my death nineteen guineas [£1346.13 today] and give to every man and boy in my employ on my farm in Millbrook, Ampthill and Marston Moretaine at the time of my death and who shall have been so employed for one month a fortnight's ordinary wages in Witness whereof I have hereunto set my hand this third day of February in the year of our Lord One thousand eight hundred and sixty two – SAMUEL SWAFFIELD.'

Signed by the said Samuel Swaffield the testator as a Codicil to his Will in the presence of us who in his presence and in the presence of each other subscribe our names as witnesses – JOHN GREEN Woburn – DUNCAN COLLET SANDERS.

The Will was proved in London.

The Bedfordshire and Derbyshire Swaffields visited each other as often as they could. Henry Richard James and his future wife, Emmeline, became acquainted when HRJ visited Ben Bailiff who, by then, was farming at Pilsbury Grange on the Devonshire Estate near Hartington.

Sam had also managed extensive estates in Warwickshire and Essex and, on his death, he was succeeded in the estate agency by his eldest son, Henry Richard James. Some years afterwards HRJ went into partnership with George Greene, an auctioneer in Ampthill, and eventually took the business over on the death of Mr Greene.

The two girls, Harriet Exton and Alice were twenty-nine and seventeen when their brother, HRJ's marriage took place in Derbyshire in 1866. Ampthill is Georgian and stylish, and the ladies were conscious of fashion. Wedding invitations prompted dress-making and the practising of new hairstyles. No doubt the girls, eyes shining with excitement at the thought of an outing, were part of the wedding party that accompanied HRJ to his nuptials in Derbyshire. And that is where Alice met her cousin Tom.

Henry Richard James Swaffield, senior son of Sam, who took over his father's business.

Chapter 5

BEDFORDSHIRE ~ HRJ and EMMELINE
Henry Richard James and his large family 1838–1922

Henry Richard James Swaffield 1839–1909 and Emmeline Jepson 1842–1922

Emmeline	Henry	Exton	Norman	Charlotte Ethel	Ella	Dorothy	Beatrice	Alan	Hugh	Richard	Hilda	Mildred	Basil
(Minnie)		(Eck)		(Bridget)		(Dot)	(Queenie)			(Dick)	(Jo)	(Kitty)	
1867	1868	1869	1871	1872	1874	1875	1876	1878	1879	1880	1882	1884	1885
1934	1964	1950	1958	1965	1945	1962	1967	1878	1918	1937	1965	1973	1972

Before their marriage at Edensor in Derbyshire, Emmeline, with her father John Jepson, had visited the Swaffields in Bedfordshire. HRJ wrote in his diary on 29 January 1866, 'Mr J and Em came over to spend the day. Four days later he, '… went to Ampthill to make arrangements about doing up house at 18 Dunstable Street.' Later in the month he attended a meeting at the White Hart to nominate a captain for the Volunteers. Private Barton was nominated.

Poster in the White Hart Hotel dated 1899

After his big family wedding, HRJ took up the reins his father had released. He had already been working alongside Sam as a farmer, estate agent, auctioneer, valuer and land agent. The newly-weds first lived at White House in Ampthill but, after two years, they moved into Park Farm, where HRJ had been born, and where they lived for thirteen years, during which time eleven children were delivered. If you enter Ampthill Park from the top road, and walk to The Katherine's Cross, the buildings can be seen below. The traditional farmhouse is red brick, with a huge 1950s barn alongside. The house was built by Samuel and occupied by his widow Harriet until she died in 1867. The present owner, John Parish, farms the surrounding 1300 acres of arable land. His mother, Margaret, remembers tales of the Swaffield family, and has much information on the building of the railway and the construction of Swaffield's Bridge. HRJ took over his father's farms, adding Houghton Conquest, and also managed the same estates plus

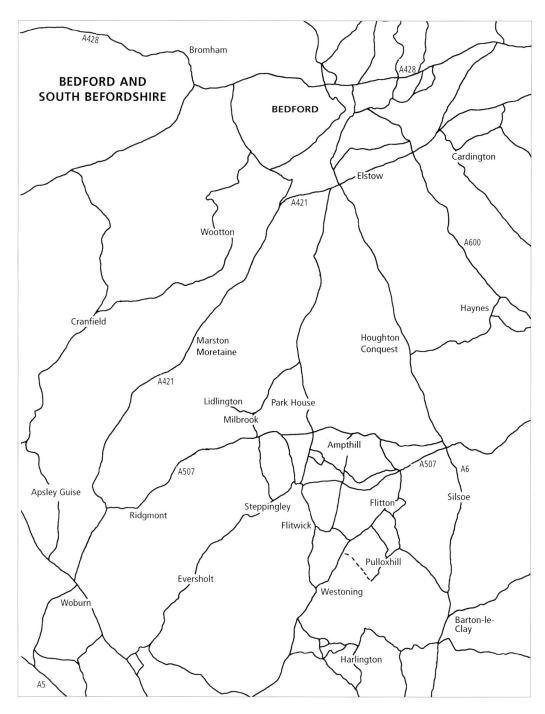

BEDFORD AND
SOUTH BEFORDSHIRE

new ones. A staunch member of the 5th Ampthill & Silsoe Co, HRJ received a quotation from W Stearn, Tailor, Ampthill for making uniforms: '… the Tunic, Trousers and Cap to be made of the cloth provided by a Government … and properly shrunk … to be trimmed with the facings, decided upon by the Clothing Committee. Suit complete comprising Tunic, Trouser, Cap with cover ornament and ball, and waist and Cross Belts with proper pouches for same … £5 15s 0d.

To an extent, family life has been documented by rescued photographs, and it was a thrill to see the first group of HRJ and his thirteen surviving children posed outside the house at Beckerings Park. This was taken on a glass plate which, latterly, was given to Queenie. Cameras were fairly primitive, and shutter speeds very slow. Emmeline posed through the years in various crinoline dresses, a fashion which arrived from Paris in 1850. Prior to that she wore six full length petticoats to make her skirts stick out into a bell shape. Discarding these cumbersome petticoats, she tied a metal 'cage' round her waist to support the new style. Perhaps the cage was loosened during her many pregnancies. Notable for elegance and charm, she brought into the family a formidable nose and jawline which she passed on to her children, her grandchildren and even one or two great grandchildren. The Dorsetshire Swaffields also claim to have a special nose, flatter and wider.

1867 – Emmeline, Baby Minnie and HRJ

The first of their fourteen children, Minnie, was born at the White House ten months after their marriage. She spent a lot of time with Nurse, and was rocked in a wood and cane cradle. As an established middle-class family, the Swaffields had three or four resident female servants. Victorians considered they owned their servants every moment except for 'what God and nature required', and the edict 'Cleanliness is next to Godliness' demanded high standards. The girls

Summer 1886 – The completed Swaffield family outside their front door at Beckerings Park.
Top L–R, Exton, Norman, HRJ, Henry. Middle and front L–R, Charlotte Ethel, Beatrice, Hugh and Hilda, Emmeline with baby Basil, Dorothy, Minnie, Richard and Ella. On the ground, Mildred and a rabbit.

started at 6am lighting fires and polishing boots, continuing until late into the evening with the washing up and carrying of coal. Open fires, candles and oil lamps produced soot, and the crammed rooms needed frequent dusting. Every day the stone-flagged kitchen floor was scrubbed, as were the wooden draining boards. Soap and soda crystals made hands raw, and 'housemaid's knee' was a real complaint. The family had dogs – spaniels and pugs were favourites – and there were working dogs on the farm. Cats lived in the cellar to keep down the mice.

Henry, the first son, was born In 1868, followed by Exton, then Norman in 1871 – the year Stanley found Livingstone in Africa. At the time of Ella's birth in 1874, Disraeli was Prime Minister. When he was old enough, HRJ took Henry into partnership and the firm became Swaffield & Son. For over forty years they managed several estates in Bedfordshire and Buckinghamshire, notably Leyton-Lowndes, Wilstead and Wootton; also the Flitwick Manor Estate, and several glebe estates. As valuers, the firm was involved with most of the properties lining the proposed enlargement, from Harlington to Bedford, of the Midland Railway, and similarly when the L. and N.W. and Hitchin lines were constructed. By the 1840s Britain had a network of passenger railways and, by the end of the century, over 20,000 miles of track had

been laid. The steam trains that ran on these lines were the first means of fast and cheap travel for everyone. Ampthill Station was opened in 1868 Not one for taking things quietly, HRJ was angry when the line was planned, as it split his land at Park Farm. After much correspondence it was agreed that a cast-iron vehicle bridge be constructed – known today as Swaffield's Bridge.

Swaffield's Bridge

The children were taught to read and count at an early age. The girls were educated at home, the three elder boys were eventually sent off to school in Derbyshire, perhaps on the advice of the Jepson family, for Uncle Ben Bailiff had now died. The little ones had slates and slate pencils, the elder ones wrote with ink, using a wooden pen with a metal nib. Text books covered all ages. Primers used simple passages, 'My dog is in the bog. My hog is in the bog.' For older children the books might ask questions – 'Q. What shape is the earth? A. It is nearly round. Q. How do you know that? A. Because ships have sailed round it.' Story books held warnings about terrible things that would happen if they were naughty. Struwwelpeter was the

The house at Beckerings Park

worst. It told of Harriet who burnt to death because she played with matches, Augustus who died because he would not eat up his soup, and 'naughty little Suck-a-Thumb' whose thumbs were cut off by a 'great, long red-legg'd scissors man'. They learnt to play the piano, to draw and to paint. They had dolls' houses, a Noah's Ark with wooden animals, and tin soldiers. A rocking horse, always dapple grey with a horsehair mane, was part of the nursery scene. In the garden they played skipping and clapping games, marbles, football, races with hoops and chasing games such as 'he'. When they went to parties they were entertained by Punch and Judy or a juggler.

Over a period of eighteen years, Emmeline gave birth at home to fourteen children. The ninth child, Alan, was born in 1878 when Emmeline was 36 and HRJ 39. He was a sickly baby, and died before his first birthday. Little boys were made to look like little girls with curls and ringlets. They wore frilly dresses and pantaloons until they were five or six, when they would be put into soft breeches or knickerbockers. Little girls played in cotton smocks and caps, and wore dresses for proper occasions.

Above, Four Swaffield boys and four Swaffield girls in the woods at Beckerings

Right, Growing up – bicycles and fun

Like his father, HRJ kept up a correspondence with ex-workers who had emigrated. In 1876, Mark Facer, Lyons Wayne Co, N America wrote: [transcribed literally]:

'Friend Sir i now rite you to let you know i am quite well and all my people thank god … I don't like it so very well as England not yet i may do another year when i get more used to it perhaps i have everything to buy this year and things is verry dear ere. my Son bil is planting some ground on shares and i help him … when I go to work with anybody else i have a dolar a day and my board … people work a great deal on shares ere and help one another … their ploughs are not even half so heavy they are wooden ploughs … please to tell Whitemore never to leave therre to come to this country i have wisht many atime i never had … Mark Facer 1871'

HRJ read this letter in his comfortable drawing room, stuffed with heavy mahogany furniture and the windows swathed in thick curtains. Lots of paintings were on the walls, the side tables and 'what-nots' were covered with stuffed birds, inlaid boxes or artificial fruit under a glass dome. A piano was almost a household god. Girls were taught to play as it made them 'sit upright and pay attention to details'. With a family such as the Park Farm Swaffields, the piano also proved a centrepiece for sing songs.

The girls stayed in the schoolroom until they were eighteen, when they put their hair up and went to parties. The Swaffield family was a large and happy one. The girls, Minnie, Bridget, Ella, Dot, Queenie, Jo and Kitty, led a fairly liberated life although they were chaperoned in public. At home they made their own fun and were always romping and larking about. They loved picnics at Gypsy Lane and, at Beckerings, they had bicycles, made more comfortable by Mr Dunlop's Pneumatic Tyres. They had the whole of Woburn Park to roam in. The boys were polite, affectionate and good humoured. They were a popular family and well-liked in the community.

HRJ 'at home' at Beckerings early 1900s.
Courtesy Andrew Underwood Collection

Below, Emmeline and her Girls c1895.
Top L–R, Jo, Emmeline, Ella, Queenie. Centre L–R, Governess?, Minnie with baby Phyll, Dot, Ethel. Bottom, Two little boys

HRJ farmed very extensively, and was considered a practical agriculturist. His management of large estates, wide experience as a valuer, and extensive connections as an auctioneer, gave him a high standing in the profession. Much of nineteenth-century farming was done by hand. Carthorses pulled ploughs and heavy farm wagons, and crops were planted by throwing handfuls of seed onto the ground from a leather bag. Underprivileged children stayed away from school at busy times to help with the farm

The garden at Beckerings Park, with a group of girls posing under a tree

work. They scared crows away from the freshly sown seed with huge rattles, herded cattle and cleared stones from the fields. There were some mechanised reapers, but most farmers relied on their workers to cut the grain with scythes, whilst women and older children tied the cut corn into bundles.

The family moved from Park Farm to Beckerings Park, Steppingley in 1881 where HRJ became a tenant of the Duke of Bedford. The younger boys were sent out to school in Bedford, and travelled from Lidlington Station. Here the last three children were born and the family remained seventeen years. The three-storeyed house is some way off the road set in sweeping grounds with big trees. It has high gables, large chimneys and three generous floors with plenty of room for the thirteen surviving children to practise sliding down the banisters. Allegedly on coming into the house one day, HRJ tripped over his youngest child, Basil. "Which one are you?" he asked in jest as he went to find Emmeline. In conjunction with Beckerings Park, he also farmed Sampshill Farm, at Westoning

A portrait of Emmeline taken at Blake & Edgar's Studio in Bedford

During this time he farmed close on 850 acres of land, as well as carrying on the business at Ampthill. As a farmer he bred a cross between Shorthorns and Herefords, kept a good flock of Hampshire Down ewes, and also favoured the first cross of Tamworth and Berkshire pigs. He often exhibited cows and sheep at the County Show. But farming was becoming unprofitable, and there was an agricultural depression during the latter part of the nineties. HRJ had an acrimonious correspondence with the Duke of Bedford concerning rent. He could have been described as an 'unruly but desperate' tenant. He retired from farming in 1898 and moved to Bedford and they settled into 10 Lansdowne Road. Described by travel writer, Sara Wheeler, "It was a quiet street. The loudest noise was the bell of the butcher boy's tricycle and the muffled clatter of housemaids polishing brass door knockers."

It was perhaps as Secretary for 27 years to the Bedfordshire Agricultural Society that HRJ was best known to the public at large. His son Henry, and Henry's son Leslie, also followed in his footsteps, whilst the younger boy, Hugh, was Secretary of the Chamber of Agriculture. The organisation of the various exhibitions fell largely upon his shoulders, and his efforts did not go unnoticed A report in a Bedford newspaper stated, '... these columns have often testified to the ex-cellence of the arrangements, the diligent attention that he gave to his responsible and multitudinous duties, his courtesy to exhibitors and all who had to do business

No 10 Lansdowne Road, Bedford

with him, and the general success of the numerous shows which were held during a long term of years under his secretarial direction.'

HRJ was a social person. In 1876, before he became a tenant of the Duke of Bedford, he attended a dinner to celebrate the marriage of the Marquess of Tavistock at the Corn Exchange in Bedford. A selection of vocal music was enjoyed, also 'performances by the Band of the Grenadier Guards'. In May 1900, in full evening dress complete with top hat, for some inexplicable reason, HRJ was photographed standing before the County Sheriff's coach in front of the Swan Hotel in Bedford, obviously waiting for the Judge of the Assize to appear. The Sheriff was Colonel Algernon Mercer, and the Trumpeter was Joseph Tildersley, a shoemaker. A letter dated 1968 was written to explain this photograph, signed Chris Carter, 'Touchstone',

which was his nom-de-plume as an historical writer for the Bedfordshire Times. In the same year, HRJ attended a Jubilee Dinner at the Trocadero, London and brought the menu home. This, amongst many other precious though badly-stored papers, has been rescued, by Mabel Swaffield – w/o HRJ's grandson – and is now in the Bedford Record Office.

Above, May 1900 – HRJ posing in front of the County Sheriff's Coach at the Swan Hotel, Bedford

4 August 1907 – A family group in the garden at Lansdowne Road.
Top L–R, Basil, a friend with a little boy, Ethel
Centre L–R, Hilda Milligan, Hugh, Norman, Tich Jepps, Henry Hamilton aged 4?, Dot, Emmeline, HRJ
Bottom L–R, Tom Smith, Queenie, Kitty and Fred Potter

Bridget, Dot and Jo were unmarried and would have been considered 'on the shelf' by outsiders. But they were always included and remained within the heart of the family all their lives. Lansdowne Road had a big walnut tree in the back garden and, subsequently many family photographs were taken there. Right to the end, HRJ worked at the office in Ampthill and was present at the last Stallion Show at Bedford, afterwards attending at his stand in the Corn Exchange. He was taken ill that same evening.

Before he died Henry Richard James was almost eligible for the Old Age Pension, introduced in 1908 and payable to those over seventy. The allowance was 5 shillings a week for a single person, and 7s 6d for a married couple. For the very poor this money was a godsend. Flora Thompson in 'Lark Rise to Candleford' wrote about her Oxfordshire village, 'At first when they went to the Post Office to draw it, tears of gratitude would run down the cheeks of some and they would say as they picked up the money, "God bless that Lloyd George ..."

NEWS REPORT – April 23rd, 1909 – DEATH OF MR HRJ SWAFFIELD

During the greater part of his life of sixty-nine years, he enjoyed very fair health, which has enabled him to grapple with a considerable variety of business and to lead a very active career. He seemed, however, to be ailing during the last two or three months, but was kept to his bed by serious illness for about three weeks previous to his death, which took place at his residence at five o'clock on Wednesday morning. Just before Christmas he had a bad attack of influenza, from which he never really recovered. His death was due to cerebral haemorrhage. He is survived by Mrs. Swaffield, six sons and seven daughters, with whom sympathy in their bereavement will be felt, by social and business friends, over a very wide area of this county.

He relinquished farming when he went to live at Bedford, but retained his connection as head of the Ampthill business. The present offices of the firm on the Market Place were originally Messrs. Sharples & Co.'s bank, and were taken over by Mr. Swaffield when the banking firm bought the building opposite. Mr. Swaffield was actuary for many years of the Ampthill Savings Bank, which was carried on at his office. He previously had offices next to the Mote Hall, which have since been taken into the King's Head Hotel. In the time of the old turnpikes he was Surveyor of Highways between Bedford and Woburn, and retired from that position when the district highway boards were formed.

Always fond of sport, in the prime of his life he was often out with his gun, and rode to hounds. For many years he walked puppies, and held a cup for first prize for foxhound 'Warrior'. [Lord Charles Russell presented one of only 36 copies of a collection of essays, 'A Horn of Chase' inscribed to, 'HRJ Swaffield, Warrior'. The dog is referred to on P14–15 – '... as fine a hound as I ever saw.']

Among the various offices he held in Ampthill he had been Trustee of the Ampthill Feoffee Charities and, at the death of the late Mr John Wright, solicitor, he was appointed correspondent for that body. He was also Guardian of the Poor and Churchwarden at Ampthill for several years. He was one of the first to join the Volunteer movement at Ampthill, was Lieutenant in the Corps under the late Captain Barton, and had a great deal to do with the organisation of the Volunteer camps in both Ampthill Park and Houghton Park.

If Mr. Swaffield had lived to July 27th next he would have been seventy years of age.

The funeral is appointed to take place on Saturday, at Holy Trinity Church, 11.30 a.m. and at the Bedford Cemetery 2.15 p.m.

Henry Richard James Swaffield was '… interred in Bedford Cemetery on Saturday amid many manifestations of the great respect in which the deceased gentleman was held by the community generally.' Funerals were strictly Men Only, so his sons attended, as did Samuel Swaffield, nephew, and son of HRJ's only brother, Samuel John of Leagrave Marsh, who was unwell. '…The body was conveyed in a glass hearse, followed by four carriages one of which contained a number of beautiful floral wreaths and other devices. Most of the congregation attended at the cemetery … the grave was lined with yew, studded with white roses and narcissus. The flowers surrounding included a beautiful cross from his wife and family, and wreaths from members of the family mentioned by Christian names.'

NEWS CUTTING – 1922

The death occurred on the 21st inst at her residence in Lansdowne Road of Mrs Emmeline Swaffield, Widow of H R J Swaffield who came to Bedford in 1889 after living at Ampthill Park and Beckerings Park.

Henry and Emmeline are buried in Bedford Cemetery, and Emmeline, who died in 1922, was remembered variously by her youngest granddaughters as 'she could be a bit of a dragon', 'she was always elegantly dressed' and 'she had a very sweet nature'.

Emmeline Swaffield

WILL of Henry Richard Swaffield aged 69 of Ampthill and 10 Lansdowne Road, Bedford, Estate Agent & Auctioneer, died 21 April 1909. Proved by Henry Swaffield, Land Agent & Auctioneer. £5,491 15s 2d.

WILL of Emmeline Swaffield, aged 79, of 10 Lansdowne Road, Bedford, widow, died 21 March 1922. Proved by Exton Swaffield, Commercial Traveller. £1,026 13s 5d.

Chapter 6

DORSETSHIRE ~ STOKE ABBOTT
Village life in Stoke Abbott from 1851

John Swaffield 1819–1849
and
Caroline Canterbury 1821

After John's death, Widow Caroline Canterbury Swaffield then had two boys – Frederick and Edwin – before marrying Job Wakely

George Swaffield	John Swaffield	Tom Swaffield	Ann Swaffield	Martha Mary	Frederick Swaffield	Edwin Swaffield	Emily Wakely
4.4.1841	12.1842	6.5.1845	3.1848	1850	1854	1857	1862
29.7.1936	1910	17.3.1944		1850	1923	1930	1952
Postman	Inn-keeper	Flax Dresser & Quarryman			Farmer	Postman	Servant
m	m	m	m		m	m	m
Harriet Wakely 1845–1929	Sarah Hallett 1840–1917	Ellen Davy 1874–1934	Wm Canterbury 1839–1887		Emma Conway 1851–1926	Emma Chubb 1854–1913	Robert Notley

Caroline Canterbury Swaffield

George b 1841

Emily Wakely b 1862

The 1851 census lists Caroline Canterbury Swaffield as a 'widow and pauper', she was also illiterate but a believer in education for her children. Four years after John's death, she was pregnant again and gave birth to Frederick and then, after another three years, she had Edwin. Despite there being no apparent father, both boys were baptised Swaffield. Eventually she married Job Wakely, a flax dresser, and uncle of her daughter-in-law, Harriet. He was more than likely the father of these boys. Both her weddings were solemnised in Stoke Abbott church, as the chapel was not licensed for marriages.

Caroline's first-born, George, joined the postal services. The second boy, John, eventually became an inn-keeper. The third son, Tom, lived almost all of his ninety-eight years in Stoke Abbott. He worked in a flax mill and then in a quarry. Frederick became a successful farmer and Edwin, like big brother George, was a postman. They all loved their baby sister, Emily Wakely, who settled in Upwey.

John b 1842 , inn-keeper,
who married Sarah Hallett

In 1861 son John lodged in Green Lane in Hooke, in Dorsetshire. He had travelled from Stoke to find work as a labourer, aged 19. Two years previously he had fallen in love with pretty Sarah Hallett, daughter of George Hallett, labourer, from Waytown, Netherbury. Sarah was already the mother of Elizabeth Hallett, who was baptised in Waytown on September 25, 1859. Her name is in the Netherbury Parish Register, Entry No 541. Hooke was a fair distance from Waytown, but John was diligent in his attentions, walking, or riding, frequently to visit Sarah and her baby. When he reached twenty-one, and Sarah Hallett was twenty-three, they married. Sarah signed her name with a cross, John could write and the witnesses, Henry Travers and Sarah's sister, Mary, both signed with a cross. John took the toddler, Elizabeth Hallett, into his home. There is no record of adoption, or that Elizabeth Hallett took the Swaffield name. She was brought up by John and Sarah, looked on as a senior daughter, playing her part within the family. Subsequently, she married three times and had nine children by her first two husbands.

John is registered in the 1871 census as a brewer. He and Sarah had nine of their own children, all born in the Netherbury/Bridport areas, but two died. Their first son, John, is registered in 1881, aged seventeen, as a Militiaman and based at New Depot, Fordington, where he was enrolled and drilled as 'home service' soldier. Once grown, their second son, George, left for the South Wales coalfields as so many Dorset boys did, and Frederick sailed over to Northern Ireland. William, the last child, followed the family pub trade, and kept the Five Bells Inn at Bridport. John left the Militia whilst still young and married Mary Jane Bagg (Jane), who had raven hair and a pretty face.

John Swaffield 1864–1939 and Mary Jane (Jane) Bagg 1865–1936

Frederick James (Fred) 1888 1963 m 1909 1) Alice Meech	Beatrice Lucy (Lucy) 1890 1972 m 1917 Alfred Clarke	Alice Emily (Emily) 1892 1953 m Herbert W Howe	Wilfred John (Wilf) 1894 1917	Hilda Mary 1896 1994 m 1931 Charlie Holman	Christina Florence (Crissie) 1899 1992 m Reuben Long	William George (Will) 1901– 1927 m William J Record	Lily May 1903 1986	Louis Charles (Lou) 1904 1968	Reginald Edwin (Reg) 1907 1919 aged 12	Winifred Margaret (Winnie) 1909 2002 m 1939 Len Jones	Kathleen Myrtle (Kath) 1911 1982 m Fred'k Collin

They moved from Bridport to the New Inn, Stoke Abbott at the end of the 19th century when their oldest, Fred, was seven. He wrote a memoir in pencil in exercise books.

'Old Caroline Swaffield used to live in a cottage right on the corner by Mr Smith's barton [farmyard]. She was very old and was my great-grandmother. As soon as we arrived in Stoke, I went into her house and she said, 'Come yer less see if yon got the Swaffield nose.' Caroline married John Swaffield who came from Coker near Yeovil. He was killed up around Lewesdon Hill, with a gun, getting through a hedge. A man named Symes was with him. Of course that was a good many years before my time, and Old Caroline died very shortly after we came to Stoke.'

Fred chronicles his childhood, and that of his siblings, as seen from the pub. The old codgers related fanciful stories in their broad Dorset accents, whilst swilling a few jars of cider. Fred was in his forties when he completed this work. He died in Stoke Abbott in 1963, having spent many years as a carter for Edward Smith at Lower Farm, before taking up stone masonry work. Fred's brother, Wilfred, was killed in France in the Great War aged 22. He died of wounds, and his memorial is in the British Military cemetery in Beaumont Hamel, Somme. His sister Lucy's husband, was drowned in action in HMS Courageous on 17 September 1939 at the onset of WWII.

In 1903, when Lily was just a baby, John asked the local photographer to take a picture of their completed family of eight children. Mary Jane had had enough. She was so busy helping in the pub, always with a little one hanging on to her skirts. So they dressed up in their best, and the children stood like statues, as good as gold, not even able to wriggle or giggle, whilst the slow exposure was made. But this was too soon. The family was not complete. Over the next eight years, four more children were born, making a healthy dozen. A great sense of achievement must have overcome them when the last child, Kathleen, was born safely. A lot was dependent on nutrition and hygiene, and good common sense.

The New Inn, Stoke Abbott

John Swaffield and Mary Jane Bagg
with their first eight children.
Back L–R, Lucy and Fred
Centre L–R, Wilfred, Emily, John
Swaffield, Mary Jane, Hilda
Bottom L–R, William (in a frock),
Baby Lily, Christina

Originally the New Inn was Stocks Farm, named after the stocks placed outside under an outer wall. Once there were four pubs in the village, but only the New Inn and the Anchor remained. They were central to the lives of the villagers, some of whom never left Stoke, and some who travelled no further than Beaminster or Bridport, and then only once a year. When Fred was a boy, a conjuror named Professor Arnold pitched his tent in the yard. He, and his sisters and brothers, clustered round waiting for the excitement to begin:

'He fairly mystified the people. He had his show early in the evening, about nine or just after. One night he said to old Harry Slade, "Would yew like to toss for a drink?"

"Ess I'll toss wi thee," Harry was excited.

So the Professor borrowed Fred Wakely's box hat and the coin he did put under the hat, and Harry did cry. "Head!" or "Tails!" He went on two or three times like that, and then the next times he lifted the hat instead of a coin t'was a ball in under the hat. Next time t'was a quart cup. However it come there we didn't know. Harry got proper wild with him an said, "Yews trying to do en me out of my drink."

Poor old Jack Hitchcock, his eyes nearly coming out of his head said, "Pon my soul, well whatever is the wurld coming to?"

Old Jane Hann who was next to Jack said, "Oh my God! Look at that! I won't bide yer. I can't bide yer. My God! Whatever sort a feller is it? He'll have we all bewitched."

During all these shenanigans family life in the New Inn continued. The children lived in an atmosphere of cider dregs, tobacco fumes, hearty laughter and much drunkenness. John and Jane were good parents, the children always well fed and dressed, with tidy manners. John Swaffield was a large man, and is remembered for 'his very big tummy' and 'at weddings and funerals, wearing a bowler hat and a suit with a big, bright gold watch and chain stretched across his stomach'. They all courted and married locally except Louis who remained a bachelor. He inherited the family's musical talent, and played the cornet with the Beaminster Town Band, which provided a guard of honour at Kathleen's wedding in 1938. Big brother Fred, and he grew bigger than his father John, at one time conducted the band. It would be interesting to count up just how many Swaffield boy cousins learnt to appreciate music and perform well in public, through the auspices of this band. George Swaffield, postman and founder of the band, must have relished their enthusiasm.

c1958 – Taken at the rear of Christina Swaffield's cottage.
Back L–R: *Cecil Long, Christina Swaffield Long, Sid Long, Winnie Swaffield Jones, Lucy Swaffield Clarke, Lou Swaffield*
Front L–R: *Ben Jones, Jane Jones and Len Jones*

There were several farms and mills in the area, and family names such as Davy, Meech, Slade, Hallett, Wakely and Guppy. The Canterbury and the Swaffield families have a long unbroken record of continuity in the village. Charles and Sarah Canterbury owned the Stoke Abbott Carriers, later joined by their grandson, Johnnie. In the 1970s, Sally Bartlett, granddaughter of Mary Ann Canterbury, married Ben, the son of Winnie Swaffield Jones, keeping the families intertwined.

Fred wrote that the men drank their fair share of cider, and many of the women could swallow a quart or more. This with griddled tidies and cheese, and griddle cake cooked on a hearth, was the staple diet. Stoke Abbott then was a mass of apple blossom, and the whole village was surrounded by flourishing orchards. Along the village street, the apples fell off the trees and rolled under the cart wheels. The church was shaded by beech trees, there was a big chestnut near the Reading Room, and several very high sweetnuts by the chapel.

Wilf – killed in action 1917, aged 23

The barns and homes were constructed of mud and thatch which ignited quickly. Fires were common and the Beaminster Brigade raced over and emptied the horse trough of water. Some said there was more cider drunk those nights than there was water in the trough. The men were busy during the day. The land was richly agricultural and sown with corn, barley, potatoes and flax, with fields full of sheep and cows. Corn was cut by scythe, wheat by reaper or trapper and tied by hand. Flax was a big crop and created a lot of employment. Locally it was known as 'vlex' and was 'pulled', then the seeds were stamped with wooden beadles and spread on the ground to colour up, before the flax was put into a rick to dry out. In the winter they dried the 'shoats' over a fire of 'skimps' and crushed them next day, removing the 'skimps' as well as they could. The waste was called 'tow', and the best was sent to the factory for spinning into linen. It was dry work, and there was usually a barrel of cider handy for wetting dusty throats.

Six bellringers called the villagers to church on Sunday mornings, and in the summer there were school treats with tables loaded with cakes until ' we fernear busted'. In winter the village band played, lit by lanterns and candlelight, with the wind chasing round and blowing out the flames. The Moore family kept the Post Office and made bread. Ted was the baker and delivered as far as Dottery. Sometimes Fred went with him in the chap:

'When we got to the Inn at Salwayash, I had to do down to Ford and then to Strongate while he went on to Dottery. I used to be half afraid – not being very old – sometimes it was pitch dark before I came back from Ford. Then I had to wait at Salwayash till he came back along. The men used to try and frighten me in the pub and say Teddy was gone back to Stoke long ago, and I should have to walk home. When Teddy did arrive he would have a glass of beer and give me some ginger beer and wasn't I glad when we started for Stoke.'

'There was a man named Freddie Hamblin – an umbrella mender. He used to come by day and mend a few umbrellas through the village, and by night he would come in the pub and step dance at which he was very clever. He always carried a pair of clogs with him. He earned a lot of money like that.'

He asked Levi Bartlett one night, "Do yew go to work?"

"Yes," say Levi.

"How much do yew earn?" asked Freddie.

"Two shillings a day," says Levi.

"Well," says Freddie, "I can earn that in less than ten minutes." So he got up and went through several different steps, and then went round with his hat, and all the men put in a penny each and he counted it out and he had two shillings and threepence.

"There," he said, "Yew've worked all day for less than that Levi!" He was short and stout with a little box hat cocked on top of his head. He used to lie rough at night up Anchor Lane – sometimes down Horsehill in the carthouse.

One Sunday morning I went out in Pounds Orchard and under the wall by Emplote Gate, Freddie was sound asleep. There had been a very heavy frost, and he was as white as the grass around him. I roused him up and he shook himself like a dog and said, "I'm blowed – bean't I coold."

'We used to have a lot of timber haulers and throwers lodge there at different times. They kept their horses there and a fine lot of horses they were, especially some that came from Exeter, great powerful animals. There were scissor grinders and umbrella menders travelling the roads and, of course, they had to put in a good deal of their time at the village pub. One old scissor grinder used to come round and his wife would go on in front and shout:

> "Bring 'em out for Sammy's about,
> Rusty knives and scissors to grind.
> For my old man is coming behind!"

Will, outside the New Inn, he died aged 26

'Once a strange woman came in as drunk as a Lord. What a going on there was! After a time they tried to get her to go, but she wouldn't. She said that she wanted a ride, so she got up in Albert Heck's trap and sat back in the bottom of the cart with her head hanging over the tailboard.

"Give me a ride," she shouted.

So Albert said, "I'll give thee a ride!" He got up in the cart and drove out around the yard and galloped through the village with her head swinging from one end to the other as if she was on a swivel.

She refused to get out so the policeman said, "Better drive her on down to Union." Nobody knew who she was.'

The village normally had a constable who dealt with poachers. One constable was savagely beaten by a resentful gang, who left him for dead, and continued their poaching. After that they got a proper policeman in.

John and Jane Swaffield outside the New Inn, c 1920s

'Sometimes Saturday nights my mother used to cook tripe suppers for the men, and a jolly good time they used to have. The tripe was two pence each and they had as much as they liked. Cider used to be very cheap. Father sold many a hogshead [52½ gallon cask] at a penny a pint. Times will never be again as they have been. There weren't many teetotallers in those days!'

As a youngster Fred earned a few coppers going bird starving after the fields were sown. They had to chase the birds, waving sticks in the air. Farmers were prudent and sowed seed right to the edges of the fields. But the boys were careless and trod much of the ground 'hard as a road' making Mr Smith, the farmer, angry:

> He collared George, Fred's friend, and hollered, "What be yew doing here?"
> "Bird starving" says George.
> "Well," hissed Mr Smith, "Whose thism boy up there?"
> "Fred Swaful, Sir," said George.
> "Fred Swaful? Wass he doing yer?"
> "Bird starving, Sir"
> "Who sent he yer?"
> "Mr Edward, Sir," George was shivering with fear.

Haymaking – Kathleen and Winnie with their niece, Sylvia Clarke

"What!" Mr Smith was disgusted, "Two boys fer two fields side by side. Look how yew be treading the ground all around yer. I never seen nothing like it."

Fred ran away towards Woods Lane, much against his better judgement as he knew the ghost of a murdered maid wandered there. Mr Smith gave up and went back to his field.

"Wasn't I glad!" said Fred.'

Another opportunity to earn pocket money was pig-keeping:

'I had to look after a beautiful white sow and nine or ten young ones from Lower House. There were two big black sows from Chartnoll and I had all my time cut out to keep them from fighting my sow, and chasing them off the two splendid great barley ricks at the bottom of Elvoll. Sometimes I had to go up Netherbury Lane with my pigs in the cornfields up there. That is another thing that is gone, a lot of the villagers used to have their pig killed and sell out a part of them and keep the rest for their own use. On pig killing days you would see the women around the horse trough cleaning the innards for making blackpot.'

Hilda photographed at the Geoffrey Stuart Studio

All highly agricultural villages had a collection of blacksmiths and carpenters, as well as wheelwrights, carters, shepherds, cowmen, hurdlemakers, flax dressers, rabbit catchers and farmers. Forty or fifty would turn out from the surrounding hamlets to the two pubs on a Saturday night:

'… like a great family to discuss the week's work, what yarns we used to hear if a carter had ploughed a field with crooked furrows or a labourer had sown a field casty. Generally everybody was good tempered though sometimes I have seen amongst the older men a few arguments. They would have words and soon up-fist. Then they wanted Wakely to fetch his 'cordion and they would dance the four-handed reel, and didn't their clamps [tread] sound on the kitchen floor! Jimmy Staple was one of the very best I have ever seen dance the four-handed reel. He could step it out. He could make his hobbs noddle. Some of the old men was fond of singing. When they used to sing, "The flag that guides the sailor on the wave" – they used to roar it out. Old Jack Norris, when he had a drop, used to holler at the top of his voice. If anyone tried to stop him, he would cuss and bring his fist down across the table and make the cups jump up in the air. A young man wanted to sing after Jack had sung only one song. Didn't that set Jack up? He wanted to sing all night. He wanted to fight this young man. "I ood die vore I'd led a boy like that sing," he shouted out, "Young fellars wodn't gwine a cock walk over ee. He'd cheat the world all to pieces vore he'd gie in to em." And didn't he bring his fist on the table. He made the table fair jump.'

Hannah Harris kept a shop and is remembered as a very nice woman, but … could be difficult:

'Twas always a pantomime on Saturdays, Charles Frampton used to travel round with meat in those days. When Hannah had chosen her meat, Charles used to weigh it and say so much, but she wouldn't have it, she would carry it in and put it on her weights and too'd and fro'd so much. Charles did cuss and say her weights were all wrong. Hannah did carry it out and chuck it in the cart. Charles did bring it in again and throw it on the counter. Hannah had it out again and say 'Shan't have it' and he'd say 'Ess yew will', and when they got tired of running backwards and forwards, Charles would go on and settle it for next week.'

Tom Swaffield was Fred's uncle who married Ellen Davy, and they lived in Stoke Abbott. Ellen took in washing. She was very short and it was distressing to see her heaving wooden buckets and heavy sheets, and struggling on her stocky legs to hang the clothes on ropes to dry in the wind. Both Ellen and Tom survived to a good age, and Tom eventually moved to Bournemouth to live with one of his two daughters. A real character, Tom was a cheerful man. He once said to postman George, his elder brother, 'I wish thee be as happy as I be, George!' It was one of his boasts that he never missed the Club Day for well nigh fifty years. He seldom returned home on these occasions without having indulged in a game of skittles, of which he was no mean exponent.

Tom, flax dresser, quarryman and 'fighter'

'On Stoke Abbott Club Day there were lots of different amusements and swingboards outside the Anchor Inn, and dancing on the Rectory lawn. The pubs opened all day, and I could tell of some lively goings on. Tom Swaffield, who wasn't as spry as he used to be, he was getting on for seventy, chucked down his stick and started climbing a tree. When he got some way up the limb broke. Down comes Tom, limb and all, right down across the tables, upset all the cups with beer all over the place. Poor Tom had a nasty jar. On another occasion a young women fell under the water wheel at Horsehill Spinning Mill. All the workers rushed out and onto the bank fearing she would be drowned. Tom Swaffield rushed to the rescue, well he pulled off all the clothes he had on and jumped in and got her out. However he done it I don't know? They nearly got sucked in under the wheel. Of course as he got out all the men and women started laughing at Tom, but he didn't care a bit, and 'pon my soul if he didn't bide there and danced and kicked up all manner of capers in front of them, wet and mud all over as he was!'

Emily (aged 23) sent this photo to 'Dear Crissie' (Christina) as a Christmas card in 1915

'Tom liked a glass of beer and he would follow the hounds or play a game of skittles as good as I have seen. He used to be a flax dresser and work on the farm sometimes. In his young days he worked at Horsehill Mill also at Chenham Mill as a comber. He said that Stoke was a very rough place. I have seen Tom fight a few times, and he was pretty nimble too. I saw him once down by the allotment gate, he and a Beaminster man. Tom was coming up the road, the other was coming down. When they came within thirty yard of each other they started taking off their jackets, never having spoken a word. When they met they started fighting. And didn't they fight? And then they both went down and still they fought on the ground. They couldn't stop to get up. Another day I saw them fight at the New Inn the day before Tom was nearly sixty. Tom said they used to go crudgel playing up in the New Inn Plot. 'Two of em did challenge one t'other an ave two girt crudgels and whack et in to one t'others heeds and the vust of ee to draw blood was the winner.' For a time Tom was Stoke's champion fighter, and was challenged by other villages like Broadwindsor. He would go over and face his opponent in the square with a good crowd cheering, hissing and booing. The constable tried to stop the fights, but they, '… didn't take nar mosel bit of notice.'

Christina c 1917

Christina married Reuben Long in 1927. He worked on a farm in Winsham, near Chard. They had three children. Christina was great friends with her 'next up' sister, Hilda – and the two would meet often for a gossip. When Hilda married Charlie Holman in 1931, the wedding reception was held at the New Inn. Christina went with her children, but they were not allowed to join the main party. They were put into a separate room, given separate food and, to the children's delight, they were given sixpence each by their grandfather, John. Sixpence could buy all manner of treats dear to a child's heart. So it is sixpences, rather than segregation, which is remembered. It was a confusing incident, and not talked about. Both Hilda and Christina were brought up in the Church of England, but Christina became interested in evangelism, and once went to London to see Billy Graham. It is Gwen, Christina's daughter, who kindly rummaged in shoe boxes, and sent so many lovely sepia photographs of this large Swaffield family.

Wedding of Hilda Swaffield and Charlie Holman in 1931.
L–R, Lou (best man), Kathleen, Charlie, Hilda, John Swaffield and Sylvia, d/o Lucy

Kathleen inherited her mother's lovely heart-shaped face, and colouring. All the children had dark, shiny hair and were a good looking lot. They all went to school, and Kathleen won a place at Beaminster Grammar. She had to walk, to and fro, every day, two miles each way. Her mother tucked a baked potato into her hands, to keep them warm. The potato would be eaten, hungrily, at dinner time. But there was no hot potato for the homeward journey, and if she was delayed in winter, the light had gone. It was scary walking down the lanes in utter darkness, not a glimmer of light, and the hedges and trees eerie and beckoning. Kathleen taught when she left school, at both Stoke Abbott and Netherbury, before taking a Nanny/Governess job in Bournemouth. She married Fred Collin, and after Heather was born, they had two sets of girl/boy twins to cope with.

Kath's wedding, 1938: R of Bride is her father, John, and in suit, buttonhole and trilby, is her elder brother Frederick James [of memoir fame], peeping from behind is Lou. Bridesmaid on R of bride is Winnie, next to Michael Record and his mother, Lily.

Fred kept on with his writing and, just after the outbreak of WWII, he wrote to his sister, Kath, who was living at 12 Pattle, Beaminster.

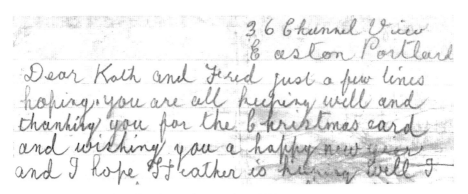

Three short extracts are shown here from Fred's 4-page letter, 1939

they get a revolution in Germany
Dear Kath you know I get some very funny
happenings sometimes well I had it about
Alf and the Courageous. I was hear in this very
old house where our Post is the night, as it
must have happened I wasnt thinking about
war nor Alf nor ships. The room seemed
different seemed a very funny light
and all at once I saw the inside
of that ship and Alf and the

as only a few are at work in the stone trade
a lot are gone to the dockyard to
work and at Whiteheads. Mrs Stone
husband is at Plymouth. I had something
in my stocking Christmas a bottle of beer so I had
a swig between 5 and 6 in bed that morning
her little boy come in bed with me with all his
toys. he is a lively young boy. Well dear Kath
I must close give my love
to Fred and Heather I
remain your loving Brother Fred

36 Channel View
Easton Portland – December 29th 1939

'Dear Kath and Fred Just a few lines hoping you are all keeping well and thanking you for the Christmas card and wishing you a happy new year and I hope Heather is keeping well. I suppose she is getting a big girl now. Has Fred plenty of work. The works where I used to be has hardly anything to do. Shouldn't be surprised to hear they are closed next week. You know I am on this A R P job. Don't get hardly anytime off. We had last Monday. I had to be on at ten that night. And then we hadn't to leave the island in case of an air Raid. What a Christmas Some difference what we used to have I had to spend my Christmas night out here in this hut all alone. I have only been to bed every other night since the war started and there is two of us at each post and we relieve one another every 8 hours day and night Saturday and Sundays. Sometimes I feel like a tiger chained up but as we volunteered for it we must go through with it. What a job about poor Alf wasn't it I don't hardly realise it is true and how it has upset everything for Lucy [Alfred Clarke m sister Beatrice Lucy but died in 1939]. I am glad she is keeping up and that she came with you for a time what a good job she had such good children. Bob is good taking to it like he has as it is no joke what they have to do. It upsets the whole life for Lucy I don't know what is going to be at the end of it. Some think it will soon be over but it is going to be a tough job unless they get a revolution in Germany. Dear Kath you know I get some very funny happenings sometimes well I had it about Alf and the Courageous. I was hear [sic] in this very old house where our Post is the night, as it must have happened, I wasn't thinking about war nor Alf nor ships. The room seemed different, seemed a very funy [sic] light and all at once I saw the inside of that ship and Alf and the engines, seemed to me Alf had a big spanner in his hand and I heard him say that's a devil of a bump and it was real to me as if whatever struck the ship was just ahead of him towards the front part of the ship. I did not think anything of it at the time but next day heard the news about the ship. I told Missus Stone about it and I said to her I felt sure Alf was gone. Wasn't I upset from the time I heard the ship was gone, as I felt sure. Now why should a thing like that come to any in an out of the way place where I am. And not thinking anything about such things. I seem to be not in this room at the same time but was where the ship was as I saw Alf plain and heard it. I'm only telling you and Fred this at present. So don't say anything to anyone now nor Lucy as it only freshens things up. Some might say I am crack. But it is quite true, I tell you Kath there is things we dont understand I should just like to know which side of the ship was struck to me it seemed what we call the off side. I suppose you know I go courting I dont know if you have heard she is a bit younger than me she is a smart girl about as tall as you and as big as Lucy. She has knitted two jumpers and given me for Christmas one with the V for tie and one that covers up to the neck, dark grey, they do look smart. I shall be glad when this is over as well as everybody else will be. It seems to alter ones life. If I hadn't been on this job I should sure have been stopped as only a few are at work in the stone trade. A lot are gone to the dockyard to work and at Whiteheads. Mrs Stone husband is at Plymouth. I had something in my stocking Christmas a bottle of beer so I had a swig between 5 and 6 in bed that morning, her little boy come in bed with me with all this toys. He is a lively young boy. Well dear Kath I must close.

Give my love to Fred and Heather.

I remain your loving Brother, Fred.'

HMS Courageous sinking Courtesy Lee Francis Wilhelmsen

Lucy and Alfred Clarke farmed at Court Orchard Farm. Lucy was forty–nine when she was so suddenly widowed. Sylvia was twenty-one and Bob was eighteen. Lucy decided to stay on at the farm, and did so, until very shortly before she died. She sold the property, but kept two rooms, and helped the new owners. It was an arrangement which worked well for all of them.

Lily aged about 20

None of the Stoke Abbott Swaffield boys had children. Sadly the end of the line of a fine family, remembered with pleasure in the village today.

Ann Swaffield b 1848

Ann Swaffield, the only daughter of John and Caroline, married her first cousin William Canterbury. They had two boys, one of whom was a hunchback, William John, always known as Jack. He played the organ, as well as the piano, and composed his own musical pieces and enjoyed symphony concerts in Bournemouth and London. When he was in London, Jack called on his Ealing cousins, and the Swaffields in Harrow. He was born in 1880 and died aged 80.

Frederick Swaffield b 1854, farmer and Edwin Swaffield b 1857, postman

Frederick and Edwin Swaffield were popular and successful men, brought up with integrity and honesty. Fred was a successful farmer at Portesham and a well-known agriculturist. His funeral at Beaminster was attended by all his surviving siblings, and by his children, and was reported in the Western Gazette in March 1923. His son, Herbert, owned three farms and had a racehorse, 'Hyland Myth', which won hurdle races at Exeter, Newton Abbott and Stratford. When Herbert died in 1967 he was described as a '… farmer, former church and local government worker'. He first farmed at Beaminster and married Lilian Alberta Daubeney of Coombe Farm.

Like his big brother, George, Edwin became a postman. He was given a pony and trap for the Stoke Abbott–Broadwindsor run. Arriving at either of his little huts, he blew his horn so that anyone who wanted a stamp or to post a letter could come along. Edwin Swaffield was Chapel, while Emma, his wife, was a member of the Parish Church. Their only son, Charles, was killed in WWI. Postman George, then aged eighty-nine and known as Dad Swaffield of Beaminster, felt very sad when he attended his younger brother's funeral

Kath (née Swaffield) and Fred Collin with their family at Pilson Pen, Dorset. Back L–R, Twins Mary [Reed] and Terry, John Crabb and Heather, Kath and Fred. Front L–R, Twins John and Anna with Ashley Crabb, aged one.

Pilsbury Grange in the Dove Valley

Chapter 7

DERBYSHIRE 1853–2002
Ben Swaffield's family

Benjamin Swaffield 1767–1840 and Hannah Burdett 1765–1857

Thomas	Hannah	Mary	**Robert**	**Benjamin**	Elizabeth	Judith	Samuel	Martha	Sarah	John
1791	1792	1794	1795	1797	1799	1801	1802	1804	1805	1806
1859			18S7	1879	1831		1863	1877	1856	1891
			Sarah	Sarah						
			Emily	Seaward						
			m	m						
			Ephraim	James						
			Cridge	Milward						

Ben, Frances, Sarah and the four boys settled into their new life at Pilsbury Grange. Here they did not have the chatter of neighbours, the comings and goings from house to house, this was a more secluded country life, with a large property and plenty of land. Pilsbury Grange became another holiday home for various Swaffields, who travelled great distances to reunite with the family.

Ben's daughter, Sarah Swaffield, now married to James Milward, Librarian at Chatsworth, was a frequent visitor. She travelled from Edensor with her own daughter, Sarah [later Craigie], and two small sons, Charles James and Benjamin William.

Although Robert Swaffield, Ben's elder brother, has not yet featured in this story, recently discovered letters have produced a thin chink of light. He appears to have been the least successful of Benjamin and Hannah's sons, and to have caused the greatest concern. As early as 1837 Ben received a letter from his father, Benjamin, from Wootton Fitzpaine. Transcribed literally from his generously large writing. His letter is dated 27 November 1837:

The address side of the folded sheet from Benjamin Swaffield
to his son, Ben, at Edensor

Extract of letter from Benjamin in 'Wotton' Fitzpaine

'My dear Son,

The first thing I shall ask of you is to forgive me for not writing to you before I assure you my time hath been so much taken up for this last two month with Referances and survey that I have not been home two days together the whole of the time and to make the better of it I had two sheep stolen and I had rode a 100 miles on that account, but however not in vaine for we have taken the Thief, we took him near Exeter and he is in Dorchester Prison for trial, I set forth a Reward of 20£ which with the Expences will cost me 40 altogether. I hope this will find you Mrs Swaffield and the dear little girl [Sarah Seward Swaffield] quite well, and I have the Blessing to inform you that we and all of us are in good health I have been to Melbury & Corscombe in the last few days they are all well, I slept at Merryland one night Mr & Mrs Meech are quite well and beg to be remembered to you when I did write if I had not written to you this day I think your Mother & Mrs Dawe would been Frantic. Mrs Dawe desires her kind Regards to you and a thousand thanks for the Grouse you sent them they were butifull and came the very day that she wanted them. Robt came down from Wayhill Fair to Wotton he is looking very well. Mr Fox hath been kind enough to offer me a very nice Farm near Ringwood in Hampshire if I wanted one for either of my sons, it is about 300 acres. Mr Fox was thinking where Robt wanted a situation or not he told me there was no hurry as no one should have the offer of it till after Lady day nearly when you have an hour to spare we shall be glad to hear from you and forgive me in not writing to you before, what think you of the Wool and corn trade I have not sold my Wool and I have out about 100 2w[s] of Old Wheat by me the best price for Wool is 15 bb and Wheat from 7/6 to 7/9 Bus[1] for the best your mother, Sarah and John [his two youngest children] joine me in kindest Regards to you M[rs] S [Frances Watkinson] and Dear Sarah

Benj Swaffield'

The part of the letter which refers to Robert

Mr Fox, a relation of Lord Ilchester, continued the Fox family tradition of helping the deserving Swaffields, but there is no record that Robert took up this offer. He and his wife, Charlotte, had moved away from Dorsetshire to Eltham in Kent, now part of Greater London. Sam, from Ampthill, made a particular journey to visit them on 23 April 1826: 'Coach hire and expenses in going to London and to Eltham to see Elizabeth and Rob[t], &c, &c, – £5 0s 0d.' Robert's next sibling is named Elizabeth. Sam's visit was made seven years after Robert's own marriage, in Halstock, to Charlotte Farmer and they had a daughter, Sarah Emily.

There are several family tie-ups between Derbyshire and Dorsetshire, but the strangest is that of the mysterious Ephraim Cridge, whose name is on Robert and Charlotte's family gravestone in the tiny churchyard at Lewcombe, but his bones lie in Australia.

~o~————————~o~

Sacred to the Memory
of ROBERT SWAFFIELD of Corscombe
who died March 24th 1857
aged 61 years
CHARLOTTE SWAFFIELD
wife of the above who died
April 3rd 1869 aged 70 years
Lord Remember me when Thou come into Thy Kingdom

EPHRAIM MATTHEWS CRIDGE MRCS
Son-in-law of the above
Robert & Charlotte Swaffield who died at
Grafton, N.S.W
on May 2nd 1867 aged 35 years.

~o~————————~o~

Thirteen years prior to his death Ephraim was married to Robert's daughter:

DERBY MERCURY – October 18th 1854:

On the 12th inst at Eltham, Kent, by the Reverend Alfred Snow, Ephraim Mathias Cridge Esq., Surgeon of Bank Top House, Sheen, Staffs to Sarah Emily Swaffield, youngest daughter of Mr Robert Swaffield of Corscombe, Dorsetshire and niece of Mr Benjamin Swaffield of Pilsbury Grange, Derbyshire.

Cridge came from Woodbury, near Exeter and on 14 July 1853 he was listed on the Fellows, Members & Licentiates in Midwifery of the Royal College of Surgeons of England. His address was at Stoke Devonport. Three years later, on 4 August, he also appeared on the List of Persons Qualified to Practise as Apothecaries in any part of England and Wales except the City of London, and within ten miles of the said City. Thirdly he is listed in the London & Provincial Medical Directory 1855, as residing at Allstonefield, Ashbourne, Derbyshire. In the same year Sarah and Ephraim's son, Thomas Matthews Cridge, was born at Sheen and registered in the Leek District, close to Pilsbury Grange.

```
ROCKY MOUTH.
Dr. E. M. CRIDGE,
MEMBER OF THE ROYAL COLLEGE OF
SURGEONS OF ENGLAND,
LICENTIATE OF APOTHECARIES HALL,
LONDON ; and registered as a duly qualified
practitioner of GREAT BRITAIN, begs to inform
the settlers of the CLARENCE RIVER
DISTRICT, that he has
Commenced Practising as a
Surgeon, &c.,
and can be consulted temporarily at Mr. Powell's,
South Arm, until a permanent residence is com-
pleted at Maclean.
     Dr. C. dispenses his own medicines.
Rocky Mouth, 23rd November, 1865.
```

Dr E M Cridge's Advertisement dated 23 November 1865

A bit of a rolling stone, Ephraim Cridge left Derbyshire several years later and sailed to Australia, no doubt promising to send for his young son and wife. He is registered in 1867 in the Australian Pioneer's Register at Grafton, New South Wales, certificate number 5225. Grafton lies on the Clarence River close to Nymboida National Park, north-north-east of Coffs Harbour on the coast, and inland from Woolgoolga. Cridge opened a surgery there in 1865, and then moved on to Rocky Mouth and started practising surgery in 1867. Records have proved that Cridge was a respected man, although he had once been fined for drunkenness. It seems more likely that he was lonely without Sarah Emily and Tom, and became unwell. His death, at 35, was premature and occurred at the Freemason's Hotel in Grafton. He owed the innkeeper for hay, cover for his horse, wine, ale, brandy and his washing. The Swaffield family have recorded his death with the respect it deserved.

Ten years previously Robert had already died, in Corscombe, where he was living as an Annuitant, or pensioned, probably by his brother Ben. In 1856, he wrote to Ben at Pilsbury Grange:

'London Sunday Nov^{em} 22 - 1856

My Dear Sir

I beg Acknowledge the receipt of your Letter which I duly rec^{d} with a Sovereign inclosed for which I rite in you my verry sincere thanks that will carry me through this journey very well we shall return on Wednesday next if please God. I find myself something better in spirits – but still my Throat is the same – I cannot keep down any Food that is the least solid and from that I am got verry thin and weak. I am still taking Medicine but I do not think that it does me any good – however I stick to the Doctors directions – I believe that Emily [his daughter] intend to return about the end of this Next Week. Mrs West will attend to Mrs Swaffields order. As soon as I get back [to Dorsetshire] I will Write to you and tell you how I am getting on. We all unite in our kind love and best Wishes, I remain yours Faithfully Robt Swaffield.

God bless you for your many kindness towards me.'

Medicine but I do not think that it does me any good - however I stick to the Doctors directions —

I believe that Emily - intend to return about the end of this next Week Mrs West will attend to Mrs Swaffields order . —

As soon as I get back I will Write to you - and till you how I am getting on - we all Unite in our Kind love and and best Wishes I Remain Yours Faithfully Robt Swaffield

God bless you for your many

*Small envelope inscribed by Robert Swaffield to his brother, Ben, at Pilsbury Grange – and additionally inscribed by Ben in pencil
'Poor Rob⁵ Last'. It is franked on the back* AA NO 24 1856 *and, on the front* ASHBOURNE NO 25 1856

Ben had been settled at Pilsbury Grange for five years, and had become a well-known breeder of fat stock.

1858 – February 15th – Forthcoming Sale, Martock Market, near Yeovil, Somerset.

Superior Pure-Bred Short Horn Bull

'Mr W G Palmer respectfully announces that he is favoured with instructions from Mr G P Gard, [Ben's elder sister, Mary, married John Gard of Somerset in 1814] to sell by auction, on Monday, the 22nd day of February 1858, bred by Mr Benjamin Swaffield, Pilsbury, near Ashbourne, Derbyshire, got by Lord Palmerstone, dam. Lavender by Rothsay, grand-daughter of Lady of the Peak by Gustavus the Hero, great grand-daughter Dowager, by Belshazar. The Auctioneer can with great confidence recommend this noble animal to the attention of the Public.'

When at Pilsbury Grange, Benjamin was presented with a silver cup engraved: 'To Benjamin Swaffield for the best managed farm in South Derbyshire – November 8 1859' which was left to his grandson, John Ernest. The letters from Wootton Fitzpaine, photographs and small cuttings, were handed down and finally preserved by Ben Bailiff's grandson, Clement Louis, who died in 1949. His wife, Dorothy, survived another forty years and, in 1960 whilst sorting drawers, she came upon them. She sent them for safe-keeping to Ben's great grandson, John 1916–1974, and they have been kept in Uncle Ernest's writing box by John's widow, Joan. Auntie Dorothy wrote on Jan: 14th 1960: 'At last, I am sending you the old letters I promised, and I hope you will find them as interesting as I think they are! I suppose the two minus envelopes and stamps must have been sent by stage coach! I wonder how long they took to get to Edensor from Wootton Fitzpayne? [sic] It is amazing to think how difficult it was to contact folk in those days, in these times of cars, wireless, telephones, telegraphs etc.'

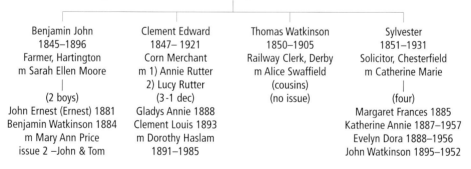

Benjamin Swaffield 1797 and 2) Frances Watkinson 1812

Benjamin John 1845–1896 Farmer, Hartington m Sarah Ellen Moore	Clement Edward 1847– 1921 Corn Merchant m 1) Annie Rutter 2) Lucy Rutter	Thomas Watkinson 1850–1905 Railway Clerk, Derby m Alice Swaffield (cousins)	Sylvester 1851–1931 Solicitor, Chesterfield m Catherine Marie
(2 boys) John Ernest (Ernest) 1881 Benjamin Watkinson 1884 m Mary Ann Price issue 2 –John & Tom	(3 -1 dec) Gladys Annie 1888 Clement Louis 1893 m Dorothy Haslam 1891–1985	(no issue)	(four) Margaret Frances 1885 Katherine Annie 1887–1957 Evelyn Dora 1888–1956 John Watkinson 1895–1952

Whilst researching this book, we have made several visits to Derbyshire. Locating Pilsbury Grange was difficult, and we had to stop several people to get directions: "The Grange? Pilsbury? Now let me think. Yes, you'll find it on the gated road from Sheen, anyone will direct you." The gated road runs along the Dove Valley and is no more than a track, well used by hikers. The first time we made our way from the Bank Top House end, but were nervous to open the gate as we thought it private land. On another occasion, we did a wide detour and approached from the north, and wound our way down a steep lane, soon coming across several large houses, but none seemed right, and some were way off the track. There was no-one to ask, only a stray heifer escaped from a field and very terrified of our car. It would not go backwards or forwards. We had to stay still and then edge round the frightened beast. Again we reached the Bank Top House end, and turned around. We then met a man, so poor we were almost embarrassed to stop him. But he knew the place.

"A Devonshire house," he said, "One of three at t'other end". So we edged past the poor heifer again, and stopped at the first of three imposing houses with magnificent views across the valley. It was empty and almost derelict, the second in poor condition with no-one at home. In the yard of the third was a man working on the outhouses. After he had called off his dogs, I went to speak to him, "Excuse me," I said, "I'm ancestor hunting."

"Oh," his smile was friendly, "You must be looking for Ben Swaffield's house, yes – this is it." After over 120 years I was impressed that Ben's memory lived on. It was a magic moment. Ben Swaffield was hard-working, a country lover and well respected. He died at Hartington and is buried there, with Frances Watkinson, in the churchyard of St Giles', under a flat stone.

Ben's grave, shared with Frances, amongst the others, well preserved in clean Derbyshire air

~o~————————————-~o~
Sacred to the Memory of
Benjamin Swaffield of Pilsbury
who died in Hartington in 1879
aged 81 years
Also of
Frances
his wife
Who died December 5th
1893
aged 81 years
~o~————————————-~o~

On the death of his mother in 1893, their first son, Benjamin John, a fervent member of the Dove Valley Volunteers, and his wife Sarah Ellen moved from Pilsbury Grange to Bank Top House,

Sheen. This large stone farmhouse is on the outskirts of Hartington on the Derbyshire/Staffordshire border. Benjamin John died there in January 1896, aged only 50.

Envelope to Mrs Swaffield

Almost immediately, Sarah Ellen received a black bordered letter from Captain C P Frinney dated Jan 27th 1896, then living at Broadmeadow, Hartington:

'Dear Mrs Swaffield

It was with extreme sorrow that we received the sad news of Mr Swaffield's death.

I write on behalf of I Company 2nd Vol., Batt. Derby Regt., to express our deep sympathy, and to say that with your wish & permission, not without, we should like to accord our Late Commander the Military honour due to his rank. If you would kindly let me know your wishes I will act accordingly. I am sure there is not a man in the Company or that ever has been in, but what would wish to join in a tribute of respect to their late Captain.

I remain

Yours faithfully

C P Frinney Capt.

The following account comes from the local newspaper:

"The Late Captain Swaffield" – 'The district around Hartington was thrown into something like the nature of a sensation on the 26th ult. when the bell tolled for the late Captain Swaffield. The deceased was for many years a tenant on the Devonshire Estate [Pilsbury], until at last, two years ago, the deepening agricultural depression drove him away, and he took a small farm on the Beresford-Hope Estate, near Hartington, and died there last week after a ten days' assault of pneumonia.

It was as a Volunteer – an earnest and painstaking Volunteer – that Mr Swaffield was most and best known. He joined the Hartington sub-division of the Dove Valley Volunteers as a private at or soon after its formation, and ultimately became captain of the company, retiring at last with the honorary title of Major and receiving the long service medal when it was issued.

He was buried at Hartington on Wednesday in last week. The funeral was with military honours, and of a character at once impressive and pathetic, on account partly of the presence of the Volunteers and a few members of the Yeomanry, all of whom were in full-dress uniform, and partly on account of the manner and the swiftness with which death overtook him whilst still within the bounds of what is known as the prime of life.

The widespread respect which Captain Swaffield years ago had already won from all classes of people – won by kindly and inoffensive demeanour over a long series of years – was enough, along with a bright and beautiful day, to account for the considerable number of spectators who gathered round to see the last of a well-known man; and though Hartington is now getting accustomed to military funerals, that of Captain Swaffield will not soon pass out of the spectators' recollection.'

The grave of Ben John Swaffield, backed by St Giles' Church, Hartington

Portrait of Benjamin John Swaffield

Inside St Giles' Church, high in the roof, are worn coloured banners and the drum of the Hartington Volunteer Band. The graveyard is set in the hills a little above the small town. There is a gate, steps up, the entrance on the right faces the roof tops. In spring the pathways are bright with brilliant purple, mauve and lavender aubretia. The churchyard is well maintained and the Swaffield graves are at the rear, left hand side. The church guide states that 'there are no amusing or scurrilous rhymes on the tombstones …'. Ben John's is a good example.

~o~————————————-~o~
"In Affectionate Memory of Benjamin John Swaffield of Pilsbury Grange
who died January 26th 1896 aged 50 years"
~o~————————————-~o~

Although space had been left for the name of spouse, Sarah Ellen, she moved to be near her son, Benjamin Watkinson Swaffield, who lived with his wife Mary Ann at Kingstone, near Hereford. Their marriage was short-lived as he was taken prisoner in 1918, a young father of two sons – Benjamin John and Thomas Watkinson.

'Gunner B W Swaffield, Kingstone – Mrs Swaffield, Green Villa, Kingstone, has received a postcard from her husband Gunner B W Swaffield, R.F.A., saying he is a prisoner of war in Germany and wounded. Up to now he has been reported as missing since 21st March, the opening day of the first German Offensive.'

Gunner B W Swaffield, Kingstone, near Hereford – 'The official lists published this week of British Prisoners of War who died in German hands includes the name of Gunner B W Swaffield, husband of Mrs Mary Ann Swaffield, Green Villa, Kingstone. He was reported missing as from March 21st last. He joined the Army Veterinary Corps on March 20th 1916, and in July 1917 was transferred to the Royal Field Artillery and drafted to France in the following November. He was the younger son of the late Major B J Swaffield, Pilsbury Grange, Hartington, and the late Mrs Sarah Ellen Swaffield, Green Court, Kingstone.'

NUMBERS OF WAR DEAD 1914-18	
Germany	1,770,000
Russia	1,700,000
France	1,360,000
Austria-Hungary	1,200,000
British Empire	910,000
Italy	460,000
Romania	450,000
Turkey	330,000
Bulgaria	240,000
Serbia	190,000
Belgium	60,000
USA	50,000
Portugal	13,000
Montenegro	13,000

1917 – Gunner Benjamin Watkinson Swaffield aged 33

A typed letter was sent to Mary Ann, [who later remarried] from Army Records at Woolwich, on 14 June 1922 regarding 'the death of the late No 245347 Gr B W Swaffield … that the late soldier is buried at Aubencheul Au Bac German Cemetery about 5½ miles NNW of Cambrai.' Blank news for a widow left with baby Tom, who had never set eyes on his father, and two-year old, Benjamin John.

1920 – L–R, Tom, Mary Ann [widow] and Benjamin John Swaffield

Ben Bailiff's four sons were successful men. Wills were left and proved. Benjamin John left nearly £2000, his brother, Clement, corn merchant of Derby who died in 1921 left £15,000, whilst Tom Watkinson Swaffield left £13,000, a goodly sum for a Railway Clerk in 1905.

This Tom, married his cousin Alice, daughter of Sam Swaffield of Ampthill. Alice had attended the Edensor wedding of her brother, HRJ to Emmeline Jepson, and Tom was one of the family guests. Tom's sudden death was recorded in the Derbyshire Telegraph on 14 September 1905:

1903 – Alice Swaffield with her two little dogs

SUDDEN DEATH OF DERBY GENTLEMAN – The Inquest

The Deputy-Coroner (Mr W J Holbrook) held an inquest at the Town Hall, Derby, this (Thursday) evening, with reference to the death of Mr Thomas Watkinson Swaffield, aged 55, of 2 Highfield Road, Derby, which event occurred with startling suddenness on Wednesday afternoon. Mr Clement Swaffield, corn merchant, of the Duffield Road, identified the body as that of his brother. He retired from business about five years ago. Witness said that he last saw him alive on September 4th, and he then appeared in very good health. He had been cautioned by doctors, who told him that he had a weak heart, and should take care of himself. Mr George Cornwell, restaurant proprietor, of 25–26 Railway Terrace, said he had known the deceased for about two years. They were both members of the Derby Photographic Society, and the deceased was greatly interested in the art. About 1–20 on Wednesday afternoon the deceased came to witness's house in company with a friend named Mr Huxley. All three had arranged to go to Hemington and Lockington for the purpose of taking some photographs. Upon arriving at witness's house the deceased took a seat in the arm chair, and he was laughing and talking. He seemed in good health, and witness left him and Mr Huxley whilst he had his dinner. He had not got many yards from the door of the room when Mr Huxley put his head round the door and called, "Mr Cornwell, just a minute." Witness went back, and saw the deceased still sitting in the arm chair. His head was back, and he was gasping. Witness exclaimed, "What on earth is the matter? Is it a fit or what?" and asked Mr Huxley to run for a doctor. He did so and Dr King came within about seven minutes, but the deceased had in the meantime died in the witness's arms. Dr King declared that death due to sudden heart attack. The body was removed to mortuary and afterwards taken to his home. The jury returned a verdict in accordance with the medical evidence.

Alice remained in Derby, and died there aged 76, leaving a curious Will in that her pets were to be poisoned, and her money divided equally between her nephews and nieces, down to the last penny. It was a difficult job for the solicitor to track down so many beneficiaries.

She was 'laid to rest' in Darley Abbey churchyard. Mourners were Eva May [niece] and Clement and Ernest Swaffield [nephews], Mr & Mrs Edward Swaffield [brother & sister-in-law], Mr & Mrs Norman Swaffield [nephew]. Many friends attended and floral tributes came from Mrs Benjamin George Swaffield, Annie and Ena [Ampthill], Mr C Swaffield, Miss Rutter. The coffin was of unpolished English oak with brass appointments.

The thread of agriculture, and love of the land and its creatures, runs right through the Derbyshire Swaffs. Gunner Swaffield's eldest surviving brother, John Ernest (Ernest) lived in Cheltenham, the house situated in an orchard of fruit trees.

20 October 1950 – Mr Ernest Swaffield with bag at Coln St Denys. 4½ brace pheasants, 16 rabbits. Photo by Harold Winterbourne

He and his wife Sarah Annie had no children. She was a busy lady and spent much of the summer bottling and preserving fruit. In 1967 Ernest received an award of merit from Lord Shackleton, and the British Beekeeper's National Honey Show at Caxton Hall, London. The Gloucestershire Echo reported: 'The award is for services to the craft of bee-keeping over a long period of years and one well earned.' Bees were Ernest's passion, and he organised bee and honey sections at all the big country shows, and acted as a judge. He also served on a Ministry Committee to decide a national mark for honey. He eventually lived with his nephew John, and his wife Joan, at Hoxne in Suffolk. John pre-deceased Ernest by three years, and Joan continued to care for Uncle Ernest until he died in 1977.

Hartington gets several visits a year from ancestor hunting Swaffs. One was Richard Swaffield, brother of Audrey – our family genealogist – himself hailing from the Beaminster clan. Richard's wife, May, left a note in a jam jar on Ben John's grave, giving Audrey's address in Peterborough. This note was found by Tom Watkinson Swaffield of Shawbury, who made contact with Audrey. His bee-keeping Uncle Ernest had left him Ben Bailiff's silver cup, he has the family Bible, and stories that his mother told him. This link

Richard and May Swaffield from Port Elizabeth, South Africa

destined this book – a complicated link originating from my own cousin, Sue Lindley d/o AC Swaffield 1902, who lives in South Africa. She looked up 'Swaffield' in the Port Elizabeth telephone book, made contact with Richard (Dick) and May, wrote to me about them, put me in touch with Audrey … finally resulting in 'The Swaffs from the Shires' or, should I have entitled it 'A Note in a Jam Jar'?

Tom was born in 1918, the year his father, Ben Watkinson, was killed. He was educated at Newton School in Herefordshire and left at fourteen. His mother, Mary Ann, had superb domestic skills and frequently entered her goodies into local agricultural shows. Tom helped carry the dressed poultry, eggs, butter, cakes and pies, but was more interested in watching the ploughing matches. Sometimes he tended Uncle Ernest's bees. He was happiest when he farmed on his own in Shropshire. He first married Lilian Altree, and had one daughter, Margaret. Tom has strong memories of the outbreak of WWII, and served with the ARP – Air Raid Precautions.

All local authorities had ARP schemes covering wardens, first aid, emergency ambulance, gas decontamination, rescue, repair and demolition services as well as first aid posts, gas cleansing stations and casualty clearing stations.

Tom's second marriage was to Margaret Gosnay, and they have three children, Anthony, Sylvester and Mary. Tom and Margaret farmed until 1972, and then took up a dairy/newsagent business. They live in Shawbury. Anthony lives in Hayes, Middlesex and

1971 – Anthony, Sylvester & Mary Swaffield

works with the BBC as a Trading Standards Officer. Sylvester is married and has two little girls. He has his own printing business in Ellesmere. Mary is a trained Nanny, lives in Richmond in Surrey, and works in Kew. She has travelled and worked with her job both in Canada and Australia. Until recently, Margaret was an auxiliary nurse working within the community. She has written books, one on local history, and has been the Methodist archivist covering the area between Walsall and Chirk, "It has been fascinating," she said, "I have had people coming from all over the globe trying to trace their ancestors."

THE WILL of **Benjamin Swaffield** of Pilsbury Grange who died March 26th 1879.

I GIVE AND BEQUEATH to my son, Benjamin John, the service of silver plate which was presented to me on my leaving Edensor. To my son, Thomas Watkinson, the silver cup presented to me by Francis Hurt Esq. To my son, Clement, the silver cup presented to me by his Grace the Duke of Devonshire.

All real estate and personal estate unspecified by my wife, Frances Swaffield, and sons Benjamin John and Sylvester who I appoint Trustees and Executors. To my daughter, Sarah Seaward Milward, the sum of £600. £400 to Thomas Watkinson Swaffield. £400 to Sylvester Swaffield. £50 to Clement Swaffield. Lands at Brampton to be vested in Trustees. £50 to wife together with furniture, plate and linen etc. £20 p.a. annuity to be paid by son Benjamin John to Frances, wife, from the Trustees. Surplus money to be divided between Thomas, Sylvester and Clement.

Benjamin John will continue at Pilsbury Grange Farm and therefore both the live and dead farm stock is left to him in the hope that he will be allowed to continue the tenancy.

Benjamin Swaffield left under £6,000 [in today's money = £386,282.60], District of Bakewell, Derbyshire.

WILL of **Frances Swaffield**, aged 81, widow of Pilsbury, Hartington, Derbyshire, died 5 December 1893. Proved by Benjamin John Swaffield, farmer, Clement Swaffield, Corn Merchant, and Sylvester Swaffield, Solicitor. £542 6s 6d – Chesterfield District.

WILL of **Benjamin John Swaffield**, aged 50, of Bank Top House, Sheen, Staffordshire died 26 January 1896. Proved by Sarah Ellen Swaffield, widow, and Clement Swaffield, Corn Merchant. £1,991 – Leek District.

WILL of **Benjamin Watkinson Swaffield** of Kingstone, Herefordshire. Gunner in Royal Field Artillery died 27 March 1918 in France. Proved by widow, Mary Ann Elizabeth Swaffield. £355 1s 4d.

WILL of **Thomas Watkinson Swaffield** of Derby, aged 55, died 13 September 1905. Proved by Alice Swaffield, widow. £13,029 12s 9d.

From Lucy [Rutter] Swaffield's Will. She died 1924:

'Executors to be husband Clement, son Clement Louis and daughter, Gladys Annie.
To my son 200 Ordinary Shares in Strarton Iron Works and also the portrait of my father.
To my sister Lizzie Bassett Rutter £50 free of tax etc.
To my daughter Gladys Annie all real estate and residue of my personal estate.
Left £4,096. Probate 26 September 1924.

LOCAL WILLS

News cutting 1926 – *Derby Mercury*:
Pets to be Poisoned. Derby Lady's Curious Request:

> "I desire that my pet dog and birds be mercifully destroyed by poison by a reliable man, and both carefully and deeply buried in my garden immediately after my decease."

'This curious instruction is contained in the Will of the late Mrs Alice Swaffield, widow, of 2 Highfield Road, Derby.

Mrs Swaffield left £9,403 11s 1d gross estate, of which £4,142 10s 4d was net personality. Two public bequests are included in the will. She left £300 each to the National Society for the Prevention of Cruelty to Children and the Royal Society for the Prevention of Cruelty to Animals.

Personal Legacies: Other legacies were as follows: Elizabeth Williams £50, Mary Milward, wife of her late husband's nephew, Charles James Milward, £50. Ellen Riley, her servant (if in her service at the time of her death), £25. George Betts, King Street, £5. All her jewellery, wearing apparel and other articles of personal use and ornament she left to her niece, Eva May Swaffield [d/o Benjamin George 1842]. The residue of her property she ordered to be divided in equal shares amongst all the nephews and nieces of herself and her late husband, living at the time of her death, except two whose names are not mentioned.

Mrs Swaffield appointed as executors and trustees her friend, Elizabeth Williams of 63 Park Grove, wife of Mr C B Williams, the police court missioner, her niece Eva May Swaffield, and her solicitor John Henry Powell.'

Her estate was distributed in December 1926 and £5537 6s 8d was left equally divided between 41 Swaffield relatives allowing them £135 1s 2d each, although some received only £135 1s 1d. Her list of bequests still exists.

Hereford Times
10 November 2002

Tom Swaffield, great-grandson of Ben Bailiff, holding his great-great-granddaughter, Ellen.

Top L–R, Tom's daughter Margaret and granddaughter Jenny, at bottom left is great-granddaughter, Angela Lewis

Photo courtesy Hereford Times, David Griffiths

Norman on the horse, Henry standing, then L–R, Baby Ella, Ethel, Exton [in skirts] and Minnie sitting on the stool

George Parker and his wife, Minnie Swaffield Parker

Chapter 8

THE SHIRES ~ 1867–2002
Bedfordshire, Yorkshire, Devonshire and Suffolk

Henry Richard James Swaffield 1839–1909 and Emmeline Jepson 1842–1922

Emmeline	Henry	Exton	Norman	Charlotte Ethel	Ella	Dorothy	Beatrice	Alan	Hugh	Richard	Hilda	Mildred	Basil
(Minnie)		(Eck)		(Bridget)		(Dot)	(Queenie)			(Dick)	(Jo)	(Kitty)	
1867	1868	1869	1871	1872	1874	1875	1876	1878	1879	1880	1882	1884	1885
1934	1964	1950	1958	1965	1945	1962	1967	1878	1918	1937	1965	1973	1972
m													

Minnie Swaffield 1867–1934) and George Adamson Parker 1866–1964

Phyllis Dorothy	Hilda Beatrice	Kenyon Shiercliffe
1895–1987	1897– 1990	1904–1989
m 1922	m 1930	m Pamela Coxhead
1) Edward C Milligan	George Shepherd	of Budleigh Salterton

Alice Jane Parker [sister to G A Parker]
m Harry Lockwood

Marjorie	Alan	Geoffrey	Donald
(Mish)			

Minnie was the eldest of thirteen siblings. Her youngest brother, Basil, was born when she was nearly nineteen. We have a glimpse of this large family in a small photograph [opposite] taken of the first six children. Minnie coped with the rapid arrival of three brothers and two sisters before she reached her eighth birthday. Park Farm was already bursting at the seams, and there were more to come.

When she was twenty-six, Minnie married George Parker of Sheffield. George was a great walker and, whilst exploring Bedfordshire, he stayed with the Swaffields at Park Farm on several occasions. Gradually his relationship with Minnie grew. They married at Steppingley in June 1893, and spent their honeymoon climbing in Switzerland. Minnie's childhood was one of constantly 'helping Mother with the babies'. Elder children often get the blame for their brothers' and sisters' misdemeanours, and Minnie's serious little face, when she was less than ten, suggests that being elder sister had its disadvantages. Despite her own mother's productivity, Minnie stopped having babies once her son Kenyon arrived in 1904, after the birth of two daughters, Phyllis Dorothy (Phyll) and Hilda Beatrice, known as Bea.

George was a wealthy steelmaster, cutler and ironmaster. Steel was invented ten years before George was born, and Sheffield began to produce stainless steel table knives and sharp tools. George's great-grandfather, Kenyon Stevens Parker QC (1790–1866), was one of the founder directors of the Legal & General Assurance Company, established in 1836. At the age of 76, in London, he was knocked over by a runaway horse and, according to his family, 'Died in agony.'

George's father married into the cutlery business. He was rather a delicate man so 'to strengthen him up', it was decided that he and his wife should 'explore Africa' with their young sons, James Kenyon and George Adamson Parker. They left their baby daughter, Alice Jane, at home. The trip was too much for George's father, and he died. His wife returned to Sheffield and went straight into the family business, becoming successful and earning enough to educate the children and maintain a home. Her eldest boy went into Law and George followed his mother's footsteps.

Once married, George and Minnie settled in Sheffield. He was a no-nonsense Yorkshireman, a meat and two veg man. He liked a big roast chicken on Sunday, and put up with cold chicken and salad on Monday, but Tuesday was:

"What's this?"

"Oh? Just wings and things," said Minnie cheerily.

"Wings? You're giving a man wings?"

Known as 'Ga' to his grandchildren, he did not suffer fools gladly. Once when his sister-in-law, Ethel, was worrying about the young men in WWII, she said, "I don't know how they can carry all their muskets."

George replied tersely, "They must be having trouble with their flintlocks."

The Parkers retired to Budleigh Salterton, Devon in the twenties and called their house 'Endcliffe', named after the Sheffield area where George and Minnie had originally lived. Minnie died in 1934 at 78 Clarkhouse Road, Sheffield, and there was a request for no mourning and no flowers. Her Will was proved by her son, Kenyon, Chartered Accountant. Her younger sister, Ethel, came to live with George and act as housekeeper. This suited her as they lived 'the

life of Riley'. Ably assisted by her faithful maid, cook and friend, Bessy, Ethel relished her new role as 'Miss Swaffield of Budleigh Salterton' where she enjoyed the company of Anglo-Indians. One day, after a coffee morning, she commented cheerfully, "The whole of the British Raj seems to have retired to Budleigh Salterton."

Ethel was tough, and broke away from the trappings of home in October 1901 when she sailed to India, aged twenty-nine. Her brother, Henry, helped her draw up a contract to work as a Lady's Nurse for a Mrs MacKinnon in Calcutta. Unfortunately Mrs M's name did not appear on the contract, which was negotiated by her mother:

Early 1900s – Ethel

' ... salary of Thirty Five Pounds for services as Lady Nurse to Mrs Hervey's daughter commencing 17th day October 1901 – ending 16th October 1902, my passage 2nd Class to be paid to and from India by Mrs Hervey. Should I leave Mrs Hervey's service of my own free will (only) before expiration of twelve months I agree to refund the passage to and from England. In the event of illness through Climatic Influences my return Passage to England to be paid by Mrs M Hervey.

Dated this 1st day of October 1901

(sgd) Ethel Swaffield

Witness Henry Swaffield (bro) of Ampthill.

India – Taj Mahal

Her journey started well, she was in buoyant mood. En route she sent a picture postcard of the P&O liner, SS Mantua, to her nephew, Leslie, at 'The Bungalow, Ampthill' dated Aden, October 15th. But her correspondence begins to tell a different story. She has her own style of writing, not typical of the time, and used small, unnumbered pages. She wrote to Kitty, her youngest sister:

Dec 17th [1901]   14 Ballygunge, Circular Road, Calcutta – Sunday

Dearest Kitty

I was so astounded at getting a letter from you this morning that I feel I must not let such an honour pass unnoticed considering how very flush you generally are with your letters. I got five letters this morning, 2 from Mother, 1 from Ella, Marion and yourself. I am sorry I shall get them all at once and only as a rule once a week, still better than none at all. We got into Bombay at day break on Sat & came ashore about 8 to Esplanade Hotel & Mr MacKinnon met us, we stayed there until Tuesday evening, I quite intended to write but it was intensely hot, in fact awfully, I fairly stuck to everything I touched. … I have not had a minute since we got here as they have moved into a new house, & Mrs MacKinnon wants everything altering. While I think of it put c/o J MacKinnon Esquire not Hervey but I will explain to Mother next time.

I was furious just before we landed, I wrote a lot of letters to send off at Bombay and the day we arrived when I opened my case for them found it had been split open and thus all taken out. I went to the Purser and kicked up a row and he put a notice up but of course I never saw them again, it was maddening as I had not time to write again, and I do not see what use they could be to anyone <u>so</u> now I shall have to write them all again. I am glad we are not living in Bombay as I do not like it nearly as much as Calcutta. … We left [Bombay] on Tuesday, with the exception of rushing out

Kitty and Ethel (seated) in 1899 at Beckerings Park

of the train twice a day for breakfast & dinner we travelled until Thursday & the dust & dirt was awful, I felt simply fearful, we used to get tea about 5 in the train, breakfast between 10 to 11 and just had time to bolt it down before the tea in the train & dinner at 6. The first day and night the scenery was very wild lovely in places and then after that it got more civilised, the stations are few & far between sometimes you run to & fro between & the trains go at a fearful speed, and when you get to them they are just a little kind of shed no pretence of a platform.

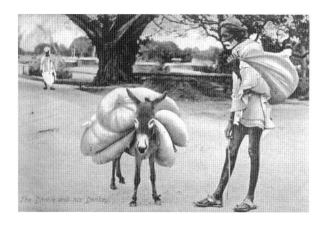

Calcutta Dhobi

Now I will tell you how I spend the days. I get up at 6-30, dress myself and then have Chota Hazri in the bedroom which means early tea, bread & butter & toast etc. Go out at 6-30 till 8. Sometimes I take Dorrie for a walk or if she goes for a drive with Mr & Mrs M I go on my own. Come in do the flowers for breakfast and do anything till eleven, then bath the kid and myself to be ready for breakfast at 12. I will tell you what I had for breakfast today just to give you an idea as it is not a bit like an English one. Soup first, roast pigeon curry, cold guinea fowl, kidney & bacon, omlet [sic] and all the time in between we are stuffing bread and butter spring onions radishes etc, & then end up with fruit of all kinds, so it is not bad for one breakfast is it? After breakfast we undress and go to bed till 3-30 then get up and dress and go for a drive till 5-30 when it is quite dark have tea when we come in and then I put the kid to bed at 7-30 and then have dinner of 8 courses so if I don't get as fat as a pig I ought to don't you think so. I wish you could all just come over and see all the trees and flowers, birds and butterflies of all colours flying about, it is almost past description.

Today has not seemed a bit like Sunday, I did not go to church Mrs M did not give me the opportunity and as we hardly seem to have found our legs at present I did not say anything about it, and outside men have been playing cricket and tennis all the afternoon and evening and the natives have all been at work just the same as yesterday.

I am very glad to hear you are working hard this term and hope you will keep it up for I don't suppose you will be at school much longer. Now dear child, I will say good night, and I want to get several letters off by the mail on Thursday. With heaps of love to you all, and don't let your letter be the <u>first</u> & <u>last</u>.

Your loving sister   Ethel.

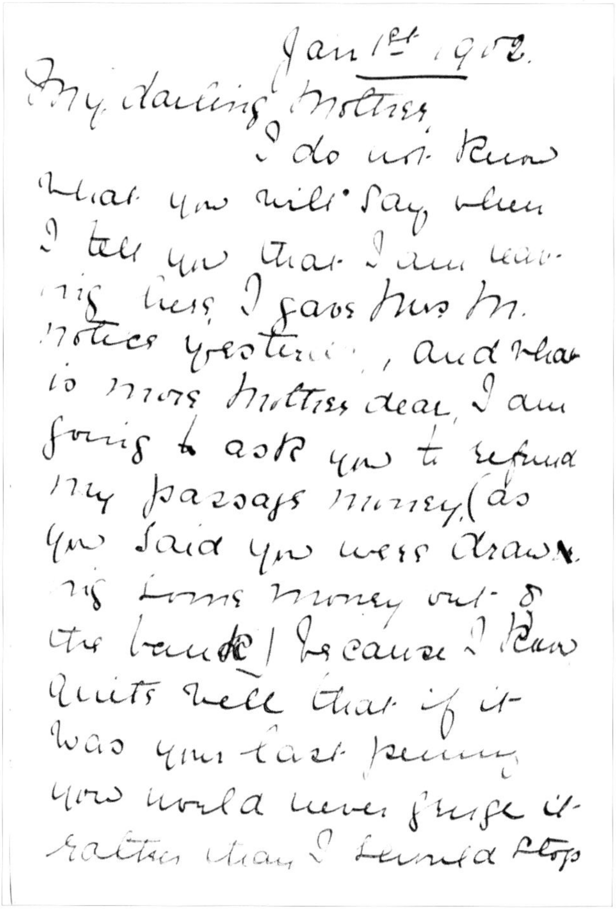

Jan 1st 1902.

My darling Mother,

I do not know what you will say, when I tell you that I am leaving here, I gave Mrs M. notice yesterday, and that is more Mother dear, I am going to ask you to refund my passage money (as you said you were drawing some money out of the bank) because I know quite well that if it was your last penny you would never grudge it rather than I should stop

Ethel's letter

Monday Dec 23rd [1901]

My darling Mother,

Many thanks for your letter received this evening and the sweet little Calendar, I was hoping someone would send me one, I also had Auntie's [Aunt Sally] letter and 2 pretty fancy handkerchiefs from Marion & Heather and last week I had gloves from George and some fancy buttons from Min and the photos from Beatrice, so think I have done very well, tho I have never had so few letters and only one card and that from Auntie, which please thank her for.

I am very sorry to hear that Hilda has started with the measles, and expect Basil will follow suit but I hope the rest will escape, it is disappointing as it puts a stop to any of the kiddies coming, which I know will be a great disappointment to you, and it would be quite funny to be quite alone.

Xmas morning 8 a.m. As you will see I did not get very far with this on Mon. & now I am furious, so no doubt you will get some grumbles. I asked Mrs M if I could go to one of the early services at 6-30 or 7-30 at the Cathedral and she said she didn't know what they were going to do, and now I have been sitting here dressed since 6-15 waiting for Dorrie to come and be dressed, and now it is after 8, but that is not surprising when they did not come in from the Theatre till <u>4 o'clock</u> —- I am sure they want to sleep <u>something off</u> !!! Then she has never given me an answer, as to whether I could go & spend part of the day with Sister Margaret, as she wrote and asked me to do. I must say I shall be glad when today and the Races are over.

There is a most awful band outside playing Ta ra ra each instrument in a different key to the others, it is as bad as a lesson. … There has been an awful row here with the servants on Sun: night the cook nearly had his life beaten out of him, and on Mon: night all the stable men got it, which resulted in the coachman & 4 syces, taking all their things outside the gate and they won't go away they are still there this morning and have sat there over night. Mon: night; I quite expect it will end in Mr M getting hurt for they are all against him and now Mother darling, the last but not least, I cannot remember if I told you in my last letter as I only wrote a p.c. last week that this was a chance of us starting for home in about a fortnight as Mr M was applying for his leave earlier, and now the other day when he went before the Dr before sending in for leave, he was drunk & of course the Dr

The Cook

told him so which he did not like, which ended in a row, and from what Mrs said I do not think there is the slightest chance of us coming which means instead of April at the latest it will be a year next Feb or March when his year and a half furlow [sic] is due, so then they cannot stop him, however I shall still hope on as he will not know decidedly until next Monday, but when you <u>get this</u> don't write to me <u>here</u> any more, as by next mail I hope to be able to tell you what we are going to do.

The Sweeper

Dorrie nearly frightened me to death last week, & you will hardly believe it when I tell you that she swallowed her little —- bracelet with a knot tied in it and the padlock on, of course it was only a thin one, but I would not have believed it if after 2 doses of castor oil I had <u>not</u> found it in a <u>certain place</u>, she swallowed it in bed one afternoon, and we only had her word for it until it appeared again, so I shall never be surprised at anything a kid eats. I have christened her the 'Gold Mine'.

It has not seemed a little bit like Xmas day, in any way, of course the climate makes a great difference for one thing, it is a most perfect day but very hot. Please give Auntie my very best love, and wish her many happy returns of the 1st, I am sorry I did not think of it having enough to write, but you have to think of this so long before when you are away and now I am afraid it is too late to write.

It is nearly 4, so I must get dressed & get the kid up to go out. I have not seen either of them today yet, so I have given up all hope of going to Sister Margaret.

With very much love to you all, hoping the measles are better.

Your loving kid   <u>Ethel</u>

Jan 1st 1902

My darling Mother

I do not know what you will say when I tell you that I am leaving here. I gave Mrs M notice yesterday, and what is more Mother dear, I am going to ask you to refund my passage money (as you said you were drawing some money out of the bank) because I know quite well that if it was your last penny you would never gruge [sic] it rather than I should stop here. I have never been happy thus I have not said much in my letters home but things have gone from bad to worse, what is making me miserable is that you should have to pay (as Mrs M says she shall not allow me or my things to leave this house until the passage is refunded) for no fault of ours, for God knows, I have done my best to stand it, & if we had been coming home in April I should have hung on, but now he does not get his leave for another <u>14 or 15 months</u>, & I know I could not stand it, I really don't know why I did not run away on Xmas night. I am sure it was only thinking that the servants would not help with my things, & I knew if I went without them I should never get them.

My time is up on the 29th & unless you telegraph the money out here which all makes it more expense, I shall have to wait 6 weeks for it, & I do not want to stay a day longer than I can help if it had not been that I shall want every penny I can get I should have gone without the month's notice.

Tomorrow morning, I am going to ask to go down to the P&O Offices & try & arrange something through them. I simply hate having to ask you to do this dear for I do not see the slightest chance of ever being able to pay you back but unless I can get my passage back through taking charge of children I shall stop out here until I can afford to bring myself, of that I have quite made up my mind, as you can come straight from India to London by some firms for less than the P&O can bring you.

I don't know what I should have done without Sister Margaret, I have been & told her everything, and she has made me promise to go there when I leave here until something turns up, and is looking out for me now. She is also going to consult her lawyer as to whether the agreement is legal in the name of Hervey, oh if only I could score one over that, I should be happy, but I am afraid it is no go. Unfortunately I have no witness to anything so have not any hold over them whatever but I assure you at times Mrs M is more like a devil than a woman for she has attacks, when she thinks all the devils in Creation are after her, does not know husband, kid, me or anyone, and fights like a fiend, I say she is either mad or has D.T's. … I have only seen her in one but that is quite enough, I cannot forget it in a hurry but I hear she has them now & again. Mr M is following in Mr Sacchi's footsteps, tho' at present they are not so frequent or violent, but from the Sun. before Xmas and for a week he was on the drink, and between the two I can tell you I live in perfect terror. When I gave Mrs M notice I told her it was [writing deteriorating here] entirely their fault had things been different, I would have stayed & gone home with them, of course she denied everything – informed me I was a servant which she is very fond of doing, she has never forgiven Henry over the Lady Nurse business and as <u>such</u> I must expect to be treated. Ask Father to find out if the agreement is legal, as soon as you get time, & of course if it is not you need not send the money, otherwise Mother dear I know I can depend on you.

Do not write me here again but address c/o Sister Margaret, Pratt Memorial School, 168 Lower Circular Road, Calcutta.

Post Office

I have just been to the P&O office, & if you will pay the money into their office in London they will pay it me here. You need not put any <u>name</u> or <u>address</u>, as I am going to call again at the office about the 26th or 27th for it. Now Mrs M says she paid £42 for me, 1st from London to Harwich & 2nd from H to Bombay, but they will be able to tell you in London exactly, as they told me today it would be £38 & then it is £3 from Bombay here, which she says I have also to pay. She took my ticket in the name of Hervey.

I have no time for more as I must get back, & you do not know how I hate the idea of having to ask you dear, but I do not see any other way out of my difficulty.

With love to you all.

Your <u>loving Ethel</u>

Exton Swaffield, Master Mariner

There was consternation when Ethel's anguished letter arrived in Bedford. Immediately Eck, her Master Mariner brother, was consulted, and on 21.1.02 he wrote from 44 Holborn Viaduct:

Dear Father,

I have cabled Ethel today I enclose copy of message sent, also receipt. I got hold of a Calcutta directory after going half over London for it & find that J. A. B. MacKinnon of 14 Ballygunge, Circular Rd is a Master Pilot & from what I saw of the Hooghly pilots when I was out there, should say that on the whole they are the hardest drinking lot of men one could find anywhere. They are really government issue, so that accounts for his furlough being stopped.

Your affect son – <u>Eck</u>

PS Hooghly pilots have very big salaries.

Cable

Swaffield, Sister Margaret, Pratt Memorial School, Calcutta.

Agreement void. Leave 29th. Demand clothes, passage money. If refused leave without either. Instruct Solicitor.

George Parker was also involved in getting Ethel home, and family photographs show that she spent some time in Bedford, but undaunted, she went out again. In 1909 – the year that their father, HRJ, died – her sister Ella went to visit Ethel in India where, rumour has it, Ethel was working for a Maharajah and was, for ever after, nicknamed 'Lady Bengal'. Ella's luggage was insured for £30 by the Marine & General Life Assurance Society, 14 Leadenhall Street, London. Ethel had caught the travel bug and, after India, in the late twenties she ran an English tea shop in Tangier, Morocco and then in San Remo, before coming home to look after widower, George Parker, in Budleigh Salterton, Devonshire.

George's granddaughter, Jane Shepherd Brettell was evacuated to 'Endcliffe' during the war. "Aunt Ethel made the house very comfortable," she recalls, "But she and Ga fought like cat and dog, he managed to make awful acid comments." As a child, Jane was scared of Ethel, but later grew to love her dearly as she mellowed and Jane matured. "She and my mother, Bea, were not unalike."

Jane and a schoolfriend spent a whole term in Budleigh Salterton, and went to school in Exmouth. "There were two boys from London living in the house too," she said, "But we were not allowed to have anything to do with them. They stayed in the kitchen quarters and caught another bus to their school. It was awful not being able to speak to them." The boys ate separately, whilst the girls had their meals with Aunt Ethel and Ga. "He had a gurgling colostomy," said Jane, "It made us giggle uncontrollably." Despite this George lived to the ripe old age of 98, surviving Minnie by another 30 years. Both he and Ethel, who in the late fifties eventually lodged with Basil and Jimmy Swaffield in Bradgate Road, died in Bedford. Basil's granddaughter, Sue, remembers that Aunt Ethel "… had a brass table in her room from India, and could make her hands into wonderful animal shadow silhouettes on the wall."

NEWS CUTTING – May 3rd, 1965

In hospital at Bedford, Charlotte Ethel (Bridget) Swaffield in her 93rd year and late of Budleigh Salterton, Devon. Funeral service at Bedford Crematorium on 6th May. No Flowers.

Minnie had been godmother to her younger brother, Eck's son, Tony, and presented Dorritt & Tony with a crate of crockery on their wedding in 1931. When the newly-weds moved into their first flat in Manchester, they had the crockery but no table on which to put it. A frequent visitor was Donald Lockwood, a young doctor, nephew of George Parker and brother to the famous eccentric Mish. Eccentricity was obviously a family trait, as he had a unique and quick method of solving the problem of frayed shirt cuffs, by cutting the sleeves off just below the elbow.

Phyllis, the eldest daughter, first married Edward Clifford Milligan of Buxton, Derbyshire. He was an engineer and much of their life was spent in Singapore. Phyllis was just ten years younger than her maternal uncle, Basil, and he too married a Buxton Milligan, Hilda (Jimmy). Phyllis and Edward had two boys, Brian and Owen. They were sent home from Singapore to school and spent holidays with Aunt Bea and Uncle George Shepherd. Brian was quite an unsettled, unhappy little boy. He joined the Navy, then the Palestine Police, and eventually worked with George Shepherd in the motor industry. He married Jean Gordon, who was tragically killed in a car accident. Brian and Jean had adopted two children. Edward Milligan died in Hemel Hempstead in 1947, and Phyllis married again, Edgar Hunt in 1949.

Bea was born at Nether Halam in Yorkshire in February 1897 when her mother, Minnie, was thirty. With her sister, Phyll, and brother, Kenyon, she was brought up in a privileged Edwardian family. Phyll and Bea fought incessantly and were sent to separate schools. Bea attended Badminton House, Clifton, where the education was quite advanced for its time and, it was assumed, that girls might well follow a career. Her best friend was Dot Irving Bell (née Gregg), who would be described today as 'very camp' or 'extravagant in manner'. She and Bea remained firm friends for the whole of their lives, and for Janet, Bea's daughter – known as

Jane – Dot's presence was fun and full of surprise. Jane remembers her as a 'mystique, poetess, raconteur and show stealer'. When Robert Falcon Scott went to the Antarctic on his second expedition in 1910 in the Terra Nova, this caught Dot's imagination, and she worked hard to raise money for Scott and his explorers. It took the combined efforts of the ship and a sledge party, which consisted of Edward Wilson, Laurence Oates, Bowers, Evans and Robert Scott, two

Bea Parker after her marriage

whole years to get to the South Pole, only to discover that Roald Amundsen had beaten them by five weeks. Scott's party was delayed by blizzards and sick, exhausted men. The party perished, and their bodies and diaries were found eight months later. Dot documented the build up to the expedition and the tragic events which followed. Her entire library was left to the Scott Polar Research Institute in Cambridge.

After school, Phyll and Bea were 'finished' in Dresden, but had to return to England because of the war. Phyll joined the Voluntary Aid Detachment [VAD] and, after much pestering, Bea joined too and became an ambulance driver. She had '… an exciting time in spite of constantly losing boyfriends'. Her photograph album brims with beautiful young men in uniform. The VAD was founded in 1909 to supplement the Territorial Army's medical services. In 1915 they were put to the test when the War Office

decided that VAD nurses should be contracted to military hospitals. They provided welfare services to the sick and wounded, and often served on front lines, and over 70,000 were at work when the war ended in 1918. Bea was not ready to return to a sedentary life in Sheffield, so her father, George, allowed her to work in his office for a time.

During the twenties Bea was sent as 'housekeeper' to her cousins, who were living in Paris. She ran the apartment whilst they went out to work. Photographs suggest that it was probably 'all play and no work'. All desperately short of money, they entertained their Parisian friends with a very limited amount of cutlery, passing off its lack by saying, "In England these days it's fashionable to eat with a knife only." She had a pretty wild time in Paris, with cousins Tony and Geoff Swaffield and Mish Lockwood. They travelled, went to parties, beaches, casinos and dances. Parental eyebrows were not raised as they were all,

Paris – Tony and Geoff Swaffield, elder sons of Eck

presumably, together. Eventually she landed a job working for cousin Geoff, who had started his design business and fashion showroom in London, and here she met Jean [née Gordon-Stewart] who modelled Geoff's hats. She and Bea became good friends.

Jean married Geoff's younger, sparky brother – Mick – or Mike as he was known to them. Mike was always close to Bea's brother, Ken Parker, they were born two years apart and had a good friendship. Ken, and his wife Pam, joined them as soon as they could after WWII on many a trip to the South of France. Travel allowance was £25 and,

Jean Swaffield in a Geoff hat

on one occasion, Mike paid for the whole holiday by selling pound notes to the French Chief of Police over many glasses of Pernod. The differently routed journeys, to and from England to the Riviera, were always an adventure and took several days. Mike's Lancia models were tested over difficult Alpine passes, such as the Lauteret. At first they travelled by sea ferry, but in later years used Silver City Airways from Lympne to Le Touquet, driving on one end and off at the other. Ken had married Pamela Coxhead and had two daughters, Rosemary and Sarah. Bea adored her younger brother and they remained close all their lives.

Mish Lockwood, George's deliciously eccentric niece, was Marjorie Lockwood, only daughter of George's sister, Alice. Mish never married, but had a married boyfriend, who took her all over Europe on the back of his motorbike. A Francophile, she taught French at the Godolphin & Latymer School in Hammersmith, and was considered 'a natural teacher'

Cousins - Bea Parker and Mish Lockwood in France

eventually becoming Vice-Principal. Quite a feminist, she dashed all over the place on her own motorbike, arriving at various destinations with a powerful roar. She travelled light, that is she wore all of the clothes she intended to use during her stay, topped off with a large fur coat. She was a good raconteur, intelligent and amusing. One summer, she urged her second cousin, Jane Shepherd, to "… parle français" but, as it was holidays, Jane found any connection with school abhorrent and said, "No French." Mish came to stay with the Shepherds in Dunstable. She said her goodbyes and straddled her motorbike,

Bea (Parker) with her husband, George Shepherd

as always fully clad. Before starting the engine she checked the state of her red-lipsticked mouth in the mirror, "Jane dear," she said, "I want you to hold my hair." She then put on her old-fashioned flying helmet, and was anxious that some of hair showed in the front, framing her face, "You see, I do like to look nice," she said, and raced off.

Bea met George Shepherd during the post-war depression. Public transport was non-existent, so George offered Bea a lift to work. With these regular meetings, romance blossomed, and they married in 1927. During WWI, George Shepherd was mentioned in despatches twice and, while he escaped physical injury, he suffered severe shell shock which affected him for the rest of his life. Early symptoms included tiredness, irritability, giddiness, lack of concentration and headaches. Eventually George, and so many other men, suffered mental breakdowns. Doctors argued that a bursting shell creates a vacuum, and when the air rushes into this vacuum, it disturbs the cerebro-spinal fluid, and this can upset the working of the brain. Some doctors insisted that the only cure for shell-shock was a complete rest away from the fighting. If you were an officer you were likely to be sent back home to recuperate.

George Shepherd came from a small uncommunicative family. Shortly after his marriage to Bea, George's mother died, and there were murmurs of 'family dispute' which were never discussed. Was it the advent of an adopted baby? Bea had discovered that she was unable to have children, so she and George agreed to adopt a baby the following year. Janet had been born in London, in October 1930, and was about six months old when she became Janet Wesley Shepherd. Her grandmother, Minnie, was absolutely thrilled with this first granddaughter, and immediately ordered a red leather photograph album. It was gilded, with the name 'Janet' embossed in gold on the cover. The Box Brownie, black and white photographs, picture Baby Janet lying in her cradle, toddling, walking, pushing her pram, the 'dollie' passenger being a large lively dog, and tumbling on the lawn with the first of many dachshunds named Oscar. The album is very incomplete as Minnie died when Jane was just four. Bea and George lived in London for six years, and then moved to Surrey, where Bea created the first of many of her gardens. Jane remembers, "… Daddy as a most benign and gentle father, a sweet man who was popular and loved by all, especially my mother's family. He used to flirt with the Ampthill maiden aunts, and they adored him."

George Shepherd in uniform

When war was declared on 3 September 1939, George immediately volunteered and joined the Royal Army Service Corps, then transferred to the newly formed REME [Royal Electrical & Mechanical Engineers]. On demobilisation he returned to his job at Algali-City Motors, taking up the director's position he had vacated. After a year he resigned and purchased an engineering works at Ashwell in Hertfordshire. During WWII, Bea joined the Red Cross and worked shifts in the depot at Leatherhead. As her daughter remembers, "It was so hard for women at that time – husbands away, young children at home, juggling with ration books, no petrol even if there was a car, and the nightly terrors of the Blitz and the doodlebugs. Add to that reports coming from school of my bad behaviour, 'If you don't stop giggling Janet Shepherd, you will be sent from the classroom,' was a constant cry of my irritated teachers."

Shell shock took its toll on George, he became very depressed and then, as anticipated, suffered a severe nervous breakdown, after which he had to undergo electric shock treatment. For Bea it was a dreadful time, but the Swaffield/Parker grit got her through and she found solace in gardening. Eventually George recovered, but had lost his sparkle, his memories of the war, and those of Jane's teen years. But not his humour – the eccentricities of life and people always made him giggle. Eventually they moved to Dunstable, Bedfordshire, and George managed the Luton Motor Company. Jane met her future husband, Mike Brettell, who was the boss's son, "Mike had Spanish blood, he was dark with hazel eyes, and handsome." George retired, Bea created another beautiful garden and became a Magistrate, sitting on the Bedfordshire Bench at Leighton Buzzard. Says Jane, "She really loved this work and took to it most conscientiously, but had to give it up when they eventually moved to Eastbourne where George died in 1971. They were a devoted couple. Bea had a strong character and complained that George was obstinate but, between them, they created a great deal of happiness. After his death Bea took up painting again, she had been a competent watercolourist as a girl. Jane and Mike Brettell settled in East Anglia, and Bea moved to Cavendish, and then to Bury St Edmunds in Suffolk. She continued painting, joined the WRVS and did Meals on Wheels, and grew yet another exquisite town garden. Even in sheltered accommodation, she amazed her neighbours by producing tomatoes in her window box. Intensely private and discreet, she was never afraid to speak her mind, and died in 1990 aged 93.

Jane has inherited artistic skills, some influenced by her adoptive mother. Her schooling at Godolphin in Salisbury was interrupted by illness. Bea was summoned and "… arrived beating drums …" to be told that Jane had a patch on her lung. It was undiagnosed pleurisy, and entailed complete bed-rest for six months at home, and then six months in a convalescent home. Here Jane was surrounded by young women from the Forces, only too ready to share the intimacies of their love lives with a wide-eyed, fascinated teenager. Illness perhaps fostered the ideas of nursing, but it was decided Jane should attend Cambridge School where "I spent two blissful years" and then moved to London to dress the Peter Jones windows in Sloane Square. "My happiest and funniest times were working as PA to the head of the newly formed Contemporary Furniture Department at Liberty's, whilst living with old school friends in a flat in the Cromwell Road."

Jane married Mike Brettell in 1954. They settled into a primitive 'Hans Andersen' cottage in a village near Dunstable, with no electricity or indoor loo. After six months they purchased another cottage with the help of a mortgage, "Ga was dismayed!" Jane was involved with the Women's Institute and Amateur Dramatics. Then Mike joined Potter's in Woodbridge, Suffolk, but was not happy and, after training, became an airline pilot with Channel Airways. They moved to Saffron Walden to be near Stansted Airport and lived, in faded splendour, in one half of a large Georgian Rectory. Civil aviation was in the doldrums, Jane worked as a Care Attendant in an Old People's Home, "… the nearest I ever came to nursing …", and they moved again, north of Bury St Edmunds, and then to manage, as joint-owners, a small filling station at South Lopham near Diss. Stress led to an early heart attack at 51 for Mike, leaving Jane with three children and half a business, which she sold six months later. Bury St Edmunds, and her charming home in Southgate Street, have proved a haven for Jane. She taught art and craft

Jane Shepherd and Mike Brettell on their wedding day

at South Lea School for eleven years, and has developed her own distinct watercolour talent, exhibiting throughout the county, and travelling here and there to paint, to study and to enjoy being with some of her many friends. Giggling is still an inimitable part of her life.

When on holiday in Italy, Bea and George, having already discussed her adoption, gently told her that they knew her father was a French architect. They filtered information, for fear of losing their precious daughter, bonded so firmly into their family. Later Jane discovered, through Social Services, that her mother was a parlourmaid, called Asenath Yeomans, but her researches have gone no further. Three children were born to Jane and Mike, the youngest a boy, George. Sue, arrived in early spring 1956, and has followed in her mother's footsteps with her love of theatre.

Said Sue, "My pinnacle of achievement has never been topped by the Pantomime and Sketch Show I wrote, cast, directed, presented and performed in when I was about eleven. My mother painstakingly copied out the scripts for me. I don't think I have ever, before or since, had such confidence in my abilities." Sue attended the quality grammar school, Thomas Mills in Framlingham, before "… switching to an enormous co-ed comprehensive at Saffron Walden. This was traumatic and, having experienced both types of education, I can honestly say that the comprehensive system is no match for grammar schooling. She moved onto Cambridge Tech and "… became highly proficient in punting, table football and, once, dabbling with pot with a member of the East Anglian Drugs Squad. Despite this I managed to pass my A levels in English

The Brettell family – Sue, Elizabeth (Bassy) with her firstborn, Emma Longland, Jane and son, George Brettell

and Art & Design and, later, I gained a Masters Degree from the Central School, London, in Three-Dimensional Art, going on to an Advanced Secretarial Course in Cambridge in the early eighties.

She works as a freelance book designer, and has been a member of Equity since 1999, doing as much acting as she can, wherever she can. Both her parents were involved in amateur dramatics, "I think my mother should have been a professional, she always stole the show, even in minor roles. My father was a charmer and bon vivant, and influenced my enjoyment of fast driving, and living a little dangerously. Her grandmother Bea was, "… a strong character, as an elderly lady she was absolutely remarkable, and served killer G&Ts. She was bright and funny and I wish I had appreciated her more."

Bassy (Elizabeth) was the middle child, and is remembered with affection by her elder sister, Sue. "Unlike me, she had a pretty clear idea from an early age of her future. As a small girl she wanted to be a farmer, or marry a farmer. As a teenager, she was more interested in horse-riding than boys. She did business studies, and then went to agricultural college, afterwards working at Lord Rayleigh's Farms. She married a farmer's son – Spencer Longland. She was a gifted artist and, I believe, she would have explored that side of herself more. She expressed her abilities with her wonderful home-making skills, and creative cake decorating. She had a great sense of humour and many friends. Her illness [Bassy died of a particularly virulent form of breast cancer aged 39] and how she coped with it, was an inspiration to all who knew her. Originally the prognosis was four months, which she didn't know, but her determination kept her going for two years. In 1995 she organised a ball for the Breast Cancer Campaign and raised £13,000. We held two more events in her memory, and raised a staggering £94,000. Bassy left two little girls, Emma and Harriet, for Spencer to bring up, much helped by Jane.

Jane's son, George, joined the Territorial Army, and then survived the punishing selection tests to become a Commando [Green Beret]. Based in Arbroath, he travelled the world, learning how to survive the jungle, the arctic and six months on active duty in Belize. Since leaving in 1990 he remained with the TA, trained as an HGV3 driver [dangerous loads] and has been working for the MoD at military air bases, also as a reserve fireman. His pastimes have included model airplane flying, mountaineering, potholing, deep-sea diving and bicycle maintenance. The worst injury he's sustained is from a model aircraft. George has trained as a potter and enjoys the craft, and has inherited Jane's talent for impersonation.

Suffolk 2000 – Swaffield cousins and partners: L–R, Sheila and Clifford, Betty S-T (d/o Kitty Potter), Jane Brettell, Bunty and Owen Milligan

Chapter 9

BEDFORDSHIRE ~ AMPTHILL 1868–1918
Swaffield and Son, Exton's Shipwreck

The family of Henry Richard James Swaffield 1839 and Emmeline Jepson 1842–1922

Emmeline (Minnie)	Henry	Exton (Eck)	Norman	Ethel (Bridget)	Ella	Dorothy (Dot)	Beatrice (Queenie)	Alan	Hugh	Richard (Dick)	Hilda (Jo)	Mildred (Kitty)	Basil
1867	1868	1869	1871	1872	1874	1875	1876	1878	1879	1880	1882	1884	1885
1934	1964	1950	1958	1965	1945	1962	1967	1878	1918	1937	1965	1973	1972

In addition to 7 girls, Henry and Emmeline had 7 boys, one of whom, baby Alan, died. The first boy, Henry, was 17 years older than the last boy, and youngest child, Basil. The business of Swaffield & Son went to Henry, as was normal in those days, the others had to fend for themselves.

Henry Swaffield was taken into Swaffield & Son by his father, HRJ, in 1899. He also followed in his father's footsteps as Secretary to the Bedfordshire Agricultural Society, leaving the position open for his own son, Leslie, at the end of his tenure. Thus three generations of Swaffs held this job until there were no heirs to either inherit the family business or the secretaryship.

1956 News cutting 'Three Generations of Service' – HRJ, Henry & Leslie

With his two younger brothers, Henry was sent far away from Ampthill to boarding school in Tideswell in Derbyshire. His father's uncle, Ben Bailiff, was not responsible for this move, as he had already died. It is more likely, that it was the prodding of Emmeline, which persuaded HRJ to send the boys to Derbyshire for a 'proper' education. She had relations in Buxton and nearby Chapel-en-le-Frith. But it was a long journey for small boys to take, and a long way from the bustle and noise of their home at Beckerings Park, Steppingley where HRJ was a tenant with the Duke of Bedford.

Three Generations of Service

It is nearly 80 years since a Swaffield was appointed secretary of Bedfordshire Agricultural Society and the post has been in the family ever since.

H. R. J. Swaffield, founder of the "dynasty", reigned from 1878 to 1904. He was son of Samuel Exton Swaffield, who came to Ampthill Park in 1824 as steward to Lord Holland.

The "Grand Old Man" of Bedfordshire Agricultural Society, Mr. Henry Swaffield, will be 89 in August. He succeeded his father in 1904 and served until 1946.

Mr. Leslie Swaffield, for eleven years the secretary since his father's resignation has taken a key role in the modernisation of the County Show and has a sharp eye and quick ear for any new idea.

The school was in Eccles Hall, a fine 3-storey Georgian building, built by Samuel Eccles, an Attorney at Law, in 1724. The Grammar School was an old-established one, which had operated in various buildings and rooms around the town. In 1827 it had 93 pupils including a few girls. The instruction was free, and the children were taught reading, writing and Latin. A fee was charged for Arithmetic. Dikes Spelling was used, and Goldsmith's History of England was read. At Christmas the boys were entertained with rum punch, whilst the girls were given

Eccles Hall, Tideswell

tea. Corporal punishment was common, swishing with a birch rod the favourite weapon. The boys played games – cricket, violent football, foot races for a hat or a pair of shoes. Fairs for fun and trading were popular, coursing with hares and minor games, such as bowling, quoits and trap-ball. The Swaffield boys had been brought up to be competitive, and entered into anything that was offered.

Mr William E Winter was the Swaffield boys' headmaster, and the roll had diminished to about forty boarders between 10–18 years. Mr Winter was assisted by two masters, a cook, housemaid, kitchen-maid and a nurse. He and his wife had a small baby son. In 1881 there was an epidemic of chicken pox, and all three Swaffield boys caught it. HRJ, their father, was furious and wrote demanding the return of fees, which Mr Winter refused. Tideswell is a delightful, small Peak District town, with pretty stone houses, walkways and lanes. A sweeping road runs through the main commercial area. It is famous for the ancient ceremony of well-dressing, and has a fine church – 'The Cathedral of the Peaks' – just opposite the school. It has been described: '… without exception the most perfect and beautiful specimen of pointed architecture to be met within the county, or perhaps in any other parochial church of its size in the kingdom.' When we visited, the church provided excellent shelter during one of the fiercest hailstorms we have experienced – the pebbles dropped like a wall of bullets on the gravestones, and bounced up with a great surge. The ground was white and crystallised, the sharp air ringing with the sound of the elements.

'The Cathedral of the Peaks', Tideswell

The boys did not stay long at Tideswell, but came home to Bedfordshire and were sent, one by one, to Bedford Modern School where they attended as day boys. In the 1880's Bedford Modern and Bedford Grammar [later known as Bedford School] were amalgamated with Bedford High for Girls and Bedford Girls Modern School – now known as Dame Alice Harpur School. Bedford was recognised as a centre for excellent education, nowhere else could

boast four such schools. Originally endowed by Sir William Harper [sic] who, in the 16th century, had acres of monastic land in the village of Holborn, just outside the City of London. The endowment enabled the Governors to keep the fees reasonable and, in Victorian times, the school was favoured by families living abroad, particularly the Indian Civil and Military Services who, on the whole, received modest salaries. In those days it was up to the pupils to 'listen and learn' if they wanted to. The Swaffs, and other boys, needed goading, "Pay attention!" was the constant cry of a frustrated Master. The boys dreamed on, staring at the sky, thinking only of tea, bread and jam, and kicking a ball about.

Henry was an athletic young man, but was unfortunate to lose a foot whilst hurdling. He was also a Freemason and attended Lodge regularly. Masonry runs strong through the family. In 1899 Henry married Alice Reynolds, of Haverhill, Suffolk, and Leslie was born in 1901. Always up to childish pranks, Leslie dropped a slimy live frog down his cousin, Bardie's, back – an act for which he will never be forgiven. Apart from frogs, he followed the same career and leanings as his father. Henry and Alice lived comfortably in The Bungalow, Ampthill, which his great-niece Sue [d/o Clifford], as a little girl, remembers visiting, 'It had a very, very long path through the garden.' And it did, it was built well back on a considerable plot of some acres in The Avenue, still a private road. It was part of the Knowle Estate, a major Ampthill development in the 19th and 20th centuries, in which the Swaffields had a major interest.

A pair of semi-detached houses were constructed nearby for Leslie and family, and for Henry's younger spinster sisters, Dot and Jo who lived carefully, even frugally, for many years. Before that the two sisters, once their mother died and they had moved from Lansdowne Road, lived in The Old Cottage, and old it was, at 85 Dunstable Street on the left side, about 400 yards up from The White Hart. The Bungalow had a tennis lawn and an orchard. Alice suffered poor health for a considerable time. Clifford, then aged eight, has a recollection of driving, with his father Basil as chauffeur, taking Henry by car to London. They visited Aunt Alice in a clinic, where she died of cancer on March 12th, 1930 aged 60.

The Prince of Wales visited the Bedfordshire Show at Ampthill and presented some of the cups. Here he is seen on a tour of inspection.
—Photograph by Planet News, Ltd.

Henry Swaffield 1931

The following year, on a delightfully summery day, HRH the Prince of Wales arrived at Ampthill Park for the 127th County Show. He was hosted by the Duke of Bedford. A newspaper report recorded:

> 'Yesterday morning all the roads to Ampthill were very busy, and the town itself was gay with bunting and flags. As soon as the site was selected, people got to work and formed a committee representative of every parish in the district. Another point of interest in the selection of Ampthill, is the fact that the Secretary of the Bedfordshire Agricultural Society is Mr Henry Swaffield, who succeeded his father in this office.'

Left: 1931 – The Prince of Wales and Henry Swaffield at the Bedfordshire Show

After Alice died, Henry was left with an old retainer, Zilipa, to look after him. He advertised for a housekeeper and employed Mrs Hall, the widow of a vicar, who acted as his travelling companion and hostess for the next seventeen years. They are reputed to have had a very proper relationship. Clifford recalls, "Uncle Henry was of course, father's eldest brother, and I was always in awe of him as a little one. Although of gruff and forbidding exterior, he had a heart of gold, and did a great deal for father later on. Sunday visits to 'the Aunts' – and they were frequent – had to include 'a walk across to the 'Bung' and often, after the formalities, "Clifford, take the jug," which entailed calling into the kitchen for a hopefully large jug, descending into the cellar beneath, and drawing on his always well-stocked barrel of best bitter to serve to the thirsty." Henry was a gruff man. Bardie, his niece, took her young children to meet him, but he had no recollection of her.

HENRY SWAFFIELD.

"Who are you?" He was fierce.
"I'm Bardie," she said firmly.
"Who?" he asked brusquely.

"Bardie. Bardie," she repeated, her children wriggling with fear, "I'm your brother Dick's daughter from Catesby."

"I still don't know who you are," he said suddenly smiling, "But give us a kiss anyway."

Norman's daughter, Mildred (Molly), also remembers Uncle Henry with affection. "He was very stiff," she said, "But he was kind. He didn't worry me."

1950s – Bardie and her children

Left: c 1937 –
Norman, Eck,
Dick and Henry

1937 – News cutting

NEWS CUTTING – October 8th, 1964

Mr. Henry Swaffield – "Grand Old Man" of Bedfordshire Agricultural Society – died at his Ampthill home on Thursday last week at the age of 96. He was Secretary of the Society for 42 years, succeeded by his son, Leslie, who served as Secretary until 1962.

During his long period of service, Mr Henry Swaffield was largely responsible for the organisation of the County Show, which was held every year except during the wars. He was also connected with the Central Association of Show Secretaries, serving as a committee member for many years, and as vice-chairman in 1937. The funeral service took place at Ampthill Parish church on Monday.

Henry's Will was proved by his son, Leslie. He left £27,962.

In 1931 Leslie married a Flitton girl, Mabel Sharpe, who originally worked in the office of Swaffield & Son. Henry held on to his position in the business for too long, during which time Leslie used the White Hart as a meeting and greeting place. It was years before Leslie and Mabel were able to enjoy some of the largesse of Henry's estate. They also waited ten years before their only child, Meave, was born. She was not academic but persistent, and gained a scholarship to be educated at Bedford High School. Her parents were very pleased. In June 1964, a few months before her grandfather passed away, Meave Swaffield married Michael Harris at Ampthill. They had two children, Elaine and Lester. The marriage did not last and Meave died of cancer in about 1990.

Mabel was a shrewd judge of important information. Encouraged by Leslie, she sorted through the business papers and records. These are now lodged at Bedford Record Office [SF – Swaffield Family] and have immense importance as they cover sales, valuations and estate management records in considerable detail, from the 1850s into the 20th century, relating to all parts of Bedfordshire and beyond. After Leslie died, it was Mabel who had sacks of personal family information, passed on from her father-in-law, Henry, and his office, to her husband, Leslie. The Bungalow garage was stuffed full of wet sacks, mostly in the roof. Mabel was persistent that the contents should be saved, and laid everything out to dry. She also persuaded as many connected nieces and nephews, to travel to Dorset to seek out their Swaffield ancestors.

This act, was remarkable for a woman who got the short straw in both her married relationship, and with that of her autocratic father-in-law, Henry Swaffield. Bedfordshire is grateful to Mabel for the preservation of family records in the Bedford Record Office under the reference SFM [Swaffield Family Mabel]. She was helped by Andrew Underwood, an archivist, pupil of Bedford Modern School and, later, teacher of religious studies there for thirty years. Andrew is the great-grandson of Benjamin George, and the son of Ena Mary Grimmer and Frank Randall Underwood

Nigel Swaffield, grandson of Exton, was seen as a possibility to take over Swaffield & Son. Living in South Wales at the time, his first National Service RAF posting was at Cardington, so he took the opportunity to visit Great Uncle Henry and Leslie, and the matter was discussed. In 1958, after three years in the RAF, then aged 23, he moved to Ampthill and became a pupil. Several of the Swaffield relatives warned that it would not work. Leslie, they said, was difficult to get along with and the going would be tough. Leslie did not enjoy good health and was considered tetchy. Nigel tried hard but stayed for less than a year, and then decided to return home and study architecture.

1956 – Nigel Swaffield in the RAF

NEWSPAPER REPORT – September 18th, 1966 – DEATH OF COUNTY SHOW STALWART

Mr Leslie J Swaffield, whose resignation as Secretary of Bedfordshire Agricultural Society in 1962 brought to an end a unique family tradition of service to the 165 years old organisation, died at his home in Ampthill last Thursday.

Mr. Swaffield, who was 65, will be remembered throughout the County as a partner and, in more recent years, sole proprietor of the old established firm, Swaffield & Son of Ampthill, auctioneers, estate agents, surveyors and valuers, which he joined as a pupil in 1917, and in which he continued to serve as a consultant after its take-over by Messrs J R Eve & Son. But it is perhaps in his role as Secretary of the Bedfordshire Agricultural Society – one of the oldest in the country – that he will be best remembered; not only in Bedfordshire, but in many other counties throughout England. Mr Leslie Swaffield played an important role in the community life of Ampthill. He was a member of the Urban District Council, sat on the Urban Road Safety Committee from which he had to resign because of ill health. He was also a member of the Wingfield Club, and had served as a former chairman of the Amateur Dramatic Society and was captain of the Bowls Club.

Exton was born at Park Farm, Ampthill and spent most of his childhood there, apart from his time at Tideswell. Although from strong farming stock, Exton saw his future as a seaman, as did his next brother Norman, and they both joined the Merchant Navy and eventually sailed together in 1897 crossing the Atlantic on the SS Urbino. Eck was Captain and Norman was First Engineer. As a twenty-one year old Apprentice Seaman, Eck joined the sailing ship Irex in Glasgow, and had a frightening voyage.

'Wreck of a Large Sailing Ship Near the Needles. Sufferings of the Crew. Six Lives Lost. Splendid rescue of Thirty Men by the Rocket Apparatus. Exciting Scenes. Narratives of the Survivors. One of the most disastrous wrecks which have occurred for many years on the Island took place last Saturday night, January 25th, when the full-rigged ship Irex ran on shore, under stress of weather, in Scratchell's Bay off the Needles Battery.'

The Irex was a new steel-built full-rigged ship, of 2,248 tons, with a crew of thirty-six hands all told, commanded by Captain Hutton, on her first voyage with a cargo of 3,600 tons of iron sewerage pipes for Rio de Janeiro. The shipwreck was the culmination of a terrifying voyage in dreadful weather. Exton had embarked at Glasgow, and his name was listed amongst the others who boarded: Captain Hutton; mate – James Irvine; boatswain – Ernest Hanson; second mate – Mr Reid; boatswain's mate – Charles Campbell; AB and OS, James Andrews, Alex Thompson, Wm Colquhoun, Robert Derrick, Stephen Carroll, James Murray, Thomas Weeks, Ned Collins, Harry Moore, John McIlroy, Dick Stearne, Sam Hughes, Isaac Rose, John Niccolls, Harry Duncan, George Brown, J Durrick, 'Old Harry'; apprentices, Laker, Hatchett, Jones, Barham, Bonner, Swaffield, two stowaways, Duffy, Robinson – cook, steward, sailmaker, carpenter, boy Ogilvie – thirty-six all told.

Apprentice Seaman Exton Swaffield was in the crew of the Irex, wrecked on her maiden voyage – 1890

Thomas Estella from Belfast was steward on board. At the inquest he told his story clearly:

"On December 10th we started from Greenock for Rio de Janeiro laden with iron pipes. When we got off the Isle of Man the cargo shifted, and we returned to Greenock. We started again on December 24th and anchored at Belfast Lough the following day, as the wind was against us." There they stayed until January 1st 1890. "There was a heavy gale on the 5th in the Channel, and six men were injured, two badly." They were fourteen days in the Bay of Biscay, and could not get beyond it. "The cargo shifted again, and the crew asked the captain to return as the ship was making water and not fit to proceed."

The Irex ashore on the rocks in Scratchell's Bay. Photo F N Broderick, Ryde, IoW

Thomas Estella continued, "The Captain put back for Falmouth, off which place he lay to for the night and the vessel rolled badly. The captain steered for Portland. On Saturday January 25th, the day of the shipwreck, it was foggy and the captain could not take observations, and we passed Portland. The same evening the captain looked for the Shambles Light. He saw a light, which he took for that of a pilot. The captain ordered the ship to be steered for the light. In a minute they struck a rock. This would be about 11 pm. The captain at once ordered the four boats to be cut adrift. The mate was in one boat looking for the plug which fitted in the bottom of the boat, and the captain was on the lee-side of the boat. A sea then struck her and carried away the boat, mate, and captain." Estella saw the boat afterwards in the water and James Irvine, the mate, called out, but no one could help him. "I saw the boat for two or three minutes, going towards the rocks, and then lost sight of it. A second boat was washed away at the same time."

Estella went on, "We all went to the rigging and stayed there during the freezing, stormy night. There were two berths left in the deck-house. One was used by the old seaman, 'Harry' – we none of us knew his other name. He had a broken leg and couldn't get up the rigging. He was an old man and had been injured some days. As the deck house stood pretty firm, we thought he would be safe till the lifeboat came alongside, for we could see the lifeboat then, and we gave the lifeboat credit for being able to save 'Old Harry' if nobody else; but when she went back, our hopes were dashed. Another drowned was a boy, William Ogilvie. He was a stupid boy, and seems to have lost his senses. When we told him to come aloft he wanted to go below, and no inducement that we could offer would make him come up. At last he sat under one of the hatches, until it was swept away; and so he went from one hatch to another till five were swept away, and the last we saw of him was about three o'clock on Sunday afternoon, trying to swim to the main hatchway, where he got jammed and was killed. The boatswain, Ernest Hanson, was drowned in the cabin, and on Sunday an apprentice named Hatchett was washed overboard."

Left: The Irex showing the damage on deck, and the extensive rigging.
Photo F N Broderick, Ryde, IoW

Opposite: Jan 25th 1890, the Irex wrecked in Scratchell's Bay

The lifeboat had been unable to reach the wreck, and the rest of the crew and the two stowaways were afterwards rescued by means of the rocket apparatus. They were only 200 or 300 yards from the land:

"I was the man who went and got the rocket line," said Estella, "It was a grand shot and our hearts went up thirty degrees. The captain was an experienced man and had been on duty ever since he left Belfast Lough on the January 1st, never having been to bed. The Needles light is red, and a pilot's light should be bright. I saw the light before the ship struck, and could see it was red. She was a fine ship, but too much for three masts – she ought to have been a four-master. She was too much for the captain, and the boatswain was frightened of her all the way."

As soon as news of the shipwreck reached the island, noon the next day, a telegram requested the Totland Bay lifeboat. The men were alerted by the firing of rockets and a mounted messenger galloping to their various homes. The lifeboat was launched, watched by a crowd of more than 200 on the cliff, and towed out by the steam collier Hampshire. The lifeboatmen then 'pulled away with a steady stroke' but soon the red danger flag was flown, the Hampshire connected again, the lifeboat changed course but was unsuccessful in reaching the Irex. A correspondent who has had an interview with one of the lifeboat crew, writes as follows: 'There were, I am informed, 15 men in the lifeboat – 12 at the oars, one at the bow, and the two coxswains, the first coxswain being Mr. Stone, chief boatman [coastguard] at Totland Bay. The crew was composed of coastguardmen and local watermen. The captain of the Hampshire steam collier, who acted boldly, towed the boat outside the lighthouse and to within about 300 yards of the wreck, and then let go. The boat was then pulled about 100 yards nearer the wreck, when a heavy sea came, which frightened some of the crew, and the coxswain then gave the order to pull towards the steamer to be taken in tow again, "We could have gone and taken the poor men off without any danger," said my informant, "It was rough but only just rough enough to call out the stuff which lifeboat crews are supposed to be made of. A good fishing boat could have done it." After being taken in tow again by the collier the rope was driven in under the stern, in consequence of which it had to be cast adrift again.

"Did you then try to reach the wreck," I inquired. "No," was the reply, "We got no encouragement from the coxswain. We were waiting for about a quarter of an hour looking at it, and then the collier took us in tow again and towed us to Totland. One of the crew – a coastguardman – said, "Are we Englishmen to leave those poor fellows clinging to the rigging?"

"When we got back to shore," my informant continued, "Ashamed enough some of us were to think that we, lifeboat men as we were, should have come back like that; but we were not all to blame, some of us wanted to go on and would have faced anything, but the majority were frightened as soon as they saw a little sea. Everyone on the cliff was expecting to see us take back the crew, and we could have saved them and been back by half-past two; but, as I have said, we hadn't a word of encouragement from the coxswain from the time we started till we got back. Mr. Seely Brooke's lifeboat crew, who were also present, offered their services, but the offer was not accepted." "Is the boat one of the Institute lifeboats?" I inquired. "She is, was the reply, "And a splendid boat she is, fit to go anywhere. It wasn't the boat's fault, sir. Could she have spoken she would have said, 'Go on! Go on! Save them! Save them!'" "And if an inquiry were held," I asked, "Should you have any hesitation in stating that, in your opinion you could have reached the ship and saved the crew?" "No hesitation at all," was the reply, "You see, sir, in being towed out we had a chance that doesn't often happen. We were quite fresh, and if we had tried we could have done it, but we didn't try. One of the poor fellows who was on the wreck afterwards told me that when they saw the lifeboat coming out they set up a cheer as well as they could, and waved blankets, and said, 'Here comes the lifeboat! God bless her!' and then when they saw us turn back, he couldn't describe what their feelings were. Let me say again that all honour is due to the captain of that collier. The sea was washing his decks, but he stood by, and did all he could, brave heart!" I have learned that amongst the lifeboat men who wanted to go on were young Jacob Cotton, who worthily bears a name honoured in the Island lifeboat service, 'Laddie' Calloway, C Calloway, W Sanders, Simmonds and Frank Hayman. It seems evident that what is wanted at Totland Bay is a thorough re-organisation of the lifeboat crew, who should be systematically practised, and placed under a management similar to that which works so splendidly at Brooke and Brighstone, whose crews have made for themselves names of glory in our Island annals. I know what a friend the lifeboat service has in the County Press, and in sending this communication to you my earnest hope is that the publicity given to it may lead to such steps as will prevent the recurrence of such a melancholy spectacle as that which Totland Bay witness on the occasion under notice.'

The Rocket Apparatus had arrived, was fired and caught by one of the shipwrecked crew on a listing deck swept with heavy seas. The crew had to climb the rigging [young Exton Swaffield clinging on for dear life] from 'the mizzen-top to mizzen-top-gallantstay, and from there to main-top, and from main-top to main-top-gallantstay to fore-top. It was planned to get the men off in canvas slings, or Breeches Buoy. The hawser was made fast, but there was not enough rope from the top of the cliff to the ship.' More supplies were called for. 'After the hawser had been tightened and as the cradle was nearing the ship for the first time a lad was seen, in his attempt to get forward, to fall from the rigging onto the deck. He climbed again, fell again and was washed overboard. John Niccolls was the first man on dry land at 4pm, and was taken to the Fort where fires had been lit, beds made, hot food prepared and medical staff were on duty. Mr Spilman, in charge of the Coastguards, yelled "Pull away lads, we're life saving," and more than once helped a fagged one to hang on again. By 5pm seven were saved, but some were severely injured with broken limbs and damaged heads. The hurricane raged making working conditions very difficult. The wind drove shingle and pieces of chalk into the eyes and faces of the rescuers that at times it was almost impossible to see, and their hands were severely blistered with rope burn. Messengers were sent to Totland Bay for supplies of bread and meat, butter, Brand's Essence, Liebigs Extract &c. Night fell, the crowds diminished, the helpers could not go on and the soldiers were called in. By 9.45, 23 of the Irex crew had been rescued. It was pitch dark, bitterly cold and wet with gale force winds. The twenty-third man was a stowaway and said that there were six more forward [one of whom was Apprentice Exton Swaffield] and one lad aft, who was afraid to venture along the main stays. The six were rescued with difficulty, the lad was left, strapped to the mast with a blanket. On the Monday morning Coastguard Machin and a coloured man belonging to the ship went off and brought the lad safely to land.'

A MESSAGE FROM THE QUEEN

The following telegram from Sir John Cowell at Osborne, was received by Mr Todd, Totland Bay, at 12.50 on Monday. "Please to telegraph to me for the Queen's information how many persons have been saved and how many lost in the wreck of the Irex, and where the survivors are now." The desired information was sent to Sir John as soon as it could be obtained, and the news that the Queen was making inquiries about them cheered the shipwrecked men very greatly. All the men who could be moved were conveyed to Yarmouth and put up at Mr Butler's on Monday night. They left Totland Bay about 7.15.

THE CAPTAIN AND THE COMPASS OF THE IREX

To the Editor of the Isle of Wight County Press

Sir, – As a good deal of blame is be-stowed on the captain of the Irex, who, it is said, did not know his whereabouts, &c., may I suggest that allowance should be made for the fact there was a great deal of steel in the ship which might have affected the compass. Cases have been known in the past. Even a steel umbrella frame has been known to alter the compass as it was brought near it, and it has refused to answer aright for the time. I do not say it was here, but there is a probability of it. Yours obediently, T Scotchmer. Channel View House, Niton, 30th January, 1890.

TO THE PUBLIC. – Printing of every description executed with neatness and dispatched at the offices of the I o W County Press

TO OVERCOME WEAKNESS. – Pepper's Quinine and Tonic gives New Life, Appetite, Health, Strength, Energy. Half-crown bottles. Everywhere. Insist on having Pepper's.

When Eck's father, HRJ, got wind of the shipwreck he rushed to the Isle of Wight to ascertain that his son had survived and was not injured.

Alan was the ninth child and the only one of the fourteen children born to Emmeline and HRJ who did not live very long. Arriving eighteen months after Queenie, he was delivered on January 18th 1878, baptised on September 28th of the same year and sadly died before Christmas on December 11th. Shortly after his death another son, Hugh, arrived in January 1879.

1899 – Hugh and Henry

Hugh was a good looking man. At one time he was probationer to A E Turnell, architect and lawyer, at Sheffield. They wrote to HRJ in 1897, '… your son, Hugh's, time of probation will expire on Monday … we like his work and he is willing to stay …'. Hugh also wished to study at Technical School and, was making enquiries about emigrating to South Africa. Instead he joined his father's business for some time and was Secretary of the Chamber of Agriculture. When he was 37, he married Mary Penfold of Bedford but they had no children. Great Britain in 1914 was rich and powerful, but British politicians were worried by Germany's growing strength. Hugh was 35 when the Great War broke out and he volunteered for the Army and, in 1918 near the end of the war, he died of wounds. His mother, Emmeline, wrote to her nephew, John Sutton, in Buxton concerning Hugh's death. His name is on the Alameda Memorial in Ampthill, as is that of his nephew Noël Swaffield (WWII), younger son of Dick Swaffield of Catesby.

"Sing me to sleep where bullets fall
Let me forget the War and all,
Damp is my dug-out, cold my feet
Nothing but bully and biscuits to eat.

Sing me to sleep where bombs explode
And shrapnel shells are á la Mode,
Over the sandbags helmets you find
Corpses in front and corpses behind.

Far from Ypres I long to be
Where German snipers can't pot at me,
Think of me crouching where the worms creep
Waiting for someone to sing me to sleep.
(Charlie Hay)

1917 – War in the trenches

An officer – Stewart Gore-Brown – at Arras, wrote home, 'Alongside me there's a lad, a subaltern in the battery, reading over and over again the casualty list that's got his brother's name on it, killed, almost the first time that he was out here. Every night before I go to sleep, I say lighten our darkness, oh Lord (but not with bursting shells) and then I get off to sleep if there's no toothache or chilblains or rats, and when I wake up in the morning and see it's daylight and I am still alive, I say, that's another night gone, thank you oh Lord, and now there's the day to get through.' Conditions in the trenches were intolerable, they were the perfect environment for lice and rats. One soldier spent 42 days in 1915 without taking his boots or his tunic off. If he had removed his boots they would have frozen stiff. Men and horses drowned in the churned up mud, whilst pigeons and dogs carried messages up and down the trenches.

War meant food shortages. German U-boats sank ships, the Government had to make sure that enough food was sent to the troops fighting in France, prices rocketed, and by 1917, rationing commenced and people had 'just enough'. Savoury Oatmeal Rissoles were often on the menu. These were made from left-over cold, stiff porridge mixed with dry boiled rice or breadcrumbs, made from baked and pounded crusts. Taste was heightened by salt, pepper and a drop of HP Sauce, chopped herbs and minced onion. The cakes were shaped, rolled in oatmeal and fried in dripping.

Exton, Norman, Richard (Dick) and Basil, the baby of the family, managed to escape fighting in the war and their stories are told further in this book.

WWI Poster

Taken in the Wilderness at Beckerings Park – 1899. Family group celebrating the birth of the first grandson, baby Frank (Tony), to Florrie and Eck. Missing are Minnie, in Yorkshire, and Norman at sea. Top L–R standing, Dot, Hugh, Henry, Ella, Dick, Eck, Queenie and Emmeline. Bottom L–R, Ethel, Kitty, Florrie [Carding], Baby Frank, Basil and Jo

Ship	From	To	Left	Arrived 1890	Days	His	Dist	Remarks
Urano	Baltimore	Amsterdam	Jany 16/99	Feby 5th	19	14	3740	Anchored 18 hours Chesapeake Bay to P.S.
"	Amsterdam	Tyne	Feby 10th	Feby 11th	1	9	285	Left A'dam 12.30 Yarmouth 4.20 Ann ed Tyne 10 h.m
"	Tyne	Baltimore	Feby 16th	Mch 5th	17	8	3639	steaming time 16.48 hrs
"	Baltimore	Rotterdam	Mch 9th	Mch 27th	18	4	3743	" 17.17 hrs
"	Rotterdam	Sunderland	Mch 30	April 1st	1	1	280	Waterway to S'land Fled 24 hours
"	Sunderland	Baltimore	April 1st	April 21st	19	22	3420	Broken down with condenser 32 hours
"	Baltimore	Rotterdam	April 29th	May 17th	18	23	3740	Trouble with vacuum 18.6.23"
"	Rotterdam	Sunderland	May 21	May 22	1	1	288	
"	Sunderland	Baltimore	May 23rd	June 8th	16	3	3709	
"	Baltimore	Leith	June 12th	June 28	16	3	3674	Speed 9.37
"	Leith	Tyne Dock	July 3	July 4	1	11	115	
"	Tyne Dock	Palermo	July 8th	July 20th	12		2472	19 Tons.
"	Palermo	Garrucha	July 28th	July 31st	3		720	"
"	Garrucha	Rotterdam	Aug 7th	Aug 15th	7	20	1548	"
"	Rotterdam	Cardiff	Aug 22	Aug 25th	2	7	560	"

Total distance steamed to Aug 25th 1899
= 22,9182 Knots to be steered
Left ship at Cardiff for a holiday 26/8/1899.
Rejoined ship at Rotterdam October 26th 1899.

An extract from the Book of Travels

Chapter 10

BEDFORDSHIRE AND BEYOND 1871–2002
Norman goes to sea and Henry Hamilton travels to Argentina

The family of H R J Swaffield 1839 and Emmeline Jepson 1842 and their third son, Norman 1871

Emmeline   Henry   Exton   **Norman**   Ethel   Ella   Dorothy   Beatrice   Alan   Hugh   Richard   Hilda   Mildred   Basil

Norman Swaffield 1871–1958 and Elizabeth Jepps 1876–1962

| Helen
1901–65 | Henry Hamilton
(Ham)
1903–1967
m
Dora Gould
b1917 | Emmeline Mildred
(Molly)
1909
m
Arthur Frank Hailstone
d1979 | Frances
(Aunt Fra)
1912–99 | Dorothy
(Dor)
1917–99 |

| Lurline (Laura)
b1949 | Norman
b1941 | Christine
b1944 | Robert
b1947 |

On 23 February 1893, when Norman was 22, he left Beckerings Park and joined the Merchant Marine Service as 3rd Engineer. He kept a detailed 'Book of Travels'. He logged every voyage, the ports of embarkation and disembarkation, the dates of departure and arrival, the time taken to sail in days and hours and the distance covered. In the first year he journeyed from Sunderland to Antwerp, Boston, Baltimore, Rotterdam, Swansea – backwards and forwards across the Atlantic – also travelling south to New Orleans. He spent Christmas Day 'off Bermuda'. After a year, and 55,376 miles at sea, he gained his 2nd Engineer's Certificate. In 1894 he did the same run, also calling at Barry in Wales and Genoa in Italy. In February he was detained in Chesapeake Bay by ice for 58 hours, and sailed some very rough and stormy passages across the Atlantic with dense fog in the English Channel. The following year he visited Spanish ports. Between Barcelona and Cartagena he recorded 'Fireman jumped overboard 8.45am on 3rd Oct'. The weather was heavy, N and NE gales and the passages were rough. Christmas Day was spent at 41N, 5920W. On March 14th 1896 he left the ship for his Chief's Ticket. Up until now Norman had engineered on the SS Ohio – but he joined the SS Urbino and 'left home Good Friday night, joined Saturday 17th April 1897' still as 2nd Engineer. 'On May 31st 'Eck [his elder brother] joined as Captain – steaming time Sunderland to Baltimore 14 days 8 hours.' The ship suffered engine trouble and they had 'several long stops' and the usual rough weather. Eventually a new propeller had to be fitted in Baltimore which entailed a delay of 26 days.

By this time Norman had met Elizabeth Jepps in Sunderland, although he often had only a day in port between voyages. In 1898 Norman had a Graphology Test, picturing his personality from his hand-writing. Tich, as she was known, would probably have agreed that concerning affections he '… showed sincerity without a great amount of ardour …', and with his business capabilities '… order and method good, not incautious …', whilst his instincts were judged '… you have the ability to express yourself with ease … 'and truthfulness '… very well marked, there is a strict sense of honour shown …'. What they did not test was humour, of which Norman had a generous ration, still very obvious in his many descendants.

Elizabeth Jepps came from a wealthy family and was training to be a concert pianist. Her daughter-in-law, Dora, believed that when she first married, Tich '… couldn't cook an egg, but had to buckle down. She made custard in crystal bowls and put them in the oven where they exploded. She was dumped into it, but she managed very well.' Eck, and his wife Florrie, were also living in Sunderland and expecting their first baby, Frank (Tony). Norman became Chief Engineer of the SS Urbino in August 1898 and spent another Christmas away. On August 26th 1899 he 'left ship at Cardiff for a holiday to be spliced.' No banns were called, and they were married by Special Licence, because he was never sure when he might have to jump on a ship. This time there were no ships to jump on and he was able to settle into married life. He rejoined the SS Urbino at Rotterdam on October 26th, 1899 and travelled through the Mediterranean to Alexandria,

Norman and Tich in Bedford

Scriphos [sic] and Syra in the Aegean Sea, and finished on a Copenhagen to Sunderland run when he had to leave ship 'owing to her being sold to Italians'. He had crossed the Atlantic Ocean 58 times and covered nearly 300,000 miles.

Britain was going through a Depression, and he took up casual engineering work whilst they lodged at 35 Blandford Street, Sunderland. He travelled on commission, and they changed lodgings several times. Jobs were hard to get and he moved from one company to another. Tich was pregnant with Helen. They had taken a house at 43 Fordland Place North, and Norman travelled to London to purchase furniture. 'Daughter born on April 26th, 1901, christened St John's Church, Sunderland.' Norman moved to London in October to work for Belliss & Morcom at a new Power Station, and lodged in Clapton. 'Wife and kid left Sunderland November 8th and went to Harpenden to board with Eck and Florrie'. Eventually Norman took rooms in Hackney Downs on April 5th and '… wife and kiddie came up from Bedford that day …'. At this time his weekly pay averaged £2 13s 11d. He travelled constantly and they moved to Stoke Newington, until Norman took up employment with the Reading Electric Supply Company as Station Fitter. They settled for a while in Caversham and '… boy born … [Henry Hamilton, known as Ham] on April 25th, 1903 at 12.45 am. Christened at Caversham Parish Church May 31st.' With the two children they took a three-week summer holiday in Bedford and Sheffield, seeing their respective families, and then moved back to a purpose-built house at the Electric Supply Works in Reading, where he was appointed Station Superintendent.

The Christmas of 1904 was spent in Bedford. In January 1905 he records, 'Boy very ill, eventually sent him to Royal Berks Hospital where he was operated on for internal tumour and was returned home end of January.' From then on life was more settled and the work steady. Their summer holiday in 1906 was spent at Bedford and Buxton in Derbyshire and '… wife and kids went to Boldon. Helen's nose operated on for adenoids. Dorothy [his sister] keeping house for me …'. On May 31st he left the Reading Electric Supply Company and started with F A Smith

Engineer as Outside Manager – but the firm got into financial trouble and the Works shut down in November and was then sold on. A private company was formed, with Norman as one of seven directors, but it was not a success. Norman took over the management in January 1909, but the company was over-staffed. At Easter his father, HRJ, was taken ill and '… got rapidly worse …' until April 21st when he died, and was buried 24th in Bedford Cemetery, all the sons being present at the funeral. Ella had left to join Ethel in India, sailing on March 6th from London. '… Number 3 in the shape of a daughter [Emmeline Mildred eventually known as Molly] born on May 5th, 1909 at 6pm and was christened at St John's, Lower Caversham. Kitty was married to F Potter in June 1909. During 1910 and 1911 business bad. Ella and Ethel in India most of the time …'

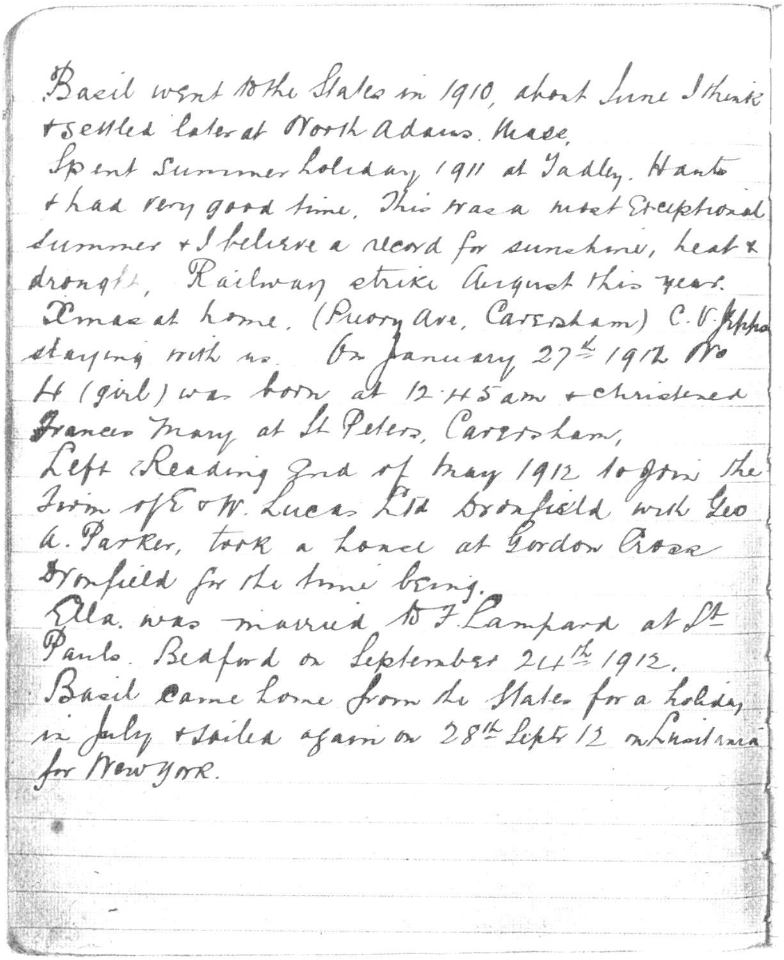

The last extract from the Book of Travels

The 'Book of Travels' peters out in 1912 – the final page full of family miscellania:

'Basil went to the States in 1910, about June I think, and settled later at North Adams, Mass. Spent summer holiday at Tadley, Hants and had very good time. This was a most exceptional summer and I believe a record for sunshine, heat and drought. Railway strike August this year, Xmas at home (Priory Avenue, Caversham) CV Jepps staying with us.

On January 27th 1912 No 4 (girl) was born at 12.45 am and christened Frances Mary at St Peter's, Caversham. Left Reading end of May 1912 to join the firm of E & W Lucas Ltd, Dronfield with Geo A Parker, took a house at Gordon Close, Dronfield for the time being.

Ella was married to F Lampard at St Paul's, Bedford on September 24th, 1912. Basil came home from the States for a holiday in July and sailed again on 28th September on the Lusitania for New York.'

Norman worked for George Parker [Minnie, his elder sister's, husband] until George sold out to a bigger group in the early twenties, and Norman was jobless. He then travelled for a Sheffield company, Stalkers, selling tools. When his nephew, Clifford, was small, Norman arrived on his circuit about twice a year and stayed with Basil and Jimmy in Bedford.

Photograph taken during a visit home. Top L–R, Dot, Jimmy, Basil, Mother, Norman Bottom L–R, Eck, Jo, Aunt Sally. Foreground, Mick, Eck's 3rd son

"He had a wonderful sense of humour, as had all his children, and in looks he always reminded me of Tom Walls. Tom Walls, twelve years younger than Norman, was an actor-producer who established himself in the West End with portrayals of eccentric old gentlemen. In the twenties he joined up with Ralph Lynn and did a series of plays by Ben Travers including 'Rookery Nook'.

Their youngest child, Dorothy, was born in Dronfield in 1917. They struggled, like many of the Swaffs, during hard times. On his retirement in 1947 they moved back to Bedford and lived in Castle Road. Dora, their daughter-in-law, remembers them as 'wonderful people'. Norman died, aged 87, in Bedford and left £8,418 8s 1d.

L–R, Frances, Dorothy, Helen and Mildred

The Norman Swaffield family was particularly handsome – the girls with striking looks and fashionable clothes. Helen, the eldest, trained at Sheffield Royal Infirmary and was a nursing sister. During WWII she joined a campaign in the Western Desert and gained an award. She was a Sister at Bedford General Hospital and had rigid standards for work and discipline. Considered at times 'rather fierce' by the younger members of her family, she kindly collected threepenny bits for Norman Jr, delivered in chinking bundles and, he thinks, spent on Dinky toys. She retired and died at the age of 64. Frances was a teacher, and in the WVS/ATS during the war. Dorothy was in commerce and personnel management. Their lives were brightened by giggling humour, they retired in Bedford, and lived together dying at each end of the same year. Basil and Jimmy were fond of 'the girls' and Christmas and Boxing Day were always great fixtures between the two families. The Norman 'aunts' are remembered with great affection by their nephews and nieces. They taught Norman Jr's first two daughters a particularly vicious version of Ludo.

L–R, Mildred, Dorothy and Frances

On the reverse of this photograph it reads: '27.5.43. Taken in April 1943, after much laughter. Three proofs were taken, and this was the best of the lot, so you can tell what the others were like! Hope you can recognise us in spite of the innocent expressions, which are not quite natural. We have sent one off to Ham & Dora, so hope they like them. Poor Frances looks as if she's had all her teeth out. Love Dorothy'

Molly Swaffield Hailstone, Norman's third child, remembers Dronfield as a 'bit of a dump'. She was educated there and attended Millhouse School for Young Ladies, "Don't forget the Young Ladies bit," she said with a smile, when she was 91. She left Dronfield at the age of 21, in 1930, and moved to Bedford to E P Rose's dress shop. She worked in various shops and department stores, in the fashion business, until she was 70, when she finally retired.

Kitty Potter and her little girls

The Potters' home

As a child she was sent by train from the north to spend her summer holidays with her aunt and uncle, Kitty and Fred Potter, and their daughters, Beryl and Betty.

"They had such a pretty house on the Cardington Road," she said, "We always had fun, and there was an outdoor tennis court. Aunt Kit was my godmother and very sweet to me. Uncle Fred had a farming business called Potter and Hall." Molly also stayed with the Richard (Dick) Swaffield's at the Red House in Catesby. Although Howard and Bardie were much younger than her, they taught her to shoot an airgun. "Uncle Dick and Aunt Ethel were kind to me," she said, "But Aunt Ethel never looked very happy."

Bardie has good memories of Uncle Norman, or 'Normie' as her mother referred to him. "He was quite an actor, and always full of 'Jewish' stories, told with a thick accent – 'Velly vell,' he would say. He would send postcards to The Red House, 'Can I be with you for cold mutton next Saturday?' and he arrived always with a huge tin of sweets. Mother would let us three children have one or two after lunch, and the tin often lasted a month."

The Red House, Catesby. Bardie, Basil, Clifford, Dick and Noël

Molly also stayed at times with Aunt Queenie, "Uncle Tom used to bring big slabs of cheese up from the cellar," she remembered. Molly married Frank Hailstone who was a regular with the RAF. They moved to Wales during the war but '… the bombing was very bad . ' and they returned to Bedford where Frank was stationed at Cardington. They had two children, Christine, who works in administration at the Chartered Society of Physiotherapy, and lives in London, and Rob who lives in Letchworth and works in computers.

1938 – Mildred's wedding.
L–R, Norman, Dorothy, Frances,
Frank Hailstone, Mildred and Helen

Christine married twice, first to Barry Moulang and secondly to Denis Cox, having two children from each marriage. Like so many she has memories of disgusting school dinners, these at the prestigious Dame Alice Harpur School in Bedford. Her method of disposing of the food, was to decant portions into a tobacco tin on her lap and, eventually, throw it down the toilet. But this did not always work, the toilet was occupied, the bell rang, and she arrived home with gravy running into her socks. She travels, walks, gardens, does up her house and, in between, has achieved an Open University BSc Hons in Politics and Economics.

Andrew her eldest son, who lives with his partner Susan Mendison, was brought up in London and educated at Holland Park Secondary School, which he left at sixteen pursuing a career in the painting and restoration of cars. He is now running his own business. At school he enjoyed metalwork and technical drawing, and has taken a course in welding and motor mechanics. Motorcycling became a hobby, but he had a very bad accident in 1985, aged twenty, and was in a coma for four months.

Robert and Christine Hailstone

At his grandmother's [Molly Hailstone] 92nd birthday party in Letchworth, Andrew took a real interest in the big box of old photographs which had been left by his aunts, Dor and Fra. He enjoys coming from a big family and said, "All of my family are great fun, we meet every Christmas, and they give me good memories." He has a sister Helen, who is married with two children, and then younger siblings – Charles and Emily Cox. Charles studies at Goldsmiths, University of London and his favourite past-time is music production. Charles' best memory is of seeing Emily's baby, Molly, for the first time. Sadly Molly died at eight months from meningococal septicaemia – a lethal type of meningitis.

5 May 1999 – Family Gathering – Two daughters (Molly and Dorothy), Grandchildren and Great-Grandchildren of Norman and Tich Swaffield. Standing L–R, Emily Cox, Jenny and Helen Oakley, Gill and Nick Hailstone, Laura Swaffield, Charles Cox, Tim Oakley, Andrew Moulang, Norman, Elizabeth and Alice Swaffield, Sally and Rob Hailstone. Seated L–R, Dora Swaffield, Molly Hailstone [90th birthday], Dorothy Swaffield, Christine Cox, William Oakley

Henry Hamilton (Ham), Norman's one and only son, was educated at Dronfield Grammar and then King Edward VII School in Sheffield. He travelled to the Argentine to work on the National Railway, and lived in Rosario, the second largest city situated on the River Plate. There he met the Gould family who had emigrated in 1914 with three children. Three more children, including Dora, were born after their arrival. The Gould family lived in the Argentine for 43 years. Dora was the daughter of Charles John Gould from London and Laura Whittingham from Birmingham. Her sister became engaged to Gilbert Henderson, a friend of Ham's, and Dora met her future husband when she was fourteen. The following year, in 1932, her parents were

1932 – Dronfield, Dora's mother, Tich and Dorothy Swaffield, Dora Gould and Frances Swaffield

due for leave after 5 years service, and she travelled home with them. It was then that they journeyed to Dronfield to meet Norman and Tich although, at the time, there was no indication that there was a faint ringing of wedding bells. Dora found the Dronfield Swaffs a very friendly bunch, and discovered that she and Dor were separated in age by just three months.

In 1937 Dora and Ham, another six-footer Swaff, were married in St Bartholomew's Church in Rosario. After two years Ham was due for leave, but as war was breaking out they stayed in the Argentine.

1937 – Wedding of Henry Hamilton Swaffield and Dora Gould in the Argentine

Extract from 'A Load of Ham' by Horatio Twinge alias Norman Jr:

'As soon as the storm clouds burst, Henry hurried round to the nearest recruiting office, but finding they had no staff vacancies he was tricked into joining up. Promised a commission (his ambition was to be a commissionaire), he trailed home to await his reveille call to the ranks. To gladden his waiting hours Dora, presented him in August 1941 with a son, a laughing lovable little darling, destined to grow into a fine upright young man, handsome, debonair, a brilliant scholar and famous author. Faced with such outstanding competition, and with the allied situation so bad, everyone was needed, Henry packed and left for the British Army.'

Norman Junior 'a laughing lovable little darling', with his mother, Dora

… 'Being a fellow best forgotten it was decided to send him to the forgotten 14th Army in Burma, and make them wish they had been more forgotten than before. Fully kitted out with pistol, gunbelt, Wells Fargo badge and hip flask, 2nd Lieutenant HH Swaffield, 23rd Foot and Mouth Regiment embarked to fight the Japanese foe.'

… 'Mentioned several times in despatches (by surreptitiously scrawling his name in the margin), he was gradually promoted to Major and a command by quietly stepping into

On the reverse of this picture Ham has written: 'Taken in Bengal May 1944, a few days before I went into hospital which probably accounts for my prim look. Taken in front of my tent, which you may note has been very cleverly raised about 3'0" to give more headroom. HHS 25/5/44'

other people's shoes when they weren't looking. His air of command was infectious, being normally heavily charged with gin.'

… 'Henry, by this time having been drummed out of the army, piped out of the Navy and dropped by the RAF, was free to return to his loved ones. The devoted Dora was waiting, along with chubby little Norman (he now had a name instead of a number), whose angel face in the photographs sent out by his Ma, had done so much to hasten world peace. With a fond farewell to his Gurkha, Mohammedan, Hindu, Zulu and Finchley troops, the battle-scarred veteran returned.'

Lurline was born in the Argentine in 1949. All babies had to be registered with Spanish names so she was recorded, like her maternal grandmother, as Laura. On his return, Ham was promoted as Chief Draughtsman of the Central Argentine Railways, but times had changed from British ownership and they decided to return to Britain.

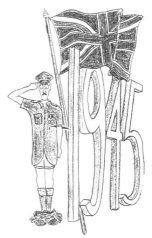

Left: c1945 – Norman Senior, Norman Junior and Henry 'Ham' Swaffield

Cartoon of HH's demobilisation

For Dora, being Argentinian born and Spanish speaking, it was hard to leave the country of her birth. All she could think of was the cold and "… wet washing hanging up in the kitchen …".

By that time Norman, Tich and the girls were all in Bedford, and they lived in Castle Road until Ham found a job and a place for his own family. He joined the Crown Agents in Millbank, London. In 1965 Ham was seconded to the East African Railways and the family moved out to another new life in Nairobi. Here he became seriously ill with cancer, was operated on, brought home by Dora and died just five days after arrival in early September 1967. Dora was well supported emotionally by the strong Swaffield family in Bedfordshire. She found them very accepting, always full of humour and really 'good fun'. She would go for tea with the other Aunts – Queenie, Dot and Jo. On Sundays they often went cycling and out for picnics to Gypsy Lane and Cobbles Stream.

1959 – Norman and Laura in England

1967 – Laura graduating from Bristol University

Their son, Norman, was already in the Merchant Navy and Laura was at Bristol University. Dora found a job as a secretary and moved to Boreham Wood. Here her knowledge of Spanish was useful in her job with the geological side of Huntings Surveys Ltd, where she stayed for 13 years. She then found a job in the Community Centre and kept that until 1990, finally retiring at the age of 73. Ham was no dancer, but Dora was always keen on Old Time and Modern Sequence Dancing and, through that, she met and married Jim Hare, who proved a wonderful dancing partner. They had three happy years together before he died of a chest infection. In her 87th year Dora is still dancing.

Now how do we describe Dora's son, Norman Jr? Do we take literally from 'A Load of Old FulHam' – Our hero' tumbling out of a porthole of the MV Somerset with a spanner in his hand clad in a Superman outfit? Or do we take verbatim that his first job, prior to joining the New Zealand Shipping Company, was as an office clerk at the Bedford Gas Works, gleaning enough money at the end of the week to purchase a Chris Barber EP. Under some misguided influence this was presented to his father, Ham – 'crawler or what?'. Norman says it was hard to please his father, a 'fairly forbidding disciplinarian', and he could never run fast enough. It is unlikely that Chris Barber's extended play jazz appeased all this. Dora, his mother, was 'always the peacemaker'. The serious side of Norman, is his family, the sea and an abiding love of it, easy-listening music, WWI battlefields and Fulham Football Club, which he follows with 'increasing desperation'.

From 'A Load of old FulHam' referring to Norman's time at Bedford Modern '… Having observed Norman's progress for a term it was noted that he was 'developing into 'a very reliable boy,' but by the age of fifteen such hopes had been much reduced by the single devastating judgement 'Slack'.

… '… the young Norman was not built to play Rugby. Indeed his school reports also chart his height and weight at every stage of his education; it is the equivalent of the gardener's diary reporting the progress of a prize string bean …'

Cartoon from 'This is Your Life Norman Swaffield'

… 'Lurline was thoroughly charmed by her big brother and frequently duped into following his lead. Not only did Norman lead the Naval Cadets at school, but he founded a troop during the holiday, rounding up the other children in the street [Allen Close] and teaching them essential skills such as Morse code and signalling systems, elementary navigation, and how to recognise particular ships should they stray into the Queen's Park area of Bedford. Lured on by the promise of promotion to even dizzier heights than Chief Petty officer, or whatever title Norman had bestowed upon her, Lurline became totally involved and had complete faith in her big, stringy brother. On one particular occasion they were practising stealth manoeuvres on their bellies through the grass, with the rest of the neighbourhood in tow, when Susan Belcher got hit in the mouth and chipped her tooth. Against all rules of naval etiquette Susan B ran home crying, and a full apology was later procured from Flight Lieutenant Norman Swaffield for his part in the casualty. Girls and chivalry were still concepts that eluded him.

Norman's own ruminations: 'I have always had an interest in the sea, odd because my father was aircraft mad. Perhaps there is a linkage with my grandfather, Norman, and a career in the Merchant or Royal Navy was always my aim. It was easier to get into the former, and engineering was the excuse as my eyesight was not good enough for a deck officer. Bedford Modern had a good cadet force naval section, and I joined the New Zealand Shipping Company as an engineer cadet on the MV Otaio trading cargo between UK and Australia and New Zealand. I loved the sea but was not a natural at engineering and left, in 1967, to get married. I then worked with nuts and bolts [Allen's in Bedford], considered the police, prison and civil services and, eventually, applied to the RAF for an administration commission. I was accepted in 1968 for the equipment branch and applied for a full commission in 1971. I was posted in Northern Ireland, Naples, Harrogate, RAF Marham, Norfolk, HQ Strike Command at High Wycombe, RAF Stanley, Falkland Islands and, latterly, Harrogate. Despite the job, the training and the involvement, none of this created any interest for aeroplanes, or cars for that matter. It's still the sea.

From a 'Load of Old FulHam' … 'In 1964 MV Somerset was harboured in Liverpool. It was, fortuitously, St Patrick's Night, and Norman was enticed to a party where he met Alice O'Keeffe. … perhaps with the intention of being enchantingly funny, he decided to make his opening gambit with a handful of ice-cubes down the back of Alice's dress. Needless to say the elegant Irish girl was not amused; student nurses were not rich in those days, and she had saved her money for weeks to buy that particular outfit. Neither was she taken with the grubby looking chap in overalls, and NHS specs, who was trying to make her laugh rather than apologise. Over the next few months Norman managed to wear Alice down without being anywhere near her. His letters were so entertaining that, unbeknown to him, they were frequently pinned to the notice board of the Nurses' Home. … It bemused onlookers that of all the eligible young men who courted Alice during this period of time, the Buddy Holly lookalike, with the mac and the bus pass was not the most startling. But there's clearly no set criteria for love and, in October 1965, Norman proposed and Alice accepted.

Alice was born at Ballysloe in County Tipperary and was the first of six children. It is difficult to tell whether she would have preferred to have been a greyhound trainer or a nurse. In the end she did both, with great success. She had a busy nursing career, but wanted to improve the lot of the elderly and infirm in a more personal way and, in 1983, they opened the Somerset Private Nursing Home, Wheldrake, near York.

But greyhounds took her heart, and her shining moment came in 1995, when her two dogs, Batties Rocket and his sister, Batties Spirit, came first and second in the Irish Derby – the world's biggest classic. Norman wrote, 'If there is one example of international acclaim for the Swaffield name, it is that of Alice winning 1st and 2nd place in the Irish Greyhound Derby. Alice followed that by being voted 'Greyhound Personality of the Year' in Ireland. The 'doggie' press was full of all this for a long time afterwards, and the name is quite well known in breeding circles to this day.'. Alice had a dream to launch a charity called Cu Cara [Gaelic for 'greyhound friend'] Sanctuary as a guide dog centre. Greyhounds are known for their sweet, gentle natures, and the project was intended to rehouse retired racing dogs, whilst providing training and employment for adults with learning difficulties. Whilst working hard to promote this project, Alice was told the devastating news that she had breast cancer on 6 April 2000. She bravely underwent radio and chemotherapy which sapped her energy, "I have so much to do," she told me on the telephone, "I need strength to fight the drugs, and on good days I work towards Cu Cara, and the day-to-day life of Somerset." Her voice was bright with enthusiasm, full of gentle Irish lilt, and a pure positiveness. "Faith and prayer are getting me through," she said cheerfully.

May 2001 – The Norman Swaffield's – Alice, Deirdra, Elizabeth, Sheena and Norman

The Nursing Home provided a challenge for Norman, recently retired from the services:

From 'A Load of Old FulHam' … 'Strangely, as soon as he shed his uniform he seemed to take on another, more familiar persona. His rapid stride became a harassed stalk, his gestures became more flamboyant and his swearing increased dramatically; he took up a bizarre vendetta against the garden ducks and would chase them over the lawn with a broom; he also began to hate pigeons and mistrust builders; he was Basil Fawlty. Fortunately his occasional lapses into lunacy were tolerated with great humour by all who surrounded him, knowing full well that this was the only way that he could be persuaded to take on his more challenging duties. To his credit, Norman did, and still does, many things with great aplomb. When the lift can't be repaired by poking the mechanism with a pen, he carries the residents upstairs to their beds; he jams himself up to the elbows in blocked toilets with great gusto, and hares down the village (and sometimes all the way to the next one) to retrieve confused and wandering residents, still in their fluffy slippers.'

Norman and Alice, over a number of years, produced three beautiful daughters – inheriting the striking looks of their forbears. Deirdra, like her mother, has followed a nursing career. She is a project manager at St Mary's Hospital, Paddington, part of a team in charge of the construction and planning of a new medical wing. She had a wonderful wedding in Dublin with the reception at Luttrelstown Castle [oh Posh and Becks eat your heart out] and married Daniel Orteu, who sported a cosmic blue waistcoat, has a French father and an English mother, and is a computer systems analyst.

December 2001 – Daniel and Deirdra Orteu

"A very good, if expensive time, was had by all," quoted Norman, drily. They partied until 2 am and 'Ireland's forty shades of green were reflected on the faces of the guests next morning.' After such a wonderful day, Deirdra will never recall that, as a child, she had a nightmare that she got 2% in a maths test, only to wake up to discover it was true. Sheena's boarding school memories are more bizarre, in that at Newhall Convent she nicked the laboratory skeleton, sat it on the nun's toilet dressed in nun's sandals, and propped a bottle of whisky into one of its bony hands. Despite this she managed an Arts degree at Queen's University, Belfast, and completed teacher training in Newcastle. Sheena is now pursuing a career in freelance journalism, a field hard to break into, and subsidising her life with supply teaching. One suspects that she may have had more than a dabble with 'A Load of Old FulHam'. Elizabeth has been, and is being, entirely educated in York, and has 'jelly and ice-cream fights' as primary school memories. She helps out in the nursing home and earns pocket money. She yearns to travel to Spain, Brazil, Argentina, Canada, Australia, Switzerland and Thailand – in that order. She lives at home, with Norman, who nurses her colds and takes her out for pizzas as a treat.

In June 2002 Granny Dora celebrated her 85th birthday in Boreham Wood. It was a lovely weekend away, and made us feel very special to be invited. It was here we had the privilege to meet Alice for the first time. I knew how ill she was, what an effort it was to attend, and was impressed with her beautiful dress sense. Earlier she had written that her Tipperary mother, Margaret Mary, '... was always busy, always looking after our needs and appearance of dress ...'.

June 2002 – Laura and Norman Swaffield in conversation

Alice told me that she now needed all her strength to counteract the drug treatment she was receiving. Nevertheless she joined in the party, laughed at the jokes, spoke to everyone and appeared next day in yet another pretty outfit with hair carefully done, make-up complete. But Alice lost her fight, the drug therapy was too fierce, and she died just two months later, on 5 September.

Dora and Ham's daughter, Lurline [Laura Swaffield], lives as a free spirit in London. She came to England at the age of five and eventually attended the 'usual nice girl grammar school'. In 1967 she got a place at Bristol University to study English, French and Drama and graduated with an MA in Drama & Theatre Arts, from Leeds in 1971. She joined a fringe theatre group [Incubus] then went into journalism in 1972, accidentally specialising in health via ten years at the 'Nursing Times' until 1983. From there she went into editing national magazines, 'Health & Fitness', 'Fitness', 'Exercise' and 'Bodytalk'. This was at the height of the aerobics boom. Laura now works partly as a freelance health writer and partly as a libraries specialist (another accident). Travel is on her agenda although, "Nothing unusual except maybe a love affair with New York that has had me going there again and again. I enjoy theatre, reading, walking around staring at nice buildings and trees, working for local community groups in connection with libraries, community facilities, regeneration etc, in an attempt to stop New Labour Tone Clones completing their disastrous orgy of destruction begun by Margaret Thatcher. Another interest is 'the psychology of Alfred Adler, the antidote to Freud. Laura is full of fun, enthusiasm and enjoys her family and friends.

1938 – Norman and Tich Swaffield relaxing at Cleethorpes.

Exton Swaffield, off duty, in America –
taken in Williamstown

Florence Anne Carding
before her marriage

Chapter 11

HAMPSHIRE ~ EXTON AND FLORRIE SWAFFIELD 1897–2002
The family spread their wings

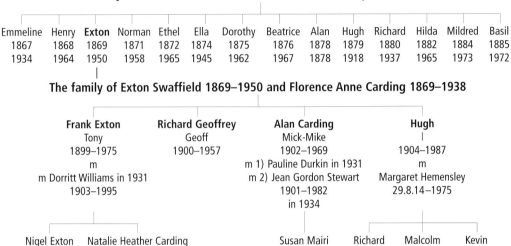

The family of HRJ Swaffield 1839–1909 and Emmeline Jepson 1842–1922

Emmeline	Henry	**Exton**	Norman	Ethel	Ella	Dorothy	Beatrice	Alan	Hugh	Richard	Hilda	Mildred	Basil
1867	1868	1869	1871	1872	1874	1875	1876	1878	1879	1880	1882	1884	1885
1934	1964	1950	1958	1965	1945	1962	1967	1878	1918	1937	1965	1973	1972

The family of Exton Swaffield 1869–1950 and Florence Anne Carding 1869–1938

Frank Exton	**Richard Geoffrey**	**Alan Carding**	**Hugh**
Tony	Geoff	Mick-Mike	
1899–1975	1900–1957	1902–1969	1904–1987
m		m 1) Pauline Durkin in 1931	m
m Dorritt Williams in 1931		m 2) Jean Gordon Stewart	Margaret Hemensley
1903–1995		1901–1982	29.8.14–1975
		in 1934	

Nigel Exton	Natalie Heather Carding		Susan Mairi	Richard	Malcolm	Kevin

Although from strong farming stock, with the Ampthill land agency business in full swing [this was eldest son Henry's domain] the rest of the boys had to look out for themselves. Exton saw his future as a seaman, as did his next brother Norman. In 1890, as an enthusiastic twenty-one year old, Apprentice Seaman Exton Swaffield, confidently joined the sailing ship, Irex, in Glasgow. The account of this terrifying voyage is covered in chapter 9. Eck continued as a Master Mariner making some sort of a living. On May 31st 1897 Eck, as Captain, and Norman, his next brother and First Engineer, joined the SS Urbino. Steaming time from Sunderland to Baltimore, USA was 14 days 8 hours. '… The ship suffered engine trouble and they had several long stops and the usual rough weather. Eventually a new propeller had to be fitted in Baltimore which entailed a delay of 26 days …'. This journey was typical of many they made, fraught with mechanical and meteorological problems.

Eck moved around the country from port to port, ready to jump onto a ship as soon as he was summoned. Somehow he managed to meet his future bride, Florence Anne Carding:

DAILY TELEGRAPH 14 May 1897:

Marriages: Swaffield-Carding – May 8, at the Parish church, Farnsfield, by the Rev R A McKee (vicar), Exton, second son of HRJ Swaffield, Beckerings Park, Ampthill, to Florence Anne, daughter of Frank Carding, The Combs, Farnsfield, Notts.

After their wedding, they settled in Sunderland, where Norman and Tich Swaffield had found lodgings. The first of four boys, named after his grandfather, Frank Carding, and his father Exton, was born there in 1899. Life for the two mariners was very difficult, and it was hard to make ends meet. Both were cheerful, good humoured and had the family sense of fun, but to forge alone in depressing times, with young children, made their responsibilities quite overwhelming. In 1901 Norman sent his wife and baby, Helen, to Harpenden to board with Eck and Florrie. Eck had then changed his on-off career from ship's captain to commercial traveller and salesman, eking out a living for Florrie and the four boys, who had come along within a period of five years.

c1907 – Eck and Florrie's four boys: L–R, Alan, Frank, Geoff and Hugh.

Written on the back by Florrie 'These are 3d a dozen. Not very flattering are they?' – presumably meaning the photos, rather than the boys.

Florrie had a sturdy nature and kept the family together. Eck was very dominating, a jolly character, whereas Florrie was small and frail, appeared at times neglected, and had to keep her end up with five males in the household. Sweetness and thoughtfulness shone through throughout all her years of ill health. Eventually they moved to Fareham in the 1920s and purchased No 17 Southampton Road, a pretty gabled Edwardian house with a long garden at the back. Geoff, Mick and Hugh all went to Price's School and made a life-long friendship with Ted Beatie who later, with his brother Dick, emigrated to Canada. They lived there until Florrie died in 1938, just a month before I, Natalie, was born. My grandmother had longed for another granddaughter.

Florrie came from Combs Farm, Farnsfield in Nottinghamshire. She was the third of twelve children, and the farm had been tenanted by the family since about 1790, latterly from the Ecclesiastical Commissioners. Like Ben Swaffield's Pilsbury Grange in Derbyshire, and Dick Swaffield's Red House Farm at Catesby, it became a happy haven for family holidays. I had to seek it out again, wanting to walk the land and feel the atmosphere of my grandmother's rural childhood. Our visit in the year 2000 was marked by a freak storm. As we approached Farnsfield, the sun from the west was a huge bright ball in the sky producing surrealistic light, and a

1905 – Florrie and her sons, Frank, Florrie, Hugh on her knee, Geoff and [foreground] Alan

wonderful green patina on the fields. Before us the skies were grimly black. Then the rain started falling in sheets, producing vivid arcs of rainbows, the first the brightest with brilliant stripes, each separated from the other, the second in the background muted and soft – the two arching across the sky and rolling countryside, as if greeting us to some special place. As we drove through these beautiful arches, I had not remembered how far out into the countryside Combs Farm was, or how high up a hill. The surrounding land is stunning, and is close to a memorial recently erected for airmen lost in a Halifax bomb disaster during WWII. Up and up to Combs Farm, the house a complete hotch potch, the gardens with idyllic views over the valley. For Florrie and Eck's boys it was a wonderful place to run, hide and play.

1910 – Postcards written in pencil

July 25th 1910 – Nottingham Station.

Dear Mother, Alan (Mick) has lost his coat when we were with Auntie Nell. I have had a nice journey. Love to all Geoff.

Postmarked Farnsfield

August 22nd 1910 – Dear Mother, I hope you arrived safely it is raining hard thank you for the postcard I caught a little rabbit in the field love to all from Geoff.

Postmarked Farnsfield

Dear Mother Please thank Daddy for his letter It is raining fast I hope you [sic] better Love from your loving son Mick.

A year later Florrie's father, Frank, died and the farm was managed by his sons, eventually coming into the hands of Charlie, the youngest boy. Of the seven girls, Althea and Win remained spinsters at home. Charlie married Dorothy late in life, and his older sisters grumpily resented her beautiful hair and energetic ways. Eventually, and reluctantly, the sisters moved from Combs into a small house in Southwell

1889 – Win, Althea, Marion and Lucy Carding

Their younger sister, Dora, lived in Barnsley, and was the proud possessor of one of the first washing machines. It was solidly constructed of wood, operated by hand and quite a novelty. Keeping up with the Jones's, Combs was the first farm in the area to have a fitted bathtub. It was of majestic proportions, panelled in oak. When it was installed, the villagers came up to gaze in wonder at the extraordinary innovation. In contrast, in the outbuildings, was a three-seated lavatory, the middle one designed for a small child. Was it possible for Mummy, Daddy and Toddler to get the urge all at once – and was three enough?

Florrie's firstborn, Frank Exton (Tony) was boarded at Elstow College, Bedfordshire. He hated it there, as did his cousin, Leslie. Elstow is the birthplace of John Bunyan, famous for his allegory, 'The Pilgrim's Progress', a quotation from which is 'A castle called Doubting Castle, the owner whereof was Giant Despair'. And for Frank it really was despair. Time spent there marred his life. Elstow was one of the new fee-paying grammar schools created after

Elstow College, then HQ for the Cosmic Crayon Company and demolished 1964

the Victorian School Boards had been abandoned. It gave more opportunity for boys, and girls, to go to University. Elstow was tough and cold with food fit for pigs. When I visited the area with my father as a child, he positively shuddered as he drove past the building. It is unlikely

1917 – The Pyramids, Egypt – Frank Swaffield on right

that Elstow pupils heard much about the Olympic Games held in the White City in 1908, or the senior boys taken to watch with wonder 'The Paris Hat' film in Bedford. On leaving school, Frank did some engineering training and, in 1917, he joined the Royal Flying Corps, the forerunner of the Royal Air Force, created in 1912 from the Air Battalion, Royal Engineers, as the air arm of the British Army. He sent his mother his address: 3/AM Swaffield FE, 125422, RN Seaplane Depot, Port Said, Egypt. Quite by chance Frank bumped into his uncle, Charlie Carding, amongst a crowd of Arabs on the platform of Port Said station. The two had only time to slap each other on the back, before being hurried to different destinations. Charlie was a corporal with the South Notts Hussars and involved in campaigns in Gallipoli and Egypt.

Geoff went to Price's but was not a good student, probably bored. In desperation, according to his cousin Tom Carding, who shared an interest in stamp collecting with Geoff, the naughty boy was sent to live with a family in France to 'learn French'. For the first month the voluble Geoff spoke not a word, and then he could bear it no longer and came out with a fluent vocabulary which stood him in very good stead in later life.

1915 – Bedford, tea in the garden. Standing, Uncle Hugh [died WWI], cheeky Geoff, Uncle Basil, Aunt Jo. Seated, Alan (Mick) with a cup of tea, his mother Florrie, Aunt Dot, Grandmother Emmeline, Aunt Minnie visiting from Yorkshire, and Eck

In 1919 Geoff wrote from Seine-et-Oise to their friend, Ted Beatie, in Canada:

'The house is shut up at home as Mother was so ill she had to go away for a long time. Hugh is a boarder at Price's, Mick's at Bedford, Frank's in Egypt, Father's in London, Mother in Derby [with Ella] and I'm here. It's really sad to be all so separated but it couldn't be helped' and then '... Frank is still in Egypt as far as we know, though this morning I've had a letter returned so he must have shifted.' By 1920 Frank had come home and was, according to Geoff '... in a big engineering place in Southsea. He's in rooms. He seems to be having an awfully good time. Frank is engaged to an awfully nice girl. Mick is doing awfully well at Bedford, while Hugh is still at school.'

The 'awfully nice girl' was but one in Tony's affections, there was another in America before he finally married Dorritt Williams in 1931. Geoff's letters continue:

Friday September 5th 1919. 'Mother seems better now thank you, and the rest of the crowd are all right. Mick has just been home for his holls, and seems to have had a good time. He seems to have got a top hole job.'

Feb 2.2.20: 'Well we all managed to get home for Xmas, and would have had an awfully nice time if Mother hadn't been so dangerously ill, she was in bed for the whole ten days I was at home. Frank has at last got a job selling light bulbs, no screw, only commission but still its better than doing nothing. He and I are seriously thinking of coming out your way to try our luck.'

30.11.20: 'Father (Eck) finds business awfully bad in fact he has nothing to do, and I'm afraid that both Mother and Father are just as poor as ever as Mick and I are the only two with decent jobs.'

January 14th 1921. 'I didn't go to England at Xmas, as the fares have gone up so that it wasn't worth it, for so short a time. Mick went home, he's working on his own at Magnetos in Bedford, and is doing very well, its just as well too, as only he and I have jobs at present, as Father and Frank are still out, though Frank is at present fitting the buildings at Price's School with lights, so is naturally getting well paid. Following your good advice Frank and I are putting off our trip to your part of the world for the time being.

Hugh, Eck and Florrie's youngest boy, and probably the tallest, also went to Price's and had made friends with Ted. On Thursday evening at 6.40pm on 6 January 1921 he curled up in the warmest place in 17 South-ampton Road, his bed, and wrote:

1928 – Hugh, Eck and Florrie in Fareham

'My dear Ted, We were awfully pleased to get your cards, it was quite a surprise. I am writing this in bed so you will have to excuse my writing which is never very grand. We have got 230 chaps at school now so we're just beginning to get bigger than a private school?? I am 17 and hope to be leaving soon.

Fareham is just the same, half asleep as usual, I don't think it has changed a bit. Daddy and Mother are both quite well. Daddy has gone to a big dinner tonight, Frank has gone to badminton.

Your old chum Hugh.

Hugh remained in Hampshire living for a long time in Brook Lane, Sarisbury Green. He was a wholesale horticulturist and married, in 1935, Margaret Hemensley who was born in Portsmouth. Margaret was the daughter of a couple who intended to marry, her mother a chambermaid, and her father a seaman. At the outbreak of WWI, he joined the Navy. His ship was one of the first to be blown up, and the marriage never occurred, although the baby was born and put up for adoption. Nan Hemensley brought Margaret up, was an affectionate foster mother, and much loved by Margaret's subsequent family. Margaret had very dark hair, black eyes and a tanned skin. The family wonder if she had a Mediterranean father. She and Hugh had three boys, all tall, dark and good looking.

From Florrie to Ted in Canada

9.1.21. Edensor, Fareham: 'My dear Ted, Your Christmas cards gave us all great pleasure, it was nice to be remembered, and we all take such interest in you and Dick; Geoff tells us that you are both engaged to be married, the very best of luck to you all, it seems no time since you two boys used to come and help get up a concert in the attic, I came across some of the scenery the other day …

Perhaps you've heard Geoff's latest news that he is training at Cox's. Frank, unfortunately, is still only doing odd electrical jobs, Mick is in Bedford with his Uncle [Basil] and Hugh is still at Price's School and growing every day.

We're having very mild weather, more like Spring than Winter. Fareham is very little changed, Mrs Dalloway always enquires after you both, when I see her, she is now living in Southsea. Very best wishes for this New Year and much love to you both, and do remember how glad we always are to hear from you both.

Yours always sincerely, Florence Swaffield.'

Some years later, Bardie [daughter of Eck's younger brother Dick] was at teacher training college in Lee-on-Solent, near Fareham. "Dear old Uncle Eck," she said, "I was very fond of him. I used to visit and he made me piles of hot buttered toast." Whilst in Lee, Bardie watched the competition for the Schneider Cup sailing trophy. She also saw the magnificent Jubilee Review of King George V and the Coronation Review of King George VI. "All the Fleet sailed past the Needles," she said, "It was a truly magnificent sight."

1936 – Mick and Jean had their first child. Florrie, with four boys of her own, had always longed for a granddaughter. She wrote to Jean in Hertfordshire County Hospital:

Fareham. Mon eve, 23 Nov '36:

'Dearest Jean

Well you did manage it in good time, to be up and about by Xmas! Dear, we were so delighted to get Mick's ring on Sat. morn. and proud I was to be the 1st here to have the good news that you and Mick have the first girl child in the juniors.

2nd May 1937 – Florrie with her first granddaughter, Susan

From what new Father says she must be a very sweet babe, born as he was, with a good crop of hair, which did not come off. So much we want to know, most particularly how you are, if you are really comfy in the HCH and what was the weight of your daughter?

Were you trying to go one better than the mother who had the babe in the cab of a lorry? I guess Mick was relieved when the hospital was reached, as he might not have been such a clever accoucheur as his Father was when Hugh was born.

I didn't write yesterday, as I felt your mail would be already large, but we talked much of you. Hugh and Jimmy were here for the day, and it <u>was</u> cold when they left at 9.45.

God bless you all Jean dear, and we are so pleased. Yours Anne S'

1

2

1936 – Extracts from Florrie's letter, signed 'Anne S'

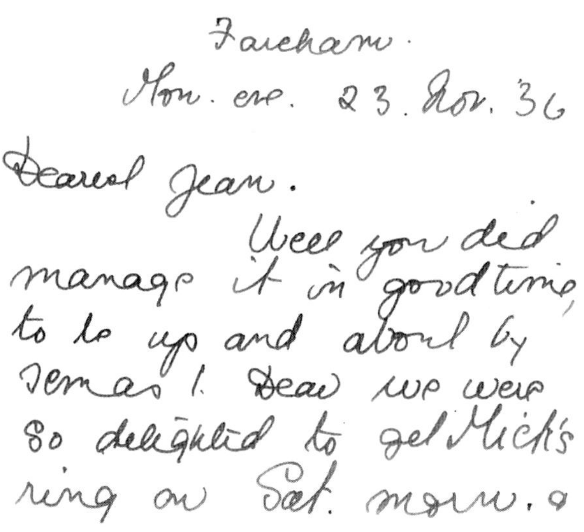

> Fareham.
> Mon. eve. 23. Nov. 36
>
> Dearest Jean.
> Well you did manage it in good time, to be up and about by Xmas! Dear we were so delighted to get Mick's ring on Sat. morn. a

> for the day, it was cold when they left at 9.45.
> God bless you all Jean dear, and we are so very pleased.
> Yours. Anne S.

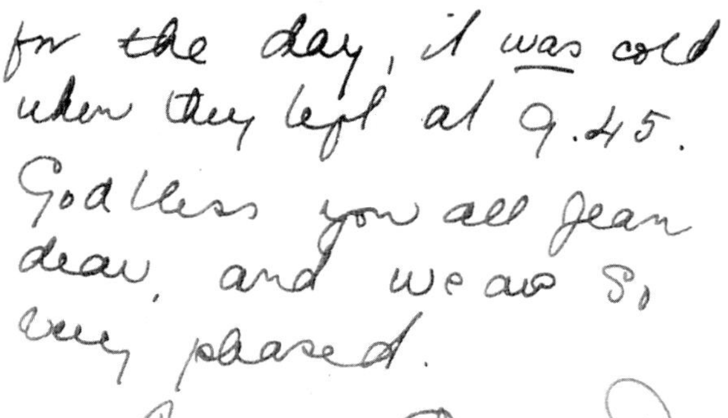

1937 – On Susan's christening Florrie wrote on four small pages of blue Basildon Bond paper:

March 18th '37.

'Dear little Susan,

As we hear from Uncle Geoff that you are christened, we send you this spoon with our love. It belonged to your great-grandfather, Frank Carding. Much love little blessing from your grandparents Exton and Anne Swaffield.'

Faeham. 18. March. '37

Dear little Susan.

As we hear from Uncle Geoff that you are christened we send you this spoon with our love it belonged to your great grandfather Frank Carding. much love little blessing from your grandparents.

Exton & Anne Swaffield

Please give the enclosed to Daddy.

1937 – Letter to Susan from her grandparents

1938 – Florrie died of cancer.

Combs was a favourite place for Geoff to visit, and in 1944 he took his young niece, Susan, and introduced her to the whole Carding family. She was eight and loved it: 'He took me to visit Lucy and Frank Howitt in Lincoln, guiding me round the Cathedral and showing me the Lincoln Imp.' The 'Imp' is a cheeky little fellow sitting high in the Angel Choir. Legend has it that when the Devil let the Imp out to play, he was blown to Lincoln by a strong wind, causing mayhem in the Cathedral. Exhausted he rested on a column and was turned into stone by an angel.

'I also met cousins, Tom and John, who were very dashing. We visited Aunt Winnie, who had a charming little villa in a garden in Southwell, and Aunt Althea. Oh yes, and Aunt Dora.'

1945 – Susan in a Geoff designed dressing gown

Years before Tony and Dorritt had spent a happy summer week with Charlie and Dorothy, and were invited for tea with Althea and Win. Tony was known for his voracious appetite, '… like a boiler with the damper out …' said Dorritt. After he had worked his way through scones and sandwiches, Althea asked Frank what he would like next.

"May I try a piece of fruit cake?" he asked.

Althea gave him an acid look. "Nobody tries my cakes," she said, "They either take a piece and enjoy it, or leave it alone."

As they were departing, Win handed Dorritt a jar of marmalade through the car window.

"Oh, how lovely, thank you very much," said Dorritt.

"It's not for you, it's for Frank," said Win going back into the house.

For Florrie, Combs, was certainly special and for me, her granddaughter, my first experience of a real farm with a muddy yard, flocks of woolly sheep in the fields, a big black bull with a ring in its nose steaming at me in its pen. I would

Althea Carding b 1872

watch Uncle Charlie take maggots out of the sheep's feet, and clean up their matted back-sides, the smell of muck and animal urine permeating the air. But the best was the back stairs. I had never been in a house with back stairs before, and climbed up and down them incessantly. It was a special creaky place for a podgy little girl to imagine all sorts of secret things. My teenage cousin, Tom, used to creep up behind me and shout 'boo'. Many, many years later he recalled how he caught me sticking metal table forks into the electric sockets, "Lucky you didn't kill yourself and set fire to the place," he said amiably.

Frank Carding [far distance] driving sheep down Long Lands Lane at Combs. The little boy is his youngest son, John Carding.

After some time Eck remarried Mary, and lived at Luton where he died, leaving Mary with very little income. She corresponded with Natalie for many years, and the two continued to meet when Mary had moved into The Priory, Worthing, to be near her sister, Honor. Both Tony and Mick sent cheques to help her out.

'RN Hospital, London – 9th December 1949

My dear Natalie,

I'm so sorry dear I had been so long in answering your two very nice letters including your good wishes for my birthday [Nov 14th], but I can't write properly and now altho I am getting better every day and shall be going home next Monday 12th, as the Specialist is very pleased with everything, and they have put me through it properly this week. …

Don't worry dear about your exam you will get through alright, but take it easily. Remember worry killed a cat once, and they have 9 lives. Please thank Nigel for his letter of good wishes for my birthday. I am answering yours because it took much longer to write and far more news in it.

Are you still keeping up your riding? It's very good exercise, but practise falling off in the right way and I am very glad you have learnt to swim so keep it up when the summer comes again, everyone should learn, you never know when it may be useful and Daddy can give you lots of hints.

My love to all of you, I shall be very glad to be home again, although I have been wonderfully well looked after here in every way. Bless you Nats, Your affect Grandad.'

1949 – Ist page of Grandaddy's letter addressed 'My dear Natalie'

Chapter 11 ~ Hampshire ~ Exton and Florrie Swaffield 1897–2002; The family spread their wings

The following year Eck died. His sons were fond of him, keeping up a continuous stream of communication by post. He is well remembered by Tom Carding as '… fine looking, larger than life, with an expansive nature …'.

During the 1920s Tony worked in the USA and in Paris. After marriage he had various jobs but his main career was on the refrigeration side of the Pressed Steel Company.

1931 – Bedford. Tony and Dorritt's wedding, Eck accompanies Sarah Williams, Florrie, in cloche hat, is with Richard Williams, father of the bride

1931 – Wedding day in Bedford

SWAFFIELD-WILLIAMS. On 16th May, at St Cuthbert's Church, Bedford by the Rev G W Byers-Jones, Frank Exton, eldest son of Mr & Mrs Exton Swaffield of Fareham, to Doris, elder daughter of Mr & Mrs Richard Williams, 16 Russell Avenue, Bedford.

Tony, then, was employed by an American firm but his position was taken by a Director's relative. He was given three months notice just before his marriage, but failed to tell either Dorritt or his parents. His salary, at £600 a year, was well above the national average. Cost of living was reasonable with eggs at 1s per dozen, bread 3½d for a large loaf, and cigarettes 1s for twenty. Nevertheless they went through a poor time, and he grabbed employment wherever he could, ending up living with Florrie and Eck in Fareham. Eck had to work as a commercial traveller and a painter and decorator to make ends meet. He was then 62, and not enjoying good health, and Florrie continued unwell. Tony was offered a job selling Nu-Swift Fire Extinguishers on commission.

Dorritt's Memoir: 'The order he was hoping to get was a big one at a large factory and he was asked to give a demonstration. Employees built an enormous pile of refuse which was then ignited. I watched from the car, heavy-hearted with pity, as my husband tore hither and thither directing a stream of foam which had as much effect on the inferno as using a pea shooter to hold back an invading army.'

By 1933 Tony got a good job with the Pressed Steel Company in Oxford, and they moved. Dorritt became pregnant but miscarried, 'My mother-in-law came to look after me. She was very kind and knew how desperate I was to have a child.'

By this time Tony was a company salesman in Birmingham, and they bought a detached house in Solihull. Both children were born in the big, back bedroom, Nigel in 1935 and Natalie in 1938.

1939 – Solihull, Tony, Dorritt, Nigel and Natalie Swaffield

Tony started gardening under Dorritt's directions, and planted potatoes to clean the ground. The yield was terrific. They had very little furniture, and the main sitting room was empty, so became 'The Spuddery' until it was furnished and deserved a better name. After the potato crop was gathered, the next job was to make flower beds and a lawn. Each time they visited Fareham they were given plants and cuttings, and raspberry canes. Florrie told Dorritt that these came originally from Combs Farm, and they fruited abundantly year after year. With vegetables Tony was less successful:

> Dorritt's Memoir: 'I remember going down the garden one Saturday morning just as he had dug up some carrots.
>
> "Something for lunch," he said cheerfully as he handed me a partly filled trug.
>
> "They've got more twists than a corkscrew, and bumps as well," I responded ungratefully.
>
> Tony looked at me, his eyes clouded with disappointment. "All my life," he said, "I've dreamt of the day when my wife would come tripping down the garden path, wearing a sun bonnet, to collect the fruits of my toil.
>
> "Sorry," I said and returned to the house feeling a real meanie.'

The Tony Swaffields then moved to the outskirts of London for the duration of WWII. Tony worked in the city. He was a member of the Home Guard in Worcester Park, an unpaid force formed in Britain in May 1940 to repel the expected German invasion. Its members worked at their normal occupation, and undertook military training in their spare time. In 1940 they were armed with a motley collection of shotguns and privately owned weapons, but by 1942 were well-trained, and liberally supplied with automatic weapons and light artillery. The family had a topsy-turvy life either in a damp shelter at the bottom of the garden, or less comfortable for the parents, a cramped 'outside' Anderson shelter in the sitting room. Flying bombs caused a real fear, and Nigel and Natalie still remember the silence after the motor cut, waiting for the big bang. Daily walks produced pockets full of shrapnel, and strange bomb craters where, yesterday, a house had stood.

After the war, in 1946, the family moved to Old Colwyn, North Wales and Tony became the Pressed Steel Company [part of the Leyland group] Branch Manager in Llandudno until 1950. He would see me off early to school each morning, still in his dressing gown, "Have you got your elevenses, your hankie and your bus fare?" He then waved from the front bedroom window, whilst I skipped down the rocky surface of Bryn Avenue. He did this every school day, making me feel comfortable and loved.

He then became South Wales Branch Manager in Cardiff. He persuaded Welsh housewives, and small shop owners, to purchase revolutionary deep freezers. I would often accompany him on long journeys during my school holidays in his silvery-blue Austin Cambridge. I would perch on the back of the passenger seat, with my head stuck out of the sunshine roof, and my plaits flying. Daddy only knew one song, 'Lili Marlene', and we would sing this on, and on, and on to make the journey go by. In Cardiff he joined the Royal Observer Corps, and became a keen Rotarian. He also dabbled with Freemasonry, became an Advanced Motorist, a reluctant plantsman, keen garden path builder, an amateur fisherman, and hard-worked house husband. Personable and popular with his colleagues, he sociably enjoyed gin and tonic at the Angel Hotel. He was a most thoughtful and loving father.

One of his employees, Reg Adams, managed his own refrigeration business in Hilton, South Africa. Now in his eighties, he wrote, in October 2001:

'Dear Natalie,

I knew Mr Swaffield since 1946. I recall that, when I applied for the post advertised, I was told that there were twenty-nine other applicants, from which they would choose six, and the successful one from these. I had just finished my leave from the RAF, and was enjoying some 5–6 months on full pay according to my rank, when I was demobilised. I was not really anxious to start work, although my father persuaded me otherwise, "You are going to look for a job aren't you, son?"

As I went through the Prestcold interviews and was finally 'the one', I wondered what I had that the other's hadn't. When I was asked, 'What do you know about refrigeration and air-conditioning?' I had replied, 'Nothing!' All the others had given such a lengthy list of their knowledge. They liked my honesty, and that's how I started. Your father – Tony – it was strictly Mr Swaffield or Sir then – did not pay any special attention to me, and I respected him as a man and my superior/boss! Perhaps, if I had made any mistakes, errors, he would naturally have called me to heel over the matter. I would not like to say that he was a strict, unreasonable driver of his staff – but fair to all …

One thing that I do remember was when I left the firm and England to come to South Africa, we both corresponded, and he was continually telling me that if I came back to England he would help to find me a good post, and he was disappointed when I didn't accept his offer. The last letter I had from him was when he had retired in the South of England and he wrote that he was getting old, and I must excuse his writing and spelling as his eyesight was deteriorating.   Your Dad was a fine upstanding man!'

Nigel went to Rydal School in Colwyn Bay, after which he did National Service in the RAF, posted mainly in Germany. He travelled extensively throughout Europe during his three years service. After a brief sojourn in Ampthill, he became a student at the Welsh School of Architecture in Cardiff. Once qualified he moved to Denmark. He has sustained a successful architectural career, living in various places such as Belfast, Reading, London, Kuwait and Taiwan. Married to Denise, they have two children, Damian and Anisa. The whole family has gradually moved to New Zealand, where they are now settled in North Island, on the Hibiscus Coast near Auckland. After years in London, Nigel describes the scenery as '… breathtaking, lush vegetation, interspersed with cultivated fields and, always, the sea in the form of river estuaries, bays and idyllic beaches. This area was one of the first settled, so there are some old houses, churches and public buildings, all white-painted, weather boarding with balconies and steeply pitched roofs.'

There are plenty of Swaffs in New Zealand, some connected, some not, and the telephone directories have lists of them. Both Nigel's children have followed careers in the computer world. Damian has a little girl, Taylor Harriet – although he is now separated from his wife.

Since childhood, I, Natalie, have been an avid letter writer and communicator – always interested in the doings of my family, and keeping up with my cousins. I loved the wildness of North Wales, less so the suburban life in Cardiff. Four years in London working for 60s architect, H T Cadbury-Brown, was more than educational. I managed to travel, ending up in America for

1960 – Accra, Ghana – Michael, Natalie and Father Ashietey

a year. By then I had met my husband, Michael, an agriculturist with British American Tobacco Company, and we married in Accra, Ghana in 1960. My bouquet was created by Mrs Noah out of creamy, perfumed frangipani, and my honeymoon weekend was spent repairing Lister pumps on bush seedbed sites at Huhunya. During our first wedded Christmas, we canoed across a crocodile infested Volta river and pow-wow'd with farmers in Sogakofe. Our first baby girl was born in Agogo. In Tanganyika we endured a week long Army mutiny. Susina and I were evacuated to Nairobi in a 4-seater Cessna. We crossed the Serengeti Plain navigating from tree to tree. Trying to be helpful, I pointed out a wide river winding across the plain, "That's no river lady, that's migrating zebra," said the Canadian pilot. We had 14 years in rural India. In Andhra Pradesh we suffered a cyclone and were cut off for three weeks. Six thousand people were killed by a tidal wave no more than ten miles away.

Our silver wedding anniversary was spent in Sierra Leone and, my last memory as a leaf wife, is of fleeing an irate farmers' meeting in Ganta, Liberia as the local bank had run out of funds, and Michael could not pay the men for their produce. The whole experience has been one of a challenging developing world.

1966 – Bangalore, India – Natalie, Michael and four children under 4

Our four children, Susina, Simon, Andrea and David, have coped amazingly well with boarding school from the age of 5, and long air journeys and separations, once sent for education in England. Michael has worked as a consultant all over the tobacco-growing world, and at times I have accompanied and worked with him. We have lived in Chinese factories, and done 3000 miles of off-road driving in Zambia, visiting small farmers – and listening to their worries as they struggle against the more wealthy farmers from Zimbabwe and South Africa. Our anchor has been a beautiful medieval house in Woodbridge, Suffolk – and this is where we gather together – and enjoy each other's company with an increasing number of grandchildren running around us. Writing is my escape and provides sheer enjoyment.

Susina has followed much in our footsteps, making her own life as an expatriate, first in Hong Kong where she met her husband, David Sutton, who works for HSBC plc. Alone, she backpacked throughout the Far East, Australia and New Zealand where, long ago, she bungee-jumped off the bridge at Queenstown. Since her marriage, and the birth of two boys, they have lived in Korea, Israel, Philippines, Panamá – and are now coming to grips with life, and commuting, in England. Laurence, their eldest boy, has taken a real interest in the writing of this family history. He encourages me, "Any new stories, Granny?", and gives me hope that I am not wasting my time. However, since he discovered Harry Potter, 'Granny's book' has lost its fascination. Nick is more interested in the FA Cup and the goal scoring merits of David Beckham.

Simon met his wife, Amy, in Sierra Leone. They have been together a long time, and have back-packed in worn-out boots and tatty clothes to many corners of the world. In Bangalore they were the only British spectators, amongst an ocean of Bangaloreans, when England actually beat India at cricket. A rare moment. Amy's background is expatriate, and she spent her first years in Burma, where her father was a United Nations geologist. She has a degree in Botany, is a trained teacher, a librarian and, now, a mother to Jackson and Thomas. Simon was educated at Greshams, has studied art, worked in PR, and wine, and is now settled in Kendal, Cumbria following a career in corporate team training. He rides his mountain bike over the hills to work

in Windermere, has a canoe and a campervan, and still manages a fair bit of globe-trotting by running events in such far-flung places as Korea and Turkey.

1992 – Simon, Natalie, Andrea, Mike, Susina and David Wheatley

Andrea, and her husband, Stewart, are also well travelled. In 1981 they started from London to Tashkent, using the Soviet railway system. They then spent a couple of years living in Kashmir, Ladakh, Madras, and Mysore. From Sri Lanka they went through South East Asia to work in Australia. They finally landed in New Zealand, broke, and lived mainly on pumpkin soup whilst seeing as much as beautiful countryside as they could. Not ones to be 'ordinary' they sailed home in a massive Russian container ship, Stewart eating boiled tongue and slurping borsch by the gallon, whilst Andrea, the almost vegetarian, crunched her way through raw cabbage and several boxes of scrooged away cornflakes. They have a pretty, late-Victorian house in Norwich, and two children, William and Fay. Stewart travels by motor-bike, 60 miles a day, to work as a packaging technologist in Lowestoft. His dream is to regenerate an old Moskvich in his garage, or sail at weekends. Instead he DIY's, changes nappies and takes William swimming.

Andrea has worked and studied, and combined her career with motherhood. She has achieved the highest academic accolade in our own small family, a 1st Class BA (Hons) in Professional Development from the University of East Anglia. She is now a tutor on one of the courses she studied – a Certificate in Counselling Skills.

David was educated, like his father and uncles, at Framlingham College in Suffolk. He joined a rigorous Outward Bound course in Eskdale, where he became team leader. Marooned on a hill top he desperately smoked his one tea bag, having previously made 5 cups of tea. He studied at college in London, living, as the others, in our flat in Chiswick. He worked as a Saturday boy in Habitat, on to Saab where he was awarded a certificate of merit, to HR Owen dealing with customer relations. Country life beckoned, and he has settled in Suffolk. He has a motorbike, a Land Rover and an elderly VW Golf. He always has time to help his friends, and enjoys the conviviality of a small town. Still looking for the right girl, he keeps in firm contact with his family and enjoys outdoor life.

The talented Geoff deserves a chapter to himself – and has no progeny.

Will of Florence Anne Swaffield, aged 68, of 17 Southampton Road, Fareham, nr Portsmouth, Hants. Wife of Exton Swaffield, died 13 July 1938. Proved by Frank Carding. £115 18s 6d.

Will of Exton Swaffield, aged 80, 1 Dunstable Court, Luton, died 7 June 1950. Proved by Leslie John Swaffield, Auctioneer & Estate Agent. £459 11s 6d.

1994 – The Wheatley family. Back L–R, Amy, Michael, Susina, Natalie, Andrea holding Laurence Sutton, Stewart Rippon, David. Front L–R, Simon and David Sutton

Chapter 12

FROM THE SHIRES TO FRANCE & SOUTH AFRICA 1900–2000
Geoff, Mick, Hugh and their families

Exton (Eck) Swaffield 1869-1950 and Florence Anne Carding 1869-1938

Frank	Richard Geoffrey	Alan Carding	Hugh
(Tony)	(Geoff/Jeff)	(Mick-Mike)		
1899	1900	1902	1904
1975	1957	1969	1987
m Dorritt Williams		m Jean Gordon Stewart	m Margaret Hemensley
issue		issue	issue
Nigel Exton		Susan Mairi	Richard John
Natalie Heather Carding			Malcolm
			Kevin

All of Eck and Florrie's sons, and they were four very different boys, went to Price's School in Fareham. It was a struggle to keep them there as Eck's employment was sporadic. In 1905 he had an unfortunate experience, losing almost six month's salary, stolen from his pocket. He wrote to his father, HRJ, on 7 May 1905, from 'Edensor', Southampton Road, Fareham:

> 'Dear Father, This week I've had a bit of very rough luck. Last Friday, coming back from Shanklin, I had my pocket picked and lost £34 0s 0d. I was never in such a rough crowd … … I've got about £30 in the bank now, but need this to get us through this year. Could you let me have £20–£25 @ 5% until next Spring? My salary is 57/- per week, don't want to realise any of Florrie's shares … I was wearing a heavy coat, buttoned up to the neck, and the money was in my back pocket ….

Your affect son, Eck'

1931 – The Swaffield family home, Fareham

Whether he received the loan is unknown. In 1909 Eck was worried, and anxious to see his parents:

'Edensor'   23.3.09

Dear Dad – I've been wondering the last few days if you would come down to us for Easter and bring Mother with you … Easter seems a very good chance as I shall have 4 clear days to trot you round your old haunts round Southsea and Portsmouth.

Now make up your mind and come for a week at any rate and longer if you care. The stay and a breath of sea air would do you no end of good and set you up for the summer. … Now d'ont [sic] write back and say you c'ant afford it as it won't cost you much, and we'll be glad to have you and the kids w'ont worry you. Think this over for half an hour then write and say you'll come and you can do anything you like when you get here. Love to all from us both, Your affect. son, Eck'

It is unlikely HRJ and Emmeline ever made the journey to Fareham for, just a month later, HRJ's death was reported in the Bedford newspapers.

All of Eck's boys made firm family friends with Ted Beatie and his brother Dick who, because of the acute unemployment problem in Britain, had both emigrated to Canada. Ted preserved the letters and they were sent to Natalie, by his daughter Sandra, after Ted's death in Canada in 1996. Geoff was the most constant of correspondents.

c1914 – Four Swaffield boys at Price's School – Frank, Hugh, Mick and Geoff

c1920 – Florrie and Eck

'Désert de Retz, par Chambourcy, Seine et Oise   June 3rd 1919

My dear Ted,

Thanks ever so much for your letter … . I have been here 3 weeks and am frightfully busy I hardly ever get time to write to anyone. I am teaching now and am having a very good time. How did you find your girl. I hope you've fixed something up with her, she deserves it after writing to you all that time.

… The weather is beautiful here and we are going to have such a glut of fruit. I had my first strawberries today.

… I shall shout so that you will hear me in Canada if you sign your letters 'your sincere friend'. Ted it's all very well but I think we've got beyond the '<u>sincere</u>' stage after all the years we've known each other … Please ask Dick to write … I shall always be at this address. Goodbye old chap. Your affectionate friend ——————— Geoff.'

'Désert de Retz, par Chambourcy, Seine et Oise   Friday September 5th 1919

Dear Ted

… I'm sorry that neither of you have got a job, and do hope you will soon hear of something; but you are awfully lucky to be able to take that Government course. I thought Dick had quite decided to go back to the land, but I suppose he's like me, mighty fed up with it. I'm at present trying to hook a job at the British Consul's office in Paris which ought to turn out A1, but I must just wait and see.

I'm glad you're still with the girl at Port Hope, she's certainly stuck to you all right. Has Dick got another girl yet? Mother seems better now thank you, and the rest of the crowd are all right. Mick has just been home for his holls [sic], and seems to have had a good time. He seems to have got a top hole job. I'm hoping to get home for Xmas, but everything is so expensive here practically treble to what it is in England.

      Yours affectionately —————— Geoff.'

'129 Avenue de Neuilly, Neuilly sur Seine, (Seine), France   Feb 2.2.20.

My dear Ted –

… Well three days before Xmas I left that awful Désert and went to England for Xmas. I started at Cox's on the 1st Jan, I've got an awfully good job here, very well paid. It's Cox's Shipping Agency so I feel awfully bucked because before I went home I'd practically tried in every corner of the earth to get a job … . Well I wonder whether you've got jobs yet? It's just a year ago since you stopped with us and Price's Pavilion was on fire. They have built a lot of new buildings there, you'd hardly know the place. Do write to me soon whether you are married or not etc. So far I haven't found any one to suit me, I always was difficult.

Old Mrs Whitlock died when I was at home at Xmas, all the good old people seem to be dying off.

Please excuse scrawl but I'm scribbling this at the office. Best of best wishes to you both, do write to me soon, and tell me all your news for old times sake. – Your affectionate chum, Geoff.'

1920 – Geoff in Paris

'129 Avenue de Neuilly, Neuilly sur Seine, (Seine).   30.11.20

My dear Ted

… I shan't be able to get home for Xmas, I did so want to, but I had a great deal of expenses one way and another lately, dentist bills, new togs etc, that I feel I can't afford it. Especially as it would cost me about £12 return, so I shall have to stop in this land I <u>love</u>!

I'm on the look out for a job, I'm awfully fed up here. I get a fairly decent screw but there's absolutely no advancement. In England they seem to be getting it hot and strong in fact everyone seems to be turning Bolshie [sic]. Frank and I are seriously thinking of coming out your way to try our luck.

I can't even get a room here, I had a nice little house, two rooms and a bathroom, but the place is sold so I've had to turn out, and now I've only got a tiny room, a proper garrat [sic] no bigger than a cupboard. I can't stand upright in it and when I'm in bed the roof is only about a foot off my head, so its lively. ... How's the girl? ... Best wishes to Dick

Cheerio Old Chap.   Yours comme toujours ——————— Geoff.'

COX & CO (FRANCE) LIMITED, PARIS   Adresse Télègraphique: COXIA-PARIS

Fondateurs: Barclays Bank Limited –   Cox & Co Télèlephone   Gutenberg   74–08, 74–09, Paris, Alger, Bordeaux

'129 Avenue de Neuilly, Neuilly sur Seine, (Seine)

My dear Ted

Many thanks for your letter of a short while ago, also the cards from your girl and self, it was good of you to think of me.

Well I hope you were successful with 'Father' when you stayed with him at Xmas, and that everything is now fixed up, if so congratulations old boy, you've made up your mind sooner than I have.

I think I told you I had to leave the shipping office where I was, as they were closing down, but I managed to get another job at the above named Bank as their French and English correspondent practically right away, so I considered myself lucky.

I didn't go to England at Xmas ... all the fares have gone up. ... Had a very miserable time as nearly all my friends were away, but had a fine time at a Fancy Dress Ball on Xmas Eve, when I went as a Baby. It was screamingly funny but I got the 2nd prize in spite of losing my petticoat during a waltz. I go to a great many dances here and generally have a jolly good time.

Following your good advice Frank and I are putting off our trip to your part of the world for the time being. ... Your affectionate chum – Geoff.'

Cox & Co (France) Limited   Paris, Le 22nd September 1921

'My dear Ted:–

... Well I am surprised to hear that Dick is married, and I am sure that Mother will be very hurt to think, that he has without even sending her a card, as she has always your interest at heart ... Well! and fancy you being married next month it really doesn't seem possible, I wonder if you have grown up at all? The last time I saw you, you just seemed the same as when you were a wee a little boy at Price's!!'

'As you will see by the above I am still with Cox's, and things are fairly flourishing, though business is putrid ... Had a great deal of trouble one way and another, all this year, things have never gone right. Frank has been out here since last March, as he has been practically out of a job since demobilisation, and as things were going very badly at home, so that they couldn't keep him any longer. I've had him out here with me, but he was out of job until about a fortnight ago, then he managed to get something at Rolls

Royce Motor place, its practically nothing at all and the pay is rotten, but it will be better than nothing. You can imagine what a pull down it has been for the last nine months, as Frank hadn't a halfpenny saved … I've had a very nice flat for the past year now, but I've to give it up at the end of the month, but have managed to get another small one in Montmartre, and move in on the 1st of Oct.'

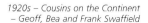

Tattered envelope from 1921, kept by Ted Beatie in Canada until he died – 1996

'Things are always the same at home, one struggles, one of us no sooner gets going, than we have to help the other out, Father was out of job and didn't hit anything for two months. Now what he has got is practically all work and very little pay, and poor Mother seems to age a good deal, it's been such a worry to her, and she is practically living the whole time by herself, as Father is very rarely at home. As we are now all away, we have made a flat in our house, as we don't want all the rooms… Well I think that this is really enough of my troubles, things might be a deal worse … we had a 10% reduction [in pay] which came as a great blow, but was better than been [sic] on the streets.

Well! Ted you rogue you might have told me something of your wife, as you know I would be interested, is she the good little pal you had all though the war???? No I am not married yet or engaged, though I am still living in hopes that she will have me!!! We went blackberrying last Sunday and got such a lot, so was busy making jam at the beginning of the week, I shall get so used to doing things on my own, that it will be really funny to get married.

I am trying to get to Spain for the winter, but I don't know if I shall succeed, nothing really ties me to Paris, and I should certainly come out your way, if I thought there were any hopes of getting a job. We have had some real jolly times this summer with the girls, I will

send you some photos next time I write, we have been everywhere in France practically … Mick is still at Bedford and engaged to such a nice girl, I was in England practically all July, so I got round and saw everybody.

Every good wish for your future old pal, and my very kindest regards to Mrs Ted. I am sure she must be nice to have fallen in love with you … I really mean every word I've put down in spite of it being such rag time. Ever your affectionate pal — Geoff'

1920s – Cousins on the Continent – Geoff, Bea and Frank Swaffield

During the next ten years Geoff started making a career for himself in the roller coaster world of haute couture as a fashion and society journalist, before breaking into the design world.

1928 – Mayfair Magazine – Les Costumes de Sport by Soiffield

How delightful Miss Helen Wills looks in this deep red dress by Patou, made of Wool Flower, a new French fabric with an English name. It is delightfully soft wool popeline uncrushable and cool

Paris au mois de Juillet, 1928.

Mes Cheres!—

It's much too hot and I'm far too weary to attempt to talk to you about the clothes that are going to be worn during the late fall and winter, but it's early yet, and most of the *grandes maisons* are not nearly ready for the journalistic world to probe into the secrets that they have been storing up through the summer.

I only got off the train late last night from Aix

MAYFAIR MAGAZINE, AUGUST, 1928 – MAYFAIR'S PARIS LETTER – By SOIFFIELD OF PARIS

Mes chères   *Paris au mois de Juillet, 1928*

It's much too hot and I'm far too weary to attempt to talk to you about the clothes that are going to be worn during the late fall and winter, but it's early yet, and most of the grandes maisons are not nearly ready for the journalistic world to probe into secrets that they have been storing up through the summer.

I only got off the train late last night from Aix les Bains, and for those of you who do not know it, I'll say it's a truly quaint and delightful old town in the Savoy country … and the excursions either on foot, horseback or by car are simply legion. As far back as 1860 the late Queen Victoria visited Aix, and since that date the town has been a very popular rendezvous for all the smartest of European society …

… Much excitement was caused on the golf links soon after my arrival by the sensational beating of Aubrey and Percy Bloomer, by Tommy Armour and his brother Willie. Another incident, which caused quite a little flutter, was a novel but very practical golfing outfit that an extremely smart girl was wearing. It started by brogue shoes, white wool stockings rolled below the knee, a delightful tartan skirt, cut with two large box pleats inserted, a double breasted navy jacket, blue shirt, and a beret basque.

Paris is still all in a whirl. And what a sensational season it has been, too. I think Lady Mortimer Davis really started the ball rolling by her sensational win with 'Mary Legend' of the French Oaks at Chantilly, one very hot Sunday in June. Then we have had the Grand Prix at Longchamps, the Steeplechase on the beautiful course at D'Auteuil all of which produced some brilliant gatherings, where one generally met the same people, but always wearing different clothes.

Until next month – Bien, bien a vous mes chères ———————— SOIFFIELD.

Dorritt Williams [Swaffield] flitted in and out of the Swaffield brothers' lives over a period of ten or more years until she married, Frank (Tony), Geoff's elder brother in 1931. For many years she was the close girlfriend of Mick (Alan), the third son, but their affectionate relationship came to a sudden finale. She also lived in Paris, working as a children's companion for Madam Devise, at the same time as Geoff, and it is she who has kept so many newspaper cuttings of Geoff's successes in the fashion world. Also two letters, carefully stored with others, and found after her death, probably written in 1928:

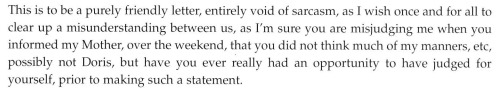

Dorritt in Paris

'c/o Cox & Co (France) Ltd,
33 Rue de 4 Septembre, Paris (Opera)   le 6 Decembre

Dear Doris

This is to be a purely friendly letter, entirely void of sarcasm, as I wish once and for all to clear up a misunderstanding between us, as I'm sure you are misjudging me when you informed my Mother, over the weekend, that you did not think much of my manners, etc, possibly not Doris, but have you ever really had an opportunity to have judged for yourself, prior to making such a statement.

… We had corresponded certainly, but I never really took anything seriously that you wrote, though apparently you took some of my letters in quite a different light … . [I took it] all as one huge joke, ie sarky correspondence between persons unknown.

… My visit to Bedford … was quite unforeseen … exceedingly short and hurried, here I must add that I was exceedingly disappointed in Mick, who is by far my favourite brother (we have always been great pals together, and always contrived to get our hols ensemble). … Considering I had come from far, and we hadn't seen each other for a considerable time, he behaved … a little selfishly. The fatal Saturday night when I was introduced to you I was feeling anything but fit, and exceedingly tired, as I had travelled since 8 o'c the night before and had not slept … I naturally did not feel much like Pictures. I had already promised my deaf aunt Jo to go to the doctors with her, and you know what relations are, but as I said to Mick I thought it rather mean of him playing hooky just the day I was there. Although not overburdened with the world's goods, the three of us could have gone out in the afternoon, and have had a real nice time, because when I do occasionally get to England I like to have a really good bust up, and I should certainly have stopped at nothing. As it was I saw nothing of Mick and had to fall back on Lewin [Smith] who I think is a real nice kid, but they do say that 'Love rules the world' and it certainly ruled me out as far as Mick was concerned … I blame myself – I should have left you entirely alone and said nothing. I am sure you will take this all in the way its meant, and not pick it all to bits and write me a very sarky reply.

Well Doris I must wind up. If I hear nothing more from you I'm sure you won't be annoyed if I wish you a real jolly Christmas and the best of everything in life. Please ask Mick to write to me, I know you can influence him more than I can.

With kindest regards believe me to be Mick's very sincere brother, – Geoff Swaff.

Although Geoff's letter was probably not the reason, the relationship between Mick and Dorritt came to an abrupt end. She stopped making entries into her diary, tried to rip out the firmly glued-in photographs from her 'Mick' album, in the end scribbling furiously over them. She was then well integrated into the Swaffield family, friends of both young and old, and a frequent visitor to many of their homes. Soon she reunited with Frank (Tony), the elder brother, then working in Manchester.

'Sunday, 11 November 1929   217, rue du Faubourg St Honoré, Paris

Tony chéri

This will probably be rather a rotten letter cos its past mid-night and writing is not the form of amusement I excel in at the 'witching' hour.

Thanks so much for sending on my gloves and for all your letters – tu me gâte beaucoup trop and you're rashly extravagant with stamps.

Yesterday I went to a 21st birthday party – and – I blush as I write it – but we drank ONLY TEA – I s'pect now I'm less than the dust beneath your great big feet.

In the evening I looked up Geoff – he was all on his ownsome. The flat … looks simply topping – the salon is the snugliest looking place I've seen for years and I bet on occasions it lives up to its appearance.

Today I've been for tea – there was quite a crowd – lots of men you probably don't know and two girls you do – Julia Woolf and Alice Wollams and of course Geoff's little playmate. The conversation dropped on various unsavoury subjects including you – and 'tween them they tore your reputation absolutely to shreds – among other things 'twas said that, when in Paris, you averaged four engagements a year. Et aprés tous ça Geoff announced to the whole crowd that you and I were to be married before Xmas and addressed me as sister-in-law throughout the afternoon. I suppose he must have received news from Fareham but he swears he just guessed – so I told him it was a jolly bad guess and left it at that. En tous cas, c'est bien enneyeux [irksome] – made me feel like one of Bluebeard's wives.

The cocktails were good, I drank 3 – so, couple yesterday's fall back, how do I stand with you now?

I'm enjoying life very much. I've so much time to look after myself that I simply don't know how I'll manage when I've a house, an Aberdeen, a canary and – Oh I nearly forgot – a husband to look after.

I hope that you will soon get a new job – p'raps you will have some replies to your applications before writing again.

Je tu dis 'Bonsoir' je suis presque endormi – et si je ne me couche pas toute de suite, je vais tomber sur terre. Dorritt'

MAYFAIR MAGAZINE, AUGUST, 1928 – MAYFAIR'S PARIS LETTER – By SOIFFIELD OF PARIS

Mes chères   *Paris au mois de Juillet, 1929*

I am convinced that Paris this season is smarter than she has been for any season since the war. The rue de la Paix is the pre-war rue de la Paix, again. One can now walk down town in the region of the Plâce Vendome, a little before the lunch hour, and then again in the late afternoon, and see more smartly dressed women than have been seen for years.

… I am having a little cocktail jacket made in silver lace to brighten up my black satin. It will carry me on for a week or two. Then I intend have a Louise Boulanger model to make a real splash when I get to Deauville … I am thrilled at the prospect, especially as Jean Patou has just sent me up two new bathing suits and wraps. One is a two-piece suit in his new Capucine color. It is a kind of burnt orange-peel in shade and will look just too marvellous against my skin. The bathing wrap is in the same shade, lined with a canary yellow sponge cloth …

… One thing I noticed during my short visits to Deauville, mes chéres, was that nearly every smart woman went about hatless in order that the sea breezes should catch her curls … the idea is to have the hair terribly flat and straight in front with masses of curls caught up in a comb in the nape of the neck … it is not a general thing, and there is every likelihood that shorn tresses will hold sway for many moons to come, but there is that tendency, to have just a little more behind.

Bien, bien a vous mes chères ———————— SOIFFIELD.

An Edwardian felt hat with feather mount, worn with a black veil drawn under the chin, and (on right) a brimmed hat of velvet and felt cut up on one side to show the hair.

1932 – Daily Mail – Curls and Rolls Out of Date. The model is Jean Swaffield, wife of Mick, Geoff's younger brother

NEWS CUTTING – 1933 – Daily Mail
EDWARDIAN HATS NEXT – AND VEILS – BOWLER CROWNED AUTUMN STYLE
by Evelyn Irons – Editress of the Women's Page

After the Victorian hats of last summer, fashion is now toying with the Edwardian period. Such, at any rate, is the view of a young Englishman, Mr R G Swaffield, who has arrived from Paris to design model hats in London. In his first collection … he showed a straw canotier trimmed with what looked like a band of steel but was actually cellophane ribbon, a Balmoral bonnet – hand crocheted by himself – in short lengths of putty-beige raffia and a joke of a hat, a skit on the feminine craze for boaters. This was actually a man's stiff brimmed straw hat with a bandanna handkerchief covering the crown.

Tuesday, July 27, 1937   THE DAILY MIRROR

How Do You Like These

3 Mad Hats!

Designed by 3 VERY SENSIBLE Hatters

Designers: Top, Nina Batchelor, left, Aage Thaarup and right, Jeff

THE DAILY MIRROR – TUESDAY JULY 27th, 1937
How do you like these 3 MAD HATS!
– DESIGNED BY 3 VERY SENSIBLE HATTERS – AAGE THAARUP, NINA BATCHELOR AND JEFF

Anne Edwards Our Fashion Expert Says:

'Hats are going forward and upward. On and on and on go the brims, up and up and up go the crowns. We know! We interviewed London's three leading creators of hat fashion, and persuaded them to tell us the secrets of next autumn.

HERE'S THE ONE THAT JEFF BUILT, AND HE SAYS: "It's a lovely thing that fits close to your head and then suddenly flares out wide at the top like a chef's hat." Jeff breaks you into the high crown movement from shallowness to height, and he gets wonderful effects with drapes, pleats and folds that slope up from right to left, so that you can get used to your high crown one side at a time.'

Jeff proudly surveys the finished job, seen in process of creation in pictures below. When he's finished, a couple of pins may be standing between it and non-existence. Helpers have to get busy at once make the hat up in permanent form.

MAN WHO MAKES HATS ON HIS HEAD

1937 – The Weekly Illustrated – The Man who Makes Hats on His Head

When he's not making hats Jeff is a great out-door person. Loves motor cycling, gardening. Fills show-rooms with floral displays from his own gardens.

Hat is being tried on on Peggy Cochrane, famous broadcasting artist and composer, who is one of Jeff's many artist clients.

Sue Swaffield [Lindley], daughter of Mick and Jean Swaffield wrote: 'Geoff was always my best and dearly loved Uncle, though we sadly lost contact after my parents separated. As a very little girl at our home, Colesgrove in Hertfordshire, he visited us frequently on day trips from London, often on his motorbike and sometimes with his friend, Francis, riding pillion. Mish Lockwood was much in evidence in those days too. He must have been in the RAF at the time.

Immediately after the war he designed children's clothes for a company called UMECO. He invited me to model, and I was paid to pose for Queen, Harpers Bazaar and other lesser publications. There was a big spread in Picture Post where he adapted the Chelsea Dustmen's hat as a fashion statement. Then came the Pack Hat in

1945 UMECO days, Susan Swaffield models in a childrens playground

the early fifties. Both Jean, my mother, and I had them. They were wonderful – a sort of tiered soft hat that you could pack, but frightfully elegant. I had navy, and Mummy a black one she wore for years – often with a brooch pinned to it. For Jane Shepherd's [Bea's daughter] and Mike Brettell's wedding, I wore a pretty turquoise dress with a rather dreary donkey coloured coat, and Geoff designed me a smashing hat using both colours.

He had a tiny flat at 39 Kinnerton Street which I visited when I was about 9 or 10. It only had one main room with a three-quarter size bed. I remember a ghastly silence when I asked, "Where does Uncle Francis sleep?" I had, of course, no idea of their orientations, and didn't have until much later. Francis was a little man with curly hair and always smiling, he and Geoff were together a long time. Geoff was an excellent cook and taught me to make a real tossed French salad step by step. I still remember his omelettes.'

The Past on Its Way to the Future
Jeff, famous London milliner, sees a rosy future in a hat which is pretty ancient history. City Volunteers wore it in the Boer War and London dustmen ever since.

Westminster street cleaner inspires new hat design.

Jean and I often went to town for the day, and this usually included a visit to his salon at 35 Sackville Street, either for a quick cuppa, or a lunch outing. We would go to a restaurant in Piccadilly called 'Monseigneur' and this was my introduction to really good food. It was not over-elaborate, and always delicious. Back in the salon in a partitioned off area, Rita, his little seamstress who always seemed overworked, sat with her horn-rimmed specs perched on her nose, sewing, pressing, steaming and trimming hats.

Geoff's clients included quite a few celebrities from the theatre and film world. We think he designed the hats for 'The Tales of Hoffman', and certainly designed some for a stage show for Patricia Dainton. My best moment was meeting Ann Todd, a faithful customer, she was a lovely lady – always delightful. He enjoyed making hats for her, swinging into his flamboyant Jeff mannerisms as she tried them on.

Jean loved hats, and now and again, he would design her one to go with an outfit that old Mr Symons, her tailor, was making. When she died, Jean still had a stack of wonderful millinery which, I believe, were later much used by the Aldeburgh Dramatic Society.

At the outbreak of war Geoff joined the RAF as a Squadron Leader. His job was that of a liaison officer between the British and the French.

Letter – June 4th, 1940 – Telephone Censorship, Faraday Building, E.C.4.

TO WHOM IT MAY CONCERN

'This is to state that Mr. R. G. Swaffield has been employed in the International Telephone Censorship as a Deputy Assistant censor for the past eight months and, for the past six months, has acted as my right-hand man.

Mr. Swaffield is a brilliant linguist, has great organising ability and I cannot do more than thoroughly recommend him for any appointment for which he may apply – particularly in connection with Intelligence Work.'

W.F. Stirling – Lt. Colonel, Censor.

Tom Carding, Geoff's cousin, said that all the work at Telephone Censorship was a cover-up, and that Geoff was a brilliant spy, using his French airs and linguist skills to their height. "He had this tremendous affinity for Les Français and anything French." Before the war, together with Mick and Jean and others, he would travel South in the summer and they all stayed at Les Sablettes, in the Golf Hotel. There was a bar close by, run for many years by a Madame Louis. Susan wrote, '… In 1954 when I was 18, together with a schoolfriend, we crossed the Channel in her parents' Citroën. We drove across France to Les Sablettes, and I remember a great welcome from Madame Louis who was then very old.

Family visits to France, Geoff with Jean Swaffield

Geoff was such a character, his French was so perfect, and his whole attitude and mien very Parisian. I loved him dearly. I wish I had seen him just before his death, but we had lost touch since my parents broke up. I did manage to send flowers to his funeral. He always called me Suze, and I signed the card 'Suze'.

The Tony Swaffields lived in North Wales during the fifties. Uncle Geoff used to visit us quite often in Old Colwyn. He was lively and his motor bike was a big draw. I [Natalie]

remember going for an exciting ride on his pillion, whizzing up and down the Welsh mountains, holding on for dear life. Before he left for London, he would ask for a cut potato, and this he would smear all over the outside of his goggles. He said that it stopped the raindrops from sticking and obscuring his vision.

He also designed one or two dresses for me, one was of blue wool with small metal studs round the collar and sleeves. He kindly involved me in his fashion world. I had embroidered a ration book cover at school, and he used the pattern for a textile design.

1946 – Aber Falls, North Wales – Dorritt, Geoff, Nigel and Natalie

News Cutting – August 15th, 1946 **Evening Standard** – By Our Fashion Reporter

'CHILDREN'S FASHIONS FLOWN TO COPENHAGEN

A collection of autumn and winter clothes for young people designed by Jeff has been bought and is already being shown in Copenhagen's top ranking store. Smartest frocks for youngsters aged four to fourteen are strictly tailored, some dresses have snappy little boleros. Scarcity of nannies and nursery maids accounts for the absence of white linen or muslin collars and cuffs.

HER RATION CARD

Rayon piqué batiste, rayon serge and rayon linen are materials suggested suitable for spring outfits. For next summer there is a printed rayon pattern with oval pendants in dual colouring. It was inspired by the industry of an eight-year-old embroidress. She picked out the design on the white cotton damask in coloured threads, and made it into a ration card holder. Her design is now being used for fashion purposes.'

Geoff remained in close contact with Jean, and was very good about taking her to theatres, particularly to Covent Garden. A year before he died, prematurely, we think of cerebral haemorrhage, he wrote to Tony from his new home – Loom House Flat, Dedham, Essex.

Dated Saturday eve January 14th 1956

'… I got up to London very late on Christmas Eve completely whacked, and spent most of the following week in bed, no flue [sic] or cold, just complete exhaustion and no voice, due I think to trying to cram in a lifetime of running a store into six months, and knowing so little about it all. … Have been in London Tues, Wed and Thursday night this week moving out of Hyde Pk St, and getting my stuff sent down here, but still have nowhere to put it. … Have kept a room in Francis' new flat which is just by Whiteleys, all very modern, central heating and boiling constant hot water, but no character.

I had a most interesting travelogue from Nigel over Christmas, he is a very lucky boy to have been able to have done all he has, at almost government expense. I now feel much better, and seem to be living mainly on vitamin K, which I trust is going to make my blood swirl around a bit more than it has lately … haven't been able to ride [his motorbike] the past few days, roads have been hellish, have a two mile walk after I get off the bus, and seem to have come out without my torch tonight. Happy birthday, and I trust all goes well, Love to you all, Geoff.'

NEWS CUTTING – 1957

SWAFFIELD – On March 25, 1957 at St Richard's Hospital, Chichester, Richard Geoffrey (Jeff Designs), after a short illness. Funeral – Fareham Cemetery 2pm Friday. Flowers by 12 noon to Messrs S Newbury, undertakers, Warsash, Hants. Memorial service in London to be announced later.

1938 – Fareham, Frank (Tony) Geoff, Mick and Hugh

Alan Carding Swaffield was the third son of Eck and Florrie. A pretty, round-faced baby, he spent his cradle days in frilly dresses, and lacy gowns. Perhaps he was named after his father's baby brother, Alan, who died in 1878. He was certainly named Carding to carry on his mother's surname and, like his brother Geoff, he visited and remained close to the Carding family in Nottinghamshire from a young age, afterwards making visits to Combs Farm with Jean, and little Susan. He was called Alan briefly as a child, never Carding, afterwards and always Mick or Mike, by his wife Jean and friends.

Mick appears in many of the Bedford family photographs. He visited often, with his parents, and went to gatherings in the Lansdowne Road garden, on picnics at Gypsy Lane and, met up with the Dick Swaffields at Catesby. He was a lively child with a cheeky smile, full of fun and full of beans. Mick had a sparkle in his eye, a penchant for naughtiness, a spirit of adventure, a zest for life. He was the epitome of everyone's favourite uncle, much loved in family circles. With a passion for cars and aeroplanes, he was a keen motor racing fan. With young Susan in tow, he was often seen at Brands Hatch, Silverstone and Goodwood, and keenly followed the careers of Mike Hawthorn and Stirling Moss. He never missed the Farnborough Air Show. He owned his first Lancia probably in the early thirties. After the war the only models available were those at the Earls Court Motor Show, where he would purchase one off the stand, and resell the previous year's at a profit.

c1920s – Mick in his AV Monocar. It weighed a quarter of a ton and was only 2'6" wide, with an air-cooled twin-cylinder engine behind the rear wheels. The torpedo body was built of plywood, papier mâché and mahogany, usually painted red with black mudguards

His first marriage was brief and childless, and then he met Jean Gordon-Stewart, daughter of Nellie [née Cullum] and Jack [JWE] Gordon-Stewart from Perthshire. Jack qualified as a dental surgeon in Edinburgh and practised in Suffolk. He collected antiques and drove one of the first cars in East Anglia. It is believed he drove at Brooklands, and won a silver rose bowl. Jean was musically talented, and a leading light in 1921–22 with her father, in the Ipswich Gilbert and Sullivan Operatic Society. After school she spent time in London and Paris, and later in the South of France.

c 1907 Suffolk, Walberswick beach, L–R, Jean, Granny Cullum, Grand-father Henry W Cullum, brother Malcolm [foreground] and Mother Nellie Gordon-Stewart on right

Mick and Jean married in St Ethelburga's, Bishopsgate, and held a reception at 17 Berkeley Square, Geoff's hat design salon. As Mick was divorced, the marriage caused a stir within the Church. The Vicar, Rev Dr Geikie-Cobb was accused by the Dean of Finchley of '... defying the ruling of the Bishop in consenting to officiate at the marriage of a divorced person ...' In his erudite reply Geikie-Cobb quotes the Judicature Act of 1925 and says '... the Bishops are advising illegally, and can render themselves liable to action in the High Court ...' St Ethelburga's was a tiny 13th-century city church. It survived the Great Fire of London, started in 1666 in a Pudding Lane bakery, spreading as far west as The Temple. In three days it destroyed four-fifths of the City of London. St Paul's Cathedral and 86 other churches were wrecked, as well as 13,200 houses. By some miracle, fewer than 20 people lost their lives. St Ethelburga's also survived the WWII bombings, but was reduced to nothing by an IRA bomb in May 1993.

Mick and Jean's only child, Susan Mairi, was christened at St Ethelburga's wearing the Gordon-Stewart family robe, complete with a Jeff-design satin and lace bonnet. At the time Mick was working with Arrow Electrical Switches in West London. His boss was an American, George Seawright, who presented his baby goddaughter with a magnificent, if rather unsuitable, silver cigar box. Mick and Jean first lived in Kensington and then moved to Colesgrove Farm at Goff's Oak, Hertfordshire. During the General Strike in the thirties, Mick drove a tube train, and became very familiar with London's Underground System.

Tim [J E] Lindley and Susan Swaffield

The marriage foundered after many years. Jean moved to Walberswick to be near her family, and had many visits from Uncle Basil, who was always kindly and supportive. Mick then lived with Irene Giddings, who changed her name to Swaffield by Deed Poll, until he died from a series of strokes. His first big one occurred at Dial House near Farnham, probably due to excitement, as Susan and family were due from South Africa the following day. He was cremated at Enfield.

As a child, Susan had wonderful long thick hair which reached her waist. Whilst at St Nicholas School, Hemel Hempstead, she persuaded a junior matron to cut it all off. There had been no discussion, Jean had not been consulted, and a huge row ensued. After school, the last being Benenden in Kent, Susan studied in Geneva and then went to St James' Secretarial College in London.

Tim Lindley, her husband, joined Imperial Chemical Industries in Britain, after Repton and the Army. In the fifties he was transferred to South Africa as an expatriate, and later joined the local company AECI, humorously known as Africans, Europeans, Coloureds, Indians. He particularly enjoyed his job as Regional Manager Eastern Cape. Their first daughter, Sarah Ann was born in St Albans, but the other two, Amanda and David, arrived in South Africa, a country they all love for its scenic beauty. The little seaside town of Wilderness has provided idyllic

times. Each year they spent a month by the sea, with lazy days on the beach, swimming in the breakers and the lagoon. They had alfresco lunches, barbecues at night, the best melktarts from George Bakery, thick cream on the milk delivered in bottles with cardboard tops. Really, truly relaxing holidays which they can still enjoy as Sue and Tim are now settled in Wilderness.

1967 – The Lindley family, Sue, Amanda, Sarah Ann, Tim with David [foreground]

The children, and each one has commented on their parents' unfailing support and their mother's wonderful cooking, were educated in various Cape Town and Johannesburg schools, and only Amanda has moved away to America. Sarah Ann recalls, '… my father comforted me during nightmares and one, special memory, he took me to town [Cape Town] to see my 'eye-exercises' lady, Miss Tomkins, a tall woman with long red hair. On the way home, we always passed a jeweller with diamond tiaras in the window. One day Daddy took me in to try one on. It was the greatest moment of my life, and I was only eight. The magic wore off in a couple of years and, at ten, 'I was reduced to tears by long division.' She married Mike Wormald, Head of Department of Accounting, a University Professor. They have brought up various chocolate coloured Labrador dogs, and three active children. Sarah Ann describes herself as a 'full-time mother', with an interest in Interior Design, which was her training. Maybe the mothering was a result of being the eldest of three as, '… I remember fights with my sister, Manda, which I now regret as a waste of precious time, and doing a lot of looking after my little brother, David.'

Amanda, at 17, travelled to London on her own to investigate Montessori training. Finally she achieved a Bachelors in Geography and Journalism at Rhodes, Grahamstown. Later she travelled to Melbourne and gained a Masters in Geography and Hydrology. One of her happiest times was during a two year stint with the Department of Forestry in Stellenbosch,

Western Cape, South Africa. She lived in a little cottage nestled in the Jonkershoek Valley, with superb views of the immense mountains surrounding the Forestry research station. She met her husband, Andrew Stone, when he was lecturing in Melbourne and they married in New Hampshire, USA. Andrew already had four children, and the family increased when he and Amanda had two daughters, Anna and Jessica. Amanda has followed a career, mainly

2002 – Standing L–R, Mike, Andrew, Simon and Emma Wormald. Seated Sue Lindley, Sarah Ann Wormald and Tim Lindley

with the University of New Hampshire Co-operative Extension Service, co-ordinating natural resource conservation assistance to local towns, and also co-ordinating the Master Gardener Volunteer program. She works from home, and is a genuine housewife, growing and preserving vegetables and fruit, and making sure the cookie tin is always full.

The Stones live in a pretty part of New Hampshire – Gilmanton Iron Works. The family enjoy camping holidays and, in the summer of 2000, they travelled to Nova Scotia and Prince Edward Island, famous for its potatoes. They visited the Bay of Fundy, home to the highest tidal range in the world. They biked all over the place, enjoyed the red sandy beaches and then travelled further north where they had to resort to walking, climbing and spotting bald eagles, similar to South African fish eagles. In the winter they go on family ski-ing trips, but the girls favourite sport seems to be very competitive soccer.

David Lindley had to enrol in national service and chose the South African Navy. He served on the mine sweeper SAS Pretoria and then studied at Rhodes University in Grahamstown. Zoology was his choice, and he obtained an Honours Degree. History during the Lindley tenure in South Africa has changed so much, with the assassination of Verwoerd, the bombing of Johannesburg Station, F W Botha negotiating with the ANC, the release of Nelson Mandela who became a real person, rather than a face in a newspaper, and the subsequent death of apartheid.

David Lindley, outnumbered by women, Ros (centre) and her two daughters

David and his wife, Ros – who has two grown-up daughters by a previous marriage – share a real love of the bush life, wine, food and their dogs. Travel is their main passion and

they back-packed to India – Rajasthan, and Ladakh in 1999. The poor value of the South African Rand inhibits serious world travel, but South Africa, and nearby Botswana, provide endless camping forays into the wilds. Both are ardent conservationists. David works in Wetlands and travels worldwide to conferences, becoming an expert in this important field. Wetlands are found from the tundra to the tropics and on every continent except Antarctica. They act as natural sponges, trapping and releasing surface water, rain, snowmelt and flood, lowering flood heights and reducing erosion. They are an important brake on surface water, that runs off from pavements and buildings, reducing waterlogging of crops. With today's climate change, the correct management of worldwide wetlands is vital.

Perhaps lorries, lorry driving and the haulage business were instilled into Hugh and his family at the time [1904] of his dramatic birth in the cab of a lorry, with his father assisting as makeshift midwife, whilst they dashed to the hospital. Hugh and Margaret remained in Hampshire living in Brook Lane, Sarisbury Green, an area which had acres of strawberry fields providing employment for local families. They had three boys, Richard born shortly after WWII broke out, Malcolm and then Kevin in 1952. Richard became a haulage contractor and married Pat Tebbett of Titchfield. Their wedding was at St Mary's Hook, Warsash on 1 September 1964. A year later Karen was born, and Jon followed in 1972. It was not until 1993 that Karen changed her name by Deed Poll to Karen Margaret, in loving memory of her grandmother.

1935 – Hugh and Margaret on their wedding day

Malcolm and Kevin

Kevin with his mother Margaret

Not much of a one for writing letters, Hugh managed this epistle on 15 December 1980 in straggly block letters:

My dear Natalie, Thank you for your very newsy letter. And am so glad all the family are doing so well – but you must all have mixed feelings about pulling your roots again [the Wheatley family were off to Sierra Leone for six years after 14 years in India, and 2 in London].

All the boys and families are well, Malcolm & Kevin send all good wishes, and very often talk about our meeting at Emery Down with your Mother. Well my dear must call it a day —— this writing is killing me!!

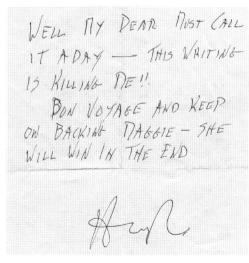

1980 – Extract from Hugh's letter

Bon Voyage and keep on backing Maggie [Thatcher] – she will win in the end ——Hugh

2000 – Karen and Richard Swaffield

Karen was married to Anthony Griffiths, who has travelled the world as an electrical aeronautical engineer. His times away overcame his times at home, and the relationship took the strain of his long absences, the marriage ending in divorce in 2002. Karen has had times of poor health, and her mother more so. Both have determination and humour to overcome illness, and they share a fighting spirit. Jon married Helen Dean, and a much welcomed first grandchild is on the way for Richard and Pat.

Like his brothers, Malcolm is full of fun. In his teens, having left school early, '… I used to help Dad on the mobile fruit and veg round, and also dig the garden. When Mum went with him, I did a bit of housework, and peeled the potatoes ready for dinner when they came home.' Malcolm remembers stories of his grandfather's shipwreck off The Needles, 'We had a picture of it hanging in the hall,' he wrote. He, too, joined the Merchant Navy and travelled to Australia, New Zealand, Japan, Canada, USA and other countries, spending most of his sea life on the SS Oriana. 'I left the sea to marry Bridget Toland from Donegal, Ireland in 1967, and then joined Richard driving lorries. Malcolm and Bridget have three children, Keileen, Shaun and Darren, but were divorced in 1987. Malcolm describes this as – my downfall.'

Malcolm and Bridget's son, Shaun

Kevin was known affectionately by his parents as 'Post War Credit', and has always been loved and supported by his elder brothers. Dogged by epilepsy, he found he had to stand his own ground at Sarisbury Secondary School where he enjoyed wood-work and science, later training as a motor mechanic. He will never forget the day his mother died, 'She collapsed in the arms of Malcolm and myself as we walked her into the entrance of Southampton Hospital.' In 1991 Kevin married Maureen Annis, twelve years his senior and the mother of four boys. They have settled near Yeovil, not far from Kevin's first-known ancestors' delightful hamlet of East Chelborough. Maureen was educated in

Richard, Kevin and Maureen Swaffield, 1991

Bedford, and enjoyed music and sports, '… I couldn't keep my hands off the piano keys …'. When they are able, Kevin and Maureen thoroughly enjoy holidays abroad.

Jeff ~ Designs

Chapter 13

BEDFORDSHIRE ~ THE AUNTS
Picnics, parties, weddings and events

H R J Swaffield 1839–1909 and Emmeline Jepson 1842–1922

Emmeline (Minnie)	Henry	Exton (Eck)	Norman	Charlotte Ethel (Bridget)	Ella	Dorothy (Dot)	Beatrice (Queenie)	Alan	Hugh	Richard (Dick)	Hilda (Jo)	Mildred (Kitty)	Basil
1867	1868	1869	1871	1872	1874	1875	1876	1878	1879	1880	1882	1884	1885
1934	1964	1950	1958	1965	1945	1962	1967	1878	1918	1937	1965	1973	1972

'The Aunts' are an integral part of our story. Everyone has aunts. Crotchety, batty, sweet, nosy, maddening and adorable. The six nicknamed Beaminster aunts – Rose, Jen, Het, Emily, Nell and Nancy all kept in touch, shared their twelve offspring, travelled away from Dorsetshire, Nancy as far away as Tasmania, and one of Het's daughters to New Zealand. But they never forgot their roots. The seven Bedfordshire aunts were close, three remained unmarried, the rest producing only nine children between them. A poor showing after their own mother's total of fourteen, of which thirteen survived. But the nephews and nieces kept in constant touch, and the maiden aunts were very special people in the lives of the whole family. All 'The Aunts' are remembered with enormous affection.

c1920s – 'The Seven Aunts' – Queenie, Jo, Minnie, Ella, Dot, Ethel and Kitty

Eight of the children were called differently from their given name. Aunt Ethel's story ties up with her elder sister, Minnie, and the Parker family. She was christened Charlotte, nicknamed Bridget and probably answered to anything. She was a forceful lady – 'a bit of a martinet' – and remained a spinster. Full of courage, she had an adventurous spirit and shook away the parental cloak and the confines of Landsdowne Road to travel abroad. First she went to India, had several unfortunate experiences, but was not put off. Travel was in her blood. In the late twenties she ran an English tea shop in Tangier, Morocco and then in San Remo. Queenie took Dot and Jo there for a much needed holiday in the sun. To her young nieces, Ethel hinted tantalisingly about her past but, was a real spinster, worried about everything, and remembered affectionately as '… a well preserved woman, quite pretty, a true Swaffield, tough, humorous and a survivor …' Her niece, Betty, daughter of

1907 – Charlotte Ethel (Bridget) Swaffield

her younger sister Kitty, remembers her aunt coming to stay with them at 30 Cardington Road. "She insisted on dosing us with disgusting little cubes of sugar swamped with cinnamon to 'keep us well'"

c1894 – Portrait of Ella

Ella was usually called Ella, occasionally Nell. She was the sixth child, sandwiched between Ethel and Dot. In 1909 she travelled to India to visit her sister Ethel. It was there that the girls heard the news, after weeks, that their father had suddenly died. On her return home she married Fred Lampard from Rochester in Kent in 1912. He was 10 years her junior.

Two sons were born, Peter and Derrick. Peter was handicapped and died in early childhood. Derrick is remembered as competitive. As a young man he used to turn up at his Uncle Dick's at Catesby with a tent tied to his back. Dick was old-fashioned enough not to want his young nephew 'sleeping rough' in the grounds. Derrick became a railway engineer and went to India. He married Rosemary Hill from Derbyshire and had two children, Peter and Michelle. Like Ella's brothers, Eck and Norman, Fred was with the Merchant Marine Service. He served on the SS Mongolian of Greenock as Third Engineer. He was another family victim of WWI when his ship was sunk on 23 June 1917. He was thirty-three. His name, which is Huguenot, is also on the Alameda War Memorial at Ampthill. Ella was a sweet woman, widowed at 42. Derby had become her home, but she returned to Ampthill where she became a keen church worker. She lived next to Dot and Jo at 'Edensor' in The Avenue before she died. In her Will she left some money to her sisters and the rest to her son Derrick.

1912 – Fred Lampard and Ella Swaffield

Margaret Dorothy was always known as Dot. She was 26 years old when she heard of the death of Queen Victoria on January 22nd, 1901.

Victoria died at Osborne and her coffin was carried to London – '… ten miles of warships line the Solent and slowly, silently passed between them the Royal Yacht. The coffin on the deck was in full view of all, covered with a pall of white satin with the Royal Standard thrown across it. Boom! Boom! go the guns … The sun is setting in a mass of flame and its last shafts flash of red upon the sparkling crown that lies upon the coffin." Great Britain was in deep mourning.

North Norfolk – jumping rocks

The new King Emperor Edward VII, aged 60, was extrovert and pleasure loving, and relieved the late Victorian gloom until he too died in 1910. During his short reign he ruled over a vast British Empire. The glittering crowned heads at Victoria's funeral, soon became leaders of hostile, heavily-armed alliances that split the Continent. Over all this hung the threat of the 1914–18 war but, before that, there was a brief spell of 'the golden age'. Consumer products such as Pear's Soap, Player's Cigarettes and Bovril were advertised in the Daily Mail. Motor cars chugged along the lanes, houses were lit with electricity, mad men flew into the sky in aeroplanes. There was a female population imbalance of over a million, and many women were not marrying. For Dot life was sedentary and, whilst walking in Ampthill Park one day, she had the unfortunate experience of being spat at by a llama. She was covered in green, juicy slime and rather upset.

Families began to enjoy seaside holidays, there were clumsy bathing machines from

Friends and family, North Norfolk coast – Dot 2nd left front

which women discreetly splashed, clad from head to toe in soggy beachwear. The Swaffs tended to enjoy their sea air from the wilder coast of North Norfolk.

Dot was carried off to the beach with the rest of the family, but probably spent more time wiping the noses and bottoms of her little nephews and nieces than having a good time. Dot was the archetypal 'middle child', the 7th out of fourteen. Dot once remarked, "Mother was always pregnant, we used to get into bed with her whilst she was resting in the afternoons, it was the only time she could give us a cuddle."

1908 – Emmeline Pankhurst rousing the crowds in London

Dot heard snippets of news of Emmeline Pankhurst and the suffragettes. Her devotees were businessmen's wives and ambitious factory girls who gathered in the Pankhurst Manchester sitting room to plot for a fairer future. They chained themselves to railings, had themselves posted in parcels to Number 10 Downing Street, and burnt slogans 'Votes for Women' in acid on golf courses. In 1913 Emily Davison hurled herself to her death under King George V's horse at the Derby. It was not until 1918 that all men over the age of eighteen had the right to vote, and it took another decade before women over the age of twenty-one had the same political liberty.

1909 – Mildred [Kitty] Swaffield in her bridal outfit

In 1909, Dot's youngest sister, Kitty then aged twenty-five, flew the nest and married Fred Potter, just two months after the death of their father. Dot was then thirty-four, she continued to live at home with Jo until their mother, Emmeline, died in 1922. Soon afterwards the two sisters moved, under the auspices of elder brother Henry, to Ampthill.

Most of HRJ and Emmeline's offspring turned out hooky-nosed and bony, but Beatrice, who was always called Queenie, was the plump, pretty, comfy one. In 1902, aged twenty-six, she married Thomas Lewin Smith who was born at Tilbrook, Hampshire, and educated at Wellingborough. He was the gregarious eldest son of wealthy farmer and corn merchant, Thomas Henry Smith, who retired near Queenie's parents in Lansdowne Road, Bedford. Lansdowne Road today has its large houses split into flats and residential homes for old people but, in those days it was described as having '… detached red-bricked houses on a tree-lined avenue in deeply respectable Bedford. There was nothing ornate about the houses in the street; they were designed for large middle-class families with more aspirations than cash …' When Tom's father died he left nearly £30,000 plus properties. He remembered his clerk and his two bailiffs, and Crown Farm, Great Staughton was left to son Tom, and New Barns, Carlton to son Sidney Smith. The farms at Croftsbrook, Northamptonshire, and Staughton Moor in Huntingdonshire were shared between his daughters Ina Jackson and Emma Ardron.

Tom entered his father's business after leaving school. He was eventually made a partner of the firm. A keen sportsman, he played cricket and tennis and was a member of the Bedford [De Parys] Bowling Club. Conkering was a sport he particularly enjoyed. There were plenty of horse chestnuts dropping in the garden and '… Uncle Tom always had a conker on a piece of string, the biggest and best making his determination to smash everyone else's conkers more acute …'. He is remembered as an affable fellow who enjoyed a drink or two. He would often bring his friends home, quite late at night, and continue to celebrate whatever needed to be celebrated, leaving his false teeth on the mantelpiece before retiring to bed.

Queenie's wedding is evocative of the frivolous Edwardian influence. Her four bridesmaids each wear lavish head pieces festooned with ostrich feathers, black velvet neck bands, long

dresses with frills and ruffles at the hem, and carry luxurious trailing bouquets stuffed with scented blooms. This was the time of The Season, of banquets and balls, receptions and of much social gathering. Life in Bedfordshire was quieter, but the five younger Swaffield girls were much in demand for parties, picnics and dances.

1902 – The wedding of Beatrice (Queenie) Swaffield and Thomas Lewin Smith; L–R, Emma Ardron [Tom's sister], Ella Swaffield, Queenie the bride, Sidney Smith [Tom's brother], Tom, Jo and Dot Swaffield

Below: 1919 – Picnic at Steppingly Woods – Queenie, her son Lewin, Dot, Jo, Norman, Kitty, Fred and Hilda (Jimmy)

Tom and Queenie lived at 12 Cardington Road and had two children – Lewin and Heather. Lewin who, as a little boy, was known as Doodie, sadly died of liver cancer when he was nineteen. When it was known that his illness was terminal, sawdust was scattered on the road outside his house so that he would not be disturbed by horses hooves. He was a

popular young man, and his tragic death shocked his many family and friends. Dorritt Williams attended the funeral at St Mary's Church, three days after Lewin died, and kept the Order of Service in her box of treasures.

Cousin Bardie went to Bedford High School and lived with Auntie Queenie, Uncle Tom and Heather at 12 Cardington Road, going home to Catesby, some thirty miles or more, for the holidays. "Auntie Queenie was an absolute dear, and very fond of picnics," she said, "But Uncle Tom didn't enjoy them at all. Uncle Fred loved them, so did Aunt Kit. So they used to scoop Queenie, Heather and I up and take us to Gypsy Lane, Badby Woods or Cobblers Lane near Ampthill. We used to dam the streams with mud, stones and twigs."

During WW II, when Bardie was older, she and Queenie went to visit the Aunts in Ampthill but, on returning, found there were no buses to take them back to Bedford.

"We'll have to thumb a lift," said Bardie purposefully.

Queenie was more reticent, but her humour came to the

In Loving Memory

OF

THOMAS LEWIN SMITH,

Died May 19th, 1925,

Aged 20 Years.

ST. MARY'S CHURCH,
MAY 22nd, 1925.

1925 – Thomas Lewin Smith died aged 20 years, son of Tom and Queenie Smith

fore when she realised that they had to get home. Bardie was quite spotty then, and Queenie had heavy legs which she joked about, "If they look at my face and your legs we'll get a lift," she said cheerfully, "But if it's my legs and your face, we'll be here all day!" When her sisters, Jo and Dot came to visit, Queenie would herald guests into the front room and say, "Come on in and meet the Three Graces."

1907 – Tom Smith

Bardie was never sure whether she should take Uncle Tom's betting telegrams to the Post Office for him, but he paid her half-a-crown, so she decided it was worth the risk. On Sunday evenings, during term time, she and Heather, Tom and Queenie would visit his parents in Lansdowne Road where Bardie was requested to play the piano, "I got half-a-crown for that as well," she laughed, "So I played the piano!" Clifford visited Tom's parents whilst they were still farming at Staughton. "I was quite small, and it was when Mother and Father went on their caravan holidays, and I was boarded out with Auntie Queenie for a couple of weeks.

Auntie Queenie

It was great, super food, a regular visit to the farm and a call at the Gery Arms on our return." The spare room where various children stayed over the years was '… next to Granny's …' and there was a big floppy bed and a massive clock in the hall that went Bong Bong Bong all through the night. It was obvious that Tom was a real character who had all the prim and proper ladies shaking their heads and muttering, "Poor Queenie, poor Queenie, she does have a difficult time." His farming terminology was rich, and he referred to his pre-harvest oats as '… brown as a fox's arse …', this said whilst cooling his tea in his saucer and sucking noisily. Fond of verse one of his favourites was:

> Listen! Listen! the cat's a'pissin.
> Where? Where? Under the chair.
> Hasten Jason, fetch a basin
> No! No! Fetch a Po!
> Too late, too late
> The carpet's in a dreadful state
> Poor, poor pussy could not wait.

Cousins Beryl and Betty Potter also went to Bedford High, an imposing red brick building in the centre of town. Betty was a sickly child growing into a healthy adult. She can hardly remember spending a whole term at school and always had something wrong with her. "I was brought up on liver," she said resignedly, "Short of blood they said." During the summer they bandaged her legs to keep the sun off them. When she was fourteen it was discovered that she had an infected appendix, just about to burst, which had been poisoning her whole body. Once removed, she was well again. Betty and Heather were almost like sisters and had great fun together in their childhood. There was a little sibling jealousy however, "Heather was always

given money for her birth-days," said Betty, "And I was always given a book. Why didn't they give me money too?" Heather, Beryl and Betty often visited the Dick Swaffield's at Catesby and Betty remembers smoking in the Catesby Woods. "We salvaged old cigar butts and bits of cigarette, and stuffed them into clay pipes."

Basil, Jimmy and Clifford often visited Catesby too. And they had picnics galore. Betty Potter remembers with

1919 – A Swaffield mix – L–R adults, Norman, Kitty, Mother Emmeline, Basil, Dot, Queenie, Mick [Eck's 3rd son], Jo and Eck, L–R children, Betty Potter, Heather Smith and Beryl Potter

pleasure, "The whole Swaffield family was, had been, were, will be mad on picnics, and many were memorable fun. When we were in Bedford or Ampthill all the Aunts used to come. There was a stream. Once Bardie sat in a very wet cow pat. She was full of tears about her 'dirty botty'. Uncle Basil rescued her by picking her up and washing her knickers in the stream before hanging them on the car radiator to dry. Eck's sons, Tony, Geoff & Mick particularly, were often around when the picnics took place, as was Dorritt Williams, who knew all three. She is remembered as being thrown into a bed of nettles and screeching with fright, "Dorritt was after one of those boys. They were a handsome lot, and always larking about. We knew she'd get one in the end."

1929 – Bardie poses with the airship directly above her head

While Bardie was at Queenie's, on October 5th 1930, the R101 disaster occurred. There is a photograph of Bardie with the huge airship over her head. "My cousin, Heather Smith, took the photograph in 1929 during flight trials." The R101 was known as the 'Ship of Dreams', and as an 'Elegant Flying Ocean Liner'. After the 1920s depression people needed dreams, and the airship was built by the government Royal Airship Works [formerly Shorts] at Cardington. It was over 700 ft long, with a gas capacity of 500 million cubic feet of highly inflammable hydrogen, but the R101 used heavy diesel engines which must have reduced the ship's buoyancy. Airships could carry a hundred passengers in comfort, and could fly for 48 hours without refuelling.

The framework, like a giant Meccano, was made by Boulton & Paul of Norwich, and covered by five acres of silver coloured linen. The women, who stitched and stretched the fabric, found it very hard work. When it was ready for trial it was steered out to its mooring mast, "You'd have to leave go or you'd have gone up with it," remembered Nellie Brewerton who had worked on the linen. Luxurious inside, it had royal blue carpet, mirrors and fine furniture. Tables were covered in damask and silver service waiters produced high class food. Ironically an after-dinner smoking room was provided. Eleven trials were made but the R101 did not fly well, the nose dipped and the ship surged, however it was imperative to get 'The Largest Flying Object Ever Conceived' launched. Lord Thompson, Viceroy of India, was anxious to arrive in Delhi in style, and he overloaded the airship with magnums of champagne and Persian carpets.

It was a miserable drizzling October night in 1930 when the R101 took off hesitantly with 54 aboard, "It was low over Bedford Bridge," said Nellie, "It could hardly get up." It crossed the Channel and there was thought of making an emergency

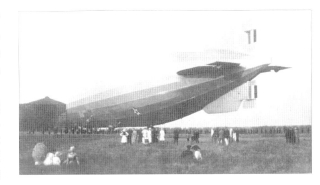
c 1920s, Cardington is visited by an American Naval airship

landing at Orly, but it lost height over Beauvais Ridge. There were strange wind patterns, and the outer material had absorbed too much rain. Airships float, and the R101 floated down erratically, "Let's get out!" screamed the terrified passengers, but the airship exploded and only six survived. "The crew were all young fellas," said Nellie, "It was the biggest thing since the Titanic in 1912, it was dreadful."

Clifford, Basil's boy, was just short of ten years old and remembers the launch, the bright lights over Goldington, and that Putnoe was '… all lit up …'. "It went off to India," he said, "And it was only next morning that the milkman told us it had come down in France.

Mrs Gent, the wife of the Chief Engineer, was a great friend of Mother's – it was an awful time."

There was a memorial service in London, and then the massed coffins were brought back to Bedford. Bardie and Heather sat with Auntie Queenie in the bay window as the cortège went past, "All the shops were closed and the flags were at half mast," said Bardie, "It was a personal tragedy for the town. Forty-five coffins went by, draped with forty-five Union Jacks, on their way to Cardington Church."

1938 – Heather Smith marries Sidney Banks

NEWS CUTTING – JUNE 1938 – MISS HEATHER SMITH MARRIED AT ST MARY'S

'Heather the only child of Mr. & Mrs. T Lewin Smith of 12 Cardington Road, Bedford, was married to Sidney Charles, the only son of Mr. & Mrs. C Banks of Waresley. It was an all-white wedding.

The church had been specially decorated by the bride's mother and aunts with lupins and mixed flowers. Mr F. Grey, head clerk to Mr Sidney Banks, and organist at Eaton Socon, was at the organ. The hymns were 'Lead us Heavenly Father' and 'Praise my Soul the King of Heaven'.

The bride was given away by her father. Her gown was of heavy satin duchesse, cut on very voluminous lines, with the train in one with the skirt and trimmed with rouleaux of same satin, the yoke, of net, finished with a slight heading. The veil was of ivory silk Malines net, held in place by a small coronet of orange blossom buds, and finished with sprays of old orange blossom which were worn by the bride's mother on her wedding day. An antique diamond, lent by her aunt, was her only ornament.

1938 – The Three Bridesmaids – Meg Watson, Mary Ardron, Barbara Swaffield

The three bridesmaids were her cousins, Miss Mary Ardron and Miss Barbara (Bardie) Swaffield, also Miss Margaret Watson [friend]. They wore dresses of white net posed over taffeta, with full skirts, pockets of the taffeta being filled with white apple blossom. They wore halo hats of white held under the chin by net and clusters of apple blossom. Their bouquets were of deep red roses, and they wore marquisite pendants, the gift of the bridegroom. The bride's mother was attired in an ensemble of dove grey carrés d'ombre, trimmed with lace to match, and grey fox cuffs. Her picture hat was of blueberry colour, with cyclamen and blue roses. She carried aquilegias to tone. Mr J. Hilton was best man.

After the reception, held at the Crofton Rooms, the bride and bridegroom left for their honeymoon, which is to be spent touring Scotland. Mrs. Banks wore a tailored suit of natural linen, with jade georgette blouse, gloves and bag, together with a Breton sailor hat of natural Baku, and shoes to match.

The bridal gown, bridesmaids' dresses, and hats, and the bride's travelling costume, together with the bride's mother's ensemble, were all made by Madame Hamilton.

About 50 guests, all the employees of Mr Sidney Banks, were entertained at 'The Cottage', Waresley on Friday evening to celebrate the occasion. Opportunity was taken of presenting Mr Banks with an electric standard lamp, and Mr Banks expressed thanks. The employees were granted a half holiday on Wednesday.'

Heather and Sidney had three children, Michael, Richard, and Judith.

DAILY TELEGRAPH – 1954 – 100–6 WINNER OF CESAREWITCH

'French Design, whose owner, Mr Sidney Banks, at one time tried to sell him for £50, won the Cesarewitch at Newmarket yesterday by three-quarters of a length from the outsider Earlswood, the jockey was Doug Smith. The win gave the Manon trainer, G Todd, his first Cesarewitch success. Mixed Vermouth was third, and the favourite, Mortification, tenth.

The race was worth £2,864 to the winner, which started 100–6. It was French Design's fourth Cesarewitch venture. He was the second seven-year-old to win the race during the last 30 years. The other was Flush Royal two seasons ago.'

Heather sadly died of breast cancer in 1979. Her sons, Michael and Richard, ran the public company of Sidney C Banks plc, one of the large agricultural merchanting companies in the UK. Both married. Michael and Ros have two daughters, Melanie a film producer, and Nicola a land agent. Richard and Susan have three children with diverse careers. Emma is an agent in the music industry, Benjamin runs a company importing fashion garments. He and his wife Amanda have a little girl, Betsy. William was in the Marines, is now a pilot and, in his spare time, renovates houses.

Jane Shepherd Brettell was, once, their au pair and remembers vividly, "... two rather naughty boys with a borrowed Nanny aged 17 (me), who lay on the floor helpless with giggles at their antics!". Judith is their sister, married at one time to John Clements, and running the family farm as well as being a Social Worker dealing with Child Protection. Judy has two children – Guy a paediatrician married to Claire a teacher, and Fiona who works in Quality Assurance, who married Neil Spavins in May 2003.

Everyone loved Jo, she was friendly and had a sweet nature, she was also profoundly deaf, but this did not dampen her kindly enthusiasm. Her deafness may well have been caused by a severe attack of measles in 1901, when she was nineteen. She was the sixth daughter and twelfth child. She had a great love of the outdoors and joined the Women's Land Army, an organisation founded in 1916 for

1907 – Portrait of Hilda Jane [Jo] Swaffield

the recruitment of women to work on farms during WWI. At its peak in September 1918 it had 16,000 members. It re-formed in June 1939, before the outbreak of WWII. Many Land Girls joined up to help the war effort and, by August 1943, 87,000 were employed in farm work. In her later years, clad in her favourite breeches, Jo supervised vegetable growing in Bedford gardens.

Bardie remembers Aunt Jo coming to stay often at The Red House in Catesby. "We made pretend little homes and Aunt Jo would fashion real washbasins with drainpipes so the water went down," she said. Jo has to be remembered by most of the younger cousins for her smiles and her wish to communicate. She taught everyone who wanted to learn, how to speak deaf and dumb language with their fingers, she was so anxious to get to know the children of the family. It is a skill once learnt that never disappears. Even the younger ones were taught, Natalie and Sue, Eck and Basil's granddaughters, by Jo herself. She was a good teacher and it didn't take long to chatter away, share smiles and giggles and make good friends. Mary, Bardie's daughter, was tutored in 'finger spelling' in the car by her mother, whilst they travelled to visit the Aunts in Ampthill.

1909 – Kitty Swaffield and Fred Potter on their wedding day

In 1909 the youngest daughter, Mildred [always known as Kitty] was married to Fred Potter of Muswell Hill and born within the sound of Bow Bells. His baby photographs, with blonde hair and blue eyes, were taken in Crouch End. Fred moved to Bedfordshire, trained at Cardington and shared a farm with Frank Hall. The family lived at 30 Cardington Road, a delightful home with a picturesque garden. Fred wooed Kitty on the River Ouse and bought her chocolates.

On her wedding day she wore a long white gown, a huge beribboned picture hat adorned her thick, piled up hair and she carried a luxuriant bouquet of white lilies. Fred was almost overshadowed by his bride. One wedding photograph of the happy couple includes a small and favourite teddy bear sitting by Fred's shiny shoes. Soon afterwards social parties were jazzing up with American music. Pianos tinkled with ragtime syncopated music, and toes tapped. But Kitty and Fred had to turn a deaf ear to these invigorating tunes as they then were busy with babies.

Two daughters were born – Beryl and Betty. Betty remembers her mother always as an elegant woman with a beautiful figure, "All the Swaffield girls had lovely hands," she remembered. Fred rode a motorbike and used to take Betty for rides sitting on the tank. Then he bought a Lanchester which had no clutch. Kitty drove this beauty, and Fred taught Betty to drive when she was old enough. As children they had a very happy time. Fred owned a boat called the Elf and sailed at Potter Heigham with George Parker on the Norfolk Broads. "Mother hated it," said Betty, "She couldn't swim."

1914 – Betty in her pram

Beryl had beautiful curly hair, Betty's was not so thick so she had it cut and shaped. When she came home her father turned her upside down and said, "Well, we can always use her as a mop!" Jane Brettell [Shepherd] spent lovely holidays with the Potters. "It was a wonderful established home and Aunt Kitty was sweet," she said, " Uncle Fred adored her. My mother, Bea Shepherd, was Kitty's niece, but only thirteen years younger. She used to pull her aunt's leg and nicknamed her Kitsy-Witsy." At her own home, Jane practised tennis against the garage door, "The noise drove my mother, Bea, mad," she said, "But when I went to the Potters there was a whole brick wall I could play against. It had nothing growing on it, and it was huge, I could hit balls to my heart's content." Jane often visited the larder and scooped the thick yellow cream from the top of the milk bowls, "There was a fig tree, and plump figs to eat and there was always the heady smell of fermenting plums."

East Runton – Fred, his girls and cousins

East Runton, on the North Norfolk coast, was a favourite place for summer holidays. The Potters and the Swaffs rented several houses and a large group would go there at the same time. Queenie and Tom Smith preferred Sheringham and went there summer after summer. There was much cooking, playing of games and plenty of fun and laughter. Fancy dress was a favourite occupation, and outfits were fashioned out of what they could find locally. Bardie went too.

Clement Spencer Thomas came on the scene when he took Heather to the Farmers' Ball at Bedford's Corn Exchange. Betty was there as well, and met Clement. Eventually they fell in love and married. Betty had been having trouble with a perforated ear drum, caused by chicken pox, so went to Switzerland where it healed completely. Clement called her his Swiss Miss. For a time she nursed at Middlesex Hospital in London. The Potter family worshipped at Elstow Church on the outskirts of Bedford. It was not in their parish, but the vicar had lived next door to them in Bedford and the church was always special.

1936 – Heather Smith and Beryl Potter, bridesmaids at Betty Potter and Clement Spencer Thomas' wedding

NEWS CUTTING – Friday November 6th, 1936

The wedding took place at Elstow Abbey Church on Wednesday of Miss Betty Potter younger daughter of Mr. & Mrs. F. J. Potter of 30 Cardington Road, Bedford and Mr. Clement Spencer Thomas, eldest son of the late Mr. R. Spencer Thomas and of Mrs. Spencer Thomas of Upper Honeydon near Bedford, and formerly of Treprenal near Oswestry, Shrewsbury. The bride was given away by her father. The bridesmaids were Miss Beryl Potter, only sister of the bride, and Miss Heather Smith, her cousin.

The bride was attired in a silver brocade dress of full length. It was made with a slight train, cowl neck and long sleeves, the only trimming being buttons of the same material. Her veil was lent by her godmother, and was held in place by a wreath of fresh flowers – roses, lilies of the valley, and white heather. Her bouquet was of similar flowers.

The bridesmaids' dresses were of turquoise taffeta with short coats to match. They carried bunches of anemones, and wore stud ear-rings of marcasite, the gifts of the bridegroom. Among the guests were: Mr. George Parker & Miss Ethel Swaffield of Budleigh Salterton, Mrs. Shepherd of Berbera, British Somaliland, Miss Dorothy & Miss Hilda Swaffield from Ampthill, Mrs. Ella Lampard & Mr. Derrick Lampard of Derby, Mr. Henry Swaffield, Ampthill, Mrs. I. Spencer Thomas, Honeydon, Mr. & Mrs. R. Shepherd of Ashtead, Mr. R. G. [Geoff] Swaffield from London, Mr. & Mrs. A. C. [Mick & Jean] Swaffield from Goffs Oak, Herts, Mr. & Mrs. R. N. [Dick & Ethel] Swaffield, Red House, Catesby and Mr. & Mrs. F. E. [Tony & Dorritt] Swaffield from Birmingham.

A year later, at Elstow, Beryl married William John Kynaston Lloyd [known as Kynaston] a chartered civil engineer from London. They had three girls Michelle, Amanda and Victoria (Vicki).

Beryl was a very keen and talented flower arranger. She died of cancer in Harrogate in 1977 aged 66. Kynaston died in 1985 near Otley. Michelle followed her mother and aunt to Bedford High School, then the family moved up to Harrogate in Yorkshire. Here they all enjoyed going

1976 – L–R, Rodney Archard, Peter Townley, Michelle Lloyd and Vicki Archard, Amanda and Christopher Townley, Beryl and Kynaston with Clare Townley

'up the dales' and out into the countryside and moorland. They joined the local Claro Beagles and the females of the family made sturdy efforts to run after the hounds, whilst Kynaston sat on his shooting stick behind a stone wall and waited for the hare to come back to him. This it usually did – to the annoyance of the rest of them, who arrived muddy and exhausted considerably later.

Clement Spencer Thomas' parents farmed at Upper Honeydon, Eaton Socon and Betty moved there straight after their marriage, "We had no running water, no electricity and hardly two pennies to rub together," she said. The farm has always been arable and at that time amounted to about 800 acres. Brenda was born within a year of their marriage, and then Jenny.

1915 – 'The Good Old Days' – harvesting at Honeydon

c1970s – Ewan and Brenda Mackintosh, Clement and Betty Spencer Thomas

c1940s – Kitty with her granddaughter, Jenny

Betty was a busy mother. She used to visit her own Mother and Father, [Kitty and Fred] in Bedford. She travelled the ten miles of country lanes, with the baby in a basket, in a pony and trap, "It took about one and half hours, and I would have to wait quite some time for the pony to have a rest, before we could start the return journey."

During this time Clement had to work hard and, for years, they had no holidays. But things got better and there were occasions when they hunted on horses with their two daughters. Clement enjoyed all country pursuits such as shooting and fishing. He had a boat and flew an Auster with his two Jack Russells, Dollar and Mite, on board.

1969 – Golden Wedding Anniversary – Kitty & Fred Potter

Much later Clement entered into partnership with David Bates and the land had increased to over 2000 acres. Betty was still on various committees, including the Women's Institute, when Clement died in November 1989. Brenda and Angus Mackintosh had four boys, Ewan, Robert, Alexander and William. Ewan died tragically in a motorcycle accident at the age of 17. Brenda too died, of breast cancer, just four months after her father had passed away.

Jenny married Desmond Longfield who became a Brigadier in the Army. They have four children – Melanie, Harriet , James and Charlotte and enough grandchildren to provide Father Christmas a busy time delivering gifts.

Betty loves to play Bridge, "Do you like cards dear," she asked hopefully, "I am really happy with a pack of cards in my hand." She goes to Bridge parties at night and drives back to her isolated house with one of Clement's old trilbies perched on her head, "They'll think I'm a man," she says comfortably. She has creative pastimes, painting in oils and writing children's stories. In 2001 she self-published a charming volume entitled 'Mr and Mrs Knife and Fork and Baby Spoon'. Independent, gregarious and active she still drives, travels abroad and is a busy church member. Bardie's daughter, Mary, once took Betty punting on the River Cam, "In all her years of living on the doorstep she'd never been, and she loved it!"

c1940s – Five of the Aunts – Jo, Queenie, Ethel, Kitty and Dot

1937 – Five of the Uncles – Basil, Dick, Eck, Norman and Henry

Chapter 14

NORTHAMPTONSHIRE
Richard Nash Swaffield and his family 1880–2002

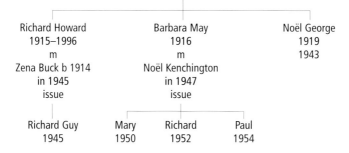

Henry Richard James Swaffield 1839–1909 and Emmeline Jepson 1842–1922

Emmeline	Henry	Exton	Norman	Ethel	Ella	Dorothy	Beatrice	Alan	Hugh	**Richard**	Hilda	Mildred	Basil
1867	1868	1869	1871	1872	1874	1875	1876	1878	1879	**1880**	1882	1884	1885
1934	1964	1950	1958	1965	1945	1962	1967	1878	1918	1937	1965	1973	1972

m
Ethel Harper in 1914

Richard Nash Swaffield 1880–1937 and Ethel Harper 1880–197

Richard Howard	Barbara May	Noël George
1915–1996	1916	1919
m	m	1943
Zena Buck b 1914	Noël Kenchington	
in 1945	in 1947	
issue	issue	

Richard Guy	Mary	Richard	Paul
1945	1950	1952	1954

From the Scrapbooks of Ethel Mary Harper Swaffield and her daughter, Barbara (Bardie)

1914 – Ethel Harper

1914 – Dick Swaffield

Richard Nash (Dick) 1880–1937 married in 1914 Ethel Mary Harper of Cheddon Fitzpaine, Taunton, Devon. He served with the Royal Engineers at Woolwich Arsenal during the First World War. In 1919 he was a Farmer and Estate Steward at Catesby Estate owned by Mr A H Attenborough. Mr & Mrs Swaffield have three children.

FOREWORD

The Catesby Estate lies between the Villages of Staverton and Hellidon on the borders of Northamptonshire and Warwickshire.

The house, standing 500 feet above sea level, has magnificent views over the well-wooded countryside and the vale of Shuckburgh.

Catesby is of considerable historical interest and is mentioned in Domesday Book.

In the time of King Edward the Confessor (1042-68) Gitda or Githa, the widow of Ralph, Earl of Hereford, son of Goda, sister of the King, held Catesby.

In 1229 Hugh de Neville received a mandate from the King to allow the Prioress of Catesby to have timber from the forest of Silverstone for the building of her Church.

In 1535 the Priory was suppressed.

John Onley became owner in 1537 and the estate was subsequently sold to John Parkhurst, Esq.

On his decease in 1730, the property passed to his grandson, John Parkhurst, who was succeeded in 1765, by his eldest son, Rev. John Parkhurst, M.A., the celebrated lexicographer. It then passed to his sons and his nephew.

About 1849 it was purchased by James Attenborough, Esq.

The present Chapel at Lower Catesby was built in 1861/2 by James Attenborough, Esq.

The Parish Church at Upper Catesby is now a ruin, but the Churchyard is still used as a burial ground.

Catesby House was built in 1863 and enlarged in 1894 and stands on high ground near Upper Catesby.

In the year 1379, the Electoral Roll listed four hundred people living and working in Lower Catesby. It was a thriving agricultural community. When, at the beginning of the 20th century, the Attenboroughs purchased the vast estate it was felt that they 'owned' the whole village. They worshipped at what was known as 'the Chapel' although it was a church. The front two pews were heated to keep the family cosy. George Lane, who worked on the estate for over sixty years, went early and lit the coke burner. When George was unwell it was Jack Badger, another stalwart agriculturist, who worked for the family for many years, who fanned the flames and produced a modicum of heat. It was unsaid but expected that the Estate workers attend chapel, but once the Attenboroughs sold up, the congregations dwindled.

To illustrate the hold that the Estate had on people's lives, a story is told of a lady in her eighties who turned up at the church in the mid-1990s. Her mother, Rose Briar, a young widow with two children, was employed by the Attenboroughs as a housemaid, and they had lived in the row of Priory Meadow Cottages. Rose stayed in the job only 18 months when she tragically died of a brain tumour, leaving her son and daughter orphaned, to be brought up in a children's home in Guildford. Whilst at Priory Meadow – in about 1923 – the little girl had a photograph taken of herself holding a rabbit, standing beside her brother. When she returned to Lower Catesby as an elderly lady, she was clutching this crumpled photograph, which seemed to be the only remaining memory of living as a child with her mother. When she walked into the church she burst into tears. Catesby was the nearest she ever got to her childhood and, although she had been living in America, she moved back to England and kept in contact with some of the parishioners and embroidered a kneeler for the church.

'1925 – THE MONEY THEY MAKE – PAWNBROKER LEAVES £273,678 – striking contrasts in the amount of profit accruing from various trades and professions are revealed in the Wills issued for probate yesterday – these include Mr A H Attenborough, Lord of the Manor of Catesby and of Fleet Street, London EC – pawnbroker. A year earlier Mr R P Attenborough left £325,000. He was a money-broker.'

1927 – THE DAYLIGHT SAVING BILL – Catesby, Daventry, 6 October 1927

'Sir – As the above Bill shortly comes up for discussion, I should like to be permitted make a few observations – "What does the Daylight Savings Bill actually do?" It simply misleads the townspeople and factory workers inasmuch as that, by altering the hands of the clock, these people quite willingly start work an hour earlier in the mornings, and consequently finish an hour earlier in the evenings.

If this hour's extra recreation is so beneficial to the factory workers (I don't doubt it is) what on earth is there to prevent shops and factories opening an hour earlier from an agreed date to an agreed date, in order that their workers can still have this extra hour of daylight, and leave the clock alone, to the benefit of the rural population.

The Great Creator provided us with the best clock there is – the sun – and surely His creatures should be happy to abide by His ruling. The urban population lose sight of the fact that through the above Bill the rural workers, especially those connected with the milk business, actually start work at 4 o'clock am.

Cannot the town workers get up earlier without the clock being 'faked' by an Act of Parliament – for this is obviously all that the Bill accomplishes?

Yours Faithfully, R N Swaffield.'

Dick Swaffield was a chip off the old family block, for it was one of his relatives in Dorset who also objected to this new fangled method of 'timing'. Fred Swaffield 1888–1963 from Stoke Abbott wrote in his family exercise book:

'When the Daylight Saving Bill came in we wouldn't have that at no price. Do you think my Grandfather clock what been going two hundred year would go if I altered en too this newfangled bloody gingerbread time? No he wouldn and I shouldn spect en to. Not her.

1916 – Howard and Baby Barbara [Bardie] Swaffield

One of them men said, 'S'pose you was to altered en and he went wass that to do do do?' and t'other said, 'I'd bweat en up. I bweat en up ass whad I'd do!' There was much scratching of heads, 'Well s'pose theest had to catch the eight o'clock train t'woudn be no good to git out there at nine, he'd be gone.' 'I oodn goo wi tha thing,' was the quick response, 'I'd catch the next. Thad ee ood. I'd wait for the next. Or I oodn go with the fust one if he didn go proper time.'

1920 – Howard and Bardie

1928 – The Northampton and County Independent

'Mr R N Swaffield of The Red House, Catesby, will be honoured by election of the Northamptonshire Chamber of Agriculture on Saturday. He is one of the best known and respected agriculturists in the county. The sixth son of the late Mr H R J Swaffield of Bedfordshire, his forebears were farmers for many generations in that county. He was born at Ampthill Park, where his father farmed for a number of years, leaving there on taking Beckerings Park Farm in 1883. Mr R N Swaffield was for four years at Ashton Grammar School, Dunstable, and later finished school at Bedford Modern School. After leaving School he assisted his father at Beckerings Park Farm, until the farm was given up, and his father went to live in Bedford in 1898. For the next two years R N assisted his father and eldest brother in the auctioneering and estate agency [Swaffield & Son] at Ampthill & Bedford, which was established in 1849.

While Mr Swaffield was fond of, and made good progress with the 'outside' part of the business, he did not take to office work. He went on to a large mixed farm in Monmouthshire, and gained practical experience and eventually was assistant manager to a large farm in Kent, where he remained until he came to Catesby in 1918, to take over the management of the Catesby Estates and to farm the Home Farm for the late Mrs Maude Attenborough and was then appointed to the same positions by Major G Attenborough.

Mr Swaffield is a useful member of the Daventry Rural District

1920 – Ethel, Baby Noël, Howard, Dick with spaniel, and Bardie

Council, and serves on the Hospital, Rating and Roads Committees of that authority. He is Chairman of the Catesby and Hellidon Conservative Association, and is also a member of the Church of England. A Freemason, Mr Swaffield is the Worshipful Master of the Beneventa Lodge 2389 Daventry. He is very fond of all field sports, particularly shooting and agriculture. He and his wife, Ethel, have two sons and one daughter.'

1928 – DAVENTRY – MR R N SWAFFIELD

'The hay harvest is now almost completed in this district and owing to the lack of sunshine it has been a very tedious job. Nevertheless, the crops on the whole have been good, and some excellent hay, which has been gathered very slowly, has been ricked, and as one goes about one sees some ricks which are quite 'warm' enough and an instance or two where 'boring' and cutting has had to be resorted to.

The corn harvest will, I am afraid, be disappointing, wheats are very patchy and the ears short, oats vary considerably, but beans have a good length of haulm [stalk] and are very well corned. The heavy thunderstorms of a few weeks ago have 'laid' the crops badly, and cutting will be a difficult and slow job. Potatoes look well but like mangolds and swedes, which are a good plant, would benefit with rain. Beef cattle and sheep have done well, and the trade for both is definitely better than a year ago. This is encouraging.

There is usually some 'snag' in farming, and the growing difficulty now is the question of labour More and more good men, chiefly the younger ones, are leaving the countryside for the towns and the shortage of skilled labour is acute. A few years ago, about half-a-dozen men would follow the threshing tackle from place to place, but now in this district no farmer can thresh without borrowing men from neighbouring farms.'

Bardie remembers having to attend St Mary & St Edmund Chapel at Catesby at 3-00 pm on Sundays.

'Mother would drag us across three fields in the mud. The vicar arrived from Hellidon on his horse with his cassock tied up with string. Our dogs always came too, spaniels and one red setter, and would settle by the stove. We had to take our slippers. If you kneel down in gum boots you get a muddy bottom.

1920 – Red House Farmyard – Bardie, Cousin Gwen and Howard

Once my Jackdaw appeared in the chapel and was walking just like the Jackdaw of Rheims. 'That little Jackdaw kept hopping about. Here and there, like a dog in a fair …' I tried desperately to catch him but he peered down at us from the eaves and did not utter a single Jack.'

Later she wrote about another incident to Dorritt Swaffield:

'… When it stopped we came out to the sideshows and it started again. We rushed into a tent, but then we only got on the outside. A man had a cap and when he let it down, the water poured into my shoes. When the rain had stopped they thought of putting the side up. A little girl gave us each a balloon for a race. We let them go and they landed on the roof garden. Then we came home. I thought I might be going for my holidays to Southsea on Thursday. I expect I shall. With lots of love from Bardie X X X X

PS: Jack has not gone back to Mrs Wing yet.

1928 – Bardie, Basil, Clifford, Dick and Noël

1928 – NORTHAMPTON HERALD – Interview with Mr R N Swaffield.

'I still try to think optimistically about farming and I am certain that the industry has touched bottom. I am of the opinion that arable farms will in the near future come into their own again. The younger farmers today have the great benefit of training colleges and research stations, and are educated up to the use of fertilisers which will, I think, alter the whole business of farming in a few years' time.

Had I an adaptable farm, I should be interested in pedigree stock, but, this not being the case, I try to make both ends meet, handling commercial stock only. I am very fond of arable farming, but at the present time this is not a paying proposition.

1926 – Red House, Bardie and Howard on Dorritt Williams' motorbike

With regard to the present regrettable depression in agriculture, I can only see one remedy, ie to impose import duties on commodities we can grow ourselves. I have not the least objection to the phrase 'Tariff Reform'. As an example I would give this illustration: I suppose the largest weekly tradesman's bill in any household is the grocer. What do we buy from the grocer that is grown or manufactured in this country? Practically nothing, not even matches. Now many commodities, such as tea, sugar, coffee, cocoa, etc etc, already bear an import duty, and we CANNOT GROW these articles. Why not reduce or abolish import duty of say 2s per lb on imported meat and bacon. This, while giving farming and stock-breeding a tremendous impetus would, in my opinion, LOWER the cost of house-keeping.'

1932 – R N Swaffield [Dick] was succeeded as presidential chairman of the Northamptonshire Chamber of Commerce by the Marquess of Northampton.

1931 at Fawsley Park, Noël, Howard, Bardie and Dick. The boys were both educated at Bloxham

1950 – Particulars of the Conditions of Sale – Catesby House

LOT I
(Coloured pink on Plan)

Area : 70 Acres   0 Roods   3 Poles

The Charming Residence

Catesby House

occupies a picked position standing on high ground, about 470 feet above sea level, with magnificent views. The approach is by a short drive off the road leading from Upper to Lower Catesby.

The house is substantially built of stone and slate and is partly creeper clad, a feature being the curved gables. The accommodation comprises:—

PORCH.

ENTRANCE HALL, 37ft. by 12ft., separated by dividing doors from the Staircase Hall, fine linenfold panelling and mirror overmantel over fireplace.

DINING ROOM, 23ft. by 16ft. 8in., panelled in Spanish oak from floor to ceiling, polished floor, panelled ceiling and service hatch.

DRAWING ROOM, 26ft. 7in. by 16ft., plus bay, beautiful Adam fireplace, walls panelled in satin, mirror with seat.

6

1932 – August – The Banbury Guardian

FEARED DOOM OF PUBLIC SCHOOLS – MOTHERS' DEMAND FOR COMFORTS

Mr Valentine Armitage, the Headmaster of Bloxham School giving his Annual Prize Giving address quoted, "One competent judge told me that he gave the unendowed public schools, ten years of life and no more."

Mr Armitage continued: "Incomes have dwindled and fees have risen. A man must cut his suit according to his cloth, and so he sends his boy to a secondary school. Before the 1914–18 War the father chose the son's school. He made the arrangements and discouraged complaints that the boy made. The mother was not supposed to know anything about schools and was not consulted. With the war came a radical change. The father was engaged elsewhere, and the mother, who took educational charge, insisted on increased comforts and these cost money. She had no respect for tradition, and she sent her boy where it was most comfortable. The father has not taken charge again, and matters have gone from bad to worse, until there is a danger that the public schools will soon be empty. That is a situation fraught with gravest consequences to the nation."

1932 – August – NORTHAMPTON HERALD

A CATESBY CELEBRATION – COMING OF AGE OF MR H G ATTENBOROUGH [MASTER HARRY] – GIFTS FROM TENANTS AND HOUSE STAFF

On Monday Catesby had another Red Letter Day – the Coming of Age of Master Harry son of Major George Attenborough, Lord of the Manor of Catesby. Early in the morning 'holiday' was the order of the day, nevertheless everyone connected with Catesby elected to 'do their bit'. Carpenters were busy in the marquee on the bowling green, erecting tables, forms etc, while others were engaged in erecting scaffolding on the west side of Catesby House in preparation for the display of fireworks which took place later in the evening.

Soon after 7pm the whole of the outdoor and indoor staffs, and their wives, numbering about 60, were entertained to a sumptuous repast in the large marquee. After the meal Master Harry was called for, and on his entering the marquee, he was received with much enthusiasm. Mr Ben Vince (butler) presented him with a very handsome inkstand and pen holder, subscribed for by the house, gardens, farm, stables and maintenance staffs.

About 8pm Major & Mrs Attenborough, and Master Harry, entertained a large house party together with the whole of the tenants and their wives, Mr R N Swaffield (Estate Steward) and Mrs Swaffield to supper in the oak-panelled dining room. During supper Mr Swaffield proposed the toast of Master Harry, which was received with acclamation.

Mr Doble Reed (Hellidon House) then gave the toast of the 'Host and Hostess' which was received with enthusiasm. Major Attenborough replying in his usual racy manner.

During supper, guests had the opportunity of inspecting the presents, which were both numerous and costly, displayed on tables in the hall. Dancing took place on the lawns to excellent music supplied by Mr Collett's Band. Despite inclement weather during the day, with a large and willing staff of farm hands, Mr Leeks of London was soon enabled to get the set piece into position and at about 10–15pm the firework display commenced and lasted for about three-quarters of an hour.

1933 – 18 July

'UNATTENDED – A feature of the wedding of Miss Constance M Attenborough, only daughter of Major & Mrs George Attenborough and Mr F D Proctor Dawnbarn of London, at Catesby near Daventry, was a negative one inasmuch as there were no bridesmaids.

The ceremony was performed in the small private chapel of Lower Catesby and the bride and bridegroom passed under an archway of old shoes and horseshoes.

Generous presents were received including from Mr & Mrs R N Swaffield (tea knives) and staff at London residence (coffee pot).'

Mr Green, a timber merchant, was the new owner of Catesby Estate in the Fifties. He moved in, chopped down the majority of the trees, sold them for more than he paid for the entire land, then moved away. Then Tom Darby bought Red House Farm in 1960 from Mr Macaness. The once lovely garden and tennis court was in a mess, mainly because his wife suffered from ill health. The Darbys worked hard and got the grounds back into some sort of order. Later they purchased, from David Shaw, Catesby House which was in the middle of their land, which the family were farming. Gwen Darby says that Monica Thomas, who has lived in the village for years, has enjoyed many games of tennis with the Swaffields on the lawn. "Red House was the Home Farm for the Estate," said Gwen, "And each farm was marked with footpaths so that workers could wend their way to Red House to collect their wages." The history of the land goes back centuries and many old farming methods, such as the remnants of criss-crossed twig drains, have been discovered. The Darbys, now, have sold up and moved away.

1934-ish

Bardie learnt to drive on a 'Bean Harper Lions Bean' – it had a right-hand gate change, accelerator in the middle and you "… always had to double declutch …".

LOT 8
(Coloured green on Plan)

Area :   444 Acres   0 Roods   9 Poles

The First-Class Mixed Farm

Red House Farm
CATESBY

The gentleman's house is approached by a short road off the Catesby to Hellidon Road and occupies a pleasant position on high ground.

It is of modern construction being built of brick, stucco faced with slated roofs, and contains:—

　　Hall, Dining Room, Drawing Room, Kitchen, Pantry, Scullery, Dairy.

　　On the *First Floor* are 5 Bedrooms and Bathroom with bath (h. & c.).

　　On the *Second Floor* is an attic.

　　Electric Light from Mains.   Water Supply from Ram.

　　Pretty Garden with flower beds and tennis court (dis-used).

Red House tennis lawn and a spaniel

Left: 1950 – Particulars of the Conditions of Sale – Red House Farm, Catesby

1940 – Peshawar – Noël Swaffield

1937 – Friday 8th October

THE RUGBY ADVERTISER – DEATH OF MR R N SWAFFIELD – PROMINENT DAVENTRY FREEMASON AND RURAL DISTRICT COUNCILLOR

'The Rugby Advertiser regrets to record the death, which took place last Friday afternoon, of Mr Richard Nash Swaffield of the Red House, Catesby, from pneumonia, after an illness lasting only a week.

Mr Swaffield, who was 57 years of age, was very well known over the whole of the county and his passing is a great loss to agriculture in the district.

The fifth son of the late Mr Henry R J Swaffield, well-known auctioneer of Ampthill, Bedford, Mr Swaffield had lived at Catesby for the past twenty years where he farmed extensively. He was Land Agent to Major George Attenborough.

Mr Swaffield was a regular attendant at both Rugby and Northampton markets, and was a member of the Daventry Christmas Fatstock Show Committee.'

Basil, Eck, Dick and Norman

Basil was upset at the premature death of his brother, they were close and 'as alike as two peas in a pod.' Dick's passing, and the loss of a bolt hole at Catesby, saddened the family. After her husband's funeral, Ethel had to leave the Red House quite quickly. Dick had been his own man on the estate where he had bred cattle. Finalising his affairs was difficult as his own business was intertwined with that of Estate work. Ethel moved to a rented property in Flitwick Road, Ampthill to be near to the Swaffield sisters-in-law and their families, as they had always been kind and welcoming. Then, unsure how to spend her time, she went back to her home town of Taunton and obtained a job as a Housekeeper. She so enjoyed the job that she kept on working for quite some time. Meanwhile her youngest son Noël, with the winds of war blowing across Europe, had joined the RAF. Because she was on the move, Ethel had given Ella's home – 'Edensor', The Avenue, Ampthill as her permanent address. And it was here that the first postcards were received. Noël, escaped from Java, was at Butterworth Airport near Penang, which was the first in Malaya to be bombed. Noël was taken prisoner of war:

1941 – Post card from Noël Swaffield – CAMP JAVA "y"

3 'My health is excellent.

6 My daily work is easy and we are being paid according to the number of days we work. We have plenty of food and recreation.

12 The Nippons treat us well so don't worry about me. I never feel uneasy.

Dear Mother, I hope you are well. Four years today I left you. Hope to return soon. Keep smiling. Love Noël

Put on transport ship from prison camp to another one.'

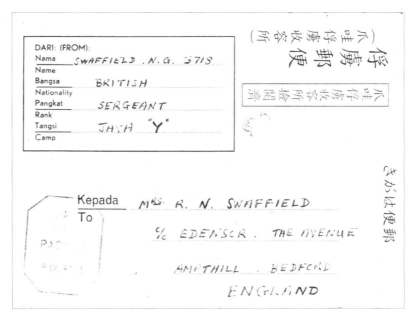

1942 – The address side of the first postcard

25/12/42 December 1942 – CAMP JAVA –
Rubber stamped – DAMAGED BY FIRE IN TRANSIT

'I am now in a Nippon Prisoner of War Camp, in Java.

I am always wishing that this miserable war would be over and that I should return home again. I am constantly thinking of you. It will be wonderful when we meet again.

Today is Christmas Day. My thoughts are with you. I am well and hope you are. Goodbye. God Bless you.'

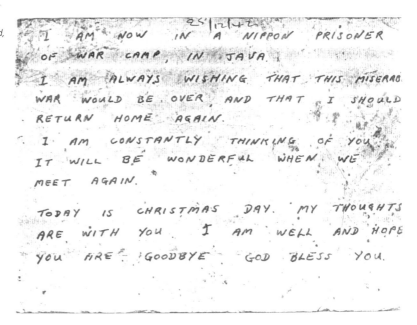

1942 – The message side of the fire-damaged, final postcard

1943 – PRISONERS WERE ON SUNK JAP SHIP

'A list of British prisoners of war who are stated to have lost their lives on November 29 last, when a Japanese transport ship carrying British prisoners of war from Java was sunk, has been received from the Japanese Government, states the War Office.'

1943 – MISSING – Swaffield – 'Officially reported missing, Java, Sgt N G Swaffield. Information gratefully received by his mother, 38 Whitmore Road, Taunton – late of Catesby.

Information has been received from the Air Ministry that Sergt Noël George Swaffield, RAF, lost his life by the sinking of the Japanese transport carrying prisoners of war from Java on 29 November 1943. He was the younger son of Mr Richard Nash Swaffield late of Ampthill and Catesby, and Mrs Swaffield. He was educated at Bloxham. Previous to being at Java he was on the North-West Frontier of India for two years, and was sent to Singapore in February 1941. He was 23 years of age.'

1943 – BUCKINGHAM PALACE – TO MRS E M SWAFFIELD

'The Queen and I offer you our heartfelt sympathy in your great sorrow.

We pray that your country's gratitude for a life so nobly given in its service may bring you some measure of consolation. GEORGE R.'

DICTATOR'S SOULS

'The Rev J G Hillam, Rector of Ampthill, requested his congregation on Sunday 6 May, to pray for the souls of Hitler and Mussolini. This has aroused indignation and many people have expressed disapproval.

One member of the congregation, a regular churchgoer and holder of an important office at the church, told a reporter of this newspaper, "I most certainly do not approve of it."

Another man said, "To hell with the souls of Mussolini and Hitler."

A third, who is also connected with a church movement in Ampthill said, "Our Lord taught us to pray for our enemies, but I think the Rector was wrong in mentioning those two by name." '

1944 – Richard Howard Swaffield married Zena Buck

At the time Howard was working with a milking machine company and was sent up to the Bristol area. Zena met Howard (who she called Richard and he called her Brat) at a dance. "He got on the bus with the village butcher," she said, "And we went to a dance at Keynsham, then Richard brought me home, it was lovely." Howard worked for the Alfalaval Company and retired at sixty, after 37 years service. To begin with the couple were sent to Northern Ireland, to Londonderry, and then moved to Castle Rock – 30 miles away. Guy was born there and they were anxious to move back to England once he reached the age of five so that he could go to school. They moved to Leicester which suited them well. They bought a little house and whilst there they often visited Catesby although the family had left by then. They stayed with Aunt Bess and Uncle Lorraine who had been an Estate worker, and had built up a great affection for Howard.

1947 – January

Dr N S KENCHINGTON AND MISS B SWAFFIELD

'The engagement is announced between Dr Noël S Kenchington of Warwick Hall, Bromsgrove and youngest son of Mrs Kenchington and the late C W Kenchington of Edgbaston, Birmingham, and Barbara Swaffield of The Priest House, Grafton Manor, Bromsgrove, only daughter of Mrs Ethel Swaffield of Taunton and the late Mr R N Swaffield of Catesby, Northants.'

1947 – Bromsgrove, Noël Kenchington and Barbara Swaffield, L–R, Noël's mother, Mr K Lloyd, Noël, Bardie and Ethel

1947 – 11 June – Bromsgrove Times – BROMSGROVE DOCTOR MARRIED

'The marriage took place at Bromsgrove Parish Church on Wednesday of Doctor Noël Kenchington, youngest son of Mrs C W Kenchington of Edgbaston and Miss Barbara M Swaffield, daughter of Mrs Ethel Swaffield of Taunton. The bride came to Bromsgrove as a student of Nonington College during the war and has since made her home at Priest's House, Grafton Manor. During the past four years she has held an appointment at Waverley Grammar School, Small Heath.

Given away by Mr Havelock Trevorrow, the bride was attired in a gown of white glacé silk, and her Brussels lace veil, loaned by Mrs Trevorrow, was secured by a headdress of delphiniums and carnations. She carried cream roses. Over 100 guests attended the reception in a marquee at Priest's House. Later the young couple left for a honeymoon in Scandinavia.'

DR KENCHINGTON – 'Dr Kenchington is the first local doctor to be appointed a magistrate since Dr F W J Coaker who retired in 1945. Dr Kenchington is an MA from Cambridge and also holds the degrees of MRCS and LRCP. He came to Bromsgrove in 1946 after service with the RAMC in India and Burma, and between 1950 and 1952 was District Commissioner of the Boy Scouts. Apart from general practice he is one of the anaesthetists at All Saints Hospital.'

1948 – Bedfordshire Times –
WE MUST LOOK FORWARD SAYS ARCHDEACON – IMPRESSIVE
CEREMONY AT AMPTHILL WAR MEMORIAL

'Many of the comrades who fought with them on battlefronts the world over, and the mothers and wives who waited in vain for their return were present at the Service of Remembrance at the War Memorial at the Alameda, Ampthill on Sunday afternoon to honour those who died in both World Wars. In his address the Archdeacon said, "… to look back

1957 – Bardie ski-ing

at the bitterness of remembrance was not enough. We must look forward too … Faith in life after death was very much at zero in this age. For the majority of people the Creed was 'Eat, drink and be merry, for tomorrow we die'. And then when we did die people went into mourning and dressed in black.

The early Christians went to burials dressed in white because they knew that their comrades were entering into a fuller and eternal life. We must look forward to rejoining our loved ones in a life which is greater and more wonderful than this one …'.

There are eighteen names engraved on the new panel for those who fell in the 1939–45 War.' These include Noël George Swaffield. Engraved amongst the many names of those who fell in the First World War are those of Hugh Swaffield fourth son of the late HRJ Swaffield, Bedford – and Frederick Lampard husband of Ella Swaffield d 1916.

1949 – 3 May – KENCHINGTON – 'Peter Noël, new-born son of Barbara (née Swaffield) and Noël Kenchington of 'Catesby', College Road, Bromsgrove. (Spina bifida)'

1950 – KENCHINGTON – Mary Janet b 27 August

Like all the Kenchington children, Mary was born at Bromsgrove. Mary's life has turned out in many ways like her mother's with strong interests in the church, sport and music. Educated at the Alice Ottley School in Worcester, Mary savoured the richness and mystery of carol services in the lofty Cathedral and was introduced to Early Music and associated instruments. The exposure to this special music lay dormant for three decades, when she learnt to play pre-16th century music on her recorder, and to sing anything from madrigals to large choral works. Another musical memory was a wonderfully exciting concert put on by the staff at school when Mary was in her fifth year, she implored her friend Jo, "You scream, I can't scream any more."

Each year the family holidayed at Parrog in Pembrokeshire where they enjoyed as many sporting activities as possible. Once she was happily sailing with her young cousin, Guy, in a particularly rough sea. "We were having a great time," she remembers, "But Mum and Dad thought we should come back, so came out to get us as they were worried." End result was that Bardie and Noël capsized. Guy has his own recollections, "Funny," he said, "I thought we were concerned about them, they were the ones who needed rescuing!"

1961 – Trafalgar Square – Paul, Noël, Mary Bardie and Richard with pigeons

Physical Education was studied at Bedford College leading to a certificate, followed by a year B Ed at Cambridge, and then an MA at Leeds. Not content with these degrees she carried on to gain a PhD – her thesis being to assess children's ability to estimate motion – a project funded by

Transport and Road Research. All this followed by a further three years at the London Bible College where she gained a BA in Theology. Mary then joined the Church Army until, after several retreats at Burford Priory, she made the big decision to become a noviciate in her late forties. "It's a mixed (5 men and 4 women) Anglican monastic community and I'm learning to be a nun – yes, really! It's not all sitting about being holy. There's lots of domestic work, garden and conservation work, thinking, talking and praying about everything under the sun and interacting with our many visitors. We are learning to be more truly the people we are, individually and in relationship with each other – which is sometimes quite a tricky task! However I think it is ultimately what the whole of the ball game of life is, and what we are doing here – building a community – is in a mysterious way of significance far beyond ourselves." Mary will have to make the ultimate decision as to whether or not she will remain in this monastic life.

1952 – KENCHINGTON – Richard Scott b May

At Bromsgrove Preparatory School Richard discovered the dominance of games, which he hated, particularly rugby and cricket, '… in the public school psyche of those days. On the other hand, I also discovered that there was a modelling room, and I used to win competitions with my flying balsa-wood aeroplanes fitted with little diesel engines. The main literary experience I remember was being treated to the adventures of Nigel Molesworth, namely 'Down With Skool' and 'How to be Topp' …'.

1961 – Richard

Bromsgrove School had a vigorous regime, even for a day scholar. Saturday was not free, there were constant and dreaded games, and compulsory attendance at chapel on Sunday. Chemistry, with all its fascination, and the school .22 rifle range provided some light relief, and Richard was soon shooting for his house and his school. '… When the Summer term of 1967 came, I put my name down for .303 shooting, and thereby started a lifelong, passionate interest … I seemed to have a flair for shooting and went in the team to Bisley in July, and was Captain for my last term, as well as achieving three × A grade A-Levels.' He was disappointed not to get into Cambridge, '… Instead I accepted a place at Imperial College London to read Aeronautical Engineering …'.

May 1974 – Extract from Press Cutting

A varied career followed working with structural steel contractors, interspersed with study as a chartered civil engineer. Match rifle shooting tops the lot, however, and it's '… now 36 years since I first fired a large calibre rifle, and the fascination of hitting the distant bullseye is still there. I first competed as an individual at Bisley in 1969 and made my one and only appearance in the final 100 of the Queen's Prize in 1970. Since then, although continuing to shoot Target Rifle (that used for the Queen's Prize) until 1984, my main interest gradually shifted to Match Rifle, a specialised and esoteric form of the sport only practised at distances of 1,000, 1,100 and 1,200 yards. At that distance a force 5 straight across the range can blow your bullet 20 feet sideways. The target is only 10 ft wide and the bullseye 2 ft diameter. It becomes an exercise in wind judgement and, believe me, when the wind is turbulent it can be very difficult (and hugely enjoyable), especially at 1200 yards. I've shot for England four times, in 1973, 1990, 1995 and 2001.

Richard and Jane have two daughters, and all enjoy the beautiful scenery of the South Cotswolds. Jane is an ordained Priest of the Church of England, and licensed to St James the Great at Dursley, Gloucestershire.

1955 – DAILY TELEGRAPH – DIFFICULTIES FOR PRINCESS – METHODIST VIEW

'Dr Leslie Weatherhead, President of the Methodist Conference, last night issued the following statement: "Princess Margaret and Group Captain Townsend are popular young people in love with one another, and everyone would wish that they could have the right of any other young British couple and find happiness in marriage. But clearly the status of the Princess raises difficulties in regard to a fiancé who is divorced and whose wife and two children are living. Should anything happen – an aeroplane accident for instance – unfortunately end the lives of Prince Charles and the Princess Anne, or if they both died without issue, then at Princess Margaret's death her eldest child would be heir to the Throne. Yet that child would be the fruit of a marriage which many Anglicans would not recognise as valid. This is bound to be a matter of vital public concern for, among other things, such an heir would be doomed to disapproval or worse in the eyes of many of the people of this realm."'

1945 – King George VI with his daughters, Elizabeth and Margaret (right)

On a more frivolous note, Noël Coward wrote in his diary on 3 November 1955: 'Poor Princess Margaret has made a sorrowful, touching statement that she will not marry Peter Townsend. This is a fine slap in the chops for the bloody Press, which has been persecuting her for so long … She cannot know, poor girl, being young and in love, that love dies soon and that a future with two strapping stepsons, and a man eighteen years older than herself, would not really be very rosy.'

1953 – Howard, Zena and Guy move South

Still with Alfalaval they moved into the Tarrant Rawston Valley where they lived in a little cottage for five years before they moved to Bournemouth. It was in this rural valley that Guy was taught to shoot by his father – both .22 and shotgun – and both shared a passion for the sport. Guy still has a cartridge case and a gun which he uses, and knows that they came from Catesby – either from his grandfather Dick, or from his young Uncle Noël who was lost in the War. "Dad taught me to tickle trout," said Guy, "And he loved woodwork, he was very clever with his hands."

Guy enjoyed his schooling at Clayesmore, Iwerne Minster in Dorset. Academia took a back seat apart from a fascination with History – and sport and sailing were the most enjoyed activities. His reports were constant, "Could always do better." After leaving school he went to College and then joined J J Allen, Complete House Furnishers in the Sales Department. He then 'went on the road' with Platignum Pens before joining Bulmer's, the cider company, in 1970, and took early retirement at the age of 56 in August 2001. "As Regional Sales Manager for the whole of the south of England," he said, "It was a wonderful job but I became fed up with driving 40,000 miles a year, getting up at six, coming home late with the phone ringing until nine o'clock at night, and having no life of my own." He does not regret this decision and sounds a happy, relaxed man with lots of hobbies. His favourite toy is a blue and silver AC Cobra Snake – known as a Fake Snake as it is a 1993 rebuild with a Q Reg, and fitted with a 4.5 litre V-8 race-tuned Rover Engine. "I can go at over 140 mph," he said, "Fortunately we have a handy airport where I can let rip." Shooting is another passion, both clays and rough and enjoyed 'at least once a week'. Guy married Ginna [Virginia Bernadette Geraldine Hole] at Camford Magna in 1977. They enjoy travel and two memorable trips were a visit to Hong Kong and China in the early nineties and, more recently, a glorious Mediterranean cruise on the SS Oriana.

Ethel Harper Swaffield had sometime previously moved to Taunton and then relocated to live near Howard and Zena. Zena admits that '… Grandma liked her own way … but, as long as you went along with Grandma, everything was fine …'. Guy knew his grandmother properly when she was quite old and he used to mow her lawn each week, "She walked a lot," he said, "She was a grey lady with a strong personality and very fond of playing Canasta, always wanting to win." Mary Kenchington was taught to play cards by her grandmother, "She huffed and puffed when we got good enough to beat her," she laughed affectionately.

Howard enjoyed the countryside and loved being at home. After retirement he busied himself with the garden and his craft work, "He made some wonderfully intricate farm wagons," said Zena. In 1976 he started suffering from emphysema and this dogged him for the rest of his life until he died on 28 September 1996. "I miss him terribly," said Zena in 2001 [aged 81], "He was very brave and we had fifty-one and three-quarters very, very happy years together." She had tears in her voice but is resilient, "But I am lucky, I have a wonderful son, a lovely daughter-in-law, and a very special grandson, Richard. I manage very well and all I need is better sight."

Zena's grandson, Richard, was educated in Wimborne and then, at seventeen, joined Sunseekers at Poole, they build magnificent cruisers for the rich and famous. He has learnt his trade through the company and has been with them for seven years. He was enthusiastic, "They have taught me everything I know, it's a brilliant job." From time to time he joins the sea trials, and loves the life.

Paul, the youngest child of Noël and Bardie, was born in 1954, and followed much the same school education as Richard. He remembers learning the names of all his mother's aunts and uncles by rote – and still retains the younger ones in his head – Alan, Hugh, Dick [his grandfather] Hilda, Kitty and Basil.

1967 – Paul

His life has been one of travel. After studying languages at Oxford, he went abroad as a volunteer with the Church Missionary Society. He landed in Macao where he taught English in a Chinese School. At the end of that contract he travelled home, much of the journey overland via India, Pakistan, Afghanistan and Iran. Religion has played a large part in his life, and he studied Theology at St John's, Nottingham and was ordained at York Minster. Bible study was intermixed with managing toys, sweets and stationery as he worked for some time as stockroom manager in a branch of Woolworths. Paul then married Clare, who is a trained Norland Nanny, and their first son, Philip, was born whilst he was a curate in Scarborough. Three more boys came along and Paul was vicar of Hucclecote, nr Gloucester. The family have now returned to China, and he is vicar of St Andrew's in Kowloon. There they lead a busy life and Paul has made a couple of trips to East Timor.

Wheels within wheels, have provided yet another link with the Kenchington story: In December 1988, Jon and Kim Swaffield [Jon, grandson of Basil] lived in Glasgow, and were

driving down the A74 to spend Christmas with Kim's family in Birkenhead. The night before, Pan Am Flight 103, a jumbo jet, had exploded in a split-second over the sleepy village of Lockerbie, killing all 259 people aboard and eleven people on the ground. Amongst those on board was Flora Swire, flying on the eve of her 24th birthday to spend Christmas with her boyfriend, Hart, in America. Her father, Jim, was at the time, Bardie and Noël Kenchington's GP in Bromsgrove. He has worked as a seemingly tireless campaigner to discover who planted the bomb. Coincidentally, Flora's mother, Jane Thompson Swire, was at prep school with me, Natalie, in Colwyn Bay. The family have planted 'Flora's Wood' in her memory – four hundred trees shaped into the letter F.

2000 – Noël and Bardie

After 32 years as a Bromsgrove GP, Noël Kenchington retired. He had been a Magistrate for 25 years and interested in Scouting [as Bardie was in Guiding], music and travel, as well as being a Divisional Surgeon in the St John's Ambulance. Avid travellers, Bardie and Noël soon set off on their first world cruise to Malaya, Macao, Bali, New Guinea, Solomon Islands, New Caledonia, New Zealand, Tonga, Fiji, Honolulu and San Fransisco.

Noel has the sweetest temperament, adores Bardie as she adores him and, as an addition to all his qualities, will be remembered for his most useful tip of 'How to Remove a Stuck Stopper from a Sherry Decanter'.

"Simply," said Noel quietly, "By tapping glass on glass." Carefully he got a jam jar, tapped round the edge of the stuck stopper and, heigh presto, out it came!

1920 – Studio portrait – Howard, Noël and Ethel, foreground Bardie with toy

USA, c1910–1915 – Basil in his car

Chapter 15

BEDFORDSHIRE ~ BASIL 1885–1973
Basil, his son Clifford and family

Henry Richard James Swaffield 1839–1909 and Emmeline Jepson 1842–1922

Emmeline (Minnie)	Henry	Exton (Eck)	Norman	Ethel (Bridget)	Ella	Dorothy (Dot)	Beatrice (Queenie)	Alan	Hugh	**Richard** (Dick)	Hilda (Jo)	Mildred (Kitty)	**Basil**
1867	1868	1869	1871	1872	1874	1875	1876	1878	1879	1880	1882	1884	1885
1934	1964	1950	1958	1965	1945	1962	1967	1878	1918	1937	1965	1973	1972

Basil Swaffield 1885–1973 and Hilda Marion Milligan 1882–1967 m 1917

Basil Clifford	Elisabeth Page
1922	1927
m Sheila Orchard in 1951	d 1930

Clifford Swaffield 1922 and Sheila Orchard 1927

Simon	Susan	Jonathan	Christopher
b1952	b 1956	b 1960	b 1965

Basil was one of the last two children born at Beckerings Park. His great-uncle, John Sutton, came to visit from Buxton, and asked Basil to post some letters for him in Ampthill. He gave Basil half-a-crown, a small fortune for a young boy who would have been willing to walk to Bedford, even London, for such a tip. Basil lived in Lansdowne Road with his parents, studied at Bedford Modern School, and was then apprenticed to the Bedford Electricity Works. Eventually he worked with a firm in Bedford which made cars, and he drove these to London for sale. In 1906 he was despatched to the United States with a few sovereigns in his pocket to make his fortune. He came home, and then sailed out again in 1910 on the Lusitania. Whilst on board he won a wheelbarrow race. Was he the barrow or the wheel? Whatever, he won a silver-plated ashtray, embossed with a red enamel ship's flag sporting a brass rampant lion. Basil joined various railway companies and, for the rest of his time in the US, he worked on an electrified section of a line in Vermont and Massachusetts. The trains were hauled by electric-loco through the very long, and ill-ventilated, Hoosac Tunnel where, at times, there were horrifying accidents. Whilst in America he enjoyed driving large open sedans and limos. The automobile always held a fascination for him. Early in the 1900s Basil had a huge car into which he packed 12 of his family, including his mother perched at the top, his sisters clinging onto their hats and he, with a jaunty wing collar and flat cap, organising an erratic motorised outing around the big trees of Woburn Park.

War was on the horizon and, in 1915, Basil decided to come home to do his bit aged 30. Because of his engineering knowledge, he was directed into munitions, and worked in a factory in Staines. During this time he married. Like his Aunt Phyll Parker, he found the Milligan family in Buxton congenial and, at thirty-two, in August 1917 at Chapel-en-le-Frith, he married Hilda Milligan, always known as Jimmy. She was three years his senior. Jimmy's mother and Basil's mother, Emmeline Jepson Swaffield, were first cousins. Elder brother Henry was good to them when times were hard, and Basil always assisted on the gate at the Agricultural Shows.

c1900s – Hilda Milligan (Jimmy) in Bedford

Jimmy, who is remembered for her cloche hats and dangly earrings, came from a prosperous middle-class Derbyshire family. Grandfather Milligan was a draper, milliner and furnisher with a large emporium in Buxton's centre. Jimmy was schooled at home by a governess, and sent to Switzerland to a finishing school in the late 1890s. She returned home, and joined two big fashion houses, Bradley's and Woollands, becoming a buyer before her marriage. It was five years before Clifford arrived. Dorritt Williams Swaffield, who lived in Russell Avenue, was already familiar with the Swaffs of Bedford, and wrote in her 1990s memoir:

'Clifford was, like me, born and brought up in Bedford and, when he was three or four I regularly took him for walks. He was a good looking little boy with golden hair, a peach-like skin and blue eyes. I enjoyed the company of this bright, animated, child and thought how lucky I was when his mother enthusiastically accepted my offer to take him off her hands every so often. Later when I had children of my own, I thought that the balance of good fortune was tipped towards her. I soon discovered that he had a contrary streak, and never wanted to do what I suggested, so I always proposed that we went in one direction when, usually for climatic reasons, I preferred another, to which he immediately objected. This stratagem meant that we were always in perfect harmony, he thought he was getting his way, whereas I invariably got mine.'

1928 – Family visit to Fareham: Basil, his nephews Hugh and Mick, Uncle Eck holding Baby Elisabeth, Auntie Florrie and nephew Frank. Clifford is the little boy, aged 6, in front of Hugh.

When Clifford was five, a little sister, Elisabeth, was born bringing great joy to Basil and Jimmy. In later life he wrote, 'Although I never realised it at the time, looking back I can now understand how bitter a blow it must have been to Mother and Father with the death of my sister, Elisabeth, who was born when Mother was 45.'

News Cutting 1930 – Mr & Mrs Basil Swaffield's Loss – Sudden Death of Their Little Girl

'Mr & Mrs Basil Swaffield of 32 Bradgate Road, Bedford, have been receiving the condolences of their many friends this week in the death of their daughter, Elisabeth Page, at the age of three years. Elisabeth was on holiday with her parents last week, a few miles from Hunstanton, when she was suddenly taken ill on Friday. A doctor was called in, but he did not consider her condition sufficiently serious to prevent her return home. Within an hour of the doctor's visit Mr Swaffield set out with her for a Bedford nursing home, which he reached at 1-00 am on Saturday, but she died the same afternoon.

Elisabeth was a bonny, bright girl and the sympathy of all will go out to Mr & Mrs Swaffield in their time of bereavement.

The funeral took place at Bedford Cemetery on Tuesday at noon, the officiating clergymen being the Rev G W Byers-Jones. Members of the family were present and a large number of floral tributes were received.'

In the late forties the family moved back to Bedford where Basil set up his own electrical engineering business. Technically he was very able, but running a business was more complicated. He always had an interest in cars and, over the years, he owned a Bullnose Morris, a Morris Cowley and a Humber 16 – as well as a varied collection of caravans rather more ancient than modern.

1923 at Catesby – Basil, Jimmy and Baby Clifford in the Bullnose Morris

Grandson Simon remembers 'Dabar' and 'Gran Grans' vividly:

'They were real Victorians, and dressed and acted in that tradition. Indeed my memories of all the Swaffield aunts and uncles are of elderly ladies dressed in black, and bewhiskered old men, living in dark houses full of heavy furniture. I recall visiting the aunts in Goldington Road as a regular event, and also visiting Uncle Henry at Ampthill. When I was very young we lived in the flat above my grandparents in Bradgate Road. We went for frequent picnics out in the Bedfordshire countryside, which Dad recalls with pleasure and amusement.' Sue, their only granddaughter, remembers 'Gran Grans whistling under her breath as she shuffled round the house, Dabar and his pipe, climbing into Dabar's old car and avoiding the spiders that were always in it.'

The East Anglian coast was a favourite with the family and caravanning provided their most memorable holidays, often at Walberswick with its wide views over marsh, heath and sea, everywhere a spectacle of sky, scudding clouds and infinite spaciousness. There are some lovely walks, well signposted, that traverse the fields and rush-strewn marshes, idling along the river bank, and criss-crossing the Common. In later years Walberswick has become a magical place for so many Swaffields, and those connected to them. It is a place almost unchanged by time. When the fishing boats come in on the

Walberswick's magical atmosphere [photo courtesy Russell Edwards]

tide, the terns wheel and hover over the turbulence. They dive vertically, with deadly precision, and snatch up unsuspecting little fish swimming too close to the surface in their own quest for food. Artists are often seen with palette and easel on one of the village greens, painting the houses with the sea in the background, their pictures full of colour graduation, play of light, ripple of wind on water, the swish of grasses and the sheer emptiness of sand, sea and sky. Philip Wilson Steer, master of Impressionism, was often there and, wrote Robin Ironside: 'The painter has gathered up all the entranced sensations of youthful visits to the seaside'.

Basil and Jimmy caravanned at Walberswick before and after the war, for a period of thirty to forty years. Like his elder brother, Merchant Seaman Norman, Basil kept cryptic diaries, known as Dabar's Scribbling Diaries. At the age of 79 he finally gave up work and 'sold up shop' in April/May 1964, leaving only a small amount to live on, allowing for '8s house help'. That year they made trips to Dunwich and Lenham [Kent], and the Castle Road girls [Norman's] came

c 1919 – Elder sister, Dot, Jimmy and Basil, Basil's mother, Emmeline, and his elder brother, Norman

to supper. In mid-November 'Jimmy in bed' for 3 days. 1965 told a chapter of deaths: '3 May Ethel died. 6 May Ethel cremated. 24 July Helen died suddenly. 29 July Helen cremated. 26 August Jo died. 31 August Jo buried at Ampthill.' 1966 started badly, '9 Jan Jim had blackout. 5 Feb Cliff and Sheila and

John and Elsie came. 17 Feb Jim into North Wing. 27 Feb Cliff, Simon and Sue came. 10 Mar Jim back from hospital. 16 July Cliff and family came. 6 Aug Cliff Simon Sue and J came. 18 Aug Leslie died. 20 Aug Leslie cremated. 20 Oct Jim into hospital. 29 Oct to Hull (Public Schools Lodge gathering – route and mileage noted).' In March 1967 Jim was back in hospital again. '24 April J very ill. 26 April J died 10am. 29 April J cremated.'

Walberswick was Basil's solace where he stayed with Jean Swaffield, now living on her own after separation from her husband, Mick. Basil stayed with Jean until 8 June when he returned to Bedford. To a home without Jimmy.

NEWS CUTTING – April 26th, 1967.

'In hospital peacefully after a long illness Hilda Marion Swaffield aged 84 years, beloved wife of Basil, 32 Bradgate Road, Bedford. Dear Mother of Clifford. Cremation at Bedford tomorrow (Saturday) 29th April at 12 noon. No letters or flowers please.'

The deaths of dear ones continued. His cousin, Ham, died on 14 September and his older sister, of whom he was very fond, Queenie, died on 23 October. The winter of 1968 was very cold with severe frosts, and the summer was very hot with high temperatures. Whatever the weather, Basil got in his car and continued travelling from Bedford to see Nobbie [Queenie's companion, in Halesworth in Suffolk], then on to see Jean, to Lenham [Ciff and Sheila], back to Dunwich and Walberswick, and to see Phyll in Eastbourne.

Basil died five years after Jimmy when his grandson Jon was eleven. The children, with their father Cliff and mother Sheila, would visit 'Dabar' in Bedford as often as they could, playing 'Dog' as they drove through London. Jon remembers, '… Wonderful fish and chips for lunch in Bedford, rock cakes, a quiet house and a ticking clock, a coal fire and a shed, full of mystery, in the garden.' Basil will always be remembered as a kind, cheerful, friendly man. Recently Clifford wrote, 'I must have about 80 or so very old photographs pre-Great War, most of which were taken by my father who, in his young days, was a keen photographer and did all his own processing from two old plate cameras which reside in my roof.' Even though Basil is in many of the pictures, he set them up, told everyone to sit still and ran like the wind to get in at the back. Fortunately he was tall [and thin] like most of the Swaff boys. His ashes were scattered in Ampthill Park.

Clifford, when asked for his potted history, replied with the smallest of pots:

'As to me, school in Bedford, joined the Sun Insurance just before the war, went into the Navy (Fleet Air Arm) and travelled through the Panamá Canal. Came back and foolishly returned to the office, worked Bedford, Cambridge, Wisbech, Maidstone, Chatham, Canterbury and here we are!' Cliff is a private man, reminding his children of their grandfather with his traditional ways and characteristics. They respect his steadfast values which include kindness, honesty and service to the family: 'He has an incredible memory for places and directions, a very broad general knowledge and solves crosswords with ease.' When requesting more information he filled in with, '… went to Froebel Kindergarten from age 5 to 8, then Bedford Modern School until the summer of 1939. Obliged to leave, earn a crust, war imminent, went into Sun Insurance office, early 1942 conscripted and volunteered for the Navy. After initial training as seaman decided it would be nice to fly. Went into Fleet Air Arm as Observer, sent to Trinidad beginning of 1943 for flying training, came home and commissioned that autumn with squadron in various remote, or not so remote, parts of the UK until August 1944. Then on Formidable and out to join the Pacific Fleet and to see the Japanese, relieved in June 1945, eventually got home later that autumn. Demobbed in April 1946, sent back to Sun Insurance in Bedford, later nine years in Wisbech, and the rest of the time down here in Kent until retirement, a little early, in 1982 at the age of 60. I cannot say I ever really enjoyed my work, but very few of us are able to do what we want in that respect, but at least it kept the wolf from the door. Back in those early days University was only available to those few who, or whose family, could afford it.'

At his Fleet Air Arm training squadron, he struck up a friendship with a pilot, Reg Elliot, and swapped crews. A week later his initial original crew were killed, and he flew with Reg for the rest of the war. They trained in the West Indies and had a fun time, in a great environment, with lots of friends. By coincidence he met his cousin, Geoff Swaffield, in Port of Spain, Trinidad. He then flew from land bases in the UK, and travelled out to the Far East, via Suez.

May 1945 – HMS Formidable after the first Kamikaze strike

The British Navy had a group of aircraft carriers, amongst which were Indomitable, Indefatigable, Illustrious and Formidable. They sailed to the Far East at the end of the war in Europe, making up part of the British Pacific Fleet. Clifford, a navigator with the Fleet Air Arm, flew spotting and bombing missions from Formidable as part of Operation Iceberg, formed to strike at Japanese airfields on the Sakashima Islands. It was at this time the Japanese performed their terrifying kamikaze attacks. The American fleet had carriers with wooden decks which, when bombed, could collapse causing huge amounts of damage. The British carriers were protected by thick armour plating and, often, the bombs would bounce off them. The Formidable was built by Harland and Wolff in Belfast in 1939. In the Spring of 1945, the Americans were completing their big push through the Japanese islands trying to take Okinawa. Vice-Admiral Chuichi Nagumo of the Imperial Japanese Navy was, at the time, one of the finest naval tacticians using craft that, in 1941, were modern and superbly equipped but, by 1944, had become outdated.

Life for the seamen on board the carrier in the sweltering heat and humidity was pretty unbearable. Water and fresh food were short, prickly heat, boils and rashes caused great discomfort and stomach illnesses such as diarrhoea and gastroenteritis sapped their energy. Despite this, morale was high. In Chambers Dictionary the word 'kamikaze' is described as '… a Japanese airman, or 'plane, making a suicide attack, an act of certain or deliberate self-destruction in pursuit of a cause.' The ships never knew when the suicide bombers would attack, or where or how – it was the most frightening thing in the world.' Clifford was on Formidable, on 4 May 1945, when a kamikaze attack was made with 'superficial damage' although eighteen aircraft were lost. Five days later he had just completed a foray in the three-seater Grumman Avenger bomber, and had landed back on deck. "We were having lunch," he said mildly, "There was

May 1945 – Mayhem on HMS Formidable after kamikaze strike

a big thud and we wondered what was going on. The tannoy was peeping away merrily, and all the men were at Action Stations." The official report states that, 'On 4 May 1945 a Zeke Kamikaze aircraft from Sakashima Gunto crashed onto the flight deck with a 600lb bomb, causing damage to radar and flight deck, which was then out of action for five days. On 9 May 1945 the ship was damaged by another aircraft, off the same island. The aircraft dived from astern, and hit – carrying a 600lb bomb. Six aircraft and the deck were wrecked, and ten others damaged in the hangar, by fire.'

Cliff was nearly thirty when he married Sheila Orchard from Birmingham. Their eldest son Simon wrote:

> 'Cliff met my mother at a tennis club in Bedford. Her parents were Frederick 'Cherry' Orchard and Anne [née Taylor]. Grandpa Orchard was then working for the Electricity Board in Bedford, he was an innovator and introduced a new form of electrical street lighting in London. He also wrote text books, Mum has always said we would have enjoyed each other's company now that I've followed an academic path. I remember him as Area manager of Eastern Electricity based in Cambridge.'

Nanny Orchard is described as having a 'volatile temperament' – without perhaps the same easy-going acceptancy of a lot of the Swaffs. The families were different, and tolerances were less guarded. According to Sheila her mother was 'very difficult', and it is a testament to their love and loyalty that Cliff and Sheila celebrated their Golden Wedding in 2001. There are four children. Simon, Sue, Jonathan and Christopher. Sue, their only daughter and second child, is applauding:

> 'The absolute core of it all, is the incredibly strong, close, loving family created by my parents. We could not now be more dispersed geographically, which in some ways is a real shame, because we miss the day to day contact. I get on so well with my brothers and my sisters-in-law that, even if they were not family, I know they would all be very special friends. My mother is absolutely amazing, to me she is characterised by fairness, kindness, always thinking of others, cheerfulness, determination, a positive outlook, and never expressing any feelings of being sorry for herself. After her first heart attack in 1986, I remember a conversation with the doctor who was explaining just how serious the situation was, and added, 'But sometimes our patients surprise us' and I thought at the time, 'My Mum will surprise you!'

1996 – Simon, Sue, Jonathan and Christopher

Simon's first memories are of the early sixties in Wisbech, Cambridgeshire, where the family had happy times. He attended Ramnoth Road Primary:

> '… all high windows, tarseal and railings', and Miss Pearce's, where they studied in a room at the back of her house. 'My strongest memories were of family days out to the North Norfolk Coast, to Holkham or Brancaster. Everyone piled into the little A30 my father drove for work. When we arrived we trekked from the car park, along the beach,

until we were out of sight of anyone else – my father was never one for crowds. It was like the retreat from Moscow, Sue and I staggering along under heavy bags, Mum carrying Jonathan, Dad weighed down with a vast wind shelter he had made, plus enough water to wash an army. We also had family holidays in Devon and Cornwall, or Pembrokeshire. We were woken at 1am and set off across country, travelling overnight to avoid the traffic, Mum sitting in the back with Sue and Jon, me in the front with Dad. This was a great adventure, with early morning stops in small towns, finally arriving at the caravan in the late morning.'

Coincidentally Jenny, Simon's wife, has very similar memories of her family travelling from Hertfordshire to Devon in the same way. Every Whitsun the Swaffields travelled to Walberswick, 'I can recall now the smell of the gas cooker in Dabar's old caravan, the smell of wet grass in the mornings, and the canvas ablution tent.' On other occasions they visited Walberswick and, across the Blyth, Southwold with its inland lighthouse, ivy-clad Swan Hotel, Adnams Brewery – where still the barrels are loaded onto drays and drawn by Suffolk Punches through the town. Here, for several summers, a house was rented on South Green and shared by the Clifford Swaffields and their children with Owen and Bunty Milligan, split-generation cousins from Basil's eldest sister, Minnie Parker's, side. Owen and Bunty have four boys who enjoyed playing on the beach with their Swaff cousins.

Lenham, Kent – Sheila Swaffield with her eldest son, Simon

Cliff and Sheila made good and lasting friends in Wisbech, some through Cliff's involvement with the Round Table, but also mixing with the farming fraternity, as had so many members of his family before him. Perhaps he had wanted to study agriculture, but the war got in the way. They visited friends on farms, and it was not long before they were helping here and there. Simon remembers, 'We would all pitch in at shearing or dipping, or haymaking, even after Dad retired.' Peter Turner has remained a firm family friend and, after university, Simon went to Wisbech and spent the summer working on his fruit farm.

'In later years I enjoyed geography, perhaps influenced by the day trips I took with Dad. He did his rounds as an insurance agent in the Fens. I would sit in the car and look at Ordnance Survey maps, of which Dad had a large collection. Occasionally I went with him into offices, smelling of polish and tobacco. On some days we would have our packed lunch (brown bread sandwiches, boiled eggs, Thermos of tea) watching trains on the main east coast line. Looking back, the most amazing thing was the way I was allowed to spend Saturdays with my friend Sammy Sampson, train spotting at Peterborough North. Sammy's mother would collect me and my sandwiches, which were in an old gas mask bag. She took us early to Wisbech station and the two of us, both 10 years old, travelled across to Peterborough via March, and set up camp at the south end of the down platform. We ate our sandwiches early and, by lunchtime, we had had enough.' Then Clifford got a new job and they moved to Kent, where Simon went to Maidstone Grammar until 1971.

'We had a radical lively young teacher who introduced us to Steinbeck and Hemingway. I suffered in French and Physics and breezed through Maths. I remember as much about the travelling to and from school, as of the days themselves. I caught a train from Lenham where we lived (usually by the skin of my teeth after a sprint down to the station), and met up with the other boys and girls from the village, and we went through our adolescent rituals in a rattling carriage, or waiting on a windy station platform. Simon joined the Scouts and Venturers, and the Combined Cadet Force, despite his opposition to military games. A naval section was started during his sixth form years, and he spent an enjoyable three years messing around on river boats, rising to the dizzy heights of Coxswain, 'The CCF camps were good, particularly a memorable week on a coastal patrol boat in the Clyde.'

Maidstone Grammar encouraged Simon to apply to Cambridge, and he was offered a place in December 1971, 'It was a great Christmas present for my parents, who have been as proud as punch ever since!' He read Geography, learnt to row, joined an acting group, and drank to excess, 'A typical student. Throughout Mum and Dad provided cash, taxied us to and fro, and kept a bed for us to sleep off each hectic term.' All the children had tertiary training. And then it was the question of finding a job. 'Mum kept worrying about my lack of career ambitions, and sent adverts she cut from the Daily Telegraph. One was

for an architectural assistant (landscape) at Lewisham Council. After demonstrating that I could indeed draw, I found myself in an office with a great bunch of radical young architects, working on public housing and environmental improvements in south London. A lot of time was spent putting the world to rights in pubs, but we were also committed, and I designed a major scheme which was still there last time I visited Catford. It was quickly obvious to me that I enjoyed this new activity, called landscape architecture, but that I needed a qualification. So my long-suffering parents supported me for two more years at Manchester. Again, taxi service provided, plus furniture and housing utensils from the ever growing store at Lenham. Dad is an inveterate hoarder, he will not dispose of anything. The attic and garage at Lenham rapidly became full of furniture, as did every room in the house after my Grandfather died. But it was useful when we were all students. There is still furniture circulating amongst the four of us.'

1997 – Simon and Clifford

'The most significant event for me at Manchester was at the beginning of year two, when I met Jenny Moore at a student party. Although she was on the undergraduate landscape architecture programme, we are the same age, as she had worked to gain her financial independence before going to college. I don't know how she put up with me as, in addition to the design course, I was rowing for the university, which entailed three hours training each day, six days a week. Whenever we met I was tired and hungry, and usually fell asleep on the couch. Jenny's family are from Dublin. Her father, Arthur Moore, was eldest of four boys, sons of a father who was a builder in Dun Laoghaire. Her mother, Florence [née Dickens] was also from Dublin. Both families were 'Anglo Irish' and they left Dublin before she was born, moving to London and building a house in Cuffley, Hertfordshire. Arthur Moore became contracts director for a major building firm Trollope and Colls.

After completing Landscape Architecture at Manchester, Simon took a job in Edinburgh, working for Scottish Special Housing Association, living in an attic flat on the Royal mile, 'Cold but very atmospheric.' He and Jenny married at Northaw, Hertfordshire, she continued her studies at Manchester and eventually they bought a flat in Edinburgh, and both spent time on projects in Orkney and Shetland. After a couple of years they moved out to a small cottage in the East Lothian village of Garvald. Then the travel bug hit them, and Simon started applying for overseas jobs in universities. 'Finally I got a telegram from New Zealand, offering me a position at Lincoln College, as it was then. We travelled via Japan to arrive in New Zealand in November 1982. I have taught at Lincoln ever since. We fell in love with the South Island; particularly the southern Alps. It was like a warm version of Scotland, few people, wide open spaces. We spent weekends either tramping, sailing or house renovating. Jenny easily got a job as a landscape architect, and won two major awards in her subsequent work. I was promoted to leader of the small landscape programme at Lincoln College in 1985, enrolled part time on a PhD, introduced an undergraduate degree in 1988, became head of a new department in 1991 (completing the PhD that year), and was appointed to a personal chair as Professor of Landscape Architecture (New Zealand's first) in 1998. Lincoln College was the first agricultural college in the southern hemisphere and has now become Lincoln University.'

In May 1989 their first boy, Matthew, was born in the middle of a cold, wet, southerly storm. Matthew has special needs and is a Downs Syndrome child. There was immediate acceptance from the family at home, and complete support. At four months old, they took Matty home and there was a natural bonding between grandparents and their first grandchild. There have been constant comings and goings between Christchurch and Lenham, Simon using sabbatical leaves to visit the family, and Cliff and Sheila making long journeys to visit them in New Zealand. Pleasurable holidays in beautiful surroundings, a place where they too would have settled, if it were not for the ties of England. During WWII, Cliff had spent leave in Australia and had sensed the opportunity to create a more independent life, away from the crowded conditions of the UK.

Simon, Jenny, Matty and Martin live far away, but hold close ties with the family, 'I feel generations away from Dabar Swaffield, but was amused when I discovered that my great-great Uncle, Ben Swaffield, was Head Bailiff at Chatsworth when Joseph Paxton, the famous landscape gardener, was redesigning the grounds and building glasshouses. It's a nice connection to my present occupation. It's an interesting thing, generational cycles, I have colleagues at work in Christchurch, who are sixth generation New Zealanders, but that only takes their family back to the 1850s. If the Swaffields count back six generations we find ourselves in the midst of typical agrarian economy of the early 1700s. I think that a long generational cycle is critical to the understanding of the family, and its characteristics.'

Sue and Jonathan were born when the family lived in Wisbech. Sue wrote:

'Simon always the big brother, but a close friend, Jonathan (now) even-tempered, funny, knowledgeable – different from when we were at primary school. He was always the one being told off, did not know his alphabet, or who had cast the whole of his new fishing rod into a pond.'

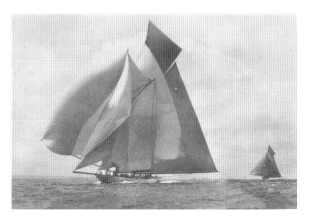

More sail than boat – Cowes

Chris, who is ten years younger, and Sue have enjoyed sailing together with the Ocean Youth Club, Chris as skipper and Sue as cabin boy, on a 76 ft gaff ketch with youngsters from a variety of backgrounds. The most memorable, was a trip to Iceland encountering whales, the aurora borealis, battling with a Force 9 gale and dealing with a sick crew miles and miles off the north-east of Iceland. Sue (or Swaffs as she is known) has travelled a lot, is a trained teacher (enjoying Geography and Maths), and a BEd (Newnham). She enjoys her present job as Lecturer at Cambridge University, Faculty of Education, having completed her tertiary training at Homerton. She finished her schooling young, and unable to start college, spent six months working in Islington as a Community Service Volunteer for a charity called 'Highbury Horse', giving rides on rag-and-bone ponies to local children on Highbury Fields, 'Leading a string of broken-down ponies across the Holloway Road was always quite eventful.' That wet summer she and Simon helped a charity 'Children's Relief International', taking kids from Leeds on a camping activity holiday. She has vivid recollections of Simon '… walking a heavy, wet marquee up the hill to repitch it away from the mud …' After initial studies, Sue had various teaching jobs including being an Exchange Teacher to Mater Dei College, Tuggerah in New South Wales, Australia. Her studies continued with Open University courses, Teaching English as a Foreign Language, and an MA in Applied Research in Education. Sport has not been neglected, and she has studied the Royal Yachting Association theory and practical exams. Sailing is a great love, as is ski-ing, swimming, gym and Korfball – a game of Dutch origin resembling basketball played by teams of six men and six women a side.

Jon Swaffield was working in Raleigh in North Carolina, at the State University as Assistant Professor in the Department of Genetics. He finds languages a chore, but is a PhD in Biochemistry and Molecular Biology, studied at Manchester after schooling in Kent, where he joined the CCF and was confronted with 'Arduous Training'. This produced a love of outdoor pursuits such as hiking, camping,

1995 – Jonathan and Clifford Swaffield

swimming and ski-ing. Things that have stuck in Jon's mind are Churchill's funeral when he was only 5, 'Maybe it was the sonorous tones of the Dead March of Saul booming over the radio, as the sombre funeral procession wound its way though London's streets.' When he was seven the Torrey Canyon tanker, loaded with 120,000 tons of crude oil, struck rocks off the Scilly Isles and produced Britain's worst pollution disaster. The beautiful Cornish coves and bays were blanketed in thick oil, and over 200,000 birds died. The following year saw the Swaffields leaping about with joy when Manchester United [a professional football team since 1885] won the ultimate prize of the European Cup against Benefica. The global population experienced man's first landing on the moon, when Neil Armstrong, on 20 July 1969, stood on the moon's surface and uttered the words, 'Man's small step for mankind' must have thrilled the heart of any nine-year-old boy.

1982 – Freetown, Sierra Leone

Another occasion which has stayed in Jon's mind, is the Falklands War between Argentina and Britain in 1982. There was fierce conflict on the Falklands, and more than 1000 lives were lost from both sides, before the Argentineans surrendered, and the islands were returned to British rule on 15 June. My husband [Michael Wheatley] and I {Natalie] were living in Freetown, Sierra Leone at the time. Freetown has one of the largest deep bay ports, where liners such as QEII can sail right up to the dockside. The children had come out for the holidays and, the night before we got wind of a ship coming in to collect stores. There was instant activity as we dragged out various Union Jacks, got up in the dark and were down at the Oil Refinery at dawn. We were the only Britons to greet the P&O Cruiser, SS Canberra, stuffed with troops. The men on board had spotted, through their gun sights, our flag-waving family under the palm trees. Easing into the tight dock, the Canberra refuelled rather slowly. Coverage of the lusty conversation between camouflage-clad paratroopers, and our tropically-dressed teenage daughters, was reported by Brent Sadler and shown on UK's 'News at Ten' that night.

On 16 January 1991 (Jon's 31st birthday) Saddam Hussein of Iraq invaded Kuwait. A Gulf War initiated originally over argument about a shared oil field, and missiles were fired at Tel Aviv and Haifa, as well as cities in Saudi Arabia. The Gulf War, known to the Americans as 'Desert Storm' and to the British as 'Operation Granby', was the first large-scale demonstration of modern technological warfare, in which guided missiles, 'smart' munitions, night vision equipment, infra-red sensors, Global Positioning Systems, cruise missiles, free-flight rockets with multiple warheads, anti-missile missiles, and modern data communications systems, were deployed. The Iraqis were impotent against the technology waged against them. In 1993 Jon was working at a teaching hospital in Dallas, when David Koresh, cult leader of the Branch Davidians [offshoot of the Seventh-Day Adventists who believe in the literal apocalyptic end of history], was killed in a fire as a result of a siege by the FBI at the Davidian Headquarters in Waco, Texas. Jon watched the army helicopters bringing victims, landing on the roof opposite his window.

Whilst chronicling these devastating events that have taken place during his lifetime, the phone has rung and our frightened daughter [Susina] in Panamá said, "Mum, put the TV on, something terrible has happened in America, it looks like the Third World War…". At the same time there was a flash message barking on my radio of the terrorist destruction of the World Trade Centre in New York and the Pentagon in Washington. The world today, 11 September 2001, is in furore, people are in turmoil and it is an unbelievable act of pure violence that is difficult for any human being to take in.

DAILY TELEGRAPH – Wednesday 12 September 2001

WAR ON AMERICA – Bush Vows revenge on Terrorists who Rained Death on New York

America suffered the worst terrorist attack in history yesterday, with thousands feared dead as hijacked planes, full of innocent passengers, crashed into the financial and military centres of the world's most powerful nation. Two airliners hit the twin towers of the World Trade Centre, an unmistakable part of the most famous city skyline, causing both 110 storeys to collapse in flames and dust. The attack happened at just after 9am local time. America goes to work early. Fifty thousand people work in the Trade Centre, and it has eighty thousand visitors each day. An ordinary Tuesday morning was suddenly transformed into a tragedy of almost unimaginable proportions. George Bush, President, appeared to be in no doubt that terrorists were responsible. The attack caused jubilation in Iraq, and among some radical groups in the Middle East, which saw it as revenge for America's fifty years of support for Israel. Suspicion for the atrocities immediately focused on Osama bin Laden, the multi-millionaire Islamic terrorist, possibly shielded in Afghanistan.

Jon's reaction to this disaster, was that of so many living in the States. His first thought was of a friend who worked on Wall Street. He got the address off a website, plugged it into a digital map, and sent an email. Next day he heard that the friend worked next to the Twin Towers, and got out into the street just after the second plane had hit, with débris and bodies raining down on him. He sheltered for five hours, and then walked up into the centre of the city devastated and shocked. Shock and outrage is the big thing – terrorism had not hit America before. "This kind of thing happens to people over there" … was the reaction of American citizens, "Let's shoot them back to the Stone Age, we are for freedom, we are the greatest democracy the world has ever known. We are the good guys."

'Now', says Jon, 'Americans are sitting up and smelling the coffee – although I would hesitate to estimate what percent of Americans could have located Afghanistan on the map. There is a real ignorance of foreign policy. The government is interested in keeping the oil flowing, the markets open irrespective of how this is achieved.'

Jon's wife, Kim [née Grannon] met him whilst she was studying Japanese and Business Studies at Sheffield University, later working for Japanese Airlines. A talented needlewoman, she established her own soft furnishing business, tailoring covers and drapes for clients when they were living in Raleigh. They have three children, Elizabeth, Thomas and Robert. Jon has always

been interested in moving into industry, and the family now live in Texas, where he is a Senior Scientist with Pharmaceutical Discovery at Lexicon Genetics.

2001 – America – Tom, Jon, Kim, Robbie and Elizabeth Swaffield

Christopher Swaffield came into the world at 12 Ham Lane, Lenham on St Swithin's day in 1965, interrupting the 9 o'clock news. Like his brothers he attended Maidstone Grammar, and then went to Plymouth Poly to follow a course in computer studies, a subject he did not enjoy. However he did enjoy horse-riding and walking on Dartmoor, and off-shore sailing. He travelled to New Zealand, and there got to know his elder brother Simon, who had gone to Cambridge when Chris was five. He then joined the Island Cruising Club at Salcombe, taught youngsters to sail dinghies, before being promoted to sail classic yachts, "The kind of sailing one dreams about," he said, "I then joined the Ocean Youth Club which trains young people with sailing/life skills, and has more than a dozen boats scattered around the UK coastline. Chris skippered his own boat, and the highlight was the trip round Iceland when Sue was part of his crew, "It was here I discovered that whale breath is very smelly, and the sea inside the Arctic Circle is too cold to swim in!" In 1997 Chris married Yvette Lewis, a nurse trained at Addenbrookes in Cambridge. He is now training to be a chiropractor. Clifford, though sparse in words about his own life, has taken a keen interest in Swaffield and Milligan history and genealogy. His genuine affection for both sides of the family has developed into a life-long hobby. He has a bursting attic, albums of photographs, and stacks of family trees. The one he customised for me, Natalie, has been rolled and unrolled continuously.

Chapter 16

DORSETSHIRE ~ BEAMINSTER AND FAR BEYOND 1900–2002
Tom, poor Nell, Nancy goes to Tasmania

George Swaffield (1841–1936) and Harriet Wakely (1845–1929)

Ann Rosetta-	Julia Jane	Still born	Mary Jane (Jen)	Caroline Esther	George William	John James	Fred'k Job	Emily Eliza	Harriet & Tom	Emily Agnes	**Tom Edwin**	**Ellen Harriet** (Nell)	**Annie Louisa** (Nancy)
1867	1868	1870	1871	1873	1875	1877	1879	1880	1881	1882	1884	1886	1889
1951	1871	1870	1966	1969	1963	1969	1879	1880	1881	1966	1961	1917	1975

Tom Swaffield 1884–1961 and Alice Hopper 1890–1976

Audrey Mary	Arthur Thomas (John)	Richard George (Dick)	Evelyn Olive (Olive)
1917	1919–1992	1922	1926

Nancy Swaffield 1889–1975 and Edward Alexander Crane Benham (Ted) 1877–1959

Eileen Mary 1917–1987	Alfred (Bill) 1919	Tasma Joan 1921	Barbara Annie 1924–1971

Beaminster is where our story began. Here, and in Stoke Abbott, many of the Swaffield clan remain. Beaminster is a pretty Dorsetshire town, which in 1755 when John & Betty Swaffield were married, was already much ravaged by fire. Later it became known for its successful Town Band, started by George Swaffield in 1878, and for its hard-working Fire Brigade. The alarm would sound, the fire engine was dragged out, the bell clanging in unison with the drums and triangles practising for the Saturday competition. The engine clattered past in a cloud of dust. "They'll be off Stoke way," the bandsmen would nod knowingly, "Dry as tinder summer time, thatch all scrimpy. Best not spread it to Beaminster."

Stoke Abbott

Fred Swaffield wrote his pencilled memoir in his exercise book, mostly in Stoke Abbott, but he had many family living just two miles away in Beaminster.

'[Now] … there are not so many houses as there used to be – a lot have been burned down or fallen to pieces … [there are] two at the bottom of Broadclothes and they were pulled down when Mr Smith's new cowstalls were built. Just inside of Pounds Orchard gate used to be a big barn, where the Laurels are used to be three houses.

Over right the horse trough used to be two up in the little garden. They were burnt down one night. When they were alight Beaminster fire brigade came over – it was a night all hands on the pump and the horse trough was empty in a few moments and then the fire did gain up again. There was nearly as much beer and cider drunk that night as water used. One man that lived close to the house that was burnt was at the New Inn sat by the fire when his wife came running in:

"Yer" she said, "Come on whoam."

"Wa far?"

"Well they houses be avire just above."

"Well wast that da do wi I?"

"Well look sharp an come on."

"Well I can't help it can I? Wast thee spect I da go up an dout ern then. Let Georgie come down an dout ern heself."

"Well be you coming on. I never seed a fellar take anything so cool in me life sit there so comfortable with a house avire a few yards from his own."

"I see thest spect I to gid up on the roof and keep the sparks off. Doesn I should have all the blooming parish looking at me instead of the vire. I can seen myself sot up there wi me legs hanging down over each side wi a bucket of wader in each hand waiting var the house da catch vire. I should be in a nice place if did catch vire, theyed think twas a blooming cockspar up there ur tomtit."

c1906 – Beaminster, studio portrait L–R, Rose, Nell, Tom, Emily and Nancy Swaffield

George and Harriet got news of the fire, and wondered at the damage. But life had to go on in Beaminster, there was much to do to tend the children, look after visiting grandchildren, grow the vegetables and maintain community involvement. George continued his postal round and, in the evenings, encouraged his young Band of musicians. At home, Harriet calmly got on with her cooking, washing and other chores. Upstairs in the attic, their youngest boy, Tom, seriously practised on his trombone, night after night, not disturbing too many of his family as, by then, the older ones had moved away. By 1914 agriculture had declined, and Britain was importing half its food. Whole families were leaving rural areas, and the Swaffields of Beaminster gradually disseminated to the London suburbs of Paddington and Lambeth, to Harrow and Wealdstone in Middlesex, to Wokingham in Berkshire, but the real adventurer was Annie Louisa (Nancy), George and Harriet's youngest daughter, who courted Alexander Edward (Ted) Benham and went to Tasmania.

c1912 – Tom with Nancy before she left for Tasmania

Nancy had attended Beaminster Grammar School and then became a pupil teacher there, before moving on to Allington in Bridport. She never qualified and complained about her poor pay as she was uncertified. But she preferred teaching to housework and cooking, returning to

Phyllis with her parents – Jack and Cissy

it in later life in Somerset. She taught her granddaughter, Linda, at Lamport School in Northamptonshire. Linda remembers being shown how to crochet and knit, "I thought I could play around as it was Granny," she laughed, "But I couldn't, I had to sit still and concentrate." Once he was finished with school, Nancy's one-up brother, Tom, moved up to Middlesex and lived with his sister, Jen, whilst training as a clerk/typist.

Tom loved music and was talented. As well as playing the trombone, he later became an amateur conductor. His elder brother, George, played the triangle in his father's band when he was nine years old, and the cornet in the Maidenhead Town Band. John James (Jack) played the clarinet for many years in the Pleasant Sunday Afternoon Orchestra at Wealdstone, and was soon joined by his daughter, Phyllis who was a gifted pianist, and sang in public.

Tom also played with them at Wealdstone, and started off another group once he moved to Peterborough. Jack was a gardener for forty years to a Jewish family at Hatch End named Falk. Early on in his employment, Alice Hopper, was nanny in the same household. One day she noticed that Jack had a gentleman visitor, so asked the Cook if she might take the men a tray of tea. Jack's visitor was his younger brother, Tom, who Alice later married and they had four children.

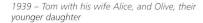
1939 – Tom with his wife Alice, and Olive, their younger daughter

The eldest is Audrey. She attended Vaughan Road school in Harrow until she was thirteen, and then took an exam for the Chiswick Polytechnic where she studied, travelling each day from home, until she was fifteen. She then joined Baker Perkins at Willesden and took the train each morning with her father. The Company relocated to Peterborough and the family moved north in 1933. Audrey was then sixteen and remembers holidays:

'We often took a pony and trap to the station, and then we took the train eastwards to Clacton, I loved Clacton, or to Westcliff, Felixstowe, Yarmouth or south to Folkestone. Other holidays were spent in Beaminster with Grandad and Mam, assorted aunts, uncles and cousins.'

Audrey developed an interest in genealogy when she discovered that her cousin, Owen Swaffield, had married into the family of Sir Goldsworthy Gurney. He was a Cornish inventor who built a series of steam carriages, one of which in 1829 ran from London to Bath and back at the rate of fifteen miles per hour. Audrey has a picture of this remarkable carriage, puffing steam and spilling over with people. The picture is hung on the wall of her flat situated within the shadow of Peterborough Cathedral. She has tirelessly searched for details of Swaffields, Wakelys, Canterburys and Hoppers amongst others. She receives requests from all over the world for genealogical information, and she has gone through all available sources of Public Record Offices, Baptismal Lists, Wills, census, newspapers and has written thousands of letters. At one time her searches were so intense she was travelling to London each week by train getting off at Liverpool Street to catch a number 63 bus. If one failed to come, she walked along the Farringdon Road to the Public Record Office at Clerkenwell. She has an old typewriter which sits on the floor of her flat, and is lifted onto the table when she has more details to record.

Her brother Arthur, known as John, became a Baptist Minister and he and his wife, Catherine Mary Saul, had two sons, Richard and Peter. Peter, also trained as a Baptist Minister and as a teacher, and is now Assistant Chaplain at Berkhamsted Collegiate School and teaches

1987 – Arthur [John] and his wife, Mary, baby Luke, Rachel and Peter Swaffield

Religious Studies and English. His wife, Rachel, is Head teacher of a middle school in the same town. Richard tragically died in 2003 of a sudden heart attack. He was a Bank Inspector in London. Audrey's second brother, Richard (Dick), was in the Merchant Navy during the Second World War. He married May La Cock, a South African who comes from a Huguenot family. Dick emigrated to South Africa and became Area Representative for the Dickinson Robinson Group, and they have settled in Port Elizabeth. Olive, the youngest, had a beautiful soprano voice and took the lead in operatics. She became a school teacher, married Tom Hodson, a Quantity Surveyor, and had two sons, one Richard died in 1981 and Robert has become a solicitor.

At seventeen Audrey continued working as a typist with Baker Perkins, whilst her father became Commercial Correspondent. Audrey became engaged at the beginning of WWII but

her fiancé was killed in the Greek Islands. Later, in 1944, she married Bill Bartron from Seattle, who was seven years her junior. He was in the United States Air Force based at RAF Conington. It was not an easy relationship, marred by the war and frequent separations. For some time Audrey lived on the West Coast of America. But Bill was away often and, eventually, she travelled home with the children by train across Canada, from Vancouver to Winnipeg.

"The train was powered by coal and wood," she said, "It was bitterly cold … Margaret was only four but soon found the Men's Smoking Room which had a spittoon and was warm." They eventually joined a ship at Halifax, Nova Scotia and returned to Peterborough and moved in with her parents, Tom and Alice. Bill Bartron was sent to Japan, then into the Korean war, later to Germany. He visited England but hated the life, the cold and the atmosphere. The couple were divorced in 1955, and Bill remarried and remained in America.

1973 – Paul, Tom, Margaret and Clive Bartron

Margaret is the only one of the four children living in Britain. She studied Domestic Science, is married and has two sons, one in Singapore. Audrey's eldest son, Paul, lives in Tacoma, Washington State, USA. He is a pianist and composer, as well as being an excellent chess player. Young Tom learnt violin at school and now plays classical guitar. He is an Architectural Technician, married with one daughter and lives in Seattle. Clive, a nurse, lives in Narrogin, Western Australia. He is sporty and excels at squash. He has been married twice and has three children. The first, Graham, lives in Yaxley, Peterborough and the other two children are also musically inclined.

1998 – Australia – Clive's children, Stephen and Claire

Audrey is now in her mid-eighties, does her photocopying at the Indian newsagents, shops in the market, goes on holiday with friends, visits her sister Olive, is a member of the History Society and still rides her bike, although with less enjoyment since an unpleasant mugging. It is a joy for her to return to Stoke Abbott and Beaminster, and she is presently busy finding out more about her grandmother's Wakely family.

The year Audrey was born, a letter from England dated 9 January 1917, arrived in Tasmania for Nancy from her older sister Ellen (Nell) who was a teacher. Nell complained of the freezing weather at home. The school in Beaminster was closed because of an outbreak of diphtheria from which several children died, 'A little girl named Mary Watts died yesterday morning in Fleet Street, and two more in the family are ill.' Nell was ill, 'I don't get up only occasionally now. Some days I feel a little brighter, but I have such a cough and bring up phlegm still. I got up a little Boxing Day, and again today, but it is bitterly cold. I was to have gone to Ventnor on December 18th, but the doctors thought it best for me to wait until I was stronger, and the weather not so cold, for it is a long journey to the Isle of Wight. I was in very much pain last week for several days.' Nell died soon afterwards of tuberculosis. She was thirty-three.

Ted and Nancy met at a dance party at Bridport, soon after which, they became engaged, and Ted emigrated to Tasmania. Ted Benham was born in Leicester in 1877. It is believed a fire ruined his father's business forcing the family to move to Bridport, where his grandfather had a gentleman's outfitters in the High Street. Ted worked as a cutter, but it was a job he always hated. He formed a branch of the Scouts Association in Bridport and later was Commissioner of Scouts in Tasmania deputising, on one occasion, for Lord Baden-Powell. His children remember being told that, in 1912, Ted was the first man to greet Norwegian explorer Roald Amundsen when he arrived in Tasmania. Amundsen had completed his epic Antarctic journey travelling hundreds of miles overland with dogs to triumphantly reach the South Pole on 11 December 1911, thus beating Robert Falcon Scott and his brave expedition companions by five weeks.

1917 – Tasmania – Ted Benham and Nancy at home

Five years after Ted had sailed they were married in Hobart by licence in November 1916. They had four children, two in Tasmania Eileen (Mary) and Alfred (Bill). Soon after they returned home, Tasma Joan was born in West Ealing in September 1921 and later Barbara, who died at forty-seven.

Eileen Mary married Edward Smith in 1938, a year before the outbreak of WWII, and they had two daughters, Thelma and Marilyn (Lynn) both born at Bath. Eileen and her husband divorced in 1965 and she went to live in the seaside town of Clevedon in a delightful cottage with a pretty garden. She died in 1978. Both girls married, Thelma had twin boys and Marilyn

and her husband, Chris Lacey, whom she met at the University of East Anglia, have a daughter, Eleanor. Eileen was very interested in family history research, and was particularly involved in discovering about the Canterburys and their tie-up with the Swaffields in Stoke Abbott. Some of her findings have been consolidated into this book She appreciated her cousin Audrey's help and, together, they stayed in The New Inn in Stoke Abbott for a few days in the summer of 1980. She was also glad to have the loan from her cousin Phyllis Swaffied of Grandfather George's Sunday School notebook, and that of the 'narrative' of Fred Swaffield from the New Inn, Stoke Abbott, from Fred's sister Winifred. Eileen also appreciated her niece, Deborah Brown's research abilities and wrote as acknowledgement, 'Deborah delved into her late mother's papers and photographs. I thank her for her encouragement and interest.'

Bill Benham was christened Alfred George Swaffield Benham after his two grandfathers. He was born in Tasmania in 1919 and came to England when he was two years old. He got his nickname as 'Captain Bill' from the Captain on board the ship of the White Star Line on their homeward voyage. At sixteen he joined the RAF as an Instrument Fitter Aircraft Apprentice, and left the RAF when he was thirty. He then worked for a civilian aircraft firm for five years, followed by thirty years on rocket motor production and development at the Summerfield Defence Centre near Kidderminster. After retirement at sixty-five, he took an Open University Degree studying Geology and History, and graduated at the age of seventy-four. During WW II, whilst serving in France in 1940, Bill had a narrow escape. He recalls, 'The ill-fated Cunard

c1940s – Shropshire, Tasma Joan and Richard Harding

Liner SS Lancastria was sent to St Nazaire in the Bay of Biscay to evacuate about 9,000 RAF personnel as the French surrendered. Although we were keen to board and get away, we missed the boat by a day. No-one can imagine how many more lives would have been lost had we caught it. A lone German 'plane dropped a bomb down the funnel and the ship rapidly sank. More than five thousand RAF men were drowned, but the news was censored and does not seem to be widely known today.' In retrospect it was a disaster much greater than that of the widely publicised sinking of the Titanic with fifteen hundred lives lost in 1912.

In the year 1999, Bill reached his 80th birthday and had a party. Sadly his son, Christopher, had died seventeen years previously. Treated for indigestion it was discovered he had terminal stomach cancer in 1983, leaving a widow, Gina, and two little boys, Stuart and Nicholas. Before he died, Christopher held down the job of Control Manager of a large power station near Huddersfield. He was very interested in steam trains. Hazel and Bill's next child, Andrea, was born in 1953. She gained a BSc and became a school teacher. Ten years later girl twins, ten minutes apart, came on the scene. They were so alike that their mother, Hazel, had to put name badges on their uniforms. Catherine and Julia have both had careers in the business world. Catherine gained a Private Secretary's Certificate and has become a Personnel and Training Officer. She follows in Granny Benham's footsteps in enjoying artistic activities such as watercolours, flower arranging and sewing. She has a husband, Robert Harris, and a son, George Alexander. Julia is thankful to be a full-time mother with two healthy children, James and Clare. She trained as a Secretary after attending school and college in

1951 – Northampton Boys Clubs – Scottish boys brought down to the steelworks at Corby – off to the South of France in a coach for a holiday. [Back rt of centre] are Richard and Tasma Joan Harding

Kidderminster, though she was born in Bromsgrove. She married David Lewis in Worcester Cathedral in 1987, and continued to work with the Midland Bank until the children came along.

Tasma Joan was twenty-two and a trained nurse when she married Richard Harding in 1943, he was a Major in the Royal Artillery. After demobilisation Richard joined the unemployed queues and landed a job running the National Association of Boys' Clubs in Northamptonshire. It was early days for foreign travel, but he arranged trips to France for the boys, and used to coach them across the Channel in the 1950s to give them a holiday of a lifetime. Tasma went too, helping with camp cooking on an inadequate Primus. Richard then took up work in the chemical industry in Cheshire and travelled all over the world as Safety Officer. He loved 'do-it-yourself' and designed and built two houses in the village of Great Mollington, and then started further house restoration in Shropshire. Born of a family of hard workers, Richard drove himself onwards and died young at fifty-eight.

Tasma and Richard had two children. Linda married Piers Norbury, a farmer's son and merchant seaman. They adopted two children, Philippa a nursery nurse and Piers who works for the Bank of Scotland. Linda is very interested in family and social history, and uses her artistic and design abilities in her job at the Boat Museum in Ellesmere Port. She deals with school groups from all over the world, and is knowledgeable about life on the canal boats. She shows the children how to knot very thick ropes, and how to paint in the Castles and Roses traditional style. Sadly, her husband, Piers died suddenly on 25 October 2001. Peter has married Ann, and has two daughters – Cheryl who is keen to emigrate to Perth in Australia, and Katie who has a career in computers.

Barbara was the youngest daughter of Ted and Nancy Benham, married and had two children, a son Roger and a daughter, Deborah. Barbara was not well and '… Nancy [her mother] did not appear to realise that Barbara's illness from cancer was terminal. She had to face it when Barbara pre-deceased her mother by four years, in 1971. Barbara's daughter, Deborah, works in art and design and has researched the book 'Pollock's History of English Dolls and Toys'. Deborah once made a dolls house which was shown on TV and worked at the Pollock's Toy Museum in London. She has a daughter, Florence, and lives in Forest Hill. The lives of Ted and Nancy's descendants have become thoroughly British, despite their own adventurous emigration to the small island beneath the large continent of Australia in the first part of the 20th century.

1943 – Barbara

Tasmania [Van Diemen's Land] was discovered in 1642 by Abel J Tasman, and was a penal settlement until 1853. It was granted local government in 1856 and united with the mainland states to form the Commonwealth of Australia in 1901. It was a brave move for Ted to think of a new life on the other side of the world. The journey by sea took months, always with the risk of disease and infection. He was sad to leave the familiar shores of Dorsetshire, to abandon his family business, and to leave his new fiancée, Nancy, who he would not see for five years. Ted was a pioneer, leaving Britain at a time when the beginnings of the winds of WWI were blowing, politics were unsettled and the quality of life at home rather poor. He was looking for a better future for himself and his family. Better than that found in the tailor's cutting room on the Bridport High Street.

George and Harriet were sad to say farewell to their baby, Nancy, particularly as Nell was so ill. For them Tasmania really was 'at the end of the world', but George had read about it and prepared Nancy for her journey. He sensed that she had the inclination to move away and try out new things. There were tears in their eyes as they waved her goodbye, and Nancy was feeling more than sad having had a last flimsy hug from Nell. Her friends gave her ribbons,

new handkerchiefs and lacy pillowcases, and told her she was a 'brave girl', 'bold' and 'mad', but secretly envious of her pioneer spirit, and the romance of seeing Ted again after so long.

1906 – Beaminster George and Harriet

Nancy sailed out to Hobart, Tasmania when she was twenty-seven. She wrote home about her experiences of sailing round the Cape. The liner docked and '… natives surrounded us in canoes. We put letters for posting in a basket, along with money to purchase the stamps, and the natives would disappear and never post the letters.' But some did arrive home in Beaminster from Cape Town and Bombay.

Ted and Nancy settled in Hobart and lived in the suburbs of Lindisfarne, Bellerive and Glenerchy the latter now a large industrial and business area of the city. Today the Tasman Bridge spans the Derwent River but Ted travelled in the Kangaroo Ferry, known as 'Old Double Guts' to get to and from the city. Nancy watched the ferry leave Hobart and cross the river, and could judge when Ted would be home for his supper. Some of her happiest days were in Tasmania, and later in old age she tried to relive them on paper, but her story ends while she is 'still at sea' sailing to her promised land. Ted went into orcharding, and farmed violets and apricots. But life was difficult so, after much heartache, they decided to leave Tasmania with their two children. They returned to an England which was changing fast … '… Some parts of England are become almost as lonesome as the veld of Africa,' wrote Rider Haggard, 'People are deserting the villages wholesale, leaving behind them the mentally incompetent and the physically unfit.' Crafts, folk songs and cart horses began to disappear whilst, for the rich, the countryside became a playground. Vita Sackville West, euphoric after a weekend away, wrote, 'Down in the garden on a lawn of brilliant green, the sprinkled figures … their laughter and the tap of croquet mallets.' This was the end of the era of servants below stairs, when the Master's change coins were scrubbed with a nail brush and his newspaper ironed.

1917 – Tasmania Nancy, baby Mary and a nurse

Things were not easy on the family's return, particularly as WWI had ended only three years previously, and a severe depression ensued. Ted got a job with Whiteways Cider in Whimple, Devon but this did not last and he returned to the trade he so disliked, tailoring. They moved to Bristol and lived in furnished rooms whilst Ted travelled for an outfitting firm, and they survived on his meagre commission. Eventually he bought a tailoring and outfitting business at Axbridge in Somerset, but said he had been swindled over the promise of good business.

1931 – Axbridge – Schoolboy Bill [aged 12] with his mother, Nancy

Nancy let out rooms, and they combined a small photographic studio with the tailoring. Life jogged along and they stayed in the area for seven years. The children went to the local Church school and Bill, alone, passed the 'free place' exams to go to Sexey's School at Blackford. When Eileen Mary was fourteen she left school and took over the housekeeping, plus the two lodgers who were bank clerks. Nancy returned to education and moved to East Brent School, coming home at weekends. She was a natural teacher using school plays and nature walks to give practical experience. Audrey has recorded that 'Uncle Ted and Auntie Nancy were buried in Salwayash churchyard.'

1958 – Nancy and Ted

Nancy's children remember her as 'quite a character' and this trip to the Antipodes was the first of many moves. She always had 'bright ideas' about moving. She would choose a destination, possibly a property, and then list the advantages and the disadvantages, the former far outweighing the latter. Then she asked her children persuasively for their 'advice' as to this proposed move, so that she could then proceed with a clear conscience. Her son Bill would convey her from the old to the new place, and Nancy would depart from the old without a backward glance – the grass over her fence was always greener. Being the youngest of a large family, with brothers and sisters old enough to be her parents, she was perhaps spoiled and able to have her own way more than most children. She remembered how her older siblings would bring her gifts of hair ribbons and trimmings for her hats. She had always thought her birthday was 23 July but, when she had to send for a copy of her birth certificate, she discovered that her true birth date was 17 July 1889, and that she was a week older than she had imagined. From then on, and to avoid a date-changing confusion, she insisted on keeping both dates, expecting presents on each.

Linda also recalls her grandmother being an ardent auction devotee, "Sold to Mrs Benham," was the frequent cry as the hammer fell, and Nancy was never sure what she had bid for – a part lot of something or other. Once she came home with four pottery pineapples made in 1840, and some two-handled cider jars. Linda said that Nancy had a peachy skin, like her own mother Tasma, and was '… not very tall and not very plump …' and that her hair went snowy white in the end. When her daughter Barbara died, Nancy moved again, her solution to difficult problems, to a flatlet in Charminster. Finally, pneumonia overcame her, and she died in Lyme Regis hospital, aged 86, with her children at her bedside.

1945 – Tasma Joan and baby Linda

Linda Norwood, Nancy's granddaughter

Her daughter Tasma Joan wrote, 'She was talented, artistic, musical – playing the piano well and teaching it later. She loved the wild flowers in Beaminster and was a gifted painter. Her letters were whole volumes, and it was a family joke that however much she had written there were always several afterthoughts squeezed in around the edges of the paper. I still miss the 'plop' of her epics on the doormat.' She kept up with many friends she had made during her travels and spent a whole winter in Nice, South of France, with one lot. Her friends were important, as her brothers and sisters pre-deceased her, leaving fewer cards to open each Christmas. Nancy was a mover, she could not stay in any place for long. First she bought five cottages at Salwayash, one of which had been her father's clock and watch workshop. This started a buying and selling project, originally to an old house in Beaminster, then she dragged Ted to Corfe Mullen 'which they both liked'. He died suddenly, so the house at Corfe Mullen was let, and Nancy moved into a flat in Bridport. Eventually she moved to Bristol to be near her eldest daughter, Eileen Mary. Part of Nancy's 'moving syndrome' was to purchase caravans, first at West Bay and later at Lyme Regis, but it disappointed her that the families left the site each morning to go to work, leaving her 'feeling abandoned and isolated without a car'. She just loved riding in cars. Despite her difficult life she was very brave and always seemed to come up smiling. '… Before she died my Mother told me she liked Frank Sinatra's song, 'My Way' – which was so appropriate as she always did it 'Her Way'. She left Christina Rossetti's poem, 'Remember' for us to read."

"Remember me when I am gone away,
Gone far away into the silent land;
When you can no more hold me by the hand,
Nor I half turn to go, yet turning stay.
Remember me when no more, day by day,
You tell me of our future that you planned;
Only remember me; you understand,
It will be too late to counsel then or pray.
Yet if you should forget me for a while,
And afterwards remember, do not grieve;
For if the darkness and corruption leave,
A vestige of the thoughts that once I had,
Better by far you should forget and smile,
Than that you should remember and be sad."

Nancy Swaffield, thank you for your poem. A perfect way to leave
a family story, to continue its journey with future generations.

c1910 – Beaminster – young Nancy as Princess JuJu

Appendix 1

~ FAMILY TREE ~

Note: Information collated from many sources, rigorously checked but authenticity cannot be guaranteed.
Layout inconsistent to include additional data.

BEGINS IN DORSETSHIRE

JOHN SWAFFEL and ELIZABETH GILLINGHAM and their children; Thomas 1756, John 1758, George 1761, Elizabeth 1762, Joseph 1764 and Benjamin 1767

John Swaffel [Swaffield], son of John, was born at Beaminster and baptised on 31.12.1731 at St Mary's Church.
He married Elizabeth Gillingham, who was born Beaminster in 1728, in St Mary's Church, Beaminster on 18.5.1755.
She died on 26.3.1812. John died 14.5.1818 and both are interred St James Church, Lewcombe, Dorsetshire.

They had six children.

JOHN SWAFFIELD 1731–1818 and ELIZABETH GILLINGHAM 1728–1812 m 1755

Thomas	John	George	Elizabeth	Joseph	Benjamin
born	born	born	born	born	born
1756	1758	1761	1762	1764	1767
bap 19.4.1756	bap 27.3.1758			bap 24.8.1765	bap 24.7.1768
Beaminster	Corscombe			Lewcombe	Lewcombe
d 5.9.1788		d 6.3.1792	d Aug 1835	d 1854	d 5.4.1840
interred		interred	interred		interred
10.9.1788		11.3.1792	24.8.1835		16.4.1840
Lewcombe			Lewcombe	Halstock	Lewcombe
unmarried	**married**	married	**married**	**married**	married
	Anne Neal	Elizabeth ?	**John Neal**	**Mary Swaffield**	Hannah Burdett
	Wood Farm, EC	(Betty)	**Wood Farm EC**	Lewcombe	at Halstock
	in c1782	in c1781	15.1.1782	28.5.1787	7.3.1791
	issue	issue	issue	issue	issue
	(five)	(seven)	(nineteen)	(five)	(eleven)
	John 1783	Thomas 1783	John I (1782 dec)	Joseph 1787	Thomas 1791
	Joseph 1785	John 1785	Elizabeth I (1782 dec)	Mary 1788	Hannah 1792
	Jane 1787	Mary 1786	John II 1783 dec	**Thomas 1791**	Mary 1794
	Susanna 1791	George I 1787 dec	John III 1784-1787	Elizabeth 1792	Robert 1795
	Edward 1794	Elizabeth 1789	Elizabeth II 1785-1812	Hannah 1794	**Benjamin 1797**
		George II 1790 ←	Thomas 1787 dec		Elizabeth 1799
		Benjamin 1792	Eve 1789 dec		Judith 1801
			Susanna 1791-1829		**Samuel 1802**
		married └→	**Catherine 1792-1847**		Martha 1804
			William 1794		Sarah 1805
			John IV 1795 dec		John 1806
			Mary 1796-1882		
			Edward 1798-1844		
			Martha 1800-1807		
			John V 1801-1878		
			Phyllis 1802 dec		
			Benjamin 1803		
			Jane I 1805 dec		
			Jane II 1808 dec		

Note – Intermarrying of:

Neighbours
John Swaffield 1758 m Anne Neal d1835
Elizabeth Swaffield 1762 m John Neal 1755

Cousins
Joseph Swaffield 1764 m Mary Swaffield in 1787
George Swaffield 1790 m Catherine Neal 1792

JOHN SWAFFIELD 1731–1818 and ELIZABETH GILLINGHAM 1728–1812

John Swaffield 1758–1807 and Anne Neal d 1835 m c1782

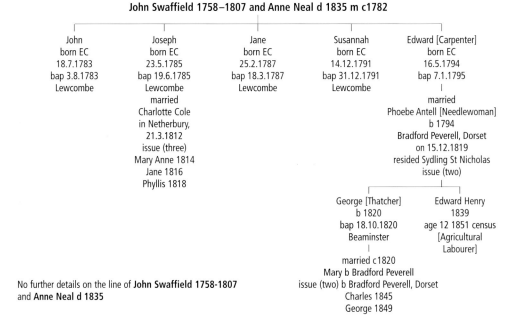

John	Joseph	Jane	Susannah	Edward [Carpenter]
born EC	born EC	born EC	born EC	born EC
18.7.1783	23.5.1785	25.2.1787	14.12.1791	16.5.1794
bap 3.8.1783	bap 19.6.1785	bap 18.3.1787	bap 31.12.1791	bap 7.1.1795
Lewcombe	Lewcombe	Lewcombe	Lewcombe	

Joseph:
married
Charlotte Cole
in Netherbury,
21.3.1812
issue (three)
Mary Anne 1814
Jane 1816
Phyllis 1818

Edward [Carpenter]:
married
Phoebe Antell [Needlewoman]
b 1794
Bradford Peverell, Dorset
on 15.12.1819
resided Sydling St Nicholas
issue (two)

George [Thatcher]	Edward Henry
b 1820	1839
bap 18.10.1820	age 12 1851 census
Beaminster	[Agricultural
	Labourer]

George [Thatcher]:
married c1820
Mary b Bradford Peverell
issue (two) b Bradford Peverell, Dorset
Charles 1845
George 1849

No further details on the line of **John Swaffield 1758-1807**
and **Anne Neal d 1835**

JOHN SWAFFIELD 1731–1818 and ELIZABETH GILLINGHAM 1728–1812

George Swaffield 1761–1792 and Elizabeth (Betty) m c1781

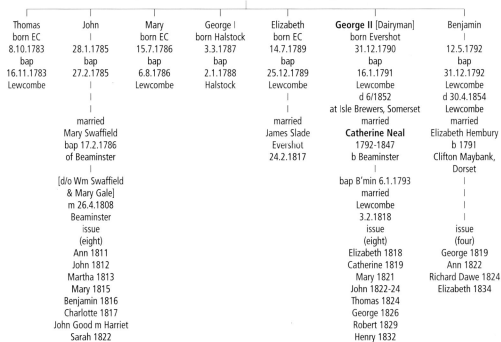

Thomas	John	Mary	George I	Elizabeth	**George II** [Dairyman]	Benjamin
born EC		born EC	born Halstock	born EC	born Evershot	
8.10.1783	28.1.1785	15.7.1786	3.3.1787	14.7.1789	31.12.1790	12.5.1792
bap	bap	bap	bap	bap	bap	bap
16.11.1783	27.2.1785	6.8.1786	2.1.1788	25.12.1789	16.1.1791	31.12.1792
Lewcombe		Lewcombe	Halstock	Lewcombe	Lewcombe	Lewcombe
					d 6/1852	d 30.4.1854
					at Isle Brewers, Somerset	Lewcombe

John:
married
Mary Swaffield
bap 17.2.1786
of Beaminster
[d/o Wm Swaffield
& Mary Gale]
m 26.4.1808
Beaminster
issue
(eight)
Ann 1811
John 1812
Martha 1813
Mary 1815
Benjamin 1816
Charlotte 1817
John Good m Harriet
Sarah 1822

Elizabeth:
married
James Slade
Evershot
24.2.1817

George II:
married
Catherine Neal
1792-1847
b Beaminster
bap B'min 6.1.1793
married
Lewcombe
3.2.1818
issue
(eight)
Elizabeth 1818
Catherine 1819
Mary 1821
John 1822-24
Thomas 1824
George 1826
Robert 1829
Henry 1832

Benjamin:
married
Elizabeth Hembury
b 1791
Clifton Maybank,
Dorset
issue
(four)
George 1819
Ann 1822
Richard Dawe 1824
Elizabeth 1834

GEORGE SWAFFIELD 1761–1792 and Elizabeth (Betty) m c1781

George Swaffield 1790–1852 and Catherine Neal 1792–1847 m 1818

Elizabeth	Catherine	Mary	John	Thomas	George	Robert	Henry
b 1818	1819	1821	1822	1824	1826	1829	1832
b Witcombe	Witcombe	Witcombe	Witcombe	Halstock	Halstock	Broadwindsor	Broadwindsor
bap	bap	bap	bap	bap	bap	bap	bap
8.10.1818	11.8.1819	24.12.1821	28.8.1822	24.10.1824	7.4.1826	6.7.1829	16.9.1932
Martock,	Martock	Lewcombe	Halstock	Lewcombe	Lewcombe	Broadwindsor	in 1851 he
Somerset	d 13.4.1878	lived at	d April 1824		d 1849 at	1841 census	was Dairyman
	at Crewkerne	home at	at Halstock		Isle Brewers	Robt living with	living at home
	interred	Broadwindsor	interred		interred	parents. In	at Isle Brewers
	Crewkerne	1851 census	2.5.1824		23.2.1849	1851 he was a	
	20.4.1878	Dairymaid/	Lewcombe		Lewcombe	servant at the	
	married c1844	Spinster and				farm of Joseph	
	at Evershot	living with				Taylor at Withel	
	Job Loveless	widowed				Florey, 300 acres,	
	1818-1871	father and				nr Watchet in	
	from Netherbury	brother at Isle				Brendon Hills	
	[s/o Sam Loveless -	Brewers,					
	né Lovelace &	Somerset					
	Susannah Guppy]						
	issue (seven)						
	Catherine Susan 1845						
	Samuel George 1847						
	Job 1848-1925						
	John Swaffield 1853-1927						
	Mary 1856						
	Henry 1860						
	Robert 1862						

Catherine Swaffield 1819–1878 and Job Loveless 1818–1871 m c1844

Catherine Susan	Samuel George	Job	John Swaffield	Mary	Henry	Robert
1845	1847-1865	1848-1925	1853-1927	1856	1860	1862
b Crewkerne	N Perrot, Somerset	ditto	b Crewkerne	b Crewkerne	b Crewkerne	
	Axminster	d Bridport	d Crewkerne				
	m Elizabeth	m Rosina	m 1) Mary Bessy	m Laura Eliz		
	Norman	Parker	James 1855-1897	Roope		
	issue	issue	issue	issue		
	(nine)	(seven)	(eleven)	(five)		
			m 2) Martha Julia			
			Harrison 1868-1917			
			issue			
			(six)			
			(total seventeen)			

No further details on the line of **George Swaffield 1761-1792** and **Elizabeth (Betty)** m c1781

JOHN SWAFFIELD 1731–1818 and ELIZABETH GILLINGHAM 1728–1812

Elizabeth Swaffield 1762–1835 and John Neal 1755–1824

m 1782 and had 19 children, many of whom appear to have died young

>>>

John<twins>Elizabeth I	John II	John III	Elizabeth II	Thomas	Eve	Susannah	Catherine
twins born EC	b East Chel	b E Chel	b E Chel	b Beaminster	b E Chel	b Beaminster	b Beaminster
1782	1783	1784	1785	1787	1789	1791	1792
bap	bap	bap		bap		bap	bap
7 June 1782	10.7.1783	29.2.84		11.3.87		24.4.91	6.1.93
Lewcombe	Lewcombe	Lewcombe		Beaminster		Beaminster	Beaminster
d June 1782	d July 1783	d 10.1787	d 31.12.1812		d 22.2.89	d Mar 1829	d 1847
interred	interred	interred	aged 27		interred	interred	Somerset
12.6.1782	15.7.1783	8.10.1787			Lewcombe	Lewcombe	interred
Lewcombe	Lewcombe	Lewcombe	Lewcombe				Lewcombe
			married				married
			Edward White				George Swaffield
			c 1808				1790
			no issue				issue
							(eight)

continued from above

Elizabeth Swaffield 1762–1835 and John Neal 1755–1824

>>>

William	John IV	Mary	Edward	Martha	John V	Phyllis	Benjamin	Jane I	Jane II
b Beaminster	b Beaminster	b Beam	b Beaminster	b Beam		b East Chel	b E Chel	b E Chel	b E Chel
1794	1795	1796	1798	1800	1801	1802	1803	1805	1808
bap	bap	bap	bap	bap	bap	bap	bap	bap	bap
11.5.94	23.8.1795	13.1.1797	6.1.1799	4.5.1800	28.12.1801	5.1.03	18.3.1805	19.03.05	9.2.1909
Beaminster		Beaminster	Beaminster	Beaminster	Lewcombe	Lewcombe		Lewcombe	Lew
William		d 6.1882	d Corscombe	d 10.1887	d Wood Farm				
was a		aged 85	Jan 1844		1878				
Blacksmith			int 31.1.1844		interred		married		
			Lewcombe		Lewcombe		Ann		
married					married		b 1799		
Euphemia					**Mary Ann Guppy**		in Hartington, Dorset		
issue (twins)					1811-1879		issue (two)		
Charlotte and					issue (six)		Eleanor 1828		
Christopher 1831					John 1840		b Cerne Abbas		
					Harry Sam Guppy 1843		in 1851 census aged 23 and		
					Mary Ann 1845		working as schoolmistress		
					George 1846		living at home in Piddletrenhide		
					Susannah 1847		ditto		
					Thomas 1851		Edward 1833 b Chetnole		

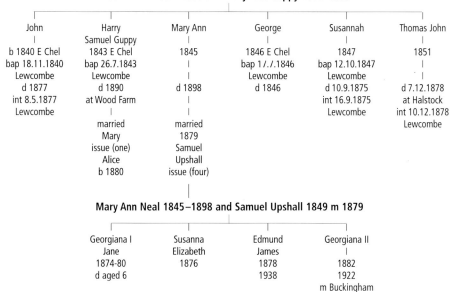

John Neal 1801–1878 and Mary Ann Guppy 1811–1879

John
b 1840 E Chel
bap 18.11.1840
Lewcombe
d 1877
int 8.5.1877
Lewcombe

Harry Samuel Guppy
1843 E Chel
bap 26.7.1843
Lewcombe
d 1890
at Wood Farm
|
married
Mary
issue (one)
Alice
b 1880

Mary Ann
1845
|
d 1898
|
married
1879
Samuel
Upshall
issue (four)

George
1846 E Chel
bap 1/./.1846
Lewcombe
d 1846

Susannah
1847
bap 12.10.1847
Lewcombe
d 10.9.1875
int 16.9.1875
Lewcombe

Thomas John
1851
|
d 7.12.1878
at Halstock
int 10.12.1878
Lewcombe

Mary Ann Neal 1845–1898 and Samuel Upshall 1849 m 1879

Georgiana I Jane
1874-80
d aged 6

Susanna Elizabeth
1876

Edmund James
1878
1938

Georgiana II
1882
1922
m Buckingham

No further details on the line of **Elizabeth Swaffield 1762–1835** and **John Neal 1755–1824**

JOHN SWAFFIELD 1731–1818 and ELIZABETH GILLINGHAM 1728–1812 m 1755

Joseph Swaffield 1764–1854 and Mary Swaffield (cousin) m 1787

Joseph
b East Chelborough
16.9.1787
bap 18.11.1787
|
d 1860
married
Lucy
Sprake
|
|
issue
(one)
James
1810-1881
he married Amy Hollis
in 1841 at Lambeth
issue (nine)
James 1842
William 1843
Edward 1845
Rebecca 1846
Eliz Hollis 1851
Henry Hollis 1853
Charles 1855-1953
Ernest 1857
Lucy 1859
Charles 1855–1953 m Hannah Seary
issue (one) Charles 1878

Mary
b East Chel
24.6.1788
4.10.1788
Lewcombe
|
married
William
Foot
m 16.4.1811
Dorchester

Thomas
b Rampisham
1791
|
d after 1851
married
Mary Whittle
b 1794

Elizabeth
b Ramp
1792

Hannah
b Ramp
1794

Benjamin
b Ramp
1797

Thomas Swaffield 1791 d after 1851 and Mary Whittle 1794

Thomas
1814
E Chel

Mary
1815
E Chel

Ann
1817
E Chel

John
bap 6.1819
Closworth
Sail weaver
d 1849 aged 30
m Caroline Canterbury
b 1821 Stoke Abbott
m on 4.3.1841
at Stoke Abbott
issue (five)

William
1821
Closworth
|
m Grace
issue (two)
b Corscombe
|
Ellen   Thomas
1846   1858

Thomas Swaffield 1791 d after 1851 and Mary Whittle 1794

John Swaffield 1819–1849 and Caroline Canterbury 1821 m 1841

After John's death Widow Caroline Canterbury Swaffield then had 2 boys – Frederick & Edwin – >>>>>>> before marrying Job Wakely

George Swaffield	John	Tom Swaffield	Ann Swaffield	Martha Mary	Frederick Swaffield	Edwin Swaffield	Emily Wakely
1841-1936	1842-1910	1845-1944	1848	1850	1854-1923	1857-1930	1862
m Harriet Wakely	Sarah Hallett	Ellen Jane Davy	William Canterbury	1850	Emma Conway	Emma Chubb	[Servant]
1845-1929	1840-1917	1847-1934	[first cousin]		d 1926	d 1913	Robert Notley
issue	issue	issue	issue		issue	issue	[Platelayer]
(15-9 survived)	(nine)	(two)	(two)		(six)	(six)	m 1893
Ann Rosetta 1867	+ Eliz Hallett	Gertrude 1868	Wm John 1880		Eli & [dec] Alice 1881	Margaret 1886	issue (one)
Julia Jane 1868	John 1864	Emily Annie 1870	Fred Job 1881		Eli 1881-1935	Mabel 1888	Robert
Stillborn 1870	Julia 1865	—			Ernest	Ethel 1890-1934	
Mary Jane 1871	George I d 1868	Gertrude			1883-1953	Edith 1892	
Caroline Esther 1873	George II 1870	m Barratt			Herbert	Charles 1896	
George William 1875	Mary Ann 1872	Emily Annie			1885-1967	Kathleen 1898-1983	
John James 1877	Frederick 1875	m WC Willmott			Florence		
Fred'k Job 1879	Charles 1877	her granddaughter			1888-1975		
Emily Eliza 1880	Alice and William	Mrs Preston			Emily		
Harriet & Tom 1881	(twins) in 1882	of B'mouth			1891-1962		
Emily Agnes 1882							
Tom Edwin 1884							
Ellen Harriet 1886							
Annie Louisa 1889							

John Swaffield 1819–1849 and Caroline Canterbury 1821 m 1841

George Swaffield 1841–1936 and Harriet Wakely 1845–1929 m 1866

Ann Rosetta	Julia Jane	Still born	Mary Jane	Caroline Esther	George William	John James	Fred'k Job	Emily Eliza	Harriet & Tom	Emily Agnes	Tom Edwin	Ellen Harriet	Annie Louisa
1867	1868	1870	1871	1873	1875	1877	1879	1880	1881	1882	1884	1886	1889
1951	1871	1870	1966	1969	1963	1969	1879	1880	1881	1966	1961	1917	1975
m John Welch	died aged		Cumberland William	William George Slade	Daisy Elizabeth Wheeler	Cecilia Edmonds				Frederick Harold Skingle	Alice Alma Hopper		Alex Edw Crane Benham
1869	3 yrs		Sebastopol Ascott	1870-1949	1870-1963	1883-63				1887-1948	1890-1976		d 1959
1835			1856-1940	m 1897	m 1903	m 1906				m 1914	m 1915		m 191?
m 1911			Beaminster	Beaminster	Wokingham	Wealdstone				Lambeth	Harrow		Tasmani
Paddington			issue	issue	issue	issue				issue	issue		issue
			(four)	(three)	(five)	(two)				(one)	(four)		(four)
			Hilda	Lilian	Owen	Herbert John				Peggie	Audrey		E Mary
			Elsie	Kathleen	Kathleen	Phyllis Dora					Arthur		Alfred
			Thomas	Gwyneth	Leslie						Richard		Tas Joa
			William		George						Evelyn		Barbar
					Harry								

continued on next page |>>>

continued >>>

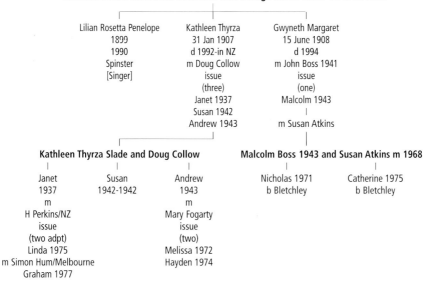

George Swaffield 1841–1936 and Harriet Wakely 1845–1929 m 1866

Caroline Esther Swaffield 1873 and Wm George Slade 1870–1949 m 1897

| Lilian Rosetta Penelope 1899 1990 Spinster [Singer] | Kathleen Thyrza 31 Jan 1907 d 1992-in NZ m Doug Collow issue (three) Janet 1937 Susan 1942 Andrew 1943 | Gwyneth Margaret 15 June 1908 d 1994 m John Boss 1941 issue (one) Malcolm 1943 m Susan Atkins |

Kathleen Thyrza Slade and Doug Collow

| Janet 1937 m H Perkins/NZ issue (two adpt) Linda 1975 m Simon Hum/Melbourne Graham 1977 | Susan 1942-1942 | Andrew 1943 m Mary Fogarty issue (two) Melissa 1972 Hayden 1974 |

Malcolm Boss 1943 and Susan Atkins m 1968

| Nicholas 1971 b Bletchley | Catherine 1975 b Bletchley |

No further details on the line of **Caroline Esther Swaffield 1873** and **Wm George Slade 1870-1949** m 1897

George Swaffield 1841–1936 and Harriet Wakely 1845–1929 m 1866

George William Swaffield 1875–1963 and Daisy Elizabeth Wheeler 1870–1963 m 1903

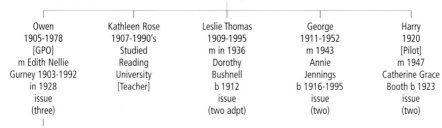

| Owen 1905-1978 [GPO] m Edith Nellie Gurney 1903-1992 in 1928 issue (three) | Kathleen Rose 1907-1990's Studied Reading University [Teacher] | Leslie Thomas 1909-1995 m in 1936 Dorothy Bushnell b 1912 issue (two adpt) | George 1911-1952 m 1943 Annie Jennings b 1916-1995 issue (two) | Harry 1920 [Pilot] m 1947 Catherine Grace Booth b 1923 issue (two) |

Owen Wm George Swaffield 1905–1978 and Edith Nellie Gurney 1903–1992 m 1928

| Brian Owen 1931 m Olive Ray b 1928 issue (three) | David John 1937 m Marion Thorpe b 1941 issue (three) | Linda Edith 1945 m John W Carter (div) issue (two) |

rian Owen Swaffield 1931 & Olive Ray 1928			David J Swaffield 1937 & M Thorpe 1941			Linda Swaffield 1945 & John Carter (div)	
Brian D 1959 m aren Mason b 1962 ssue (one) ephen b 1998	David R 1961	Clare 1964	Jennifer 1959	Wendy Jane 1964	Christopher 1967 issue Danielle 1991	Lincoln 1968	Miranda 1970 m 1990 Martin Budden issue (one) Yasmine b 1990

Leslie T Swaffield 1909–1995 and Dorothy Bushnell 1912 m 1936

Donald	Jennifer
m	m
1) Sheila Cuthbertson in 1972 (div)	Eric W Lee (div)
2) Margaret Roberts in 1990	issue (two)
	Sarah Louise 1977
	Joanna Vera 1979

George Swaffield 1911–1952 and Annie Jennings

Diana	David George
1944	1946
m in 1965	m
Harold King b 1940	Jeanette née Jones
issue (three)	issue (one)
Adrian Roy 1970	Jairun Edward
Sally Marie 1973	
>> issue (one)	
Elliott Lewis 1995	
Gary Mark 1977	

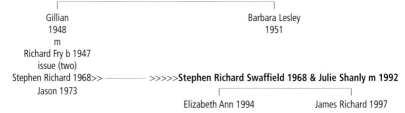

Harry Swaffield 1920 & Catherine Grace Booth 1923 m 1947

Gillian	Barbara Lesley
1948	1951
m	
Richard Fry b 1947	
issue (two)	
Stephen Richard 1968>>	
Jason 1973	

>>>>>**Stephen Richard Swaffield 1968 & Julie Shanly m 1992**

Elizabeth Ann 1994	James Richard 1997

No further details on the line of **George William Swaffield 1875–1963** and **Daisy Elizabeth Wheeler 1870–1963** m 1903

George Swaffield 1841–1936 and Harriet Wakely 1845–1929 m 1866
John James Swaffield 1877–1969 and Cecilia Edmonds 1883–1963 m 1906

Herbert John	Phyllis Dora
1907-1993	1908-1982
m Molly Impey d 1994	
issue (three)	

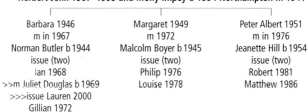

Herbert John 1907–1993 and Molly Impey d 1994 Northampton m 1941

Barbara 1946	Margaret 1949	Peter Albert 1951
m in 1967	m 1972	m in 1976
Norman Butler b 1944	Malcolm Boyer b 1945	Jeanette Hill b 1954
issue (two)	issue (two)	issue (two)
Ian 1968	Philip 1976	Robert 1981
>>m Juliet Douglas b 1969	Louise 1978	Matthew 1986
>>>issue Lauren 2000		
Gillian 1972		

No further details on the line of **John James Swaffield 1877–1969** and **Cecilia Edmonds 1883–1963** m 1906

George Swaffield 1841–1936 and Harriet Wakely 1845–1929 m 1866

Emily Agnes Swaffield 1882–1966 and Frederick Harold Skingle 1887–1948 m 1914

|

Peggie 1916

|

Peggie Skingle 1916 & Harold Littlewood at Harlestone, Norfolk (div) m 1944

Diana Kay
1945
m 1) George Rowe in 1965 at Bridport (div)
>issue Neil Rowe (now Aplin) 1966
>>m Kerry Harris in 1990 Yeovil
>>>issue (one) Naomi Kate Aplin 1996
m 2) Donald Aplin in 1970
>>issue (one) Dorothy Aplin 1971

Howard Frederick (now Burwood)
|
m Elizabeth Howell in 1968
>>issue (one)
>>Emma Louise Burwood 1970

|

Peggie Skingle 1916 m Frederick Burwood – widower with 7 children
They adopted in 1964 a daughter Eileen née Micklewright b 1959 and named
Burwood. She married Maxwell Pollendine in 1979. Issue (three) Simon 1980,
Samantha 1982, and Sophie 1978 born in Yeovil.

No further details on the line of **Emily Agnes Swaffield 1882–1966** and **Frederick Harold Skingle 1887–1948** m 1914

George Swaffield 1841–1936 and Harriet Wakely 1845–1929 m 1866

Tom Swaffield 1884–1961 and Alice Hopper 1890–1976 m 1915

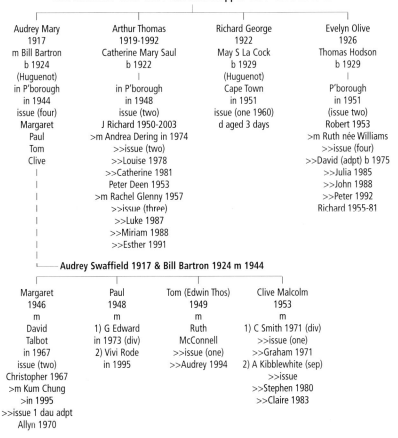

Audrey Mary
1917
m Bill Bartron
b 1924
(Huguenot)
in P'borough
in 1944
issue (four)
Margaret
Paul
Tom
Clive

Arthur Thomas
1919-1992
Catherine Mary Saul
b 1922
|
in P'borough
in 1948
issue (two)
J Richard 1950-2003
>m Andrea Dering in 1974
>>issue (two)
>>Louise 1978
>>Catherine 1981
Peter Deen 1953
>m Rachel Glenny 1957
>>issue (three)
>>Luke 1987
>>Miriam 1988
>>Esther 1991

Richard George
1922
May S La Cock
b 1929
(Huguenot)
Cape Town
in 1951
issue (one 1960)
d aged 3 days

Evelyn Olive
1926
Thomas Hodson
b 1929

P'borough
in 1951
(issue two)
Robert 1953
>m Ruth née Williams
>>issue (four)
>>David (adpt) b 1975
>>Julia 1985
>>John 1988
>>Peter 1992
Richard 1955-81

Audrey Swaffield 1917 & Bill Bartron 1924 m 1944

Margaret
1946
m
David
Talbot
in 1967
issue (two)
Christopher 1967
>m Kum Chung
>in 1995
>>issue 1 dau adpt
Allyn 1970

Paul
1948
m
1) G Edward
in 1973 (div)
2) Vivi Rode
in 1995

Tom (Edwin Thos)
1949
m
Ruth
McConnell
>>issue (one)
>>Audrey 1994

Clive Malcolm
1953
m
1) C Smith 1971 (div)
>>issue (one)
>>Graham 1971
2) A Kibblewhite (sep)
>>issue
>>Stephen 1980
>>Claire 1983

No further details on the line of **Tom Swaffield 1884–1961** and **Alice Hopper 1890–1976** m 1915

George Swaffield 1841–1936 and Harriet Wakely 1845–1929 m 1866

Nancy Swaffield 1889–1975 & Edward Benham 1877–1959 m 1916　　　　**Eileen Mary Benham 1917–87 & Edward Smith 1915–83**

| Eileen Mary 1917-1987 m Edward Smith (div) 1915-1983 m 1938 issue (two) Thelma 1949 Marilyn 1952 | Alfred 1919 Hazel Drake b 1922 issue (four) Christopher Andrea (and twins) Julia & Catherine | Tasma Joan 1921 Richard Harding in 1943 issue (two) Linda 1945 Peter 1948 | Barbara Annie 1924-1971 Leslie Brown in 1950 issue (two) Deborah 1951 issue (one) >>Josephine Florence Roger Leslie 1953 | Thelma 1949 m Nigel Matthews in 1967 issue (two) Julian & Nicholas (twins) 1968 | Marilyn 1952 m Chris Lacey in 1974 issue (one) Eleanor 1984 |

Alfred (Bill) Benham 1919 and Hazel Drake 1922　　　　**Tasma Joan Benham 1921 and Richard Harding m 1943**

| Christopher 1947-1983 m Gina issue (two) Stuart Nicholas | Andrea 1953 m Clitheroe issue (one) Jennifer 1988 | Catherine 1963 <twins> m Robert Harris issue (one) George Alexander b 1998 | Julia 1963 m David Lewis issue (two) James 1996 Clare 1999 | Linda 1945 m Piers Norbury issue (two adpt) Philippa Piers | Peter 1948 m Ann issue (two) Cheryl 1974 Kate 1977 |

No further details on the line of **Nancy Swaffield 1889–1975** and **Edward Benham 1877–1959** m 1916
No further details on the line of **George Swaffield 1841–1936** and **Harriet Wakely 1845–1929** m 1866

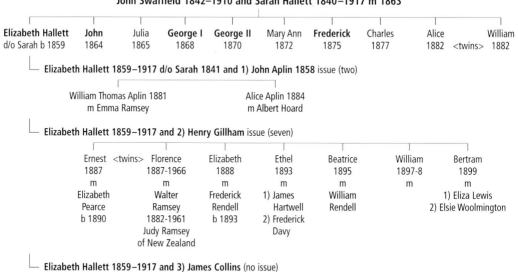

John Swaffield 1819–1849 and Caroline Canterbury 1821 m 1841

John Swaffield 1842–1910 and Sarah Hallett 1840–1917 m 1863

| **Elizabeth Hallett** d/o Sarah b 1859 | **John** 1864 | Julia 1865 | **George I** 1868 | **George II** 1870 | Mary Ann 1872 | **Frederick** 1875 | Charles 1877 | Alice 1882 <twins> | William 1882 |

　　Elizabeth Hallett 1859–1917 d/o Sarah 1841 and 1) John Aplin 1858 issue (two)

| William Thomas Aplin 1881 m Emma Ramsey | Alice Aplin 1884 m Albert Hoard |

　　Elizabeth Hallett 1859–1917 and 2) Henry Gillham issue (seven)

| Ernest 1887 m Elizabeth Pearce b 1890 | <twins> Florence 1887-1966 m Walter Ramsey 1882-1961 Judy Ramsey of New Zealand | Elizabeth 1888 m Frederick Rendell b 1893 | Ethel 1893 m 1) James Hartwell 2) Frederick Davy | Beatrice 1895 m William Rendell | William 1897-8 | Bertram 1899 m 1) Eliza Lewis 2) Elsie Woolmington |

　　Elizabeth Hallett 1859–1917 and 3) James Collins (no issue)

John Swaffield 1842-1910 and Sarah Hallett 1840–1917 m 1863

John Swaffield 1864–1939 and Mary Jane Bagg 1865–1936 m 1886

Frederick James 1888 1963	**Beatrice Lucy** 1890 1972	**Alice Emily** 1892 1953	Wilfred John 1894 1917	**Hilda Mary** 1896 1994	**Christina Florence** 1899 1992	William George 1901 1927	**Lily May** 1903 1986	Louis Charles 1904 1968	Reginald Edwin 1907 1919	**Winifred Margaret** 1909 2002	**Kathleen Myrtle** 1911 1982
m 1909 1) Alice M V Meech 1887-1937 no issue 2) Florence Sampson at Weymouth Reg Office 12.9.1941 no issue	m 1917 Alfred Clarke d 1939 issue (two) Sylvia 1918 Robert 1921	m Herbert W Howe | issue (two) Kenneth 1922 Keith 1927 |		m 1931 A Charlie W Holman 1906 1976 issue (two) >John >Joan	m Reuben Long issue (three)		m William J Record issue (one) Michael 1931 m >Rita Charvill >b 1937 issue (two)		age 12	m 1939 Len Jones 1914-88 | issue (two) Ben Jane	m Fred'k Collin b 1911 in 1938 issue (five) Heather Mary Terry Anna John

Alice Emily line:
Ken 1922 issue (one) Janina b 1962 >m John Barlow >>issue (one) >>James 1998 — Keith 1927 d 1998 Long Beach, California

Lily May line:
Elizabeth Emma 1965 m >Adrian Coverdale b 1953 issue >>Thomas Adrian 1997 >>Alexander John 2001 — Jane Louise 1967

Frederick James line:
Sylvia Mary 1918-2000

Beatrice Lucy line:
Robert John & Dorothy Harvey issue (two)

Robert John 1945 m Janet Mary Lane issue (two) Alison Clare 1967 >m >Kevin Morris >>issue >>Sylvia Mary b 1998 Vernon Robt John 1969 >m >>Debbie Kelly

Diana Sylvia 1946 issue (two) Elizabeth Clarke b 1970 Adam Clarke b 1983

Christina Florence Swaffield 1898 and Reuben Long 1899

Cecil John 1928 2001	Sidney George 1929 1989	Gwendoline Mary Ruth 1930
m 1950 Doris Richards issue (four) Janet Myra Clifford Susan	m 1) Sylvia Kendal issue (three) David Philip Keith 2) Peggy	m 1951 Ken Dart issue (three) Dafydd 1952 Edwin 1954 Colin 1961 >>issue (one) >>>Lavinia Christina 1987

Winifred Swaffield 1909 and Len Jones 1914–1988

Ben 1947	Margaret Jane 1949
m Monica Sally Bartlett issue (three) Simon 1974 Andrew 1977 Sarah 1984	m 1983 Richard Cadell issue (two) Laura 1985 Christopher 1987

Kathleen Swaffield 1911–1982 and Frederick Collin b 1910 m 1938

	<<twins>>		<<twins>>	
Heather	Mary	Terence	Anna	John
1939	1943	1943	1949	1949
m	m	2002	m	dec
Robert	Clement		David	
Crabb	Reed		Fowles	
issue (five)	issue (two)		issue (two)	

Heather Collin 1939 and Robert Crabb

Ashley	Nicholas	David	Samantha	Daniel
1961	1962	1964		1974
	m	m	m	
	Mary	Helen	Mark	
	Furie	Barraclough	Pearce	
	issue (one)	issue (one)	(baby due)	
	Charlotte	Laura	07/03	
	1995	1989		

Mary Collin 1943 and Clement Reed

Lorna Anne	Ellen Elizabeth
1967	1969
m	engaged
Gavin Sandmann	Giles Haywood
issue (three)	
Jennifer 1993	
Adam 1997	
Alice 1999	

Anna Collin 1949 and David Fowles m 1970

Victoria Anne	Andrew Jonathan
1972	1974
m	m
Gary Noble	Tamsin Marsh
issue (one)	
Jessica Lucia 1999	

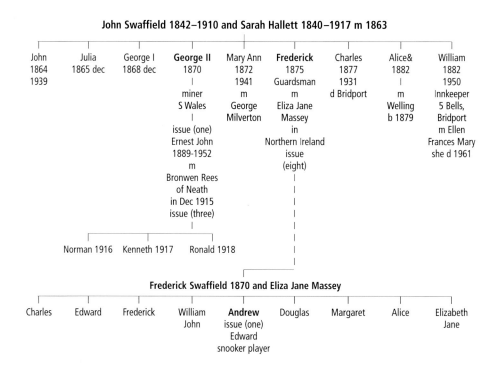

John Swaffield 1842–1910 and Sarah Hallett 1840–1917 m 1863

John	Julia	George I	**George II**	Mary Ann	**Frederick**	Charles	Alice&	William
1864	1865 dec	1868 dec	1870	1872	1875	1877	1882	1882
1939				1941	Guardsman	1931		1950
			miner	m	m	d Bridport	m	Innkeeper
			S Wales	George	Eliza Jane		Welling	5 Bells,
				Milverton	Massey		b 1879	Bridport
			issue (one)		in			m Ellen
			Ernest John		Northern Ireland			Frances Mary
			1889-1952		issue			she d 1961
			m		(eight)			
			Bronwen Rees					
			of Neath					
			in Dec 1915					
			issue (three)					

Norman 1916	Kenneth 1917	Ronald 1918

Frederick Swaffield 1870 and Eliza Jane Massey

Charles	Edward	Frederick	William	**Andrew**	Douglas	Margaret	Alice	Elizabeth
			John	issue (one)				Jane
				Edward				
				snooker player				

John Swaffield 1842-1910 and Sarah Hallett 1840–1917 m 1863

Frederick Swaffield 1854–1923 and Emma Conway d 1926

Eli <<twins>> Alice [A dec]	Ernest Frederick	Herbert Conway	Florence Emma	Emily Alice
5.8.1881–9.7.1935	1883-1953	1885-1967	1888-1975	1891-1962
b Beaminster	b Beaminster	b Beaminster	b Beaminster	
m 1) Florence	m	m		
Lydia Bennett	Annie Louisa Childs	Lilian Alberta Daubeney		
1883-1912	1875-1967	1884-1959		
at Wargrave,	Beaminster	Beaminster		
Wokingham, Berks				
on 26.8.1911	|	|		
lived	March 1916	18.10.1912		
Claycastle Farm,	lived	lived		
Hazelbury Plucknett, Somerset	North Buckham	Manor Farm,		
issue (three total)	Beaminster	Portesham		
1912 twins which died, as did	issue (four)	issue (four)		
Florence – all interred B'minster	Arthur Ernest 1917	Elsie 1913		
m 2) Maud Ellen Fry	Dorothy L 1920	Phyllis L		
at Chedington on 2.4.1923	>m Edmund A Snook	Freda A		
issue (one)	Herbert G	Edward Byron		
Vera Maud	Ralph Conway			
b 5.10.1925				
m Frank Shepherd at Merriott				
10.7.1948				
issue (1 son, 1 daughter)				

No further details on the line of **John Swaffield 1864–939** and **Mary Jane Bagg 1865–1936** m 1886
No further details on the line of **John Swaffield 1842–1910** and **Sarah Hallett 1840–1917** m 1863
No further details on the line of **Joseph Swaffield 1764–1854** and **Mary Swaffield** (cousin) m 1787

JOHN SWAFFIELD 1731–1818 and ELIZABETH GILLINGHAM 1728–1812 m 1755

Benjamin Swaffield 1767–1840 and Hannah Burdett 1765–1857 m 1791

Thomas	Hannah	Mary	Robert	Benjamin	Elizabeth	Judith	Samuel	Martha	Sarah	John
1791	1792	1794	1795	1797	1799	1801	1802	1804	1805	1806
1859	|	1857	1879	1831	1831	|	1863	1877	1856	1891
m Harriet	John Rugg	John	Charlotte	1) Frances	James	Robert	Harriet	George	Ephraim	Elizabeth
Guppy on	at	Gard	Farmer	Chubb	Storer	Meech	Nash	Squibb	Matthews	Otton
b1791-1883	Montacute	on 23rd	at Halstock	in 1829	of	of	Exton	d 12/1847	at Bridport	Wootton
m 18.3.1818	on	August	13.9.1819	F died 1832	Taunton	C'combe	at	of Melbury	b 3.1847	Fitzpaine
issue	23.6.1818.	1814	Charlotte	issue (two)	Watch-	on	Hitchin	Osmond	In 1851	no issue
(three)	John	John	died on	2) Frances	maker	3.3.1829	Herts	3.10.1826	Sarah was	
John 1820	remarried	Gard	3.4.1869	Watkinson			in 1834	issue (five)	living with	
Harriet 1821	after Hannah	hailed	aged 70	in 1836 at			issue	Sarah	her mother,	
Anne 1828	died	from	R died at	Old Brampton			(seven)	Stephen	Hannah,	
		Mont-	Corscombe	issue			Mary	George	in Allington,	
		acute	24.3.1857	(four)			Harriet	Thomas	Bridport	
		issue	issue	>Benjamin			Henry	Martha		
		Elizabeth	Sarah Emily	>Clement			Benjamin			
		m Daniel	>m Ephraim	>Thomas			Samuel			
		Biddlecombe	Cridge	>Sylvester			Alice &			
		in 1849	>>issue				Edward			
		issue	>>Thomas							
		(two)								
		Mary								
		Florence								

Benjamin Swaffield 1767–1840 and Hannah Burdett 1765–1857 m 1791
Thomas Swaffield 1791–1859 and Harriet Guppy 1791–1883 m 1818

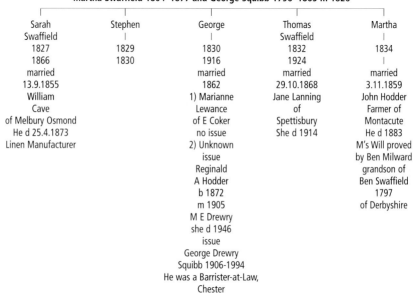

John Guppy	Harriet	Anne Guppy
b 1819	1820	1828
bap	bap	bap 3.8.1828
Melbury Osmond	Melbury Osmond	Melbury Osmond
m Eliza in 1846	m 30.09.1852	d 1847
issue (four)	George Edwards	
Thos Edward 1848	Draper of Yeovil	
Evelyn Anne 1850			
Mary Eliza 1853		
Herbert James 1860	30 in 1851	

No further details on the line of **Thomas Swaffield 1791–1859** and **Harriet Guppy 1791–1883** m 1818

Benjamin Swaffield 1767–1840 and Hannah Burdett 1765–1857 m 1791
Martha Swaffield 1804–1877 and George Squibb 1796–1865 m 1826

Sarah Swaffield	Stephen	George	Thomas Swaffield	Martha
1827	1829	1830	1832	1834
1866	1830	1916	1924	
married		married	married	married
13.9.1855		1862	29.10.1868	3.11.1859
William		1) Marianne	Jane Lanning	John Hodder
Cave		Lewance	of	Farmer of
of Melbury Osmond		of E Coker	Spettisbury	Montacute
He d 25.4.1873		no issue	She d 1914	He d 1883
Linen Manufacturer		2) Unknown		M's Will proved
		issue		by Ben Milward
		Reginald		grandson of
		A Hodder		Ben Swaffield
		b 1872		1797
		m 1905		of Derbyshire
		M E Drewry		
		she d 1946		
		issue		
		George Drewry		
		Squibb 1906-1994		
		He was a Barrister-at-Law,		
		Chester		

No further details on the line of **Martha Swaffield 1804–1877** and **George Squibb 1796–1865** m 1826

BENJAMIN SWAFFIELD 1797–1879 MOVES TO DERBYSHIRE

JOHN SWAFFIELD 1731–1818 and ELIZABETH GILLINGHAM 1728–1812 m 1755

Benjamin Swaffield 1767–1840 and Hannah Burdett 1765–1857 m 1791

| Thomas | Hannah | Mary | Robert | **Benjamin** | Elizabeth | Judith | **Samuel** | **Martha** | Sarah | John |

Benjamin Swaffield 1797–1879 and 1) Frances Chubb 1798–1832 m 1829

Anna Maria
b March 13 1830
bap May 2 1830 Edensor
d Feby 15 1832

Sarah Seaward
b April 16 1831
bap May 15 1831 Edensor
m in 1853
issue (three)
Mrs S Craigie
Charles James Milward
Benjamin William Milward

Benjamin Swaffield 1797–1879 and 2) Frances Watkinson 1812–1893 m 1836

Benjamin John
b Dec 5 1845
d Jan 26 1896
bap Jan 25 1846 Edensor
Farmer, Hartington
m Sarah Ellen Moore
b 1858

of Rowington, Warwickshire
on Feb 24 1881

at Handsworth, Sheffield
issue
(two)
John Ernest 1881-1977
Benjamin Watkinson
1884-1918

Clement Edward
Nov 23 1847
Aug 6 1921
bap Jan 2 1848 E'sor
Corn Merchant
1) Annie Hope Rutter
1854-1884
2) Lucy Rutter
[elder sister]
b 1851-1924
both from Manchester
m 1) Jan 18 1877
m 2) 1887
at Manchester
issue
(twins)
Clement (& Lucy dec)
Clement issue (two)
>>Gladys Annie 1888-1927
>>Clement Louis 1893-1949
>>>m Dorothy Haslam
1891-1985
lived in Derby

Thomas Watkinson
March 14 1850
Sept 5 1905
bap June 23 1850 E'sor
Railway Clerk, Derby
Alice Swaffield
1849-1926
[first cousins]

Ampthill, Bedfordshire
March 1876

St Andrews, Derby
issue
(none)

Sylvester
Dec 31 1851
d 1931
bap Mar 21 1852 Edensor
Solicitor, Chesterfield
Catherine Marie
1857-1928

in 1881

Chesterfield
issue
(five)

Margaret Frances 1885
Catherine Annie 1887-1957
d Skendleby, Lincs
Evelyn Dora 1888-1956 d Chesterfield
John Watkinson 1895-1952 d Sheffield
>m Winifred Ann
>>issue (three)
>>Dorothy Mary Firth
>>Winifred Alice Wild
Edward Walter 1896-1918

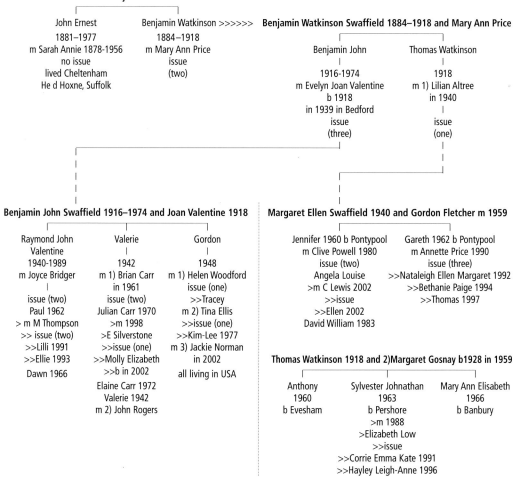

Benjamin Swaffield 1797–1879 and 2) Frances Watkinson 1812–1893 m 1836
Benjamin John Swaffield 1845–1896 and Sarah Ellen Moore b 1858 m 1881

John Ernest
1881–1977
m Sarah Annie 1878-1956
no issue
lived Cheltenham
He d Hoxne, Suffolk

Benjamin Watkinson >>>>>>
1884–1918
m Mary Ann Price
issue
(two)

Benjamin Watkinson Swaffield 1884–1918 and Mary Ann Price

Benjamin John

1916-1974
m Evelyn Joan Valentine
b 1918
in 1939 in Bedford
issue
(three)

Thomas Watkinson

1918
m 1) Lilian Altree
in 1940

issue
(one)

Benjamin John Swaffield 1916–1974 and Joan Valentine 1918

Raymond John
Valentine
1940-1989
m Joyce Bridger

issue (two)
Paul 1962
> m M Thompson
>> issue (two)
>>Lilli 1991
>>Ellie 1993
Dawn 1966

Valerie

1942
m 1) Brian Carr
in 1961
issue (two)
Julian Carr 1970
>m 1998
>E Silverstone
>>issue (one)
>>Molly Elizabeth
>>b in 2002
Elaine Carr 1972
Valerie 1942
m 2) John Rogers

Gordon

1948
m 1) Helen Woodford
issue (one)
>>Tracey
m 2) Tina Ellis
>>issue (one)
>>Kim-Lee 1977
m 3) Jackie Norman
in 2002
all living in USA

Margaret Ellen Swaffield 1940 and Gordon Fletcher m 1959

Jennifer 1960 b Pontypool
m Clive Powell 1980
issue (two)
Angela Louise
>m C Lewis 2002
>>issue
>>Ellen 2002
David William 1983

Gareth 1962 b Pontypool
m Annette Price 1990
issue (three)
>>Nataleigh Ellen Margaret 1992
>>Bethanie Paige 1994
>>Thomas 1997

Thomas Watkinson 1918 and 2)Margaret Gosnay b1928 in 1959

Anthony
1960
b Evesham

Sylvester Johnathan
1963
b Pershore
>m 1988
>Elizabeth Low
>>issue
>>Corrie Emma Kate 1991
>>Hayley Leigh-Anne 1996

Mary Ann Elisabeth
1966
b Banbury

No further details on the line of **Benjamin Swaffield 1797–1897** and **1) Frances Chubb** and **2) Frances Watkinson**

SAMUEL SWAFFIELD 1802–1863 MOVES TO BEDFORDSHIRE

Benjamin Swaffield 1767–1840 and Hannah Burdett 1765–1857 m 1791

Samuel Swaffield 1802–1863 and Harriet Nash Exton 1807–1867 m 1834

Mary Emmeline 1836-1848 bap	Harriet Exton 1837-1916	**Henry Richard James 1839-1909 Emmeline Jepson**	Benjamin George 1842-1898 Eliza Annie Smith in Dec 1863	Samuel John 1846-1914 Harriet Randall in Dec 1872	Alice <twins> 1849 Tom Wat-	**Edward** 1849 Miss Poole 1874 at
		on April 5 1866 at	1839-1928 Grocer's daughter	1858-1915 both died	kinson Swaffield	Edmonton
	Eventually lived with	Edensor, Derbyshire	from Newport Pagnell who died 1928 in	Leagrave Marsh, Beds		Resided at Greenwich
	sister Alice		Ampthill aged 89			
d age 12	d Derby no issue	Bedford issue (fourteen)	issue (five)	issue (eleven)	d 1926 issue (none)	issue (six)
		Emmeline 1867	Samuel Exton 1865-1949	Samuel 1874		Alice 1875
		Henry 1868	Laura Harriet 1866 m Gee	Herbert 1875		Harriet 1876
		Exton 1869	Alice Mary 1870-1880	Stanley 1877		Edith 1877
		Norman 1871	Eliza Annie 1874 -1969	Charles 1879		Edward 1878
		Charlotte Ethel 1872	Eva May 1881-1962	Harriet 1881		Samuel 1880
		Ella 1874		Francis 1883		Muriel 1882
		Margaret Dorothy 1875		Douglas 1887		
		Beatrice 1876		Alice 1889		
		Alan 1878		Kathleen 1891		
		Hugh 1879		Winifred 1892		
		Richard Nash 1880		Mildred 1895		
		Hilda Jane 1882				
		Mildred 1884				
		Basil 1885				

Henry Richard James Swaffield 1839–1909 and Emmeline Jepson 1842–1922 m 1866

Emmeline	**Henry**	**Exton**	**Norman**	Charlotte Ethel	**Ella**	Margaret Dorothy	**Beatrice**	Alan	Hugh	**Richard**	Hilda	**Mildred**	**Basil**
1867	1868	1869	1871	1872	1874	1875	1876	1878	1879	1880	1882	1884	1885
1934	1964	1950	1958	1965	1945	1962	1967	1878	1918	1937	1965	1973	1972
issue (three)	issue (one)	issue (four)	issue (five)	no issue	issue (two)	no issue	issue (two)	dec	no issue	issue (three)	no issue	issue (two)	issue (two

|>>>>>>   continued next page

cont >>>

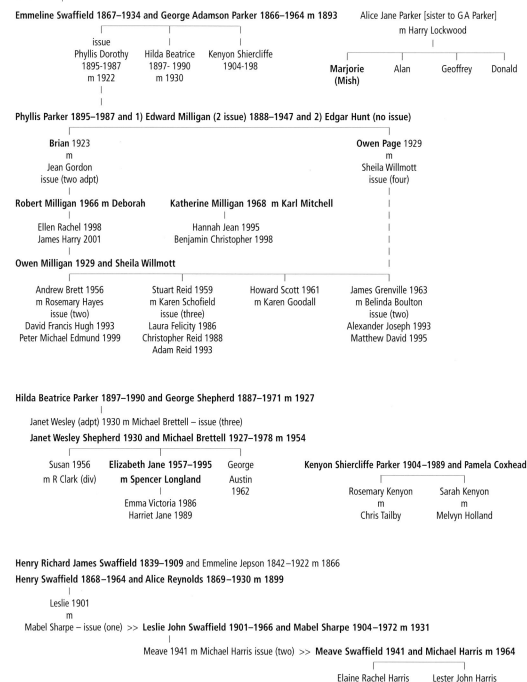

Emmeline Swaffield 1867–1934 and George Adamson Parker 1866–1964 m 1893

Alice Jane Parker [sister to G A Parker]
m Harry Lockwood

issue
Phyllis Dorothy
1895-1987
m 1922

Hilda Beatrice
1897- 1990
m 1930

Kenyon Shiercliffe
1904-198

**Marjorie
(Mish)**   Alan   Geoffrey   Donald

Phyllis Parker 1895–1987 and 1) Edward Milligan (2 issue) 1888–1947 and 2) Edgar Hunt (no issue)

Brian 1923
m
Jean Gordon
issue (two adpt)

Owen Page 1929
m
Sheila Willmott
issue (four)

Robert Milligan 1966 m Deborah

Ellen Rachel 1998
James Harry 2001

Katherine Milligan 1968 m Karl Mitchell

Hannah Jean 1995
Benjamin Christopher 1998

Owen Milligan 1929 and Sheila Willmott

Andrew Brett 1956
m Rosemary Hayes
issue (two)
David Francis Hugh 1993
Peter Michael Edmund 1999

Stuart Reid 1959
m Karen Schofield
issue (three)
Laura Felicity 1986
Christopher Reid 1988
Adam Reid 1993

Howard Scott 1961
m Karen Goodall

James Grenville 1963
m Belinda Boulton
issue (two)
Alexander Joseph 1993
Matthew David 1995

Hilda Beatrice Parker 1897–1990 and George Shepherd 1887–1971 m 1927

Janet Wesley (adpt) 1930 m Michael Brettell – issue (three)

Janet Wesley Shepherd 1930 and Michael Brettell 1927–1978 m 1954

Susan 1956
m R Clark (div)

**Elizabeth Jane 1957–1995
m Spencer Longland**

Emma Victoria 1986
Harriet Jane 1989

George
Austin
1962

Kenyon Shiercliffe Parker 1904–1989 and Pamela Coxhead

Rosemary Kenyon
m
Chris Tailby

Sarah Kenyon
m
Melvyn Holland

Henry Richard James Swaffield 1839–1909 and Emmeline Jepson 1842–1922 m 1866
Henry Swaffield 1868–1964 and Alice Reynolds 1869–1930 m 1899

Leslie 1901
m
Mabel Sharpe – issue (one) >> **Leslie John Swaffield 1901–1966 and Mabel Sharpe 1904–1972 m 1931**

Meave 1941 m Michael Harris issue (two) >> **Meave Swaffield 1941 and Michael Harris m 1964**

Elaine Rachel Harris   Lester John Harris

Henry Richard James Swaffield 1839–1909 and Emmeline Jepson 1842–1922 m 1866

Exton Swaffield 1869–1950 and Florence Anne Carding 1869–1938 m 1899

Frank	**Richard Geoffrey**	**Alan Carding**	**Hugh**
1899-1975	1900-1957	1902-1969	1904-1987
m Dorritt Williams in 1931		m 1)Pauline Durkin in 1931	m Margaret Hemensley
1903-1995		m 2)Jean Gordon Stewart	1914-1975
		1901-1982	issue (three)
issue (two)		issue (one)	

Nigel Exton	Natalie Heather Carding	Susan Mairi	Richard	Malcolm	Kevin
03.05.35	13.08.38	21.11.36	11.02.40	17.04.43	19.10.52
m Denise Lane	m Michael Wheatley	m J E (Tim) Lindley	m Pat Tebbett	Bridget Toland	Maureen Annis
issue (two)	issue (four)	issue (three)	issue (two)	issue (three)	no issue
				div 1981	

Nigel Swaffield 1935 and Denise Lane 1943 m 1965   **Natalie Swaffield 1938 and Michael Wheatley 1933 m 1960**

Damian Exton 1966	Anisa Jane 1968	Susina 1962	Simon 1964	Andrea 1966 < & > David 1966
m 1994	m 1998	m 1994	m 1996	m 1996
Lisa Eltringham (sep)	Dominic McKiernan	David Sutton	Amy Bradshaw	Stewart Rippon
issue (one)		issue (two)	issue (one)	issue (two)
Taylor Harriet 2001		Laurence 1993	Jackson 2000	William 1998
		Nick 1996	Thomas 2003	Fay 2002

Susan Mairi Swaffield 1936 and James E Lindley 1931 m 1957   **Richard Swaffield 1940 and Pat Tebbett m 1964**

Sarah-Ann 1957	Amanda 1960	David 1965	Karen 1965	Jon 1972
m	m	m	m	m
Michael Wormald	Andrew Stone	Ros Ambler	Anthony Griffiths (div)	Helen Dean
in 1981	in 1989	in 1999		(baby due 2003)
issue	issue			
(three)	(two)			
Emma 1983	Anna 1992			
Simon 1986	Jessica 1994			
Andrew 1992				

Malcolm Swaffield 1942 and Bridget Toland m 1967

Keileen	Shaun	Darren
1968	1970	1972
& Alex Edwards		& Sharon Gordon
issue		issue
Shane 1989		Jules
Danielle 1991		b 1999
Sinead 1997		

Henry Richard James Swaffield 1839–1909 and Emmeline Jepson 1842–1922 m 1866

Norman Swaffield 1871–1958 and Elizabeth Jepps 1876–1962 m 1899

Helen	Henry Hamilton	Emmeline Mildred	Frances Mary	Dorothy
b 26.4.01	b 25.4.03	b 5.5.09	b 27.1.12	b 4.9.17
d 25.7.65	m Dora Gould b 1917 in 1937 d Dec 1967 issue (two)	m Frank Hailstone 1908-1979 in 1938 issue (two)	d 6.3.99	d 21.12.99

Lurline 1947 (Laura)	Norman b 1941 m Alicia O'Keeffe in 1967 issue (three) Deirdra 1968 m > Daniel Orteu Sheena 1972 Elizabeth 1985 Alicia died 5.9.02 aged 59	Christine Mary 1944 m 1) Barry Moulang issue (two) Andrew 1965 Helen 1966 2) Denis Cox issue (two) Charles 1981 Emily 1984	Robert Frank 1947 m Gillian Mills in 1971 issue (two) Nick 1980 Sally 1983

Henry Richard James Swaffield 1839–1909 and Emmeline Jepson 1842–1922 m 1866

Ella Swaffield 1874–1945 and Frederick Lampard 1884–1917 m 1912

Peter died young	Derrick Peter m Rosemary Hill issue (two) Peter Lampard Michelle Lampard

Henry Richard James Swaffield 1839–1909 and Emmeline Jepson 1842–1922 m 1866

Beatrice Swaffield 1876–1967 and Thomas Lewin Smith 1874 m 1902

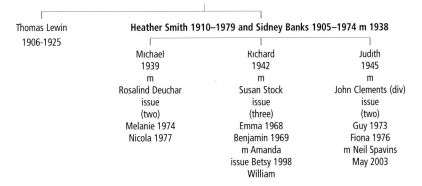

Thomas Lewin 1906-1925

Heather Smith 1910–1979 and Sidney Banks 1905–1974 m 1938

Michael 1939 m Rosalind Deuchar issue (two) Melanie 1974 Nicola 1977	Richard 1942 m Susan Stock issue (three) Emma 1968 Benjamin 1969 m Amanda issue Betsy 1998 William	Judith 1945 m John Clements (div) issue (two) Guy 1973 Fiona 1976 m Neil Spavins May 2003

Henry Richard James Swaffield 1839–1909 and Emmeline Jepson 1842–1922 m 1866
Richard Nash Swaffield 1880–1937 and Ethel Harper 1880–1976 m 1914

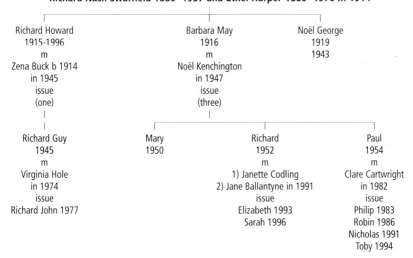

Richard Howard	Barbara May	Noël George
1915-1996	1916	1919
m	m	1943
Zena Buck b 1914	Noël Kenchington	
in 1945	in 1947	
issue	issue	
(one)	(three)	

Richard Guy	Mary	Richard	Paul
1945	1950	1952	1954
m		m	m
Virginia Hole		1) Janette Codling	Clare Cartwright
in 1974		2) Jane Ballantyne in 1991	in 1982
issue		issue	issue
Richard John 1977		Elizabeth 1993	Philip 1983
		Sarah 1996	Robin 1986
			Nicholas 1991
			Toby 1994

Henry Richard James Swaffield 1839–1909 and Emmeline Jepson 1842–1922 m 1866
Mildred Swaffield 1884–1973 and Frederick Potter 1881 m 1909

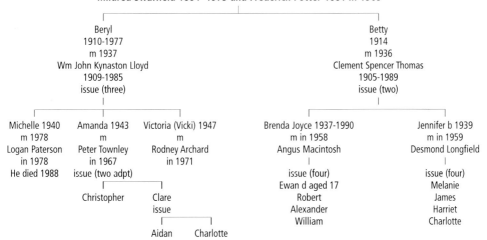

Beryl	Betty
1910-1977	1914
m 1937	m 1936
Wm John Kynaston Lloyd	Clement Spencer Thomas
1909-1985	1905-1989
issue (three)	issue (two)

Michelle 1940	Amanda 1943	Victoria (Vicki) 1947	Brenda Joyce 1937-1990	Jennifer b 1939
m 1978	m	m	m in 1958	m in 1959
Logan Paterson	Peter Townley	Rodney Archard	Angus Macintosh	Desmond Longfield
in 1978	in 1967	in 1971		
He died 1988	issue (two adpt)		issue (four)	issue (four)
			Ewan d aged 17	Melanie
	Christopher	Clare	Robert	James
		issue	Alexander	Harriet
			William	Charlotte

Aidan	Charlotte

Jennifer Potter 1939 and Desmond Longfield

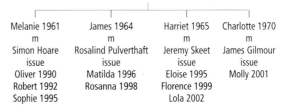

Melanie 1961	James 1964	Harriet 1965	Charlotte 1970
m	m	m	m
Simon Hoare	Rosalind Pulverthaft	Jeremy Skeet	James Gilmour
issue	issue	issue	issue
Oliver 1990	Matilda 1996	Eloise 1995	Molly 2001
Robert 1992	Rosanna 1998	Florence 1999	
Sophie 1995		Lola 2002	

Henry Richard James Swaffield 1839–1909 and Emmeline Jepson 1842–1922 m 1866

Basil Swaffield 1885–1973 and Hilda Milligan 1882–1967 m 1917

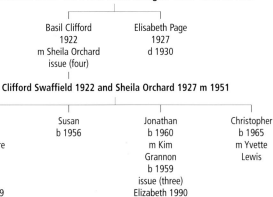

Basil Clifford	Elisabeth Page
1922	1927
m Sheila Orchard	d 1930
issue (four)	

Clifford Swaffield 1922 and Sheila Orchard 1927 m 1951

Simon	Susan	Jonathan	Christopher
b1952	b 1956	b 1960	b 1965
m Jenny Moore		m Kim	m Yvette
b 1952		Grannon	Lewis
		b 1959	
issue (two)		issue (three)	
Matthew 1989		Elizabeth 1990	
Martin 1992		Thomas 1993	
		Robert 1998	

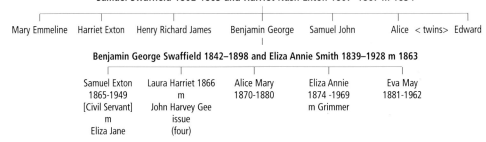

Samuel Swaffield 1802-1863 and Harriet Nash Exton 1807–1867 m 1834

Mary Emmeline	Harriet Exton	Henry Richard James	Benjamin George	Samuel John	Alice < twins > Edward

Benjamin George Swaffield 1842–1898 and Eliza Annie Smith 1839–1928 m 1863

Samuel Exton	Laura Harriet 1866	Alice Mary	Eliza Annie	Eva May
1865-1949	m	1870-1880	1874 -1969	1881-1962
[Civil Servant]	John Harvey Gee		m Grimmer	
m	issue			
Eliza Jane	(four)			

Benjamin George Swaffield 1842–1898 and Eliza Annie Smith 1839–1928 m 1863

Laura Harriet Swaffield 1866–1945 and John Harvey Gee

Dorothy Primrose	Douglas John	Gwendoline Irene	Kathleen Marjorie
1902-1966	1904	1907-1989	1913-1987
m	m	spinster	m in 1931
George Wilcox in 1927	Gladys		Louis C Osborne 1907-1988
issue	issue		issue
(two)	(two)		(five)
June 1929			Michael 1931
John 1931			Muriel Anne 1934
			David 1936
			Wendy 1940
			Nicholas 1949

June Anne Wilcox 1929 and Victor Samuel Marklew

Robert Victor	Richard John	James Lance
1953	1956	1958
m in 1973	m in 1984	m in 1985
Kay Turner	Dorinda Owen	1) Louise Gilray
issue	issue	issue
Zoe 1974	Jennifer 1985	Verity Emma 1991
Christopher 1978	m McKelvey	2) Anna Frodin in 1994
		issue
		Sofi Brigitta 1995
		Samuel Johan 1997

John Bernard Wilcox 1931–2000 and Jean Valerie Owen in 1953

Paul Anthony 1954 and Teresa Wakeman

Charlotte	Rosaline	Paul	Lee
1979	1981	1990	1992
issue	issue		
Lucy 1996	Mark 2000		

Michael John Osborne 1931 m Valerie Gale in 1960

Paul	Adrian
Michael	John
1960	1964
m	m
Julia Bigg	Julia Janes
issue	issue
Harry Lewis 1998	Joseph Clifford 1998
George 2001	

Muriel Anne Osborne 1934 & 1) Donald Peter Newman (div 1983)

Lesley Anne	Mark Peter	Grant
1956	1959	1965
m Robert Funnel	Anne-Marie Holt (div)	
issue	issue	
Alexander 1989	Gemma Louise 1983	
Louise Emily 1991	Rikki 1988	

M Anne Osborne/Newman 1934 m 2) Mr Taylor (no issue)

David Lawrence Osborne 1936 and Elsa

Neil	Robert	Jeremy

Wendy 1940

Ian	Mark	Wayne

Nicholas Robert Osborne 1949 m Anne Wheeler in 1972

Janine	Gareth
1974	1977
m Roger Andrews	
issue	
Megan 2001	

Benjamin George Swaffield 1842–1898 and Eliza Annie Smith 1839–1928 m 1863
Eliza Annie Swaffield 1874 and Albert Edward Grimmer 1877–1960 m 1863

Honora Patricia Annie	Lily May	Ena Mary	Eva Jane	Margery Bertha
1900-1991	1904	1907-1978	1911-1978	1912-2001
		m in 1933	m in 1945	m in 1944
		Frank Randall Underwood	Herbert Groves Bowles	Edgar Walter Nightall
		1907-1977	1907-1982	1912-1998
		issue	issue	issue
		(two)	(one)	(two)

Benjamin George Swaffield 1842–1898 and Eliza Annie Smith 1839–1928 m 1863
Ena Mary Swaffield 1907–1977 and Frank Randall Underwood 1907–1977 m 1933

Andrew Grimmer 1934	Rosemary Anne 1938 and Neil Wigan 1935 m 1964

Bruce Randall 1965	Anne Josephine 1966
m Robyn Thilthorpe 1968	m Allan Woodard 1966
issue (four)	issue (two)
Louise Robyn 1991	Philippa 1994
Josephine Clare 1992	Thomas Allan 1997
Samantha Brooke 1994	
Catherine Clare 1996	
Wigan/Woodard families	
all resident in Australia	

Benjamin George Swaffield 1842–1898 and Eliza Annie Smith 1839–1928 m 1863
Eva Jane Grimmer 1911–1978 and Herbert Bowles 1907–1982 m 1945

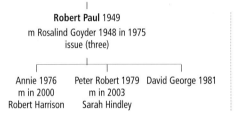

Robert Paul 1949
m Rosalind Goyder 1948 in 1975
issue (three)

Annie 1976	Peter Robert 1979	David George 1981
m in 2000	m in 2003	
Robert Harrison	Sarah Hindley	

Margery Grimmer 1912-2001 & Edgar Nightall 1912-1998 m 1944

John Richard 1945	Christopher Mark 1948
m Wendy Vowles in 1973	m Jill Coughtrey in 1971
issue (two)	issue (two)
Claire Victoria 1975	Mark James 1971
>m Nicholas Cahm 1971	Emma Josephine 1974
Timothy James 1979	>m Bradley Harris in 1998

Samuel Swaffield 1802–1863 and Harriet Nash Exton 1807–1867 m 1834
Samuel John 1846–1914 and Harriet Randall 1872–1915 m 1872

Samuel	Herbert	Stanley	Charles	Harriet	Francis	Douglas	Alice	Kathleen	Winifred	Mildred
b Wootton	Edward					Exton			Mary	Hannah
1874-1931	1875-1938	1877-1959	1879-85	1881	1883-1957	1887-1947	1889	1891	1892	1895
d Wimbl-	Houghton	Gt Easton	d age 6		Acton	Dunmow			Brentford	
don, Surrey	Regis	Dunmow			London	Author	m Leeder	Spinster	Middlesex	m 1926
m Farnham	m H Regis	m		m	m Brentford	'A Little Book	issue		m 1913	Walter
Ellen	Edith	Annie		Murphy	Elsie Higgins	of Jokes' &	Douglas		Ernest	Prance
Miller	Mary	Mary			1902-76	'All Boloney'			Maidment	
issue	She d 1936	She d 1954			F d Acton	of Grantleigh			issue	
Gerald	H was a				Green	Hotel, London			Raymond	
	Licensed Victualler								Jeffrey	

Samuel Swaffield 1802–1863 and Harriet Nash Exton 1807–1867 m 1834
Edward Swaffield 1849 and Miss Poole

Alice	Harriet	Edith	Edward	Samuel	Muriel
Mary	Emily		James Poole	Edgar	Annie
1875 (Mar)	1875 (Dec)	1877	1878	1880	1882
Greenwich	Greenwich	Greenwich	Greenwich	Greenwich	Lewisham
d Princes	d Dublin	d Bournemouth	m Edith Willington		m Mr Baker
Risborough			of Beds		

No further details of **HRJ Swaffield 1839–1909** & **Emmeline Jepson 1842–1922** m 1866

No further details of **Benjamin George Swaffield 1842–1898** and **Eliza Annie Smith 1839–1928** m 1863

No further details of **Samuel Swaffield 1802** and **Harriet Nash Exton 1807–1867** m 1834

No further details of **Benjamin Swaffield 1767–1840** and **Hannah Burdett 1765–1857** m 1791

No further details of JOHN SWAFFIELD 1731–1818 and ELIZABETH GILLINGHAM 1728–1812

Appendix 2

~ BIBLIOGRAPHY ~

AA Road Atlas of Britain 2000

All About the First World War 1914–1918, Pam Robson, Macdonald Young Books 1996

Andrew Underwood Collection, Ampthill

Antiquities of the County of Dorset 1st pub 1744, updated 1836, John Hutchens

Australian Pioneer's Register

Bartholomew's Gazetteer of the British Isles, 1887

Beaminster – Towns & Villages of England, Gerald Gosling & Alan Sutton pub 1993

Beatie, Ted of Toronto, Canada – letters written to him by R G & H Swaffield courtesy Sandra Beatie

Bound to the Soil, a Social History of Dorset, Barbara Kerr, 1968 Dorset Books

Britain & the Great War, Rosemary Rees, Heinemann 1993

Cadbury History, John F Crosfield, University Press, Cambridge 1985

Carisbrooke Museum, Isle of Wight – The Wreck of the Irex

Chambers Biographical Dictionary, Eds: Magnus Magnusson & Rosemary Goring, Chambers 1990

Chatsworth Settlement, Derbyshire – Archive Department

Cherry, Sara Wheeler, Jonathan Cape 2001

Churches & Chapels in the County of Derby, Rawlins

Complete Servant, pub USA

Crewkerne in Old Photographs, Gerald Gosling & Frank Huddy

Daily Life in a Victorian House, Laura Wilson, Hamlyn 1993

Dictionary of English Surnames, R H Reaney & R M Wilson, OUP 1995

English Agriculture 1850 & 1851, James Caird

Everyday Life in Regency & Victorian England, Kristine Hughes, Writer's Digest Books, Ohio 1998

Existing Villages That Have Undergone Change, Yeovil Library

Fellows, Members and Licentiates in Midwifery of the Royal College of Surgeons of England 1853

Fleet Air Arm Museum – Curators Office, Jerry Shore 2001

Holy Bible, St James Church, Lewcombe inscribed *The Parish Church of East Chelborough Lucam 1858*

House of Commons Research Paper 99/20 Inflation: the Value of the Pound 1750-1998

King William IV, Philip Ziegler, Collins 1971

Leland, John, 16th Century Historian

Life & Work in 19th Century Britain, Rachel Hamer, Heinemann 1995

London & Provincial Medical Directory 1855 & 1868

National Horseracing Museum, Newmarket, Graham Snelling, Curator

Pears Cyclopaedia, BCA 1991–92

Pevsner, Nikolaus, Buildings of England 1951-74

Pioneer's Register, Grafton, New South Wales, Australia 1867

Pocket Oxford Dictionary 5th Ed, FG & HW Fowler, Clarendon Press 1974

Queen Victoria in her Letters & Journals, Christopher Hibbert, Sutton 2000

Ship of Dreams, BBC-TV, 28.02.01

Swaffield, Dorritt [née Williams], memoir, cuttings, diaries

Swaffield, Ethel [née Harper], scrapbook

Swaffield, Frederick (1888–1963) – Memoir – various sections contributed by family members

[Note: Extracts taken with permission from Stephen Jones' literal translation of Fred Swaffield's memoir. Usage here cannot be considered 'true copy', but has been punctuated and rearranged, for easier reading and to add flavour.]

Swaffield, George 1875, extracts from diary of Boer War

Swaffield, George 1841, extracts from journal

Swaffield, Norman 1871, Merchant Navy Log Book

The Africa House, Christina Lambe

The Bachelor Duke, W S Cavendish, 6th Duke of Devonshire, James Lees-Milne, John Murray 1991

The Estate – A View from Chatsworth, Devonshire, Deborah Duchess, pub Macmillan 1990

Tideswell in the Days of Father Brown, Canon Fletcher, re-pub SJB Books 1986

Timetables of History, Bernard Grun, Touchstone 1975

Victorian Family Life, Jane Shuter, Heinemann 1997

Who's Who in British History, Ed Juliet Gardiner, Collins & Brown Ltd 2000

www.familysearch.org

www.google.co.uk

www.dorsetshire.co.uk

Yorkshire Post – January 1901

Appendix 3

~ VISITS ~

Bedfordshire [NW 1949, 2000-2002] – Bedford, Ampthill, Honeydon, Steppingley, Millbrook etc

Bedfordshire & Luton Archives & Records Service, The Record Office, Riverside Building, County Hall, Cauldwell Street, Bedford MK42 9AP. Telephone 01234 228833

Archive – SFM = Swaffield Family Mabel

Derbyshire [NW 2000 & 2002] - Bakewell, Edensor, Chatsworth, Hartington, Pilsbury Grange, Rowsley, Tideswell etc

Dorsetshire & Somerset [NW 1999 & 2002] Beaminster, East Chelborough, Melbury Osmond, Evershot, Halstock, Lewcombe, Bridport, Wootton Fitzpaine, Lyme Regis, Dorchester, Yeovil, Crewkerne etc

The County Record Office, Bridport Road, Dorchester DT1 1RP. Telephone 01305 250550

Hampshire [NW 2000] Fareham

Northamptonshire [NW 2000] Catesby, Daventry, Hellidon etc

Appendix 4

~ ACKNOWLEDGEMENTS ~

MY GRATEFUL THANKS TO:

Archard, Vicki [née Lloyd], photographs

Bartron, Audrey [née Swaffield] genealogy, files, records, cuttings, Wills, birth certificates

Benham, Bill, photographs, written information

Brettell, Jane [née Shepherd], photographs, written information

Boyer, Malcolm, scanning all visuals and providing photographs

Cox, Christine [née Hailstone], photographs, *Book of Travels – Norman 1871*

Darby, Gwen of Catesby, written/verbal information, photographs, *Conditions of Sale – Catesby Estate*

Dart, Gwen [née Long], photographs

Friston, Don, design, proof reading, production guidance

Hailstone, Rob, photographs

Harding, Tasma (née Benham), photographs, written information

Jones, Ben, photograph

Kenchington, Bardie [née Swaffield] – scrapbook, letters

Lindley, Susan [née Swaffield], letters, cuttings, photographs

Martin, Howard of Cardiff, Loveless family genealogical research

Perkins, Janet [née Collow], photographs

Ramsey, Judy, genealogy

Reed, Mary [née Collin] – information and photographs

Spencer Thomas, Betty [née Potter], photographs, cuttings

Swaffield, Clifford, archive, genealogy, photographs, Wills

Swaffield, Dora [née Gould], photographs

Swaffield, Joan [née Valentine], letters, photographs

Swaffield, Kevin, photographs

Swaffield, Margaret [née Gosnay], photographs

Swaffield, Norman, *A Load of Ham & A Load of Old (Ful)ham*, photographs

Underwood, Andrew, photographs, cuttings, information, guidance

and many others for their valuable contribution

Index